Essential Clinical Social \

Series Editor
Carol Tosone

For further volumes:
http://www.springer.com/series/8115

Judith B. Rosenberger

Editor

Relational Social Work Practice with Diverse Populations

 Springer

Editor
Judith B. Rosenberger
Silberman School of Social Work
Hunter College
City University of New York
New York, NY, USA

Past President: Postgraduate Psychoanalytic Society
New York, NY, USA

ISBN 978-1-4614-6680-2 (hardcover)   ISBN 978-1-4614-6681-9 (eBook)
ISBN 978-1-4939-1596-5 (softcover)
DOI 10.1007/978-1-4614-6681-9
Springer New York Heidelberg Dordrecht London

Library of Congress Control Number: 2013937826

Springer is part of Springer Science+Business Media (www.springer.com)

For my family and friends.
You make it all matter.

JBR

Acknowledgments

I would like to express my great thanks to Carol Tosone, Senior Series Editor, for her encouragement and astute guidance in moving this book from idea to reality: her vision of clinical social work is unparalleled, as is her tireless advocacy of social work's role in the helping professions. Joan Berzoff, a leading author in our field, embodied the social work principle of joining the practical and the relational by helping me gather this exceptional group of writers and supporting me through the process of integrating many voices. Clear and insightful editorial recommendations pulled me out of many a quagmire, thanks to Susan Heath, Nancy Beckerman, and Cathy Siebold. Sonia H. Martin, graduate research assistant, was responsive, pre- cise, technically gifted, and unflaggingly cheerful – all much needed and appreci- ated contributions. *I also wish to thank my study group partners of over 30 years - Monica Bernheim, Mary Beth Cresci, Andrew Karpf, Pauline Pinto, and Suzanne Zissu - whose weekly inspirational, scholarly, and friendly support have kept vital my clinical thinking, teaching and practice*.

To all the chapter authors, I offer gratitude and appreciation for sharing their scholarship and practice expertise. Their hard work and forbearance brought this work through the long process of weaving together many perspectives. I thank them for their demonstration of how our diversities can come together and make an important contribution to all clinical social workers.

Lastly, and most importantly, I want to thank my family: I am very fortunate to have had their confidence and enthusiasm every step of the way.

Contents

Part III   Religious Diversities

Part IV   Diversities of Sexual Identity

Part V   Diversities Founded on Life-Altering Experience

Contributors

Neil Altman Editor Emeritus, Psychoanalytic Dialogues: The International Journal of Relational Perspectives, New York, NY, USA

Author, The Analyst in the Inner City: Race, Class, and Culture through a Psychoanalytic Lens, New York, NY, USA

Ambedkar University of Delhi, India

John L. Bennett Callen-Lorde Community Health Center, New York, NY, USA

Silver School of Social Work, New York University, New York, NY, USA

David P. Cecil Master of Social Work Program, Asbury University, Wilmore, KY, USA

Monit Cheung Graduate College of Social Work, University of Houston, Houston, TX, USA

Cheryl El-Amin Islamic Social Services Association - USA, Tempe, AZ, USA

Detroit Public Schools Social Worker, Detroit, MI, USA

Daniel C. Farrell NYU Silver School of Social Work, New York, USA

Manny J. González Silberman School of Social Work, Hunter College, City University of New York, New York, USA

Graduate Center, City University of New York, New York, USA

Harriet Goodman Silberman School of Social Work, Hunter College, City University of New York, NY, USA

The Graduate Center of the City University of New York, NY, USA

Griffin Hansbury National Psychological Association for Psychoanalysis, New York, NY, USA

Thomas K. Kenemore Masters Social Work Program, Chicago State University, Chicago, IL, USA

Carol A. Leung Flushing Hospital Medical Center, New York, USA

Aneesah Nadir Islamic Social Services Association - USA, Tempe, AZ, USA

Retired Professor-Arizona State University, Phoenix, AZ, USA

Judith B. Rosenberger Silberman School of Social Work, Hunter College, City University of New York, NY, USA

Past President: Postgraduate Psychoanalytic Society, New York, NY, USA

Renee Schlesinger Wurzweiler School of Social Work, Yeshiva University, New York, USA

Kenneth M. Stoltzfus Department of Social Sciences, LCC International University, Klaipeda, Lithuania

Frederick J. Streets Wurzweiler School of Social Work, Yeshiva University, New York, NY, USA

Chaplain of Yale University, New York, NY, USA

Columbia University School of Social Work, New York, NY, USA

Yale University Divinity School, New York, NY, USA

Jeni Tyson Maplewood, NJ, USA

Mohan Krishna Vinjamuri Department of Social Work, Lehman College, City University of New York, New York, USA

Victoria R. Winbush Cleveland State University School of Social Work, Cleveland, OH, USA

Cleveland State University Diversity Management Program, Cleveland, OH, USA

Smith College School for Social Work, Northampton, MA, USA

Part I
Foundations of Relational Diversity Practice

Introduction

Judith B. Rosenberger

The principles of relational practice are a perfect fit for clinical social work practice with diverse populations. Social work has a long-standing creed that relationship is key to helping clients (Reynolds 1982, 1975; Hamilton 1951; NASW 2011). Precise helping methods and their rationale have been less well articulated, and their adaptation in today's rapidly diversifying social work client base (Berzoff 2011) requires an updated look that validates their continued centrality. This book provides explanation of relational theory as the grounding in intrapersonal and interpersonal skills, and their theoretical underpinnings, that prepare today's clinical social worker to respond with confidence in new and challenging treatment situations. This book has three goals. First, it explains the psychodynamic process and practice skills of relational theory that have emerged from the developments of object relations theory and self-psychology (Goldstein 2001; Meissner 1979), giving illustrations of their application in clinical social work practice. Second, it provides innovative content about the research support for relational theory in social work and its inextricability from issues like race and religion. Third, it gives a wide range of specific examples of the application of relational practice skills to the particular needs of a wide range of diverse populations. In these chapters the social work practitioner learns the rationale and methods of integration of clinical knowledge with the escalating need for appropriate treatment of clients who bring ever more complex, and perhaps unfamiliar, sociopolitical situations and internal self-organization.

This relational model of clinical practice draws on many developments in relational psychoanalytic theory, including the British school (Fairbairn, Winnicott, Klein, and others) and has particularly incorporated and highlighted American relational theory (Mitchell, Greenberg, Aron, and Altman among others) and self-psychology

J.B. Rosenberger, Ph.D., LCSW (✉)
Silberman School of Social Work, Hunter College, City University of New York, NY, USA

Past President: Postgraduate Psychoanalytic Society, New York, NY, USA
e-mail: judith.rosenberger@gmail.com

J.B. Rosenberger (ed.), *Relational Social Work Practice with Diverse Populations*,
Essential Clinical Social Work Series, DOI 10.1007/978-1-4614-6681-9_1,
© Springer Science+Business Media New York 2014

(primarily Kohut) contributions. As Tosone has explained in her paper *Relational Social Work: Honoring the Tradition* (2004), clinical social work today has not departed from but has expanded knowledge about practice by incorporation of relational theory concepts. Emphasis on relational parity rather than hierarchy in the clinical situation, on co-construction of meanings rather than a priori assumptions, and on the clinician's authentic and interactive presence rather than the blank screen therapist open the door to mutual discovery and collaborative planning of social work interventions (Aron and Harris 2011; Greenberg and Mitchell 1983; Mitchell 1997; Neimeyer 1993). This form of therapeutic exchange invites issues of bias, core beliefs, adaptive and maladaptive coping, projections and introjections, historical forces, and, especially important in diversity practice, current sociopolitical realities to become natural subjects in the direct experience of the treatment relationship (Guntrip 1975). For example, a female client living in poverty in an abusive marital relationship requires the clinician's attentive concern about her cultural and personal narrative as such, out of which can emerge experiential learning about her internalization of relational paradigms that keep her locked in a disempowered position.

The capacity to explore such dynamics with a clinician requires confidence that the sociocultural context and real life options of the client are understood and that she/he can be experienced as a full and respected individual in her/his[1] own right. The relational principle of authenticity is bidirectional: the clinician attends to the client's story as the client experiences it, confirming that the immediate reality is heard and understood (Baker Miller 2012). The relational clinician balances the interpersonal and the contextual (Tosone 2004). Manifest problems, overall situation (including in this case cultural views of marriage and child rearing), and real options for action given a client's realistic financial and social supports must be heard and acknowledged, along with her sense of self as a man or woman, as a member of a community and family, measures of self esteem, and the like. Rather than focusing on the presenting problem as an outgrowth of developmental history, as pre-relational psychodynamic theory might suggest, or addressing the sociopolitical inequities in the present situation as a nonclinical social work intervention might do, the relational social worker seeks to engage the client in a respectful exploration of the world as he now sees it, including how he experiences the clinician. This orientation to "interpersonal interaction and experiential learning" (Borden 2009, p. 159), rather than didactic or interpretive informing, underlies the relational theory stance for the social work clinician.

Relational theory weds developmental and intrapsychic theory to the central social work rubric of "starting where the client is." The relational emphasis on techniques and stages of practice equips the relational social worker to create a helping relationship that is congruent with the client's social reality without sacrificing necessary attention to individual internal structures. Recognizing that the therapeutic milieu encompasses client and clinician *in environment* resolves issues of dissonance in initial understandings, so central to diversity practice, which can stymie

---

[1]For continuity in the general discussion, the clinician will be referred to as female and the client as male, unless context, as in this example, clearly indicates otherwise.

internal change if they are not addressed directly in the clinical exchange. As Baker Miller (2012) explains, disconnection in the here-and-now relationship fosters decreased vitality, inability to take action, confusion and loss of self-knowledge, lowered self-worth, and increased isolation. These dissonant, or non-related, conditions defeat the most accurate and astute interpretations and interventions a clinician might offer. "In contrast, relational clinical practice is founded on client and clinician in environment" (Tosone 2004) as a bidirectional stance that validates inclusiveness, equality, and social provision, which are at the heart of all effective social work.

The specific relational theory precepts and techniques are described and expanded in this chapter. The remaining chapters present salient issues and applications of these precepts to work with diverse populations. Before delving into the specific issues of populations of diversity that are predictable in clinical social work practice, a brief review of the relevance of the relational model to diversity itself helps set the stage.

Diversity and Relational Social Work Practice

Viewing diversity in an "us-and-them" perspective is contrary to social work's commitment to universal therapeutic responsiveness. Sullivan (1953) wrote long ago about an internal "me" and "not me." This unconscious division reinforces social marginalization, and insularity, of groups – a particular concern in today's multicultural world. Prejudices and ignorance invite "not me" barriers, as a version of this splitting also marginalizes the social work clinician herself in the context of contemporary practice that is dominated by diversity. Clinical social workers may often be baffled or feel threatened when clients represent sociocultural populations with which they are not familiar. They may mistakenly disqualify themselves as capable of understanding how to work with such clients. They also may attempt to bridge the gap by immersing themselves in trying to learn the sociocultural context of these clients. While this last endeavor is of value, it still defines otherness as a problem to be solved for fruitful work to begin.

A further liability of the us-and-them perspective is the mistaken assumption that uniformity exists in either "us" or "them" (Altman 2007). Relational theory not only contradicts such divisions but also embraces uniqueness in the individuality of all clients as the nature of all clinical encounters. Applied to diversity, relational theory extends this core framework with particular attention, but not divergent attention, to the apparent and the less apparent dimensions of otherness in race, ethnicity, religion, sexual orientation, and seminal life experiences. In this way, relational practice with diverse populations teaches the relational social worker how to deepen the work necessary to establish rapport, congruent goals, and effective technique with all clients (Geso and Hayes 2000). As Bromberg (2011) states regarding the interpersonal/relational perspective, "There is no true dialogue that does not emerge from some collision between subjectivities" (p. 67).

Emphasis on Practice

This book uniquely describes and illustrates direct practice across multiple differences within the integrated framework of the relational theory perspective. In doing so, many issues that have constricted diversity practice are addressed. Since marginalized or alienated groups are highly sensitized to worker awareness of their social differences, the clinical social worker today must be prepared to practice the relational skills that minimize misperceptions about differences, reducing the risk of false assumptions and inadvertent suppression of an individual's personal narrative (Foucault 1980; Hartman 1992; Stern 2010). It draws on the solid grounding in techniques of social work learned in all practice curricula while enlarging the clinical theoretical underpinnings to apply them to self-other difference in an integrated and anxiety-free approach to practice. While geared toward beginning clinicians, the conceptual framework that joins relational theory to diversity practice is applicable to supervision, agency organization and services, and autonomous practice alike. The pursuit of clinical cohesion across socially constructed and powerful demarcations of difference is the unifying theme.

This book is not philosophical or political. It imparts concrete information, explanations, illustrations, and alertness to likely errors in work with diverse populations. It authenticates the clinical dimensions of practice by illustrating the fusion of the internal and external dynamics as people from diverse populations navigate the social universe (Berzoff et al. 2008; Tosone 2004). It spells out steps and methods of practice that guide respectful and useful work, applying the relational theory orientation of discovery and adaptation to meet the client where he is and to co-construct realistic approaches to problems of living. Work with unfamiliar, disenfranchised, and marginalized populations can lead to clinician frustration and the pull to resort to formulaic strategies. This form of objectification heightens clients' resistance, which then can be attributed to client limitations in using services (Altman 2000; Layton et al. 2006). The social worker's resistance, due to anxieties about success with clients who are unfamiliar with and suspicious of clinical services, is allayed by classifying such clients as unsuitable for clinical practice. The relational social worker finds in these chapters a broader path to follow: interactive assessment and collaborative treatment planning that are at the heart of the relational model of keeping both client and clinician engaged in pursuit of a meaningful working relationship.

Book Contents

The five sections of this book cover the orientation to diversity practice; the documented basis of relational practice as a clinical social work model; the larger implications of race, including Whiteness, and religion as intrinsic to all clinical practice; and a series of specific explorations of how relational practice applies and is conducted with diverse populations. These specific populations include race, religions, sexual orientation, and, unique to this volume, populations who have undergone life-altering experiences that continue to distinguish their capacities, perspectives, and relationship to the clinical social work process. This long list of topics is divided into five sections, all of which retain a consistent theoretical focus, explanation of practice implications, and case examples of direct applications of relational social work methods. The student and practitioner will find both direct instruction and supporting methodological explanation, and the instructor or trainer will find suggested study questions to any or all parts of the book adaptable to classroom use. Extensive references provide links to further study or research in the relational theory, practice recommendations, and each population.

Section One

The first section orients the reader to relational social work practice and its theoretical justification. It is followed by four sections on different frameworks of diversity: racial and ethnic diversity, religious diversity, diversity based on sexual orientation and object choice, and finally diversity based on life-altering experiences that set groups of people apart from the general population. This array of frameworks illustrates that the very concepts of diversity and diverse populations are exceedingly complex. An individual may fit into more than one definition of diversity: this is a dimension of diversity practice that is discussed in each of the chapters.

In the first chapter, Rosenberger discusses concepts of diversity itself and highlights perceived paradoxes between clinical practice and practice with diverse identification groups. This chapter articulates the macro-level forces impinging differently on populations, the mezzo-level actions of those populations in transmitting specific group beliefs and practices while contending with wider social forces, and the micro-level expression of both these arenas of internalized influences mixed with personal development of the individual. The reader will learn specific information and practice guidelines for the application of relational theory to a given population. The treatment discussions recognize the potential conflicts between an individual's identity as a member of a population and his acceptance of relational social work as a practice.

In the second chapter, Goodman supports the relational model as the treatment of choice based on analysis of research perspectives that have created, and can bridge, divisions between social work activists and clinicians in regard to diversity education and practice. Constructivism is presented as a framework of flexibility that supports relational practice. In contrast to positivism, which champions absolute known truths, constructivism is shown to support social work in general and relational practice in particular. The chapter confronts the tendency of diversity studies to make population description an end point rather than a stepping-off point for co-constructed exploration of past and present meanings to the individual. It gives both seasoned and neophyte clinicians the philosophical and scientific bases for navigating the coexistence of multiple meanings and options that are the necessary ingredients of practice with diverse practice scenarios.

The body of the book instructs students in the application of relational theory to a range of diversities beyond those typically covered in social work practice literature. This expansion of perspectives, to include religion, sexuality, and life-altering events, opens up diversity thinking itself, echoing the orienting topics in the first section. The population-specific chapters carry forward the unity/diversity nexus of relational clinical technique and its disparate applications. It specifically includes applications beyond the office or with solo practitioners, reflecting the individual's relation to the larger society's assumptions and reactions to designated diversity.

The chapters in these sections present a profile of core beliefs about the self that are linked to population of membership and explain how clinical practices can be oriented for maximum benefit with the specific population. Challenges and likely errors of assumption are described to alert the clinician to resistance, transference and countertransference, and the pull toward identification with client projections about the clinician and clinical practice itself. Ever present is the impact of the clinician's own population of identification, as experienced by herself and by the client. That the client is always informing the clinician, not only about who he is but also about their interaction, is a reminder needed by practitioners and supervisors at every level of experience. The bidirectional influences that are required to establish a meaningful working alliance is a central focus of the relational practice literature (Symington 2007). Increasingly, the clinician is being called to embrace ideas of helpful actions, such as inclusion of people and practices in the client's life that go beyond her own one-to-one efforts. As Tosone (2004) points out, treatment planning can include, as social work has from the beginning, the value of action with and for others as part of the therapeutic process. Especially in work with diverse populations, many elements of the client's social universe, unconventional to the clinician, may provide support, guidance, activities, and other contributions to an expanded but still cohesive clinical process.

Section Two

Section two, on racial and ethnic populations, includes African American, Hispanic, Asian American, and Asian Indian chapters. A White American chapter was considered but omitted because White, as Altman's chapter explores, connotes the position of social dominance more than it does a population per se. Each author addresses the significance of being designated a diverse population. Winbush explores the centrality of differential power and privilege for African American clients. The history of oppression and marginalization and the overt social struggles for equal recognition and opportunity are, Winbush asserts, always active along with "multiple other identities." Gonzalez takes a "relational-cultural" approach in his chapter to underscore values and expectations stemming from Hispanic identity coupled with the impact of migration and the ambivalence of re-acculturation. Cheung and Leung echo Gonzalez's attention to migration and to the misdirection of assumed sameness within the diverse Asian American population. Vinjamuri explains the amalgamation of religious and spiritual beliefs in the Asian Indian population. He, too, cites the impact of migration and the internal dissonance that it can bring. All these authors include attention to extended family, histories of dislocation, navigation of self and other intensified by population membership, and demands for alterations in the clinical relationship to unify relational practice with the here-and-now specifics of the client's sociocultural aspects of self. Taken together, the chapters illustrate the theme of the book as a whole: individual diversity obtains within group diversity, and relational social work practice with diverse populations requires the combined distinction of individual client needs and processes with inclusion of population-specific awareness and adaptations of approach.

Section Three

The third section, on diverse religious populations, includes Evangelical Christians, Muslims, and Orthodox Jews. These are large and growing parts of our society. Each belief system can be directive to its adherents about practical as well as spiritual matters of living. This presents an exceptionally rich opportunity for the relational social worker trained in a-religious theoretical models. She cannot attempt to work around religious prescriptions and interpretations that are core beliefs and central to the client's cohesive sense of self. The relational model of practice directs the clinician to move toward inquiry and understanding about how a client's religious beliefs may or may not be pathways to growth and problem solving in any given situation. Helping the client resolve any specific conflicts while remaining within his belief system requires relational attunement to religious convictions. Cecil and Stoltzfus emphasize primary beliefs of Evangelical Christians that can become central in connection or disconnection with clinicians. Their discussion underscores the importance of understanding the power of the key beliefs for helpful relational practice, regardless of whether the clinician shares those beliefs. Representing the Muslim population, Nadir and El-Amin illustrate the importance of the relational approach, rather than an approach of inherent clinical authority. They show how the clinician's authority rests on flexibility in problem solving that does not create unnecessary collisions with the teachings of Islam. Schlesinger adds to this understanding about working with, not changing, core beliefs as she describes the cohesion and security of membership in a population that guards and promotes Jewish rituals and practices due to a history of persecution. Her chapter on practice with Orthodox Jews demonstrates the challenges to all religious "outsiders" in diversity practice.

Relational theory de-pathologizes resistance in diversity practice, calling on the clinician to acknowledge the value of preserved separation without forsaking the quest for useful interventions with the individual that are psychodynamically informed. The conundrum of seeking connection through flexibility with what may be an inflexible prescription for living teaches the student, or the advanced practitioner, about her own inflexibility. There is inevitable resistance with a clinician who embodies an oppressing population, past or present. Similarly, there is an inevitable pull toward overidentification between client and clinician of similar population histories.

In this way, relational theory not only de-pathologizes resistance, it elevates it as a clinically critical dimension of accurate assessment, resilient engagement, and fruitful treatment.

Section Four

Hansbury and Bennett's chapter on the lesbian, gay, bisexual, and transgender (LGBT) population calls necessary attention to issues raised by creating categorizations. The very designation of the enormously varied range of experiences of people who are identified or self-identified within LGBT as constituting a population raises concerns about how constructions of social identifiers sets a powerful force in motion. Hansbury and Bennett's work reminds us that all populations include multiple identities, and that identities change over time, for individuals as well as for groups. Constructivism gives us a theoretical platform for being appropriately skeptical about the durability of explicit designations. At the same time, we cannot deny the power of a group designation to be comforting and protective or simultaneously constricting and isolating. Hansbury and Bennett illustrate that in order to practice we must construct a relational container that is not a rigid anchor.

A container stabilizes things for the moment but can move along with the tides; it does not have to remain static and restraining, as anchors do. This chapter on LGBT clients brings to light particularly well the constant interaction of irreducible differences and socially constructed diversities. People may share biological, historical, experiential, or ideational composition. They constitute a group on that basis and as such may present some consistent issues for clinical attention. At the same time, each person may be legitimately identified with another group. The moment the clinician or client thinks in terms of group membership, something is gained by way of collective knowledge and something is lost by way of individual experience. This is the nature of the attachment/separation dialogue. Relational theory embraces deconstruction of assumptions as much as it validates the power and often the value of constructed meanings as a means of communicating and experiencing a cohesive identity. The relational clinician gains facility in cutting the anchor to one set of meanings. As an example, the LGBT population membership provides an identity container, even as it has changed and grown in answer to the question "What are you?" Hansbury and Bennett's chapter reminds the clinician that the question is not "What are you?" but "Who are you?" Or even more correctly, we can ask "Who are you now?" Moment to moment understanding of the meanings to the client of his population identifiers aids relational exploration by providing some structure of communication, but it is a structure always eligible for reconstruction.

Section Five

The fifth section of this book reflects some of the most powerful life-altering events of current social existence that become in themselves population parameters.

Tyson explores the defining and separating power of military combat experience. This circle of combat veterans, themselves hugely divergent in what that experience has wrought, exists within the larger circle of the military itself as a population. Tyson explains how the relational clinician must comprehend the tensions created by before and after for the combat veteran, as well has his/her generation of ambivalence in the conflicted larger society.

Farrell's chapter in this section on homelessness as a distinct experience, points to the social construction of conditions that define populations. These conditions become absorbed in both personal and public perception in divisive ways. Farrell reminds us of the widely varied impact of homelessness, determined by extent and type of personal experience with this devastating condition. He gives us support for the clinical role in sustaining individual integrity through social provision as well as interpersonal therapeutic process. This inclusion of intentional acknowledgement of individual integrity as a clinical action also is central in Kenemore's chapter on the large reentry population of the formerly incarcerated. As Kenemore describes, individual devastation during incarceration amplifies ambivalence toward the free society and its structures, which the clinician represents. His chapter highlights the use of relational understanding and technique to be open in acknowledging aversion and suspicion as part of social reentry. Kenemore's chapter also stresses the positive use in relational practice of social action as therapeutic. These two chapters bring us back with special emphasis to our social work roots. As Tosone (2004) reminds us, the healing power of social action was there from the simultaneous inception of social work and psychoanalysis.

References

Altman, N. (2000). Black and white thinking: A psychoanalyst reconsiders race. *Psychoanalytic Dialogues, 10*, 589–605.

Altman, N. (2007). *The analyst in the inner city: Race, class and culture through a psychoanalytic lens* (2nd ed.). New York: Routledge.

Aron, L., & Harris, A. (Eds.). (2011). *Relational psychoanalysis* (Vol. 4). New York: Routledge.

Baker Miller, J. (2012). *Five good things*. Wellesley: Jean Baker Miller Training Institute at the Wellesley Centers for Women.

Berzoff, J. (Ed.). (2011). *Falling through the cracks: Psychodynamic practice with vulnerable and oppressed populations*. New York: Columbia University Press.

Berzoff, J., Flanagan, L., & Hertz, P. (2008). *Inside out and outside in: Psychodynamic clinical theory and psychopathology in contemporary multicultural contexts* (2nd ed.). New York: Jason Aronson.

Borden, W. (2009). *Contemporary psychodynamic theory and practice*. New York: Lyceum Books.

Bromberg, P. (2011). *The shadow of the tsunami and growth of the relational mind*. New York: Taylor and Francis.

Foucault, M. (1980). *Power/knowledge: Selected interviews and other writings*. New York: Pantheon Press.

Geso, C., & Hayes, J. (2000). The psychotherapy relationship: Theory, research, and practice. *Journal of Psychotherapy Practice and Research, 9*, 106–107.

Goldstein, E. (2001). *Object relations theory and self psychology in social work practice*. New York: The Free Press.

Greenberg, J., & Mitchell, S. A. (1983). *Object relations in psychoanalytic theory*. Cambridge: Harvard University Press.

Guntrip, H. (1975). *Schizoid phenomena, object relations and the self*. Madison: International Universities Press.

Hamilton, G. (1951). *Theory and practice of social case work*. New York: Columbia University Press.

Hartman, A. (1992). In search of subjugated knowledge. *Social Work, 37*(6), 483–484.

Layton, L., Caro Hollander, N., & Gutwill, S. (2006). *Psychoanalysis, class and politics: Encounters in the clinical setting*. New York: Routledge.

Meissner, W. (1979). Internalization and object relations. *Journal of the American Psychoanalytic Association, 27*, 345–360.

Mitchell, S. (1997). *Influence and autonomy in psychoanalysis*. New York: Routledge.

National Association of Social Workers (2011). *Code of ethics*. New York: NASW.

Neimeyer, R. (1993). Constructivism and the problem of psychotherapy integration. *Journal of Psychotherapy and Integration, 3*(2), 133–157.

Reynolds, B. (1975). Social Work and Social Living: Explorations in Philosophy and Practice. National Association of Social Workers/NASW Press.

Reynolds, B. (1982). Between Client and Community: A Study in Responsibility in Social Case Work. National Association of Social Workers/NASW Press.

Stern, D. (2010). *Forms of vitality: Exploring dynamic experience in psychology, the arts, psychotherapy, and development*. New York: Oxford University Press.

Sullivan, H. S. (1953). *The interpersonal theory of psychiatry*. New York: Norton.

Symington, N. (2007). *Becoming a person through psychoanalysis*. London: Karnac Books Ltd.

Tosone, C. (2004). Relational social work: Honoring the tradition. *Smith College Studies in Social Work, 74*(3), 475–487.

Orientation to and Validation of Relational Diversity Practice

Judith B. Rosenberger

Relational Diversity Practice

Social work's emphasis on person-in-environment and person-in-situation (Saari 1986, 2002; Goldstein 1995, 2001; Turner 1996; Berzoff 2011) turned our attention to the client in social context. Less a focus of these important contributions was the centrality of the clinical relationship itself. It remained for the incorporation of psychoanalytic perspectives to emphasize the here and now of the clinical encounter as a primary subject of discovery and impact in clinical social work.

Relational theory evolved in response to clinicians' direct observations of what created therapeutic motivation and efficacy. While many writers have proposed variations in metapsychological theory about the internal landscape that informs manifest client functioning (Fairbairn, Winnicott, Klein, Aron, Bromberg, and many others), those that come under the relational theory umbrella share a common belief in the clinical encounter as the place where internal dynamics are accessible to change. Greenberg and Mitchell (1983) coined the term "relational theory" and in doing so joined it to the social work tradition of the helping relationship itself as the medium of effective social work (Tosone 2004; Hepworth et al. 2006). What elements of therapeutic contact help clients engage in a clinical process? What actions are most significant in helping clients make changes that reduce their subjective distress and manifest dysfunction? Why are these motivations and actions the most powerful? And, how do these factors translate into clinical social work practice with diverse client populations? The answers to these questions propelled the movement that became relational theory, a model that contradicted classical drive theory's emphasis on instinctual gratification, asserting that the central

J.B. Rosenberger, Ph.D., LCSW (✉)
Silberman School of Social Work, Hunter College, City University of New York, NY, USA

Past President: Postgraduate Psychoanalytic Society, New York, NY, USA
e-mail: judith.rosenberger@gmail.com

J.B. Rosenberger (ed.), *Relational Social Work Practice with Diverse Populations,*
Essential Clinical Social Work Series, DOI 10.1007/978-1-4614-6681-9_2,
© Springer Science+Business Media New York 2014

"drive" was for meaningful connection with others (Greenson 1967; Strachey 1966; Freud 1957). This paradigm of relatedness as the most essential human factor in development and health shifted the definition of distress and functional problems to interpersonal misalignments (Bacal and Newman 1990; Bennet and Nelson 2010). It further shifted the framework of clinical practice to a psychosocial model – a clear connection to the roots of social work – in which the relational practitioner uses "empathic attunement, interpersonal interaction, and experiential learning in efforts to facilitate change and growth" (Borden 2009).

The forms of misalignment, such as failures of empathic relating, interpersonal neglect and disregard, embedded distortions of interpretation about other people and what things mean, and the like, apply to individual interchanges and to group interchanges. For example, because psychoanalytic theory, which informs relational theory, was developed in the context of White middle- or upper middle-class clients and clinicians, there is a tendency to fuse clinical thinking and practice with elitism and the politics of dominance and submission. Caro Hollander, in her books, *Love in a Time of Hate (2007)* and *Uprooted Minds (2010),* takes issue with the association of psychodynamic therapy with Whiteness and oppression. She sees clinical process as a pathway to reversing what Foucault (1980) previously characterized as disavowal of histories of oppression and subjugation of any personal narratives.

Relational theory in psychoanalysis derived from Greenberg and Mitchell's (1983) dissatisfaction with classical theory's elevation of an unconscious straw man to be toppled and instead concentrated therapeutic action on exploring the here-and-now communication and enactments between client and clinician. Similarly, encounters between clinicians and clients of different backgrounds and situations require real-time attention to content and exchanges that reveal problems and solutions in their existing cultural idiom. Diversity denotes identified and self-identified distinctions that can too readily become explanations, but not resolutions, of in-group and out-group misalignments (Altman 2000; Berreby 2005; Bhopal and Donaldson 1998; Brodkin 1998; Buck 2010). The motivation to form connection creates a powerful pull toward assumptions that confirm alignment or protect against painful misalignment. Shared identifiers invite assumptions of shared experience, and unshared identifiers invite expectations of unshared experiences. In this way, diversity clinical social work brings relational theory into the spotlight: the practitioner can, and must, apply the triumvirate of empathic attunement, interpersonal interaction, and experiential learning (Borden 2009; Aron 2001) with specific intention and awareness in establishing a truly helping relationship.

The clinical social worker and her client may or may not share self-identifiers, such as race, religion, sexual orientation, or a pivotal life experience, and a multitude of less obvious factors, real or projected. The relational practitioner is alert to these features and their potential to support or derail interpersonal alignment. Additionally, client and clinician specifically do not share their identified roles in the clinical practice process. All clinical encounters therefore must confront the significance of apparent sameness and difference in forming connection. What unifies or divides them in their pursuit of the meaningful help? The clinical social worker's knowledge of how to pursue authentic alignment using the relational approach is the subject of this book. Authenticity includes abandoning illusions of preexisting templates to which clients' ways of expressing feelings, concerns, and options may be referred. For example, a classically defined oedipal conflict expressed in angry behavior at the boss would better be explored openly in search of feelings of disrespect, culturally inappropriate communication, and means of redressing these wrongs in ways that are empathically resonant yet address likely and desired outcomes. The ways the client experiences equivalent misunderstandings and behaviors in the relational clinical exchange would be central to revealing and, most importantly, expressing the disturbances leading to a life problem.

In addition to empathic attunement to the client's immediate experience, mutuality in the construction of goals and methods, and continuous monitoring of the state of communication, the relational clinician makes use of mishaps and gaps in the treatment interaction as opportunities to illuminate and repair maladaptive responses that have become embedded in the client's psychosocial functioning. Reparative work resides in the immediate clinical interaction, wherein the relational practitioner embraces difference and disconnection as a road to shared discovery. As Bromberg (2011) states, "There is no true dialogue that does not emerge from some collision between subjectivites…" (p. 67). True to the core principles of social work as a profession, relational clinical social work starts where the client is and takes mutual responsibility for finding meaningful understanding and methods of moving to a place of greater internal satisfaction and interpersonal success (Tosone 2004).

Applying Relational Theory to Practice with Diverse Populations

Relational social work makes the interpersonal process central in clinical practice. Drawn from object relations (Fairbairn 1954; Winnicott 1958), self-psychology (Kohut 2000), and psychodynamic theories of development (Safran 2008; Jordan 2008; Fletcher and Hayes 2005), among other two-person psychologies (Mitchell 1993, 1997; Stolorow and Atwood 1992; Stolorow et al. 1987; Altman 2010; Aron 2001; Kiesler 1996), relational theory focuses on present interpersonal functioning, particularly as revealed and developed in the clinical relationship. Experience classified as "diverse" is inherently at risk for a non-neurotic but nonetheless non-cohesive quality of experience (Chu 2007).

The evolution of psychoanalytically informed theory in relation to a White, middle- or upper-class, European population makes it suspect regarding applicability to other populations. Contemporary thinkers have aggressively widened the framework to embrace the sociopolitical universe (Kleinman 1988, 1995; Altman 2010). In the process, definitions of intrapsychic structures and the role of interpersonal experiencing have sometimes vied with dimensions of self and social context, so that divergent areas of study have emerged. Social work clinicians remain aware that culture, race, and traumatic life experiences, and the like, are inseparable from assessment of self-experience and the mechanisms of treatment (Berzoff et al. 2008; Tosone 2004; Rosenberger 1999). The contributions and language of classical psychoanalysis (unconscious process, separation and attachment, narcissism, and so on) persist but are transformed into the two-person framework of practice.

Combined attachment and mutual exploration in relational practice promote the drive toward integrity of the self (Balint 1968; McWilliams 2011). Reactions are visceral, in the realm of unformulated experience (Stern 1997; Levenson 1983), as well as conscious and cognitive. Experience classified as "diverse" is inherently at risk for a non-neurotic but nonetheless non-cohesive quality of experience. The development of both attachment and mutual exploration in relational theory address this incoherent potential because they are responsive to what object relations theorists posit as a central drive toward integrity of the self (Balint 1968; McWilliams 1999). The clinical interpersonal field, then, will in practice reflect and address the points of collision and congruence stemming from the two individual, culturally informed, selves. Each individual simultaneously enacts experiences of development and reflects current interactional contexts (Caro Hollander 1997). The clinical interpersonal field thereby reflects and addresses points of congruence and incongruity stemming from the two individual, culturally informed, selves (Bromberg 1998; Hoffman 1998; Symington 2007; Fonagy et al. 2004).

Emergence of Relational Theory for Clinical Social Work Practice

Relational theory is a natural and valuable fit for clinical social work and especially for clinical practice with diverse populations. It reflects the pro-social principles that define contemporary clinical social work without sacrificing intrapsychic understanding. An uneasy relationship exists between psychoanalytic theories that articulate intrapsychic dynamics and itemized practice competencies (Council on Social Work Education 2010). While not overtly contesting the validity of developmental and clinical aspects of psychoanalytic theory, social work educators have at times been concerned that emphasis on internal and historical experiences of the client could eclipse attention to presenting problems and their social determinants.

This uneasiness was particularly acute when Freudian drive theory looked to unconscious conflict stemming from early fixations as the explanation of presenting symptoms and complaints. Ego psychology (Hartmann 1958) was initially embraced in social work as more inclusive, with its proposal of "conflict free" functional attainment. Pearlman's (1957) seminal work on "social casework" emphasized solving problems of social functioning (p. 4). This functional problem approach elevated adaptation without adequately critiquing the social realities to which adaptation was being made. From a relational theory point of view, both drive theory and ego psychology missed the essential therapeutic role of the clinical relationship itself, seeing what Greenson (1967) called the "working alliance" as a mechanism to permit the real work to be done, viz., interpreting unconscious conflict and developmental barriers (as in an oedipal conflict fueling an adult's conflict with an authority). As Bromberg (2011), a relational theorist, has said, particularly in such cases, "conflict interpretations are useless or even worse" (p. 101). Trauma, catastrophic or insidious and cumulative, typifies the life experience of marginalized and oppressed clients as well as many individuals in personally demoralizing circumstances. The problems that afflict the majority of social work clients may indeed contain intrapsychic conflict but are inaccessible in the absence of interpersonal alignment with a clinician who is experienced as an authentic person whose interests are collaborative with the client's goals and real-life situation.

Social work practitioners and social work as a profession remained split between those interested in intrapsychic dynamics and those concentrating on direct action with clients to ameliorate problems. An intermediate wave of psychoanalytic theorists broadened psychodynamic thinking in varying directions but shared "overlapping concerns, emphasizing the roles of relationship and social life in their conceptions of personality development, health, problems in living, and therapeutic action" (Borden 2009, p. 146). Still, the contributions of relationship and social life were viewed as impacting the client who remained the subject of the clinician's concern without directly involving the clinician as a subject of equal concern. Clinical social workers were encouraged about but still wary of the hierarchical and authoritative stance of the psychoanalyst. Licensing distinctions and advanced training selections (whether to train at a psychoanalytic institute; whether such an institute accepted social work trainees) increasingly separated clinical social workers from their peers. This schism also became linked to concerns about addressing diversity: that psychoanalytic theory was being elaborated mainly by White, Western men working with private clients was seen as implicitly segregationist and patriarchal. Clinical social workers studying and working with psychoanalytic orientation were on the defensive or dissociated from social work as a whole, which unfortunately replicated the arbitrary and conflict-laden positions that psychoanalytic theory was seeking to redress.

The emergence of three bodies of psychoanalytic thought – object relations theory (Winnicott, Fairbairn, Klein, Kahn), interpersonal psychoanalysis (Sullivan), and self-psychology (Kohut) – led the way to what Greenberg and Mitchell (1983) distilled and refined into contemporary relational theory. Spurred on also by feminist theoreticians (Baker Miller 2012), the psychoanalytic orientation became egalitarian, experience-near, and closely linked to the social realities of individual lives. The drive to connection became clearly defined as treatment dimension in which both parties negotiate their understanding of problems and solutions.

A helping relationship was redefined as one in which empathy, direct interaction, and experiential learning through clinical interactions are the therapeutic agents (Borden 2009). Thus, the relational clinical practitioner was supported in directing her work to forming and using meaningful connection with the client's direct presentation. Tosone (2004) has articulated that this reaffirms central principles of social work: starting where the client is and addressing real-life factors shaping client problems and clinician options that are the bases of meaningful assistance.

The central importance of human relationships is spelled out in the National Association of Social Work mission statement (Hepworth et. al. 2006). Relational theory expands this statement to explain how the human relationship between social work clinician and client creates a therapeutic experience. In addition to Greenberg and Mitchell (1983), two other bodies of theory support relationship, rather than interpretation, as the agent of healing and enhanced self states. Neuroscience is confirming more quantifiably the therapeutic impact of identifying and addressing ways in which actual experience has shaped, and can reshape, patterns of relating. Etiology of increased affective vitality by relational treatment is tracked to confirm that neurologically "what fires together, wires together." This phrase summarizes the establishment of existing patterns of affective aliveness and also shows that there is an open future of affective experiences (Schore 2003a). Wired in to both client and clinician are historical relational paradigms and their behavioral expressions. Through interaction and mutual influence, key dimensions of direct social work practice (Hepworth et al. 2006), experiences are refired and thereby eventually rewired (Schore 2003b; Schore and Schore 2008).

The feminist movement also championed the centrality of relating over informing as an enhancer of quality of self-experience as well as style of functioning. Baker Miller (2012) conveys the feminist perspective in her description of "Five Good Things":

Growth-fostering relationships empower all people in them. These are characterized by:

1. A sense of zest or well-being that comes from connecting with another person or other persons.
2. The ability and motivation to take action in the relationship as well as other situations.
3. Increased knowledge of oneself and the other person(s).
4. An increased sense of worth.
5. A desire for more connections beyond the particular one.

Zest, growth, motivation, self-knowledge, self-esteem, and a desire for connection and community all are proposed by the feminists as a measure of health that could be pursued directly through relational interchange, rather than as a by-product of interpretation and conflict resolution. Quality of living was the goal and outcome of the quality of relating in the therapeutic process.

All these and many other contemporary contributors demonstrate the integrity of relational theory and clinical social work practice: the relational clinical social worker seeks connection with her client in ways that allow the client to recognize and relinquish, as necessary, embedded patterns and establish new ones according to a framework brought by the client. Psychoanalytic theories help the clinician comprehend and articulate her understanding of the client's subjective experiences. Clinical social work methods help the clinician organize this process of mutual discovery and directions for change. The relational theory outlines these interactions across individual differences as the mechanisms of the therapeutic process.

Key Concepts of Relational Clinical Practice

While each theoretical model has its own language and explanation, the relational theory has distilled key concepts that, appropriately, mark points where differing theories converge. These include:

1. Empathic attunement and engagement

    This concept, drawn primarily from self-psychology, requires an understanding of empathy as encompassing all self states of the client. It is emotional recognition and reflection that includes aggression, despair, dissociation, and all forms of self-experience, including experiences of the clinician's misunderstandings or inadvertent injuries. A relational clinician therefore follows closely and attempts to acknowledge all that a client brings, which creates a container for cohesion-building and experiential learning through the interpersonal dialogue.

2. Mutuality in the dyad

    The clinical process is bidirectional. Neither party's individual perspective holds more value or power. The client is the authority on his subjective experience, including the experience of the helping process. The clinician is the authority on how to conduct the therapeutic process to enhance self-reflection and openness to possibilities, by application of the other principles of relational practice.

3. Co-construction of meanings

    Statements and other ways of conveying information are interpreted selectively by speakers and listeners alike. Interpretation can include speculation on past as well as present bases of meanings. Verification of understanding is shared in relational practice, requiring the social work clinician to be open about her understandings so as to be corrected, confirmed, or otherwise addressed as a collaborator in discovery rather than an authority about who the client is, of what problems consist, and acceptable forms and directions of change.

4. Not knowing and inquiry

    The relational clinician is not defensive about what she does not know. This includes asking for clarification or information can include dimensions of a client's cultural and social contexts and references. Inquiry bolsters the client's authority about his own life conditions and worldview, opening the door to the clinician's exploration of the impact of his background on presenting problems and their parameters of resolution.

5. Transference and Countertransference

    These concepts are reconceived in relational theory. Rather than being projections and distortions of the client and the clinician based on unresolved early life experiences, as in drive theory and earlier versions of object relations theory, in relational theory, transference and countertransference are seen as responses and creations in the real, ongoing interpersonal exchange in that dyad. Important internalized and historical forces continue to shape relationships, including the transference relationship, but the emphasis in relational theory is on the actual elements of the clinical interchange that rekindle unconscious constructions. A special value of transference and countertransference in diversity practice is its surfacing of socially induced assumptions about how differences are predefining and often anxiety producing in the clinical pair.

6. Collaborative goal setting

Irrespective of the clinician's assessment of client dynamics during assessment, an explicit contract for clinical goals is necessary. While this contract may be modified during the course of treatment, including suggested modifications introduced by the clinician, the client's endorsement of the purposes of the relational clinical social work process is required.

7. Authenticity of the clinician as a person

The blank screen of classical psychoanalytic models is replaced in relational therapy by a more open sharing of the clinician's experience in the work. Self-disclosure does not mean unalloyed sharing of personal information. Rather, disclosure of the clinician's thought process, concerns, lack of information about unfamiliar dimensions of the client's social and cultural life experience, and the like are part of the development of mutuality in the helping process.

8. Affirmation of strengths

The client's issues brought for clinical attention are surrounded by many coping strategies that have maintained him. Overt acknowledgement of the effort and efficacy of client coping redirects the relational clinical process from pathology to whole-person understanding. Even when coping strategies are implicated in failures of problem resolution and need to be deconstructed to instill more effective ones, their intentions and contributions to survival are recognized.

9. Cultural competence

This concept is introduced here as a dimension of relational clinical social work practice to emphasize the cultural/social/political context of client lives as intrinsic to creating an effective relational clinical social work process. While cultural competence is often conceived of as knowledge about a specific cultural group – in other words, content information – the relational model promotes addressing the meanings of cultural identity to the client as an individual and as a participant in a therapeutic process. Competence in the clinician resides in acknowledgement of the power of group identity in the client's self-experience and outlook on clinical social work treatment with a specific clinician. Resistance based on cultural differences therefore is viewed as a pathway to understanding and construction of a larger arena of connection. Using all the concepts described above, the culturally competent clinical social worker introduces cultural discussion by hypothesis and inquiry when it is absent in the dialogue.

Guidelines for Practice

Guidelines for practice in relational social work are instruments for charting the course in the relational field; the goal is a treatment process that is mutual and adaptive rather than a prescribed protocol (Hoffman 1998). Techniques such as active listening, reflecting, or interpreting can be learned. Their application is in the service of achieving connection and an agreed upon trajectory of work. The negotiation of this trajectory, which constitutes contracting, requires an extra measure of tolerance by the clinician for a non-predetermined treatment profile (Pizer 1998). While now heightened in relational theory, the phenomenological perspective has been part of social work practice for decades: we need to believe what we see, not see what we already believe.

The clinician remains open to what must be learned in the process about meanings and options that will be congruent with the client's agenda based on his population of identification. There is structure to remaining open and moving toward and through a mutually defined course of practice. This structure is spelled out in the stages of relational practice described below. In preparation for applying the stages and techniques of clinical practice with diverse populations, the clinician needs to be aware of how her own development and present context will be active in the building of a working alliance. Being the product of what is assumed to be the same population of identification initially can be reassuring and increase traction for engagement. At the same time, the clinician needs to be cautious: subjugation of an individual's narrative (Foucault 1980) can occur because of assumptions about similarity as well as difference. Countertransference distortion can be triggered by discomfort with any client narrative about him or the clinician that destabilizes the clinician's own construction of self-cohesion.

The relational clinician is distinguished by willingness to be active in articulating the purpose of finding clinical common ground and the problems that arise in seeking it. Rather than applying the familiar caveat to "interpret the resistance," presuming the client is defending against unconscious conflict, the relational clinician will "call attention to the dissonance." The dissonance may indeed reflect unconscious conflict in the client. From a relational practice point of view, however, micro-, mezzo-, and macro-level forces are at work; populations with which a person identifies shape self-identifications and together interact to create a worldview which is presented in the social work practice setting. Ambivalence in the clinical encounter is more likely than not and may attach to or be generated by diversity issues. Indeed, the absence of ambivalence can be a troubling sign of either developmental arrest (Mahler 1969; Mahler et al. 1975) or pseudo-connection (Benjamin 1988; Symington 2007). Maintenance of connection by acknowledgement of individual differences builds toward a cohesive self in the clinical process and thereby for the client within his own spheres of collective membership.

Being familiar with historical and present social forces impinging on people as members of a vulnerable population is an advantage to the clinician in helping the client feel understood. Starting from the manifest content of the client's presentation, which may highlight his diverse population framework, the clinician conveys interest and allows herself to be educated about the client's view of the problems at hand. At the same time, the clinical assessment must include latent, unconscious components of the client's dynamics. In *Psychoanalytic Diagnosis,* McWilliams (2011) makes the case for psychodynamic diagnosis alongside exploration of the client's reported history and presenting issues. Talking with a person is a phenomenological, moment-to-moment process of discovery and clarification of problems, issues, and strengths, whereas diagnosis condenses a detached categorization which can become reified.

Clinical Social Work Stages and Techniques with Diverse Populations

In the application of relational theory to direct clinical practice with diverse populations, the social worker need not jettison previously learned frameworks for practice. Relational theory refers to the stance of the co-constructivist clinician in interaction with the client and the theoretical framework of promoting self-integration as fundamental to human functioning and vitality (Rogers 1961; Fromm 1998; Stern 2010). The structure of case practice is familiar to all practitioners, new and experienced, who were introduced to clinical social work through the work of Richmond (1918, 1922), Hamilton (1951), Woods and Hollis (1999), Goldstein (2001), and other social work pioneers. The translation of these seminal structural elements to work in a relational model with diverse populations is offered below.

1. Engagement

   Engagement is framed as demonstrating to the client the understanding that his experience of self and his pressing problems are important to the clinician. With clients who are members of diverse populations, meanings may be constructed that have both universal and very culturally specific dimensions. The clinician facilitates engagement by establishing "potential space" (Winnicott 1971; Bollas 1987, 2008), meaning a place of safe communication where cultural idiom is welcome. Language differences are recognized as realities, not apologies. The clinician reflects and modifies as necessary her grasp of the client's problems, motivation, obstacles, and options, indicating her desire to construct a shared relationship.

2. Identification of Core Problems

   Voluntary clients typically arrive with a statement of what is the matter. For mandated clients, a perceived core problem is being required to be in the social work setting itself (Hepworth et al. 2006). Involuntary status, even more than language difficulties, requires direct and immediate acknowledgement. Because involuntary encounters are assigned by outside forces, resistance, conscious and unconscious, occurs as an expectable response to a coercive situation. A relational practice response is for the clinician to acknowledge the coercive forces as part of beginning engagement. The clinician can express that she nonetheless would like to see if there is some way she can be of help with the client's life and difficulties and thereby pursue definition of a core problem. Manifest content becomes a shared language for the relationship exchanges, even as the clinician reflects on latent dimensions such as developmental maturity, character, relational patterns, anxieties, and other content that will inform her assessment of how she can be of help (McWilliams 1999, 2011).

3. Assessment

Assessment includes more than diagnosis; it is an understanding of the client's "overall level of personality structure and functioning" (Dane et al. 2001, p. 483). It weighs the impact of age, gender, sexual orientation, physical and mental health, family structure, conditions of living, and, perhaps most importantly in the area of diversity practice, past and present social forces shaping individual and group experience. The psychodynamic assumption that unconscious process will always shape manifest communication leads the clinician to listen for the latent content of developmental level and defensive style (McWilliams 2011). These universal considerations may be more difficult to identify with an unfamiliar population: individual populations share a template of normal and abnormal communication, relational style, degrees of openness about personal matters, and so on. A frequent area of dissonance between client and clinician is perception of appropriate roles. These are perhaps particularly likely to be grounds for transference and countertransference when culturally determined roles differ.

4. Authenticity and Not Knowing

Asking counter-balances assuming by both parties. A clinician's reluctance to ask for background or current information can reflect countertransference issues about hierarchy. For example, the clinician's professional identity can mask for both parties the goal of parity in developing expertise about the client's problems. Excessive compliance as well as evasion or hostility must be overtly recognized to establish authenticity. Courage to acknowledge not knowing, and needing to know, establishes the client's power to authorize the clinician's work (Altman 2007). Many clients find clinical attention alien and suspect. Particularly among oppressed populations, deception and misdirection may be self-congruent and socially necessary. The onus is on the clinician to explain how the requested information is relevant to a viable course of treatment.

5. Treatment Planning and Goal Setting

Assessment and problem identification will fall flat unless the treatment plan that results reflects goals that are meaningful to the client. The assessment has revealed aspects of character as well as urgent presenting problems. The client's desire for concrete solutions to practical matters is not resistance, in a relational model, but rather a starting point for the clinician to reframe problems in ways that can lead to productive action. Client motivation is enhanced by a treatment plan that is goal directed (Woods and Hollis 1999; Dane et al. 2001).

Demonstrating willingness to engage the presenting problem must be balanced with empathic recognition of what the problem means to the client interpersonally, intrapsychically, and socioculturally. Solutions that destabilize the familiar situation, and call for self-awareness, provoke ambivalence (Mitchell 1993). Change also can mean potential loss of support and recognition in the present social reality (Rosenberger 2011). Goal setting therefore has to have an attainable future direction. The relational clinician demonstrates not only empathic understanding but commitment to helping the client find a safe and tolerable treatment plan. Family therapy, including extended family, pastoral counseling, home visiting, support groups, and the whole armamentarium of social work interventions can be conjoint with a core clinical relationship. Interpersonal security inspires and also protects, and the psychodynamic underpinnings of relational practice help the clinician convey that the client brought the problem, however hesitantly, for an important purpose.

6. Forming a Contract for Clinical Work

A contract for social work practice rests on mutual definition of purpose and scope, as well as practical arrangements (Woods and Hollis 1999). A contract for clinical social work practice includes diagnostic thinking and a socially conscious mental health agenda in its purpose and scope (Brandell 2011). The contract thus must reflect both the client's biopsychosocial functioning and the plan for addressing his functioning in his social context. The relational clinical social work model therefore draws on attachment theory in a socially conscious way (Brandell 2011). The contract is a hypothesis about why the problem exists and the most likely way to effect change. The contract emerges by consensus, built on relational attunement, about problem definition and pathways to seeking problem resolution.

7. Into Action: Following the Treatment Plan

A particular strength of clinical social work practice is the multitude of settings in which training and practice occur. Diversity is the norm. Therefore, the relational clinical practitioner acquires professional skills that infuse concrete problem solving with psychodynamic depth, and vice versa. The observant relational clinician receives resistance to intrapsychic exploration in contracting as a means of clarifying to the client's paradigms of help receiving and help providing (Kleinman 1988). Additionally, the relational clinician assesses her own resistances and countertransferences, whether or not they are co-members of the client's population of identification. Relational social work practice recognizes the significance of the social context of the client, balancing insight with real sociocultural options and consequences of change (Akhtar 1995; Kleinman 1988; McWilliams 1994).

8. Termination

Termination ideally is planned from the outset, as part of the assessment process (Brandell 2011), reflecting interventions that are culturally congruent. The authenticity of the working relationship in relational social work carries through from acknowledgement of limits of familiarity with a diverse population to direct discussion of any interpersonal practice disruptions to the clarification of the boundaries in time, frequency, and length of the clinical process. The code of ethics (NASW 2011) calls for this transparency in treatment planning for all social workers. The practitioner's authenticity in sharing her limits of certainty about the client's sociocultural perspective offsets the possibility that the work becomes another arena in which the client is pressured and controlled to act in ways that are inherently incongruent with the sense of individual self (Symington 2007; Kohut 2000; Hoffman 1998). Establishment of a mutual, respectful, and attuned therapeutic process, however short or long, creates hope; it also creates attachment and the feelings of loss at its ending (Basch 1995; Mann 1977, 1980).

Clients of diverse populations often have endured multiple losses as well as ongoing alienation in the dominant culture. These factors make the achievement of a meaningful clinical social work relationship all the more difficult to leave. With this in mind, the social work clinician leaves ample time for the termination process. The relational approach guides the clinician to return to her assessment appraisal of the client's patterns of dependency and history of separations and thereby anticipate and articulate the reemergence of these issues in the face of this new loss. Ambiguity and ambivalence in completing termination is unavoidable (Sanville 1982), but adequate time to reflect and review the achievements and incomplete aspects of the practice process are dealt with in a direct and transparent manner. In work with diverse populations, this summing up step may very well refer to the cultural explorations, learning, and negotiations that have taken place: this approach anchors the diversity dimension to the interpersonal dimension wherein the integration of differences into a larger whole has taken place.

Conclusion

Clinical social work with diverse populations is an extension, and a model, of the relational approach to a co-constructed, mutually conducted, and personally authentic therapeutic process. As a profession, social work has evolved toward a less hierarchical, more interpersonally congruent model. Conducting practice in light of a client's values, circumstances of living, and range of opportunities has become the hallmark of contemporary social work, and clinical social work has focused on the individual's intrapsychic experience with those social realities (Brandell 2011). Diversity practice heightens our core social work awareness of the significance of the client's developmental and continuing circumstances. It embraces open communication about what the client and the clinician do and do not know about their populations of identification. It directs the clinician to timing and stance in her own use of self as an extension of her understanding of the client's cultural idiom. What is meaningful and relevant to the clinical problem at hand is gathered in the assessment stage, including individual developmentally determined issues in tandem with socially created issues based on the client's specific cultural context and experience as part of a marginalized and oppressed group.

Theorists of the two-person psychologies, beginning with Fairbairn (1954), Winnicott (1958, 1965b), and others, up to the present-day writers (Aron and Harris 2011; McWilliams 1999, 2011), have offered a metapsychology and clinical theory that collectively underpins modern relational theory (Goldstein 2001; Wachtel 2008). The common elements are the mutuality of exploration to establish a treatment focus that is congruent with the client's social as well as psychological reality and the use of an open dialogue throughout the clinical process so that both participants help maintain the therapeutic course. Diversity practice makes central the incorporation of sociopolitical and cultural realities that inform clients' development, present problems, and future options (Altman 2007; Caro Hollander 2010; Berzoff et al. 2008; Hartman 1992). Representing the fundamental social work ethic of individual self-determination (NASW Code of Ethics 2011), relational clinical social work joins the micro-, mezzo-, and macro-levels of client dynamics and realities in a structured yet nonhierarchical model of practice particularly suited to work with diverse populations.

Study Questions

1. The change in expression of a core social work principle from "client in situation" to "client and clinician in situation" is reflective of relational theory. Explain.
2. Diversity is a natural fit with relational theory because of its emphasis, among other principles, on mutuality and co-construction of meanings. Give an example of how mutuality and co-construction of meaning bridged a cultural difference in your practice.
3. Choose one of the stages of treatment, as outlined in this chapter. Give an example of applying one or more relational social work principles in this stage of a case.
4. Relational theory helps resolve historical distinctions between clinical social work and psychoanalysis. Explain, with an example, how an interaction with a client reflects how both of these traditions inform the practice exchange.
5. Explain how relational theory conceptualizes the use of transference and countertransference in practice.
6. Cultural diversity embraces more than demographic categories. Summarize in one paragraph how relational social work expands cultural diversity thinking.

References

Akhtar, S. (1995). A third individuation: Immigration, identity, and the psychoanalytic process. *Journal of the American Psychoanalytic Association, 43*, 1051–1084.

Altman, N. (2000). Black and white thinking: A psychoanalyst reconsiders race. *Psychoanalytic Dialogues, 10*, 589–605.

Altman, N. (2007). Integrating the transpersonal with the intersubjective: Commentary on Mary Tennes's beyond intersubjectivity: The transpersonal dimension of the psychoanalytic encounter. *Contemporary Psychoanalysis, 43*, 526–535.

Altman, N. (2010). *The analyst in the inner city: Race, class and culture through a psychoanalytic lens* (2nd ed.). New York: Routledge.

Aron, L. (2001). *A meeting of minds: Mutuality in psychoanalysis.* Hillsdale: Analytic Press.

Aron, L., & Harris, A. (Eds.). (2011). *Relational psychoanalysis* (Vol. 4). New York: Routledge.

Bacal, H., & Newman, K. (1990). *Theories of object relations: Bridges to self psychology.* New York: Columbia University Press.

Baker Miller, J. (2012). *Five good things.* Jean Baker Miller Training Institute at the Wellesley Centers for Women. Wellesley

Balint, M. (1968). *The basic fault: Therapeutic aspects of regression.* London: Tavistock.

Basch, M. (1995). *Doing brief psychotherapy.* New York: Basic Books.

Benjamin, J. (1988). *The bonds of love.* New York: Pantheon Books.

Bennet, S., & Nelson, J. (2010). *Adult attachment in clinical social work.* New York: Springer. doi:10.1007/978-1-4419-6241-6.

Berreby, D. (2005). *Us and them: The science of identity.* Chicago: University of Chicago Press.

Berzoff, J. (Ed.). (2011). *Falling through the cracks: Psychodynamic practice with vulnerable and oppressed populations.* New York: Columbia University Press.

Berzoff, J., Flanagan, L., & Hertz, P. (2008). *Inside out and outside in: Psychodynamic clinical theory and psychopathology in contemporary multicultural contexts* (2nd ed.). New York: Jason Aronson.

Bhopal, R., & Donaldson, L. (1998). White, European, Western, Caucasian, or what? Inappropriate labeling in research on race, ethnicity, and health. *American Journal of Public Health, 88*(9), 1303–1307. doi:10.2105/AJPH.88.9.1303, DOI:10.2105%2FAJPH.88.9.1303.

Bollas, C. (1987). *The shadow of the object: Psychoanalysis of the unthought known.* New York: Columbia University Press.

Bollas, C. (2008). *The evocative object world.* New York: Routledge.

Borden, W. (2009). *Contemporary psychodynamic theory and practice.* New York: Lyceum Books.

Brandell, J. (2011). *Theory and practice in clinical social work* (2nd ed.). Los Angeles: Sage.

Brodkin, K. (1998). *How Jews became white folks and what that says about race in America.* Piscataway: Rutgers University Press.

Bromberg, P. (1998). *Standing in the spaces: Essays on clinical process, trauma, and dissociation.* Hillsdale: Analytic Press.

Bromberg, P. (2011). *The shadow of the tsunami and the growth of the relational mind.* New York: Taylor Francis.

Buck, S. (2010). *Acting white: The ironic legacy of desegregation.* New Haven: Yale University Press.

Caro Hollander, N. (1997). *Love in a time of hate: Liberation psychology in Latin America.* New York: Routledge.

Caro Hollander, N. (2010). *Uprooted minds: Surviving the politics of political terror in the Americas.* New York: Routledge.

Chu, B. (2007). Considering culture one client at a time: Maximizing the cultural exchange. *Pragmatic Case Studies in Psychotherapy, 3*(3), 34–43. New Brunswick, NJ: Rutgers University Libraries.

Council on Social Work Education (2010). Alexandria, VA.

Dane, B., Tosone, C., & Wolson, A. (2001). *Doing more with less: Using long-term skills in short-term treatment.* New York: Jason Aronson.

Fairbairn, W. (1954). *An object-relations theory of the personality.* Oxford: Basic Books.

Fletcher, L., & Hayes, S. (2005). Relational frame theory, acceptance and commitment therapy, and a functional analytic definition of mindfulness. *Journal of Rational-Emotive and Cognitive-Behavioral Therapy, 23*(4), 315–336. doi:10.1007/s10942-005-0017-7.

Fonagy, P., Gergely, G., Jurist, E., & Target, M. (2004). *Affect regulation, mentalization, and the development of the self.* New York: Other Press.

Foucault, M. (1980). *Power/knowledge: Selected interviews and other writings.* New York: Pantheon Press.

Freud, S. (1957). *The standard edition of the complete psychological works of Sigmund Freud.* London: Hogarth Press.

Fromm, E. (1998). *The essential Fromm: Life between having and being.* New York: Continuum.

Goldstein, E. (1995). *Ego psychology and social work practice.* New York: The Free Press.

Goldstein, E. (2001). *Object relations theory and self psychology in social work practice*. New York: The Free Press.

Greenberg, J., & Mitchell, S. A. (1983). *Object relations in psychoanalytic theory*. Cambridge: Harvard University Press.

Greenson, R. (1967). *The technique and practice of psychoanalysis* (Vol. I). New York: International Universities Press.

Hamilton, G. (1951). *Theory and practice of social case work*. New York: Columbia University Press.

Hartman, A. (1992). In search of subjugated knowledge. *Social Work, 37*(6), 483–484.

Hartmann, H. (1958). *Ego psychology and the problem of adaptation*. New York: International Universities Press.

Hepworth, D., Rooney, R., & Rooney, G. (2006). *Direct social work practice: Theory and skills*. Belmont: Brooks Cole.

Hoffman, I. (1998). *Ritual and spontaneity in the psychoanalytic process: A dialectical-constructivist view*. Hillsdale: Analytic Press.

Jordan, J. (2008). *Relational-cultural therapy* (Systems of psychotherapy video series). Washington, DC: American Psychological Association.

Kiesler, D. (1996). *Contemporary interpersonal theory and research: Personality, psychopathology, and psychotherapy*. New York: Wiley.

Klein, M. (1997). *Envy and gratitude*. London: Vintage.

Kleinman, A. (1988). *Rethinking psychiatry: From cultural category to personal experience*. New York: The Free Press.

Kleinman, A. (1995). *Writing at the margin: Discourse between anthropology and medicine*. Berkeley: University of California Press.

Kohut, H. (2000). *Analysis of the self: Systematic approach to treatment of narcissistic personality disorders*. Madison: International Universities Press.

Levenson, E. (1983). *The ambiguity of change*. New York: Basic Books.

Mahler, M. (1969). On human symbiosis and the vicissitudes of individuation. *Archives of General Psychiatry, 20*(4), 490–492.

Mahler, M., Bergman, A., & Pine, F. (1975). *The psychological birth of the human infant: Symbiosis and individuation*. New York: Basic Books.

Mann, J. (1977). *Casebook in time-limited psychotherapy*. New York: Jason Aronson.

Mann, J. (1980). *Time-limited psychotherapy*. Cambridge: Harvard University Press.

McWilliams, N. (1999). *Psychoanalytic case formulation*. New York: Guilford Press.

McWilliams, N. (2011). *Psychoanalytic diagnosis* (2nd ed.). New York: Guilford Press.

Mitchell, S. A. (1993). *Hope and dread in psychoanalysis*. New York: Basic Books.

Mitchell, S. (1997). *Influence and autonomy in psychoanalysis*. New York: Routledge.

National Association of Social Workers. (2011). *Code of ethics*. New York: NASW.

Pearlman, H. H. (1957). *Social casework: A problem-solving process*. Chicago: University of Chicago Press.

Pizer, S. A. (1998). *Building bridges: The negotiation of paradox in psychoanalysis*. Hillsdale: Analytic Press.

Richmond, M. (1918). *Social diagnosis*. New York: Russell Sage.

Richmond, M. (1922). *What is social case work?* New York: Russell Sage.

Rogers, Carl. (1961). *On Becoming a Person: A Therapist's View of Psychotherapy*. London: Constable.

Rosenberger, J. B. (1999). Heightening cultural awareness in the psychoanalytic situation. In *Psychoanalytic inquiry*. Hillsdale: The Analytic Press.

Rosenberger, J. B. (2011). Freedom from/freedom to. *Proceedings: 50th anniversary clinical conference*. New York: International Conference for the Advanced Professional Practice of Clinical Social Work.

Saari, C. (1986). *Clinical social work treatment: How does it work?* New York: Gardner Books.

Saari, C. (2002). *The environment; its role in psychosocial functioning and psychotherapy*. New York: Columbia University Press.

Safran, J. (2008). *Relational psychotherapy* (Systems of psychotherapy video series). Washington, DC: American Psychological Association.

Sanville, J. (1982). Partings and impartings: A nonmedical approach to interruptions and terminations. *Clinical Social Work Journal, 10*(2), 123–131.

Schore, A. (2003a). *Affect disregulation and disorders of the self.* New York: Norton.

Schore, A. (2003b). *Affect regulation and the repair of the self.* New York: Norton.

Schore, J., & Schore, N. (2008). Modern attachment theory: The central role of affect regulation in development and treatment. *Clinical Social Work Journal, 36*, 9–20.

Stern, D. (1997). *Unformulated experience.* Hillsdale: Analytic Press.

Stern, D. (2010). *Forms of vitality: Exploring dynamic experience in psychology, the arts, psychotherapy, and development.* Oxford: New York.

Stolorow, R., & Atwood, G. (1992). *Context of being: The intersubjective foundations of psychological life.* Hillsdale: The Analytic Press.

Stolorow, R., Brandchaft, B., & Atwood, G. (1987). *Psychoanalytic treatment: An intersubjective perspective.* Hillsdale: The Analytic Press.

Strachey, J. (1966). *Standard edition of the complete psychological works of Sigmund Freud.* London: Hogarth Press.

Symington, N. (2007). *Becoming a person through psychoanalysis.* London: Karnac Books Ltd.

The New York Times (2011, June 23). *Mental health expert reveals her own fight.*

Tosone, C. (2004). Relational social work: Honoring the tradition. *Smith College Studies in Social Work, 74*(3), 475–487.

Turner, F. (1996). *Social work treatment.* New York: The Free Press.

Wachtel, P. (2008). *Relational theory and the practice of psychotherapy.* New York: Guilford.

Winnicott, D. (1958). *Collected papers: Through paediatrics to psychoanalysis.* London: Tavistock.

Winnicott, D. (1965a). *The family and individual development.* London: Tavistock.

Winnicott, D. (1965b). *Maturational processes and the facilitating environment: Studies in the theory of the emotional development.* London: Hogarth Press.

Winnicott, D. (1971). *Playing and reality.* London: Tavistock.

Woods, M., & Hollis, F. (1999). *Casework: A psychosocial therapy.* New York: McGraw-Hill.

Relational Therapy: Constructivist Principles to Guide Diversity Practice

Harriet Goodman

Introduction

A central claim of clinical social work is its commitment to serve marginalized and diverse groups of people. Achieving cultural competence is fundamental to social work education and built into the Education Policy and Accreditation Standards of the Council on Social Work Education. At the same time, social work is a profession that asserts expert knowledge recognized by a license following an advanced degree. The purpose of diversity curricula and training is to enhance social workers' knowledge and practice with different groups of people they identify as marginalized, oppressed, or simply different. In the case of clinical practitioners, years of supervised practice and specialized training increase social worker's self-identification as authorities about the lives of other people. The irony in this relationship, where professionals claim expert knowledge about subjugated others, is that the power associated with becoming an authority about other people risks disqualifying the experiences of the very people clinicians strive to understand.

Two decades ago, Hartman (1992) recognized this paradox and described how unitary knowledge excluded the lived experiences of subjugated groups. In contrast, when people sought to define themselves, they were able to validate their own truths. In the last century, these actions were evident in the political acts and written words of Black Americans, women, homosexuals, immigrants, and people with mental illness. By advancing their own aspirations and ideas about themselves, they were able to override the ways in which powerful experts defined them. Through their own words and actions, they replaced the "expert" knowledge of others with expressions of their own experiences (Hartman 1992). Hartman wanted social

H. Goodman, MS, LMSW, DSW, Ph.D. (✉)
Silberman School of Social Work, Hunter College, City University of New York,
New York, USA

The Graduate Center of the City University of New York, New York, USA
e-mail: hgoodman@hunter.cuny.edu

J.B. Rosenberger (ed.), *Relational Social Work Practice with Diverse Populations*,
Essential Clinical Social Work Series, DOI 10.1007/978-1-4614-6681-9_3,
© Springer Science+Business Media New York 2014

workers to interrupt the power disparities between themselves and their clients, examine their roles as experts about the lives of other people, and reject the idea that clients were simply passive recipients of professional ministrations (Hartman 1992). Awareness of the theoretical underpinnings that may unconsciously guide learned expertise allows the practitioner to greater self-evaluation and relational authenticity in the relational clinical encounter.

Currently in social work education, infusion of cultural content throughout the curriculum or courses to develop knowledge about specific cultural and ethnic groups are central vehicles for producing culturally competent practitioners who can work with diverse populations. In addition, widely disseminated training programs such as "Undoing Racism" (James et al. 2008) or curricula developed through an anti-oppression lens (van Wormer and Snyder 2007) are meant to sensitize social workers to the experiences of diverse groups and the effects of White privilege, class, or cultural bias on their practice. However, the outcomes of these efforts may not be effective. Anecdotal reports suggest that White social work students may feel burdened because of their own perceived privileged status (Abrams and Moto 2007), and the persistent silence of ethnic and racial minority students in the classroom frustrates discussion of diverse life experiences (Ortiz and Jani 2010). Critics of diversity curricula note they "rely on the production and circulation of generalizations and the making of grand summary statements [that] tend to be violent, colonizing, and possessing only a pretense of objectivity" (Furlong and Wight 2011, p. 48). In addition, when cultural competence is only an add-on to professional education, it may not promote the need for practitioners to develop their own capacity for the self-reflection necessary to engage in unearthing their own ideological and cultural values (Furlong and Wight 2011) essential for diversity practice.

This leaves many clinical social workers pessimistic about the state of diversity practice and searching for alternative conceptual models to promote enduring cultural competence for practice. On a more positive note, some social work professors have integrated constructivist concepts, an epistemological way of knowing that rejects unitary knowledge, and emphasizes qualitative research concepts such as the social construction of meaning into courses with cross-cultural content (Lee and Greene 1999). For example, in Finland, educators used discourse analysis to focus on conversations of cultural meaning between social workers and immigrant clients as a methodological tool and a resource to explain the ordinary and common in immigrant's lives. In this way, they were able to access the individualistic and dynamic ways in which culture played out in a transitional and global context (Anis 2005). More recently, Furlong and Wight (2011) promoted the concepts of "curiosity" and "informed not knowing" so that the clinician positioned the client as the expert and the worker as the knowledge seeker. In addition, they asserted the clinician should regard the client as "a mirror upon which the practitioner can see the outline of their own personal, professional, ideological, and professional profile" (p. 39).

These efforts suggest that constructivist approaches might provide clinicians with strategies they can apply over a lifetime of combined self-reflection and knowledge seeking and a greater possibility for understanding the diverse experiences of clients. This supports the notion that achieving diversity practice is a lifelong endeavor (Furlong and Wight 2011; Kincheloe 2008). Even Hartman touched on the language of qualitative research methods. For example, she referenced "bracketing," a qualitative research concept that calls for setting aside one's own experiences when interacting with another person to allow for the expression of the other person's own worldviews. In this way, she advanced the idea that diminishing the power between researchers and subjects, or by extension practitioners and patients, could produce better representations of clients' experiences. She suggested that augmenting the voices of subjugated people could not occur through an epistemological approach that assumed the existence of an objective reality outside of the person under the control of elite groups (Foucault 1980; Hartman 1992).

In contrast, social worker's application of constructivist knowledge building approaches or qualitative research methods might help clinicians transcend their own worldviews in a therapeutic relationship so that those of their clients could emerge (Abrams and Moto 2007; Lit and Shek 2002; Opie 1992; Williams 2006). Methods drawn from a particular ontological view of knowledge building suggest a route for how relational clinical practice might elevate the truths of clients' experiences and reveal the highly individual, contextualized experiences of people whose lives are different from those of their therapists.

This is a radically different way to augment the perspectives of diverse groups within therapy. It suggests that the therapeutic relationship is a potential venue where the therapist and the client can build contextual, linguistic, intersubjective, and social knowledge together (Kvale and Brinkmann 2009); this would enable clients to project the subjective realities within them into the clinical relationship. Although there is always inevitable power asymmetry between professionals and their clients (Karnieli-Miller et al. 2009; Teram et al. 2005), a clinician's desire (Furlong and Wight 2011) to learn about how patients experience and perceive their own worlds positions them to transfer their authoritative knowledge to clients, the true experts about their everyday lived experiences.

This chapter makes an explicit connection between constructivist research methods, those in various traditions of qualitative inquiry, and relational clinical social worker's attunement to the experiences of diverse populations. I use the terms "constructivist research paradigm" and "qualitative methods" interchangeably and explore a modest range of qualitative research traditions that have the potential to enhance diversity practice. Similarly, I use the term "culture" or "cultural group" to refer to any group of people who interact together over time and develop distinctive features. I propose that it is unlikely through reading, conducting research that distills the experiences of diverse groups, or training and course work alone that social workers learn about cultural variation. Instead, when clinicians gain access to how individuals construct their unique and evolving identities, they can understand them best.

Strategies drawn from constructivist research methods have the potential to help us unearth the lived experiences of people who are our clients. Imbedded in constructivist transactional and subjective epistemology (Lincoln and Guba 2003) are methods that can help clinical social workers understand the cultural distinctiveness of individual people. Although knowing *about* cultural variations among clients might provide starting points for diversity practice, these can only serve as "sensitizing concepts" or conjectures for understanding other people; it is through discovery of indigenous experiences (Patton 2001, p. 278) of individual clients that ultimately confirms, disconfirms, or entirely transforms a clinician's understanding of their client's realities. Generalizations about particular groups may be useful for the practitioner, but they should never be assumed as universally true (Furlong and Wight 2011). This stance allows for the particular representation of the meaning of culture in a client's life experience to emerge both temporally and contextually. Otherwise, clinicians will not be able to keep pace with the "moving target" nature of diversity practice with clients who live with us in a rapidly changing environment (Ortiz and Jani 2010).

A constructivist approach is particularly aligned with relational clinical practice, because it assumes the active engagement of both the researcher and the informant – or the emersion of both the therapist and the client – in a process of discovery consistent with cocreated interaction and learning (Pozzuto et al. 2009). The purpose of research is to generate knowledge. This is different from psychotherapy, where the therapist's role is to enable a client in some way. However, relational therapy and qualitative research share many attributes. They both call for elements of mutual discovery within a process that involves engagement and examination. They both have transformative potential (Finlay and Evans 2009). The relational therapeutic consultation is a conversation with features similar to qualitative inquiry. It is a venue where therapists can listen and respond openly without insisting that their particular beliefs, values, or assumptions about those of others are the right ones (Barrineau and Bozarth 1989). Strategies qualitative researchers employ have the potential to help relational practitioners gain entrée into worlds beyond their own (Frie 2010).

Introducing the *Bricolage*

Bricolage is a French word that translates as a "handyman" or "jack of all trades," a person who employs whatever tools he needs to get the job done. Levi-Strauss (1968) contrasted these "tinkerers" with skilled craftsmen who operated as technicians and followed a precise method. Denzin and Lincoln (2004) extended the concept of *Bricolage* and drew parallels between the work of qualitative researchers and that of *bricoleurs*. As *bricoleurs*, researchers employ whatever methodological strategies are necessary within the unfolding context of the inquiry. With this in mind, rather than locate a single qualitative method that will inform diversity practice for relational therapists, I propose scouring qualitative research traditions for methodological elements that might prove useful for diversity practice.

By proposing a *Bricolage* of methods drawn from several qualitative traditions, I highlight the synchrony between qualitative research and relational theory in clinical social work practice with different groups and propose a flexible guide for diversity practice. Drawing on various elements from an array of qualitative research traditions, the relational therapist can develop a repertoire of strategies to enhance diversity practice rather than follow specific steps associated with a single tradition. In this way, clinicians can apply a range of tactics to uncover the realities of their clients' lives (Kincheloe 2001, 2005; McLeod 2001; Warne and McAndrew 2009). Here I familiarize relational social workers with the roots of these concepts and language for strategies they can select in their roles as *bricoleurs* as circumstances develop over time.

The *Bricolage* is particularly well suited for relational diversity practice, because of its grounding in egalitarian relationships and because it values unearthing subjugated knowledge. In addition, it demands self-awareness on the part of the clinician within the complexity of the lived world of their clients. Kincheloe (2008) describes those who practice as *bricoleurs* as "detectives of subjugated insight" (p. 336).

This chapter begins with overview of the development of scientific knowledge in the modern age beginning with a rejection of the medieval embrace of received beliefs and the adoption of positivism for research about human experiences. Following a summary of constructivist inquiry and principles associated with qualitative methods generally, I provide brief overviews of several traditions of qualitative research that have elements particularly salient for the relational therapist; methods from these traditions will form the basis of a *Bricolage* for diversity practice. Then I indicate how clinicians in relational therapeutic practice can employ methods associated with these traditions to support the revelation of diversity. Taken together as the *Bricolage*, these concepts offer a "way into" the social realities of clients towards enriched diversity practice.

Modern and Social Constructivist Perspectives

Positivism and the Modern World

Most social workers understand the distinction between positivist and constructivist research as the divide between quantitative and qualitative research methods. The positivist, quantitative approach is the more familiar (Giorgi 2005) and the most conventionally "scientific" (Thyer 2008). This is the case although qualitative research is a vibrant and growing method of inquiry in the postmodern world (Lit and Shek 2002) to the point where some describe it as an "indispensible part of the methodological repertoire of the social sciences" (Jovanovic 2011, p. 1). However, the paradigm debate extends beyond techniques. Positivist and constructivist research have divergent ontological stances and represent different philosophical approaches to the nature of inquiry. Overall, science is a systematic quest for knowledge, and within it are conceptual roots that represent assumptions and beliefs about the nature of reality, the study of knowledge, how we acquire knowledge, the relationship between the researcher and the subject under study, and the language that represents what is known (Lincoln and Guba 2003; Lit and Shek 2002; Ponterotto 2005). Different research paradigms represent different approaches to science.

Beginning in the in the seventeenth and eighteenth centuries, the Enlightenment signaled a movement away from Western ways of knowing typical of the Medieval period that relied on religious doctrine and received beliefs and towards modernity. This shift created new ways of understanding the world. Galileo and Copernicus were the first natural scientists in the modern sense of the word. In opposition to a world known only through Christian doctrine, they began the transformation of a subjective world into one that was exact, knowable, and objective (Karlsson 1992; McLeod 2001) through a process of the "mathematization of nature" (Karlsson 1992, p. 412) and a natural scientific tradition of abstracting knowledge of the world. Accompanied by improvements in measuring systems, Galileo made the ontological assertion to measure what could be measured and make measures for anything else (Weyl 1959).

John Locke and René Descartes were the earliest philosophers associated with this approach; they asserted the idea of an objectively knowable world outside of the researcher. In the early 1800s, Auguste Comte applied the label "social physics" to what he would later call sociology. This reflected the belief that the same methods of inquiry for the natural sciences could apply to the study of human affairs. His term for this perspective was "positivism," which involved developing material explanations for both natural and human phenomena (Thyer 2008). In the nineteenth century when positivism became an organized branch of philosophy, John Stuart Mill (1843/1906) also claimed that both the social and natural sciences should work towards discovering laws that explained and predicted phenomena using the same hypothetico-deductive methods (Karlsson 1992). In other words, he also promoted the idea that the methods for knowing about human beings and the natural world were essentially the same.

For 150 years since then, positivism has been the dominant force in the natural sciences and readily adopted by the social sciences (Lincoln and Guba 2003; Ponterotto 2005). The core of this research paradigm is that the world is made of publically accessible substances that people can describe and observe (Giorgi 2005). For the most part, both the natural sciences and the various human sciences claim these ontological approaches and continue to employ essentially the same methods.

Positivism emphasizes empirical research methods dominated by experimental design, where the purpose is explanation and prediction. The social sciences, including psychology and social work, have largely embraced this picture of an objective reality, and many still affirm psychosocial phenomena are a part of that reality in the same way as the natural sciences (Thyer 2008). Hearkening back to Galileo, a central feature of this paradigm is the application of valid and reliable measures. As such, the language of the positivist paradigm is the language of numbers. Consequently, the methods are chiefly quantitative and manipulative and emphasize the verification or rejection of hypotheses using statistical tests as the product of this repertoire of methodological elements (Lincoln and Guba 2003). Research involves building an "edifice of knowledge," cause and effect linkages, and the ability to generalize. The conventional benchmarks of positivist "rigor" involve internal and external validity, reliability, and objectivity (Lincoln and Guba 2003).

These are all concepts familiar to clinicians in social work practice. For some, they are the only way they understand "research," perhaps because in contemporary social work education, research courses emphasize statistics. In addition, evidence-based practice grounded in positivist methods is ascendant, and in the hierarchy of scientific rigor, the randomized controlled trial rests at the top. However, journals dedicated to qualitative research and multi-methods in social work have grown with a corresponding vibrant literature that embraces various constructivist research traditions. In addition, professionals involved in relational therapies contest unitary knowledge, because they claim the positivist paradigm cannot produce critical aspects of knowledge that inform their practice (Aisenberg 2008; Finlay and Evans 2009; Nilsson 2010). It is one reason many psychotherapists look to constructivist research paradigms when they conduct research.

Constructivist Research Perspectives

It is easy to see why Hartman criticized positivism and unitary knowledge for subjugating the voices of marginalized populations. Within the positivist paradigm, researchers establish "real" definitions of the essential attributes of variables. They assign nominal definitions that represent consensus or a convention about how a particular term is used. Finally, they propose operational definitions that specify how they will measure variables. In that sense, researchers are the masters of operationalization, because they control the attributes of a variable, and they decide how they will measure it in their studies.

This lies in stark contrast to the constructivist paradigm where the researcher's concern is to study "characteristically human phenomena" in a world where man is "an experiencing human creature" (Giorgi 1966, p. 39). Here meaning-making is central to knowledge and involves local and specific realities and constructions of subjective experiences where the context is an essential component of understanding. The intention is not to mirror reality. Instead, constructivists focus on interpretation and negotiation of meaning in the social world (Kvale 1996).

Unlike the positivist researcher who is a disinterested scientist, the posture of the constructivist researcher is that of a passionate participant and a facilitator of multi-voiced reconstruction of human experiences. The critique of positivism for research about people is that "unlike gases or gravity, human behavior is always shaped by context and shaped by time. We cannot generalize about human behavior because human behavior is not a-contextual, nor a-historical, never ungendered, un-classed, or non-racial" (Lincoln 1998, p. 15). In contrast to positivists, constructivists seek forms of knowledge that are context specific and inseparable from granular understanding of race, class, and gender (Lincoln 1998); their commitment is to depth of knowledge and probing understanding the human condition. When phenomena appear, they do so within a context that is relevant for understanding them (Giorgi 1966).

Tracing the various roots of constructivism represents a set of traditions, each of which contains its own historical origins and associated schools, often overlapping in methods and generating variant traditions over time. This is natural for an approach that promotes methodological flexibility. However, constructivist research traditions share a great deal. They reject traditional non-reflective positivist approaches to knowledge and assert that studies of the human experience are not approachable through reductionist, context-stripping quantitative methods. Researchers who embrace a constructivist perspective consider the whole experience rather than only segments of an experience. Instead of seeking to measure occurrences, qualitative researchers search for the essence of meaning they obtain through first-person accounts in narratives, informal or formal conversations, or observations of people within a particular cultural context (Moustakas 1994). In some traditions, they may also discover meaning in artifacts, such as poems, pictures, or stories that enrich their understanding.

A central focus of qualitative inquiry is how people construct meaning in a social, personal, and relational world that is complex and layered. For qualitative researchers, the objective is always to do justice to the experiences of their informants, whom they often view as coresearchers, by opening up meanings in areas of social lives not easily understood (McLeod 2001). Qualitative research emphasizes learning about phenomena inductively and in their own right; it addresses open, exploratory questions and seeks to discover unique phenomena (Elliott 2008).

Critical to establishing the connection between diversity practice in relational therapy and the constructivist paradigm is the view that our understanding that people's experiences are historic and culturally relative. "Not only are they specific to particular cultures and periods of history, they are seen as products of that culture and history and are dependent upon the particular social and economic arrangements prevailing in that culture at that time" (Burr 2003, p. 4). These approaches produce more textured knowledge and reveal subjugated and indigenous meaning as they attempt to distance knowledge production from the control of elite groups (Kincheloe 2008) who claim they have expert knowledge.

Overview of the Traditions of Qualitative Research

Efforts to categorize the traditions of qualitative research are widespread and vary. They represent an evolving set "methods" that often involve refinement, transformation, or reconfiguration by a new generation of adherents to the original "tradition." There is also considerable overlap in methods, although the language associated with each tradition may be different (Creswell et al. 2007).

In order to draw on various elements for the *Bricolage*, I discuss qualitative research traditions often referred to in the social work literature or employed in studies of clinical practice. These are ethnography, phenomenology and hermeneutics, heuristics, and grounded theory. I will briefly review the history, characteristics, and conceptual elements associated with each of these traditions; I will also suggest how each can enhance diversity practice in relational therapy. Ultimately,

I will construct a tentative toolbox for the clinician that draws on these principles. Although all constructivist research traditions call on the same ontological values, each offers different elements that may be relevant for promoting diversity in relational therapy with different clients and under different circumstances.

Ethnography

Overview. Ethnography is the earliest distinctive qualitative research tradition; it strives to understand the culture of a group of people. It involves study within social settings, where the researcher has the opportunity for emersion in that locale and access to both direct observation and interactions with particular social groups. An underlying assumption of ethnography is that when a group of people interacts together, they will evolve a culture, which is a set of patterns and beliefs that guide the members of the group. Participant observation in the tradition of anthropology is the primary method used in ethnographic study (Patton 2001). Typically, ethnographers keep extensive field notes to record their observations and interactions, generally accompanied by separate analytic notations. The purpose of ethnographic inquiry is to produce a representation of the cultural or social group studied (Tedlock 2000).

Jovanovic (2011) and others (Denzin and Lincoln 2004; Patton 2001) locate the historical origins of modern qualitative study within ethnography. The earliest practitioners of this method worked during the beginning of the last century with anthropological field investigations of different cultural groups. These early ethnographers included Bronislaw Malinowski, Gregory Bateson, and Margaret Meade. They believed they had the authority as researchers to represent the experiences of the people they studied, a situation that dissolved over time with the changing ontology of qualitative inquiry (Denzin and Lincoln 2003). However, early ethnographic studies took place among remote, nonliterate cultures, and anthropologists could become enmeshed in issues of Western colonialism by either trying to sustain a culture's distinctiveness or to act in the service of imperialism (Patton 2001).

By the 1930s, ethnography solidified around long-term fieldwork through participant observation of a particular group, which became associated with the Chicago School of Sociology (McLeod 2001). However, as ethnography developed, researchers recognized its potential for understanding more proximate cultural groups; it also trended towards revealing the processes of hidden or subjugated populations. The luminaries of this approach were Robert Park and W.H. Whyte, and Whyte's ethnographic study, *Street Corner Society,* remains a classic example of the method of participant observation, where the researcher spends time with people, listening to them, observing their interactions, and maintaining field notes. In this tradition, current ethnographic studies coalesced around modern social problems. In the case of organizational ethnographic study, these methods can also illuminate the culture of institutions.

Applications for Diversity Practice. Ethnographic study involves long periods of intimate study and a keen awareness of the stages of fieldwork, because the relationship of the ethnographer to the object of study changes over time, and the stance of the observer must be open to discovering the experiences of people they observe. In participant observation today, the researcher looks for feedback to verify their observations; in addition, direct observation allows for understanding how the context shapes cultural expectations. Ethnography enables researchers to include their own perspectives through direct observation of an experience. These conceptual features mirror the processes whereby therapists can learn about the distinctive cultural features of their clients over time.

Both the historic objectives of ethnography to learn about other cultures and the methodological evolution of participant observation methods are signal elements for a *Bricolage* of diversity practice. Although participant observation of a cultural group is generally not available to clinicians, its underlying assumptions underscore important perspectives for diversity practice. Examination of other cultures on their own terms provides the practitioner important guideposts. These include direct observation over time, where the researcher must be open to the experiences of the people they observe and the incorporation of their own experiences as reflections of their observations (Finlay and Evans 2009). For the clinician, these elements lay the groundwork to respect the unique aspects of specific groups, the important role that context plays in the development of cultural expression, and how both emersion and self-reflection can lead to fresh discoveries in the therapeutic interaction.

Phenomenology and Hermeneutics

Overview. Phenomenology originated in work of Husserl who saw it as a way to understand and describe phenomena as they reveal themselves to people's consciousness through meaningful lived experiences. Husserl was a prolific writer who left over 45,000 pages of manuscript, some of which remain unstudied (McLeod 2001). Nonetheless, Husserl's work has led to several interpretations of his ideas on phenomenological methods that focus on how researchers and subjects jointly construct meaning. Overall, the purpose of phenomenology is to understand the world from the subject's point of view and discover the world as a subject experiences it (Kvale 1996). In order to do this, the focus is on how to put together experiences that make sense of the world. Consequently, phenomenology rejects the idea of a separate objective reality. Instead, it is a search for the experiential essence (Patton 2001).

Among the most prominent groups developing a research approach based on Husserl's principles is the Duquesne school of empirical phenomenology, where the methods for achieving meaning-making and the subjective interpretations involved in understanding are central (Giorgi 1966, 2005; Moustakas 1994; McLeod 2001). These include four processes that enable the researcher to understand the meaning and fundamental nature of an experience. They include, *Epoche,* phenomenological reduction, imaginative variation, and synthesis (McLeod 2001; Moustakas 1994).

The concept of *Epoche* originated with Husserl and involved freeing oneself from all suppositions. In Greek, *Epoche* means to stay away from or to abstain. This prepares researchers to receive knowledge by allowing new events, people, and experiences to enter into their consciousness (Moustakas 1994). Carrying out *Epoche* requires putting aside anything that would obstruct a fresh vision and establish an original vantage point without authoritarian views of the world promulgated by society's experts. In this way, researchers can understand phenomena as they present themselves (Moustakas 1994). Notably, for Moustakas, the challenge of achieving *Epoche* is not only to clear mental space to enable researchers to be open to external experiences but also to "be transparent to ourselves" (p. 86) through a process of meditative reflection. The researcher strives to develop an attitude of openness and wonderment about the phenomenon under study (1994).

If *Epoche* describes the mental preparation of the researcher, phenomenological reduction describes the initial observational processes themselves, which involve an iterative process of looking and describing. This is a way of both seeing and listening to experiences in their own right; this ultimately enables the researcher to grasp fully the nature of a phenomenon. It also involves bracketing off anything except what the researcher has learned about the phenomenon. It follows the principle of horizontality, which requires the researcher to consider all meanings as equal and not to privilege any one. Only later can the researcher eliminate irrelevant, redundant, or overlapping observations, leaving the "horizons" or meanings and constituents of the phenomenon (Moustakas 1994).

The next step in this process is imaginative variation, where the researcher's task is to utilize imagination to see the experience from various frames of reference and develop thematic material from the phenomenological reduction process. There is no single truth; instead, countless possibilities unite the observations. This leads to various descriptions of the phenomenon into a synthesis of meaning. Notably, there is no unique synthesis of a phenomenon, and the essence of an experience is never exhausted. This is because the observations the researcher makes have taken place at a particular point in time and from a personal vantage point. Moustakas (1994) summarizes this process as follows: "One learns to see naively and freshly again, to value conscious experience, to respect the evidence of one's senses and to move toward an inter-subjective knowing of things, people, and everyday experiences" (p. 101).

Hermeneutics grew out of the analysis of written texts, and narrative analysis expanded the idea of what constitutes a text for study to include a broader range of materials as primary sources of research data. These include oral histories, life narratives, creative writing, and transcriptions of in-depth interviews. The concept of a story or a personal narrative enables the researcher to become a part of the cultural experience of the storyteller, and culture threads throughout discussions of discursive forms of qualitative analysis. Clearly, stories and narratives offer windows into social meanings that may not otherwise be available (Patton 2001). This approach focuses on how people use stories to communicate their experiences to others (McLeod 2001) and of particular interest is how they can inform a researcher about the ways in which people make sense of their experiences. This highlights the similarity between narrative analysis and phenomenology (McLeod 2001).

From McLeod's (2001) perspective, the two basic epistemological approaches that engage the researcher in the search for meaning are phenomenology and hermeneutics. On the surface, they appear to take opposite tacks; phenomenology is a meditative process that involves the researcher indwelling in the phenomenon until its essence is revealed. In hermeneutics, understanding always begins from a perspective imbedded in a significant cultural text. The assertion is that the research can never be entirely free of preconceptions because we ourselves inhabit our own cultural universe. Consequently, hermeneutics forces researchers to go beyond their "culture-based understandings" (McLeod, p. 56) and allows the inquiry to develop from emersion in the experiences of the other. Phenomenology does not place knowledge within a social or historical moment, whereas hermeneutics sets the topic of inquiry within a set of contextual features (McLeod 2001).

Nonetheless, both traditions assume an active construction of a social world by people and deal primarily with language or artifacts, such as pictures or physical objects that represent phenomena. Heidegger is the philosopher most associated with bringing together phenomenology and hermeneutics. Heidegger had been Husserl's assistant and was familiar with hermeneutics from his theological studies. He promoted the "natural attitude" of the researcher, which contrasted with phenomenological principles such as *Epoche* or bracketing, which involved the suspension of any preconceptions. Instead, the "natural attitude" provided the researcher with an interpretive horizon through which to understand phenomena. Although Heidegger's support for the Nazi party and failure to recognize the Holocaust has interfered with his influence, his importance for qualitative researchers was his appropriation and integration of ideas from both phenomenology and hermeneutics. If hermeneutics can only speak to what people have already assumed to exist, phenomenology opens up the possibility of revealing something entirely new. He recognized that as soon as we begin posing questions, we were making assumptions about an experience. Consequently, the examination of what guided the researcher to those questions requires understanding and exploration. For McLeod (2001), both aspects are necessary to study the experiences of everyday life.

Applications for Diversity Practice. Elements of both the methods and the underlying perspectives of phenomenology and hermeneutics are useful. For relational therapists, the actors in developing understanding include the experiences of both the client and the therapist and how language is a vehicle for revealing hidden and implicit meanings in the everyday world of each. In the clinical encounter, therapists must free themselves of suppositions in order to allow the client's life experiences to emerge. In the language of phenomenology, this occurs through *Epoche* and bracketing; both encourage therapists to focus entirely on the cultural meanings clients ascribe to their life experiences. At the same time, Heidegger recognized that it is impossible for people to rid themselves entirely of their preconceptions. Following Moustakas, this calls on the therapist to be transparent about their own cultural beliefs and ideas about people with diverse life experiences. Taken together, the concepts of *Epoche* and bracketing from phenomenology and the natural attitude from hermeneutics position the clinician to take in the unique perspectives of patients; at the same time, they remain aware of their own cultural proclivities and existing ideas about those of others. Simultaneously remaining aware of these two perspectives potentiates the relational aspect of the therapeutic encounter.

An important contribution of hermeneutics for the diversity-aware clinician is its origins in the meaning of cultural artifacts that represent the broad experience of a particular group. Reflecting on both Hartman's examples, texts written by Black Americans, women, homosexuals, immigrants, and people with mental illness are one source to expand the natural horizon of the clinician. Diaries, pictures, and descriptions of festivals and ceremonies are vehicles that enable clients to interpret their meaning for the clinician. Similarly, storytelling provides windows into cultural dimensions not otherwise available to the therapist.

Heuristic Inquiry

Heuristics is singularly associated with Clark Moustakas, who sought a word that would capture the essence of his personal investigations of the human experience. He found that term in the Greek word, *heuriskein*, to discover or find, a word he describes as a "cousin word" of *eureka* (Moustakas 1990, p. 9) in recognition that these discoveries lead researchers to new meanings about the human experience. Heuristic inquiry begins with a problem the researcher seeks to answer that represents a personal challenge to their understanding of the world. In this sense, it is autobiographical; however, it must have a universal social significance.

Researchers have employed Moustakas's principles of heuristic inquiry (1990) to study psychotherapy, including the effects of the therapist's characteristics on their practice (Stephenson and Loewenthal 2006). These studies rest on qualitative research findings founded on heuristic principles of "the internal search to know" (Nuttall 2006). The heuristic model strives to plumb the depth of others of all ethnic and cultural groups. Similar to other qualitative traditions, heuristics includes "observations" of a range of cultural artifacts. This calls for reflexivity, a concept familiar to qualitative researchers as an active questioning process that requires researchers constantly to reflect on their own assumptions (Lit and Shek 2002).

Moustakas (1990) proposed concepts that guide this process, beginning with identification of the focus of inquiry and becoming one with it. Ultimately, through self-dialogue, the researcher allows the phenomenon to speak to and question it. Through this iterative process of self-dialogue, multiple meanings emerge, which eventually coalesce into core meanings. This process requires openness, receptivity, and attunement to all of the experiences the researcher has with the phenomenon. It also requires honesty about one's own experience in relation to the question or problem. Throughout heuristic research, tacit knowing enables the researcher to see beneath the explicit perceptions of the world around us. Intuition links implicit knowledge and explicit knowledge that is easily observed and described, because it allows the researcher to utilize an internal capacity to make inferences and arrive at knowledge of underlying dynamics. Logic and reasoning are not at play; instead "we perceive something, observe it, and look and look again and again from clue to clue until we surmise the truth" (p. 23). Finally, indwelling is the process of turning inward to gain a deeper understanding of an aspect of the human experience. It is conscious and deliberate and allows the researcher to follow clues that lead to fundamental insights about the experiences of interest (Moustakas 1990; Douglas and Moustakas 1985).

Applications for Diversity Practice. Moustakas was unique among qualitative research scholars because he explicitly applied a research approach to clinical practice. His book *Heuristics* (1990) has specific sections on its application to psychotherapy and person-centered therapy. He asserted these methods could guide clinicians to put aside their received beliefs and superior roles to discover the truth of a client's ethnic and cultural experience as the client experienced them. The objective was for clients to develop and reveal a portrayal of personal significance they themselves ascribed to their cultural groups. Subsequently, others (Finlay and Evans 2009) have written about its therapeutic applications, but few (Anis 2005; Freeman and Couchonnal 2006) have applied these or similar principles as a means to bridge cultural and racial differences between therapists and their clients.

Heuristics offers the *Bricolage* unique channels for clinicians in their pursuit of connectedness and relationships with clients. The process of heuristic inquiry includes emersion, involving self-search and self-reflection; acquisition, which discloses experiential meanings; and, finally, realization, resulting a synthesis of the true nature of experience (Moustakas 1990). More significantly, the processes of this method, self-dialogue, tacit knowing, intuition, and indwelling, offer the clinician guides for linking their own inner dialogue with strategies to reveal the cultural features of their client's life experiences. Elements from heuristic methods can apply to practitioners who embrace relational theory as they seek to understand their client's highly individual representations of cultural, ethnic, and religious traditions. However, perhaps the most salient feature of heuristics for relational therapists in their search for diversity practice is the degree to which this tradition relies on the depth of understanding required of researchers about themselves. After all, the driver of inquiry is a personal challenge both the researcher and the clinician must experience.

Grounded Theory and Constructivist Grounded Theory

Although some have described grounded theory as the "default" qualitative research approach (Drisko 2008, Personal communication) or the "market leader" in qualitative research (McLeod 2001, p. 70), in actuality it lays out very specific procedures for a specific purpose. Even though numerous and varied qualitative studies claim grounded theory as their methodology, it began as an explicit attempt to formalize an inductive research process using prescribed analytic methods to develop empirically grounded theories; in this tradition, the goal of qualitative methods is inductive theory development (Flick 2002). Some assert that the popularity of this approach rests in its explicit focus and methodology, which suggests the potential for replication. In other words, the specificity of data collection and analytic procedures has made it more acceptable as a model of inquiry because it involves a systematic approach that implies rigor (McLeod 2001; Patton 2001).

Barney Glazer and Anselm Strauss, two scholars from the University of Chicago Department of Sociology, originally laid out the principles of this approach in *The Discovery of Grounded Theory* (1967). In this book, they proposed a specific method for researchers to follow, beginning with the conceptualization of the problem under investigation through a highly technical and detailed approach to data collection, analysis, and reporting. In this tradition, the relationship between the researcher and the informants is relatively unexplored; instead, grounded theory focuses on the emersion of the researcher in the data. It is primarily a set of principles for data collection and data analysis, generally done alone (McLeod 2001). Elements unique to grounded theory include indentifying a broad, action-oriented open-ended question for inquiry.

The researcher approaches the problem under investigation with an open mind, so that themes will surface from the data without any preconceptions. In other words, by not culling theoretical possibilities in advance, the researcher can remain neutral and allow the data to drive theory development. Data collection and analysis take place simultaneously, so that concepts identified in earlier observations inform those the researcher subsequently explores. Data collection ends with saturation, which occurs when researchers determine they will not gain any further ideas from subsequent observations (McLeod 2001; Moustakas 1994).

Over time, grounded theory methods have been refined in subsequent work by Strauss and Corbin (1990). Recently, Charmaz (2006) took a more flexible approach in what she describes as "constructivist grounded theory," which she contrasts with "objectivist grounded theory." She calls for a more interactive and emergent approach and elevates the significance of the meaning and actions in the lives of the subjects. In addition to emphasizing the individual's view, values, beliefs, and ideologies, her work promotes a more active role for the researcher than earlier expositions of the method. In other words, she stresses the interpretive traditions of qualitative research in her application of the principles of grounded theory.

Through careful analysis of the data that involves examination of field notes, detailed study of transcribed interviews, coding of each element, sorting of codes, and constantly comparing those codes, the researcher ultimately constructs a theory about the issue studied (Moustakas 1994). The key to grounded theory is the emersion of the researcher in the data and strict adherence to a purely inductive process, in other words, the production of theories from observations in the real world. Grounded theory involves unraveling the elements of an experience toward the development of a mid-level theory. The purpose of these theories is to propose a way of understanding about the nature and meaning of phenomena. Each study has its own detailed sequences of continuous questioning of gaps, omissions, and inconsistencies that the researcher identifies. Similar to other qualitative traditions, context and structure play important roles in an inductive proof where the researcher is continuously proposing theories and checking them against observational data (Moustakas 1990), in the case of clinical practice, what transpires in that relationship.

Applications for Diversity Practice. Certain elements of grounded theory and constructivist grounded theory have the potential to "ground" the relational clinician in practice with diverse populations. Continuously tuning into gaps, omissions, and inconsistencies in client's stories leaves room for the clinician to explore areas that clients do not easily reveal about cultural practices or differences they have with the practitioner based on ethnic norms. Charmaz's emphasis on the researcher's and the subject's views, values, beliefs, and ideologies also brings this method closer to an element of diversity practice. It suggests that clinicians must enter the therapeutic relationship with willingness for self-exploration. The suggestion that researchers should not come to the research process with theories – what Patton (2001) would call sensitizing concepts – may also be useful in certain circumstances. If therapists have their own strongly held "theories" about particular groups, they must learn to recognize what they are and "test" them in relation to the particular client with whom they are engaged. However, the central lesson of grounded theory for clinicians is its fidelity to induction. In other words, it suggests that what clinicians come to understand about a client's cultural identification comes directly from clients themselves and therapists' interactions with them. Within this approach is respect for the unique cultural representation of the individual client.

Bricolage: Methods from Constructivist Research for Relational Therapy

Kinocheloe (2001, 2005) provides a rich conceptualization of the *Bricolage,* which has important implications for multi-method and multidisciplinary research. In his vision, the *bricoleur* exists within the complexity of the real world, and his task is to "uncover the invisible artifacts of power and culture and [document] the nature of their influence not only on their own scholarship but also scholarship in general" (Kincheloe 2005, p. 324). However, others (Warne and McAndres 2009) envision an even wider application of the *Bricolage*, which draws parallels between the research and therapy. "[Any] research setting is imbued with both conscious and unconscious meaning processes and meaning. This is significant both in the generation of research/practice data and construction of the research/practice environment" (p. 857). Finlay and Evans (2009) make an explicit link between qualitative research and relational therapy using the metaphor of a "voyage of discovery" (p. 3). This chapter blended these concepts to provide relational therapists with an approach to diversity practice that drew on constructivist approaches, recognizing similarities between these research concepts and clinical practice.

Ethnography, grounded theory, phenomenology, and heuristics are only some of the historic and expanding array of constructivist research traditions. Their growth and integration over time has been an informal form of the *Bricolage* (Denzin and Lincoln 2003). It is apparent in examining the development of various qualitative traditions that scholars have adapted and expanded elements of existing models or joined models and proposed them as variations of a particular tradition. Heidegger reframed the phenomenological concept of *Epoche* as the "natural attitude" when

Table 1 Bricolage for diversity practice in relational therapy: principles from constructivist research methods

Research traditions	Methodological elements	Application for diversity practice in relational therapy
Ethnography		
	Investigation of different cultural groups	The stance of the observer must be open to discovering the experiences of people they observe
Constructivist grounded theory		
	Induction	Approach the problem under investigation
	No preconceptions, individual views, ideologies, or beliefs	with an open mind, so that themes will emerge from the people themselves; the observer's ideology is not relevant
Phenomenology		
	Epoche	The observer leaves aside their own ideas
	Bracketing	about the person's experience and how
	Reflexivity	they believe they would have responded; the observer understands how they would have responded and encourages expression of alternative worldviews
Heuristics		
	Immersion	The observer engages people about their
	Direct and active participation of the researcher	own life experiences and probes beneath their immediate responses
Hermeneutics	*Verstehen*	The observer relates to people on their own terms and point of view, rather than that of their own and promotes understanding the person

he sought to create a clearing in which the ordinary aspects of life could be revealed. The ultimate result was an integration of phenomenology and hermeneutics (McLeod 2001). Similarly, Charmaz altered grounded theory to "constructivist grounded theory," another example of the mutability of these traditions that address changes in the application of research methods over time.

Although it would be possible to draw from an even larger array of qualitative research traditions, methodological elements of the traditions presented here provide a starting point to guide diversity practice for relational therapy. Typical of the constructivist enterprise, some of these concepts appear in more than one tradition or are implicitly threaded throughout. For example, in every case, these traditions involve induction. The researcher makes meaning based on observations rather than on preexisting theories. However, the strategies involved in ensuring that the researcher's own "theories" about the world do not interrupt a vigorous inductive process vary. For example, in grounded theory, the researcher achieves induction by careful coding procedures that put the brakes on his or her own predilections. In contrast, the concept of *Epoche*, which endures throughout phenomenology and existential phenomenology, requires specific mental preparation on the part of the researcher to eliminate any preconceptions. However, in both cases, the objective remains the same – to allow the worldview of the client to emerge (Table 1).

As the earliest qualitative method, ethnography recognized that groups of people that interact together develop a distinctive culture that expresses itself in the relationships among members, sets of beliefs about the world, behaviors that the group endorses or rejects, and other characteristics that reinforce norms and modes of expression. Cultural distinctiveness was at the heart of their studies. In their practice, ethnographers recognized they could best understand the cultural features of a group by emersion in that culture and long periods of in situ observation. Although it is not feasible for clinicians, or for that matter many researchers, to engage in participant observation studies, the signal legacy of ethnography is its emphasis on the unique aspects of a culture and its influence on individual's expectations about themselves and other members of the group. This suggests that clinicians should be open to the experiences their clients report and incorporate their own experiences as they reflect on both. Field notes are a metaphor for this process in therapy. Just as the ethnographer records observations in the field, the clinician maintains a mental log of how clients construct meaning in their lives; just as the ethnographer records their own responses to their observations, the clinician examines their own responses to the client's worldview. Ethnographic study has always involved observations over time and the researcher's own reflections on those observations. In therapy, both emersion and self-reflection can promote discovery in the therapeutic interaction.

The intertwining traditions of phenomenology and hermeneutics utilize written and narrative language as vehicles for revealing the explicit and implicit meanings in the everyday experiences of both clients and therapists. In this respect, a major contribution of hermeneutics is investigation of the cultural artifacts that represent the unique experience of a group. These include diaries, religious texts, or descriptions of festivals or ceremonies that can become vehicles for clients to interpret their meaning for therapists. Similarly, storytelling is an important vehicle where therapists can learn about how clients construct meaning that would otherwise be unavailable to them.

From the perspective of phenomenology, therapists need to rid themselves of any preconceptions they have about a client, in order to focus entirely on the cultural meanings each client ascribes to their life experiences. Presumably, this occurs in a preparatory phase through *Epoche* or the conscious act of eliminating all preexisting assumptions about the client's primary reference group. Subsequently, as the client begins to reveal cultural constructions to the therapist, bracketing keeps that content separate from the clinician's own perspectives. Although this may be possible in unique circumstances, where the therapist is completely naïve about the client's cultural past, it is unlikely to occur among either researchers or highly educated clinical practitioners. Heidegger's "natural attitude" recognizes that these preconceptions are a part of the human experience. Consequently, this calls for therapists to be transparent to both their own cultural beliefs and open to those of their clients. They need to remain simultaneously aware of their own cultural proclivities and existing ideas about those of others in order to potentiate the relational aspect of the therapeutic encounter.

In their original conception of grounded theory, Glazer and Strauss also called on researchers to the inquiry without any preexisting theories, since their approach was entirely inductive and all theories developed from the data. Although qualitative methods rely almost exclusively on inductive as opposed to deductive logic, grounded theory is perhaps the strongest tradition for promoting induction and for establishing a method to ensure that it occurs. Simply put, theoretical propositions were grounded in the data. This is a useful posture for the clinician, and it represents another strategy for eliminating preconceptions about the cultural context as the client experiences it.

Another feature of grounded theory that is useful for the relational therapist is located in methods that occur during data collection or during a therapeutic interview. Therapists should continuously tune into gaps, omissions, and inconsistencies in client's stories. When this occurs, the clinician should meticulously explore those areas. They may indicate regions where clients do not easily reveal information about cultural practices or differences they have with the ethnic norms they attribute to the practitioner. Charmaz's emphasis on the researcher's and the subject's views, values, beliefs, and ideologies also brings this method closer to an element of diversity practice. It suggests that clinicians must enter the therapeutic relationship with willingness for self-exploration.

Heuristics is unique because its sole adherent, Moustakas, specifically applied heuristic methods to clinical practice in psychotherapy and person-centered therapy. In these chapters, he determined that these methods could help practitioners put their received beliefs and superior beliefs aside to uncover the true ethnic and cultural experiences as clients experiences them. Related to his autobiographical approach to qualitative inquiry, it was important for clients to develop a portrait of themselves imbedded in their cultural groups, which will lead to the truth about the client's ethnic and cultural experience as they experience them. The objective was for clients to develop and reveal a portrayal of personal significance they themselves ascribed to their cultural groups. Subsequently others (Finlay and Evans 2009) have written about the applications of qualitative methods to therapy, but few (Anis 2005; Freeman and Couchonnal 2006) have applied these or similar principles as a means to bridge cultural and racial differences between therapists and their clients.

However, perhaps the most salient feature of heuristics for relational therapists as they strengthen diversity practice is how it relies on the depth of understanding required of researchers about themselves. After all, the driver of inquiry is a personal challenge the researcher and the clinician must experience. Consequently, methods such as self-dialogue, tacit knowing, intuition, and indwelling offer the clinician guides for linking their own inner dialogue with strategies to reveal the cultural features of their client's life experiences.

Reservations and Rewards of Joining Research and Therapeutic Concepts

Clearly, the purpose of conducting a research study is different from conducting a therapeutic interview, and not all elements of any research paradigm are relevant for relational therapy or any psychotherapeutic model. However, in an exploration of humanistic psychology and qualitative research, common principles emerge, such as individual uniqueness, the dominance of the client's perspective, the essence of interpersonal connection, and flexibility of approach (Patton 1990; Soldz 1996). Nonetheless, the purpose and function of these two ventures are very different (Patton 1990). The meaning for clinicians is the therapeutic effects of the interview, while qualitative researchers seek a larger canvas to explore problems and present them in a scholarly forum. The application of the *Bricolage* in the intimate relationship between client and therapist is a much smaller canvas. It is meant to provide tools for probing the unique aspects that both the social worker and the client bring to the engagement.

Some have already explored the application of qualitative methods to promote cultural competence and rejected it. Williams (2006) analyzed how various constructivist epistemological paradigms could guide social workers achieve cultural competence; this was an original research-driven approach to the problem of multicultural education and practice. Another reservation here is the increasing interest in critical racial theory that some social work educators are using to guide diversity education and could conceivably apply to individual practice. Critical racial theory rests beneath the larger paradigm of critical theory, itself a research paradigm in Denzin and Lincoln's (2003) elegant typology. The ontological perspective of critical theory is that social, political, cultural, and economic forces shape reality. In addition, ethnical, gender, and racial values crystallize over time. Critical theory is closely aligned with a postmodern worldview, and it is imbedded in the notion that structural forces shape life experiences. Recently, some social work educators (Abrams and Moto 2007; Ortiz and Jani 2010) have proposed ways in which to apply critical race theory to augment diversity practice; this also has the potential to advance diversity practice through creative application of various constructivist concepts. Besides the implications of hanging diversity education squarely on race to the exclusion of gender, nationality, sexual identity, religious affiliation or any of the other ways in which social workers must transcend difference in their practice, an intrinsic feature of this paradigm is that it pulls the discussion towards macro issues in social work practice. For the clinician who employs a relation-centered approach, the issues are closer to the bone.

Study Questions

1. Why should relational therapists be concerned about their authority in relation to the clients they serve? What are the factors that nourish the power of clinicians in their engagements with clients?
2. What do you consider the ideal relationship between knowledge *about* a client's cultural, ethnic, religious group or group affiliation, and what a clinician can learn in their interactions with individual patients?
3. Do you consider it possible to achieve *Epoche* in initial sessions with clients? Are there other components of the *Bricolage* that you believe would be more productive in "letting in" the experiences of clients?

4. Imagine that you have a second-generation South Asian young man who has come to you with symptoms of depression. His immigrant father is no longer able work in his small business, so your client has left college and taken over responsibility for running the store. In his home country, young men normally take responsibility for the family in such circumstances. He was a promising engineering student but had to leave school. Why would it be important to understand the cultural context in both the home country and the US in working with this patient?

References

Abrams, L. S., & Moto, J. A. (2007). Critical race theory and the cultural competence dilemma in social work education. *Journal of Social Work Education, 45*(2), 245–261.

Aisenberg, E. (2008). Evidence-based practice in mental health care to ethnic minority communities: Has its practice fallen short of its evidence? *Social Work, 53*(4), 297.

Anis, M. (2005). Talking about culture in social work encounters: Immigrant families and child welfare in Finland. *European Journal of Social Work, 8*(1), 3–19. doi:10.1080/136914504200 0331341.

Barrineau, P., & Bozarth, J. (1989). A person-centered research model. *Person-Centered Review, 4*(4), 465–474.

Burr, V. (2003). *Social constructionism* (2nd ed.). New York: Routledge.

Charmaz, K. (2006). *Constructing grounded theory*. London: Sage.

Creswell, J. W., Hanson, W. E., Clark Piano, V. L., & Morales, A. (2007). Qualitative research designs: Selection and implementation. *The Counseling Psychologist, 35*(2), 236–264. doi:10.1177/0011000006287390.

Denzin, N., & Lincoln, Y. (Eds.). (2003). *The landscape of qualitative research: Theories and issues* (2nd ed.). Thousand Oaks: Sage.

Denzin, N., & Lincoln, Y. (Eds.). (2004). *Handbook of qualitative research* (2nd ed.). Thousand Oaks: Sage.

Douglas, B. G., & Moustakas, C. (1985). Heuristic inquiry: The internal search to know. *Journal of Humanistic Psychology, 25*(39), 39–55.

Elliott, R. (2008). A linguistic phenomenology of ways of knowing and its implications for psychotherapy research and psychotherapy integration. *Journal of Psychotherapy Integration, 18*(1), 40–65. doi:10.1037/1053-0479.18.1.40.

Finlay, L., & Evans, K. (2009). *Relational-centered research for psychotherapists: Exploring meanings and experience*. West Sussex: Wiley.

Flick, U. (2002). Qualitative research – state of the art. *Social Science Information, 41*(5), 5–24.

Foucault, M. (1980). *Power/knowledge: Selected interviews and other writings*. New York: Pantheon Press.

Freeman, E. M., & Couchonnal, G. (2006). Narrative and culturally based approaches in practice with families. *Families in Society: The Journal of Contemporary Social Services, 87*(2), 198–208.

Frie, R. (2010). The conversation never ends: Philosophy and therapeutic practice in dialogue: A review essay of Donna Orange's thinking for clinicians: Philosophical resources for contemporary psychoanalysis and the humanistic psychotherapies. *International Journal of Psychoanalytic Self Psychology, 5*, 198–209.

Furlong, M., & Wight, J. (2011). Promoting "critical awareness" and critiquing cultural competence: Towards disrupting received professional knowledges. *Australian Social Work, 64*(1), 38–54.

Giorgi, A. (1966). Phenomenology and experimental psychology II. *Review of Existential Psychology and Psychiatry, 6*(1), 37–50.

Giorgi, A. (2005). The phenomenological movement and research in the human sciences. *Nursing Science Quarterly, 18*(1), 75–82. doi:10.1177/0894318404272112.

Glazer, B., & Strauss, A. (1967). *The discovery of grounded theory.* Chicago: Aldine.

Hartman, A. (1992). In search of subjugated knowledge. *Social Work, 37*(6), 483–484.

James, J., Green, D., Rodriguez, C., & Fong, R. (2008). Addressing disproportionality through undoing racism, leadership development, and community engagement. *Child Welfare, 87*(2), 279–296.

Jovanovic, G. (2011). A social history of qualitative research. *History of the Human Sciences, 24*(1), 1–27. doi:10.1177/0952695111399334.

Karlsson, G. (1992). The grounding of psychological research in phenomenological epistemology. *Theory and Psychology, 2*(4), 403–429. doi:10.1177/0959354392024001.

Karnieli-Miller, O., Strier, R., & Pessach, L. (2009). Pearls, piths, and provocation: Power relations in qualitative research. *Qualitative Health Research, 19*(2), 279–289. doi:10.1177/1049732308329306.

Kincheloe, J. L. (2001). Describing the bricolage: Conceptualizing a new rigor in qualitative research. *Qualitative Inquiry, 7*(6), 679–692. doi:10.1177/107780040100700060.

Kincheloe, J. L. (2005). On to the next level: Continuing the conceptualization of bricolage. *Qualitative Inquiry, 11*(3), 323–350. doi:10.1177/1077800405275056.

Kincheloe, J. T. (2008). Bricolage and the quest for multiple perspectives: New approaches to research in ethnic studies. In T. P. Fong (Ed.), *Ethnic studies research: Approaches and perspectives* (pp. 313–352). Lanham: AltaMira Press.

Kvale, S. (1996). *Interviews: An introduction to qualitative research interviewing.* Thousand Oaks: Sage.

Kvale, S., & Brinkmann, S. (2009). *Interviews: Learning the craft of qualitative research interviewing* (2nd ed.). Thousand Oaks: Sage.

Lee, M.-Y., & Greene, G. J. (1999). A social constructivist framework for integrating cross-cultural issues in social work. *Journal of Social Work Education, 35*(1), 21–38.

Levi-Strauss, C. (1968). *The savage mind.* (trans: Weightman, J., & Weightman, D.). Chicago: The University of Chicago Press.

Lincoln, Y. S. (1998). From understanding to action: New imperatives, new criteria, new methods for interpretive researchers. *Theory and Research in Social Education, 26*(1), 12–29.

Lincoln, Y. S., & Guba, E. G. (2003). Paradigmatic controversies, contradiction, and emerging confluences. In N. K. Denzin & Y. S. Lincoln (Eds.), *The landscape of qualitative research: Theories and issues* (pp. 253–291). Thousand Oaks: Sage.

Lit, S. W., & Shek, D.T.L. (2002). Implications of constructivism to counseling and social work practice. *Asian Journal of Counselling, 9*(1/2), 105–130.

McLeod, J. (2001). *Qualitative research in counselling and psychotherapy.* Thousand Oaks: Sage.

Moustakas, C. (1990). *Heuristic research: Design, methodology, and applications.* Newbury Park: Sage.

Moustakas, C. (1994). *Phenomenological research methods.* Thousand Oaks: Sage.

Nilsson, C. (2010). A phenomenological approach to practical knowledge in psychotherapy. *Santaka Filosophia, 18*(3), 70–80.

Nuttall, J. (2006). Research report: Researching psychotherapy integration: A heuristic approach. *Counselling Psychology Quarterly, 19*(4), 429–444.

Opie, A. (1992). Qualitative research appropriation of the "other" and empowerment. *Feminist Review, 40*, 52–69.

Ortiz, L., & Jani, J. (2010). Critical race theory: A transformational model for teaching diversity. *Journal of Social Work Education, 46*(2), 175–193.

Patton, M. Q. (1990). Humanistic psychology and humanistic research. *Person-Centered Review, 5*(2), 191–202.

Patton, M. Q. (2001). *Qualitative research and evaluation methods* (3rd ed.). Thousand Oaks: Sage.

Ponterotto, J. G. (2005). Qualitative research in counseling psychology: A primer in research paradigms and the philosophy of science. *Journal of Counseling Psychology, 52*(2), 126–136. doi:10.1037/0022-0167.52.2.126.

Pozzuto, R., Arnd-Caddigan, M., & Averett, P. (2009). Notes in support of a relational social work perspective: A critical review of the relational literature with implications for macro practice. *Smith Studies in Social Work, 79*(5), 5–16.

Soldz, S. (1996). Psychoanalysis and constructivism: Convergence in meaning-making perspectives. In H. Rosen & K. T. Kuehlwein (Eds.), *Constructing realities: Meaning-making perspectives for psychotherapists*. San Francisco: Jossey-Bass.

Strauss, A.C., & Corbin, J. (1990). *Basics of qualitative research: Grounded theory procedures and techniques*. Thousand Oaks, CA: Sage Publications

Stephenson, S., & Loewenthal, D. (2006). The effect of counseling/psychotherapy practice of an absent father in the therapist's childhood: A heuristic study. *Psychodynamic Practice, 12*(4), 435–452.

Tedlock, B. (2000). Ethnography and ethnographic representation. In N. K. Denzin & Y. S. Lincoln (Eds.), *Handbook of qualitative research* (2nd ed., pp. 455–486). Thousand Oaks: Sage.

Teram, E., Schachter, C. L., & Stalker, C. A. (2005). The case for integrating grounded theory and participatory action research: Empowering clients to inform professional practice. *Qualitative Health Research, 15*(8), 1129–1140.

Thyer, B. A. (2008). The quest for evidence-based practice? We are all positivists! *Research on Social Work Practice, 18*, 339. doi:10.1177/104973150731399.

van Wormer, K., & Snyder, C. (2007). Infusing content on oppression into the social work curriculum. *Journal of Human Behavior in the Social Environment, 16*(4), 19–35. doi:0.1080/10911350802081568.

Warne, T., & McAndrew, S. (2009). Constructing a bricolage of nursing, research, education, and practice. *Nurse Education Today, 29*(8), 855–858.

Weyl, H. (1959). Mathematics and the laws of nature. In I. Gordon & S. Sorkin (Eds.), *The armchair science reader*. New York: Simon and Schuster.

Williams, C. C. (2006). The epistemology of cultural competence. *Families in Society: The Journal of Contemporary Social Services, 87*(2), 209–220.

The Color of Whiteness and the Paradox of Diversity

Neil Altman

Stevie Wonder's "Ebony and Ivory" notwithstanding, literally speaking, there are neither White nor Black people in the world. If you see a person whose skin color is white, you will most likely call an ambulance. There are people in the world whose skin color approximates black, but for the most part "Black" people are some shade of brown. "White" people are some shade of pink. So why is it so common, in the United States anyway, to refer to people as "White" and "Black"?

In my view, the language of "Black and White" speaks to the human propensity to divide things, and especially people, into mutually exclusive categories. We seem to need to think that people are like us or unlike us. Any ambiguity seems to make us very uncomfortable. I have suggested elsewhere (Altman 2009) that this sort of categorization fits well with Harry Stack Sullivan's (1953) notion that we construct a self along the dimensions of "good me," "bad me," and "not me." "Not me" comprises those aspects of "me" that are intolerable for whatever reason. We tend to define ourselves with reference to a disavowed "not me" group. The more rigidly we need to define ourselves, the more rigid are the boundaries between the in-group and the out-group, between the "Blacks" and the "Whites," to the extent that the purity of the "White" group has at times required that even one drop of Black blood disqualifies a person from being classified as White.

A substantial body of literature has emerged making it clear that racial categories are not discrete and mutually exclusive on any sort of physical basis but rather are socially constructed (Sternberg et al. 2005). For example, Ignatiev (1995) pointed out that when the Irish came to North America in the 1850s, they were not initially considered "White." Many Irish people were sympathetic to the abolitionist cause at

N. Altman, Ph.D. (✉)
Editor Emeritus, Psychoanalytic Dialogues:
The International Journal of Relational Perspectives, New York, NY, USA

Author, The Analyst in the Inner City: Race, Class, and Culture through a Psychoanalytic Lens, New York, NY, USA

Ambedkar University of Delhi, India
e-mail: Altman.neil@gmail.com

J.B. Rosenberger (ed.), *Relational Social Work Practice with Diverse Populations*, Essential Clinical Social Work Series, DOI 10.1007/978-1-4614-6681-9_4, © Springer Science+Business Media New York 2014 the time, sympathizing with Black slaves based on their history of oppression at the hands of the British. It was only when large numbers of Irish turned against Blacks during the time of the draft riots in the 1860s that they began to be considered, and to consider themselves, as White. A sure route to Whiteness, evidently, is to adopt anti-Black racist attitudes. Jacobson (1998) pointed out that many immigrant groups, including Germans, Irish, Italians, and Jews were not considered White when they first arrived in North America. It was only when the next group arrived to take on most excluded status that the previously most excluded group was accepted into the ranks of the White. And, of course, the presence of African-Americans with dark skin provided a contrast with those of relatively light skin that allowed them to identify as "White."

Demonstrating that race has no physical basis, while demonstrating the basis of racial categories in psychological and social constructions, in no way calls into question the power of racial categories *as* social constructions. Socially constructed categories of human beings are always unstable, in that the human characteristics organized by the categories in question could always be organized in some other way, yielding a different set of socially constructed categories with different meanings. I organized the categories based on skin color differently when I pointed out that skin color is never black or white, that is, dichotomous, but rather somewhere on the brown-pink spectrum, which is a continuum rather than a dichotomy. The meaning of skin color difference as dichotomy is very different from skin color as continuum. The former yields discrete racial categories, while the latter yields a potential multitude of non-mutually exclusive categories. The meaning of even dichotomous categories is also subject to socially constructed alteration, as in "Black is beautiful."

Since socially constructed categories are inherently unstable, they must be stabilized by reiteration and by some form of enforcement. Reiteration organizes social reality, the primary reality for human beings. Starting in school, the "cool" becomes the "cool" group by being regarded as "cool," acting in the ways socially recognized as cool and sometimes by treating others as uncool. Similarly, White people become White people by being socially recognized as White, acting White, treating others as non-White; Black people become Black in the same way. Once categories are stabilized in this way, there are cultures that develop associated with the categories that are passed down through generations from parents to children and grandchildren. The stabilization of the categories is given powerful reinforcement as attachment to familial and community cultures becomes part and parcel of one's social identity. Social identity is a deeply and strongly rooted element in one's personal identity.

Enforcement means social forms of coercion to inhabit your socially constructed category and not to cross lines. The most egregious forms of such enforcement in the United States are easy to recall: laws against interracial marriage, lynching of Black men suspected of having sexual relations with White women, and social disapproval. Currently, racial lines are loosening to a degree in some quarters, to the point where a man of widely recognized mixed race has been elected President of the United States. Nonetheless, the US Census Bureau asks him, along with the rest of us, to self-identify using racial and ethnic categories; it is highly significant that he identifies as Black, or in the current, more accurate parlance, "African-American." His mixed background led many in the USA to believe that he was not born in the United States, despite conclusive evidence to the contrary; his self-identification as African-American, as well as marriage to an African-American woman, yielded nearly unanimous support among African-Americans in the 2008 presidential election.

Whiteness

Perhaps the most fundamentally damaging elements in the social construction of race in the United States derive from the ways in which a "White" perspective dominates in the social construction of racial categories. When the decisive element in the categorization of people into White and Black is the psychic and social self-interest of White people, then a fundamentally alien perspective is built into the sense of self-identity of Black people. Beginning with the middle passage and slavery, Africans were stripped of their names, their traditions, and the social identities they had had in Africa. They were given the names of their owners; their social identities were stripped down to their status as slaves. The vacuum created by prohibition of African identities was filled by the denigrated and dehumanized images of slaves that served to justify slavery and to fortify the self-images of the slave holders and those who colluded with and benefited materially from its perpetuation.

From the beginning of course, African-Americans did what they could to define their own sense of identity; a strong culture has been developed with deep roots to the point where many feel that the African-American contribution is the crucial element in the sense of national/social identity of White people and not just as a point of disidentification. Nonetheless, White views of Black people, whether idealized or denigrated, created dilemmas factoring out internalized racism when building up an internally generated strong sense of identity. Currently, images of African-Americans in the media, micro-aggressions in the street and the workplace, and so on must be dealt with as an alien but internalized view of self that must be put in its proper place. James Baldwin's (1993) "Letter to my Nephew" is perhaps the clearest and most powerful statement I know of the dilemmas created by alien and denigrating elements in the social construction of a sense of identity.

Aside from the specifics, what is perhaps most insidiously damaging about the White perspective on race and culture in the United States is the way in which it presents as the *standard* perspective. That is to say, Whiteness in the USA presents itself as mainstream, the taken-for-granted cultural, ethnic, and racial position from which non-White positions deviate. For example, consider how White people might speak of "ethnic food" or an "ethnic neighborhood" as if *all* foods didn't have an origin associated with one or more ethnic groups or as if *all neighborhoods* didn't have a dominant ethnic character (or more than one).

Similarly, in mental health literature, when one speaks of "diversity" or "diverse groups" (see, e.g., Paniagua 1998), the assumption often seems to be that one is speaking of non-White groups. References to "people of color" seem to imply that there are people without color, as if White weren't a color, a particular color, and White people not an ethnic group, a particular ethnic group. In the absence of the idea that Whiteness specifies a particular racial, cultural, and ethnic position, Whiteness is set up as the simply human position, the norm, and standard; the assumption becomes that people are White unless otherwise specified. In that sense, being identified as White puts one in a superior position in relation to other groups. If all groups, including groups of White people, are particular cultural, ethnic, and racial groups, then all are on an equal level. None are entitled to be set up as standard, as the norm, as the definer of what is normal or deviant. Many justifications for colonialism, for colonial exploitation and genocide, were based on this idea of Whiteness as the norm, from the perspective of which other groups could be seen as abnormal, deviant, less developed, and so on. It is historically demonstrated that colonialism, or enslavement, even orchestrated by those who in the United States are counted as non-White (Japanese enslaving Koreans, some Indian castes dominating others, even Black freemen in pre-civil war United States having Black slaves) (Jones 2003; Robertson 2006) self-justifies social control by self-elevation. Intercultural and interracial interactions then always involve a difference in perspectives, not a deviation of one group from the norm as defined by the other group. This approach is fundamentally *relational* in that all interactions are intersubjective. All interactions are between people with different perspectives, not between one person and an "other" who represents the norm. As we shall see below, the implications for diagnosis and treatment in psychotherapy are profound.

The socially constructed Black-White dichotomy serves the purpose, for people who identify as White, of providing a basis for construction of self. As noted above, the existence of a Black "other" in the context of a Black-White dichotomy gives the White-identified self a convenient repository for attribution of unwanted psychic qualities. In the United States historically, qualities such as sexuality, aggression, hyper-emotionality, exploitativeness, and laziness have been attributed by White people to Black people, thus creating a denigrated "not me" (Sullivan 1953). Also as noted above, a challenge is thus created for Black people not to identify with these denigrated images of themselves or with the refusal to claim such characteristics as "me" among the dominant White identity. Given the degree to which a White sense of identity depends on disavowal of those characteristics and qualities assigned to Blacks, there are distortions in the social identities of Whites that are often invisible to White people. The disavowal of qualities such as sexuality and aggression can leave White people devoid of some qualities that are enriching to self. For example, the emptying out of sexuality and emotionality can leave a White person depleted of many psychic resources necessary for fulfilling relationships. White people who were raised by Black "nannies," for example, may find themselves nostalgic for the nurturance that they came to associate with the Black person, as well as with women in general. They may become confused when this idealized image encounters denigrated images of the Black person later in life (Suchet 2007).

These processes of disavowal and displaced attribution occur on both the macro social level and the micro level of individual relationships. Unthinking attribution of negative qualities to Black people by White people is at the core of what Sue (2010) called "micro-aggressions." These attributions are absorbed by individuals from the social surround where they permeate the media as well as communications from parents, other family members, and peers. These attributions and micro-aggressions also operate inevitably between therapist and client of any racial and ethnic groups. Therapists must remain alert to the socially constructed attributions and stereotypes operative between themselves and their clients, which can interfere with, or facilitate, the work of helping clients develop heightened awareness of emotional and interpersonal experiences. Noting and unpacking these attributions, stereotypes, and micro-aggressions forms a crucial part of the therapeutic work.

We will now proceed to examine in some detail how racial and ethnic forces operate in both the diagnostic/assessment process and the therapy/counseling process.

Diagnosis and Assessment

Two points must be made about the assessment/diagnostic process. First, all diagnoses reflect the value system in the culture of the diagnostician and in the culture of the larger society. All diagnoses, as they make judgments as to what is normal and what is pathological, make reference to the norms of a given society and culture. Layton (2006) has written illuminatingly about this normative backdrop as the "normative unconscious." For example, diagnoses which rely on affect regulation as a central part of the clinical presentation are embedded in a value system that defines how much affect is too much and how much is too little, as well as with respect to style of expressiveness. Cultures vary as to how much affect is considered excessive (as in "histrionic") and what is considered overly restrained and defensive. In some cultural contexts, there is a value placed on restraint in the expression of feeling; in some the direct expression of anger and affection is considered inappropriate, and in some the norm can include a good deal of direct expressiveness between people. To take another example, what is thought to be psychotic in one cultural context may be considered part of a normative spiritual experience in another.

These culturally embedded norms may be particularly clearly seen in the way children are diagnosed. As classrooms have gotten larger, as curricula have gotten more standardized (as in the failed "No Child Left Behind" policy), and as success and failure have come to be rigidly defined by performance on standardized tests, there is an increasing premium on children's ability to sit still and listen for long periods of time. Thus, "attention deficit hyperactivity disorder" emerges as a diagnosis, where it might not have if classrooms were smaller, if physical activity were more valued, and if the curriculum were more individually tailored. As economic opportunity has come more and more to depend on the ability to read and less and less on the ability to make things, for example, "dyslexia" emerges as a diagnosis in a way that would not have been the case in an agricultural society.

Symptom-based diagnostic systems (the Diagnostic and Statistical Manual of the American Psychiatric Association (2002) being the best example), in their narrow focus on individual behavior, are particularly prone to ignoring the societal and cultural context in which judgments of health, pathology, and functionality are made. These symptoms may also be blind to the ways in which the larger psychological and socioeconomic situation of the person may feed into the symptom picture. For example, deficits in attention and hyperactive behavior might reflect anxiety from any number of sources. There may be family dysfunction or material poverty with all its attendant stresses. These factors would be part of a comprehensive understanding of the symptoms necessary to do justice to the client as a person.

Consider the situation of foster children. Many of them have been subject to abuse and neglect, as well as to multiple losses of parents/caretakers and chronically unstable living situations. A comprehensive understanding of such a child's "attention deficit" or "oppositional" behavior, for example, must include consideration of the social situation of the child along with possible physiological and psychological factors. A simple diagnosis of attention deficit disorder or oppositional-defiant disorder is not enough, nor is the treatment with stimulants or tranquilizers an adequate response. Aside from a currently rampant culturally specific failure to attend to the social context of such disorders, there are economic forces at play as well. Pharmaceutical companies collude with mental health clinicians and insurance companies to make drug treatment of symptom-based disorders the standard of care. The fundamental reorientation it would take to address the familial and social forces that feed into abuse, neglect, and multiple foster care placements would be much more complicated and costly to address than simply to medicate the symptoms of children who bear the ultimate burden of society's failures.

Cultures are not monolithic in the respects I have described, and individual clinicians may vary in the degree to which a given clinical presentation appears pathological or not. Nonetheless, the diagnostic system itself, within which all diagnostic criteria emerge, bears the mark of the culture(s) in which they are embedded and which they perpetuate.

The second point about diagnosis is that the diagnostic/assessment process is an interactive and intersubjective process. The process reflects an interaction between the cultures of the clinician and the client, as well as between their unique personality makeups. All of these factors go into the mix of an intersubjective and intercultural context that crucially affects the assessment and diagnostic process.

Here is an example: Clinicians strongly influenced by a Northern European emphasis on punctuality are inclined to schedule sessions to the minute, more or less, to start and stop on time. Clients strongly influenced by a Southern European or Third World cultural background may be less punctual, or, to put it more positively, more relaxed about time. Such clients may show up late from the point of view of the clinician, leading to an assessment of the client as "resistant" to the therapy process. The clinician may be inclined to end the session "on time," which from the point of view of the client may be seen as rigid and uncaring. Is the client "resistant"? Is the clinician "rigid and uncaring"? Perhaps so, in either or both cases; but I believe it is preferable to consider that there is a cultural difference here which requires each person to see the perspective of the other. Neither necessarily represents a healthier or more functional way of being than the other, though one might always wonder how each way of being works out in a particular cultural context.

There is no question but that having difficulty, and/or a disinclination, to read is dysfunctional these days. But simply diagnosing "dyslexia" is not enough. Many children with dyslexia have strengths in other areas. A complete diagnostic/assessment process narrowly focused on dysfunction might be less inclined to note potential strengths in a somewhat altered notion of what might constitute "success" for that particular child. Such might be the benefits when the clinician is more aware of the societal and cultural context of diagnostic judgments, when the clinician is able to decenter from the value he or she might personally place on reading-based knowledge. More generally, for purposes of developing skills in interpersonal and intercultural communication, both clinician and client, and the process, can benefit from an effort to explore the point of view of the other.

This effort to see from the perspective of the other, as well as from one's own perspective, is what defines a relational approach to the diagnostic/assessment process, to therapy, and to interpersonal relations in general. Traditionally, especially in a medical model, the diagnostician is seen as holding an objective ("evidence-based") transcultural body of knowledge about sickness and health, functionality, and dysfunctionality. But when one person sets himself or herself up as holding the objective point of view about the other in any way, the stage is set for hierarchy, inequality, and objectification of one person by the other. One is the observer, the other the observed. One person is the subject, the other the object.

Treatment

Increasingly in these days of "evidence-based" practice, treatment planning flows directly from a diagnostic assessment, as when a diagnosis of "attention deficit hyperactivity" disorder leads directly into the prescribing of stimulant medication. The treatment process then accordingly reflects and reinforces the cultural bias informing the diagnostic process.

As regards psychotherapy, a relational approach emphasizes intersubjective communication as key both to the therapy process and to the goals of the treatment. Breakdowns in communication, felt as disruptions, misunderstandings, and impasses, may reflect a degree of replication or repetition of the interpersonal patterning underlying dysfunctional or unsatisfying interactions in the client's life outside therapy. They may bring to the fore anxious preconceptions the client has about self and other people. At the same time, they tend to engage anxieties in the clinician as well, often bringing up long-standing points of conflict for him or her as well. From a relational point of view, misunderstandings, conflicts, and impasses are seen as points of opportunity to find new solutions for old problems, thus bringing change to long-standing preconceptions about self and other, about what is possible in the interpersonal world, for both clinician and client.

Cultural misunderstandings are a special case of the type of disruption that can both threaten and activate a therapeutic process. Finding a way for each person to stretch his or her cultural horizon then becomes a way to expand each person's, but especially the client's, intersubjective capacity and repertoire. To some extent, cultural differences reflect splits in the psychic world. For example, cultures vary with respect to the value placed on dependence and independence. In societies where children tend to stay close to home when they grow up, perhaps following in the footsteps of their parents with respect to work and social status, children may not be raised to be independent in the same way as in societies where there is a greater degree of social mobility. Cultural influences in this respect, and others, will also be inflected by gender and more idiosyncratic familial and personal factors.

At the same time, dependence and independence form a point of internal tension and negotiation within individuals in all cultures. Children staying close to home nonetheless have desires to find their own ways in some respects, and children raised to be on their own nonetheless get homesick. So a cultural difference tends to reflect a way of dividing up the psychic world as well. In a therapist-client relationship, a cultural difference can join up with personality differences to create a collusive division of labor, on one hand, or an impasse, on the other. An example of the former would occur when the therapist and client both implicitly build their relationship on the client being helpless and dependent while the therapist is in the seemingly more resourceful role. In this sort of interaction, the client may be disowning his own potential resources, while the therapist may be disowning her own potential dependence. This form of splitting may have its origin, and be reinforced, by a cultural or gender difference. When and if the client begins to disrupt this arrangement, perhaps by making a claim to do things his own way in or out of the therapy, the equilibrium may be disturbed, creating an impasse. The resolution of the impasse can entail, simultaneously, psychic and cultural integration and intersubjective understanding. Horizons can be expanded on all fronts.

Case Example

Rosa was a high school senior who came to the clinic where I worked at the time with panic attacks and severe, intermittent depression triggered by a recent breakup with a boyfriend.[1] She was a bright young woman who went to an elite high school out of her neighborhood. Her mother and father were first-generation immigrants from Puerto Rico who had lived here for about 20 years. Rosa's mother was a bright woman, but moody and sometimes quite depressed, who had never learned English. She stayed home raising her three children, of whom Rosa was the youngest and the only girl. The father, an intelligent and energetic man, had worked his way up from being a stock clerk in a store to the store manager. Rosa began therapy talking mostly about her anger that her ex-boyfriend had left her for another young woman they both knew. Rosa was enraged, depressed, with suicidal thoughts. I began seeing her twice a week.

After the first few sessions, Rosa began missing appointments. A pattern developed between us: Rosa would come to one or two sessions and then miss one.

---

[1] An earlier version of this case appeared in *The Analyst in the Inner City: Race, Class and Culture through a Psychoanalytic Lens, 2nd* Ed., Routledge, 2009

At first she would call to cancel. Something had come up at school or she needed to be at home to help her mother. After some time, she began missing sessions without calling. I felt disappointed, sometimes angry, when she would cancel.

After the pattern of keeping and missing appointments had established itself, I developed a characteristic conflict about how to follow up on the missed appointments. I felt caught between intruding by pursuing her and abandoning her by seeming to ignore her absence. I also felt caught between revealing to her, by an overly eager phone call, how much I wanted her to show up and revealing to her, by withholding contact, how angry I was. My compromise solution was to wait a day or two to see if she would call; if she did not, I would write her a letter noting that she had missed an appointment and saying that unless I heard otherwise, I would expect to see her at our next appointment. Rosa would show up at the next appointment with some concrete reason she had been unable to come to the appointment and apologize for having forgotten to call me.

After a couple of months, Rosa did not respond to one of my letters, so I wrote again asking her to contact me about her plans for our next appointment. After a week's delay, Rosa called, saying she had not gotten my first letter and asking for a new appointment.

When we met, I asked Rosa what she had been thinking about our work while we had not met. She said she had been feeling better and thought perhaps she did not need to come so regularly. I asked her if she had considered contacting me to tell me so. She said that she felt uncomfortable about it: She anticipated I would think that she needed to continue her sessions and that since I was the doctor, it was not her place to disagree. I asked her how she thought I had experienced her absence, and she said that she had actually thought about me at one point and wondered how I would fill the time when she did not show up. When I pressed her to speculate about my state of mind, she said she thought I was probably angry to be "stood up." I said perhaps this was not unlike what she had felt when her boyfriend had "stood her up," and she agreed.

In the next session, Rosa expressed anger at her mother for insisting that she be home at midnight the previous weekend when she had gone to a party. She felt that her mother could not accept that she was pretty much grown-up. What if she wanted to go away to college the next year? Would her mother even let her go? Rosa felt that her mother had no life of her own, that she would go into a depression if Rosa did not stay home with her. I suggested that Rosa might feel similarly about me, that she had to hide her thought that she was feeling better and might not need me anymore. Rosa agreed and said that she had also been feeling angry at me for pursuing her when she thought she was making it clear by her absence that she did not want to come to her sessions, at least on a regular basis. Her mother and I were both standing in the way of her developing autonomy. Over the next few sessions, none of which were missed, we had the opportunity to explore her guilt about wanting to be more independent. She felt that she was leaving behind her mother, as well as her childhood friends, in going "downtown" to school. In subsequent sessions, we also talked about how Rosa saw me as potentially facilitating her growth away from her mother, because I was White, a professional, and a man and because we were trying to remove obstacles to her independent development. Thus, her work with me was threatening whether she saw me as representing her mother or as an alternative to her mother, like her upwardly mobile father.

Rosa continued her treatment, on and off, until she graduated from high school. She went to college away from home, dropped out, reenrolled near home, and called me from time to time in distress about ways in which she felt she was sabotaging her success. I have not seen her for many years at this writing.

Rosa's reluctance to tell me directly that she wanted to cut back on or end her therapy could be seen as reflecting a culturally specific deference to authority. On the other hand, I must ask myself, how often do I openly disagree with doctors?

Rosa's conflicts over dependence and independence can also be seen as conditioned by culturally specific factors. In a Latina family, there may be an expectation that the only daughter will indeed stay close to home and her mother. This expectation, of course, changes as the new generation adopts a new cultural framework in which the independence and achievement of women is valued.

If I were to assign dependence to Rosa while reserving the independent role to myself as the male, White therapist who will help her to become more independent, I am denying my own dependent side. As it happened, however, I had had enough therapy at that point to have questioned some of my own bravado in this respect. Additionally, and crucially, I had learned about some traditional cultural values as a Peace Corps volunteer in an Indian village. I had noted how children were not raised in that village to be independent and leave home, because, with very rare exceptions, they would not. For example, children were breast-fed until they gave it up on their own, and children and adults all slept together (separated by gender).

It was a shock to discover, once I had returned to the USA and had my own children, how eager, if not desperate, parents are in my US subculture to wean their children and to get them out of their beds (with exceptions, of course). But, of course, it all made sense when my children grew up and went away to college: They and we had been preparing for that move since the get-go. So I could sympathize both with Rosa's mother and with Rosa's desire to move away and have her own life. I could sympathize with both sides of Rosa's conflict; thus I was well positioned to help her negotiate conflicting values. If I had simply tried to help her become more functional in school, I would have been siding with the independent wishes, thus perhaps forcing her into a more dependent position in order to have that side of her feelings represented. Most interesting to me, however, is the way my own dependence on Rosa was contained in my very efforts to help her become independent. That is, in trying to encourage her to come to her sessions, I was simultaneously trying to encourage independence and promoting her dependence on me (and enacting mine on her). In wanting to leave therapy, she was simultaneously acting autonomously in relation to me while resisting our joint efforts to help her be more independent and functional. Being able to recognize my own dependence on Rosa, as well as my wish for her to be more independent, was key to my being able to recognize the paradoxical intertwining of dependence and independence for both of us in our interaction. The solution we came up with, sessions "as needed," seemed like a creative resolution to this conflict, in synch with the adolescent developmental period as well as the intercultural and intergenerational transitional period Rosa was experiencing.

Note how the intercultural interaction overlaps with the intrapsychic interaction in this case. The two forms of integration depend on each other.

Conclusion

Taking a relational approach to the role of culture, race, and ethnicity in mental health work, this chapter emphasizes the socially constructed role of all social categories. Most crucially, there is no transcultural, objective place for the therapist or diagnostician to stand in working with clients. The mental health worker occupies a culturally specific place, as much as the client does. Our expertise does not consist in standing above culture and race, but rather in the process of heightening awareness of intercultural and interracial interaction between therapist and client, between self and other. Such heightened awareness can advance the client's development both in and out of therapy while promoting the growth of the therapist as well.

Relational theory guides toward an awareness that every clinical interaction entails an interaction between cultures and personalities, between cultures as expressed through the prism of each personality, and between personalities as expressed through the prisms of each culture. The implication for practice is that therapeutic action, from this relational point of view, inheres in the unpacking of these interactions within the clinical interaction. The goal is raised consciousness and increased competence in all aspects of human relations, from the cultural to the personal levels.

Social work has been a trailblazer in paying attention to the interaction of culture and personality in both theory and practice (Sheppard 2001). For me, a psychologist trained in a relatively traditional form of psychoanalytic theory and practice, it has been enriching and rewarding to discover and join with the relational social work tradition as reflected throughout this book.

Study Questions

1. Identify some psychological functions that are served by the social construction of racial categories. How might a relational clinician incorporate these functions when working with a client?
2. What are the implications for practice that White people in the United States so rarely think about "White" as a racial category? What challenges may this present in the treatment setting with clients that are viewed as being "non-White"?
3. What is a micro-aggression? Identify a situation in your own practice where a micro-aggression was present and describe how it may have affected the treatment relationship.

4. Describe an example of how the diagnostic process may be influenced by cultural factors that are specific to race.
5. How might cultural factors influence the treatment process? Identify a specific example and how that stage of the treatment process may be influenced.
6. What are two or more interventions or observations that the author makes that reflect principles of relational practice in the case material.

References

Altman, N. (2009). *The analyst in the inner city: Race, class, and culture through a psychoanalytic lens* (2nd ed.). New York/London: Routledge.
Baldwin, J. (1993). Letter to my nephew. In *The fire next time*. New York: Vintage International.
Ignatiev, N. (1995). *How the Irish became white*. London: Routledge.
Jacobson, M. (1998). *Whiteness of a different color*. Cambridge: Harvard University Press.
Jones, E. (2003). *The known world*. New York: Harper Collins.
Layton, L. (2006). The place gives me the heebie jeebies. In L. Layton, N. C. Hollander, & S. Gutwill (Eds.), *Psychoanalysis, class, and politics*. New York: Routledge.
Paniagua, F. A. (1998). *Assessing and treating culturally diverse clients*. Thousand Oaks/London/New Delhi: Sage.
Robertson, G. (2006). *Crimes against humanity: The struggle for social justice*. New York: The New Press.
Sheppard, D. (2001). *Clinical social work (1880–1940) and relational psychoanalysis: An historical interpretive analysis of relational concepts and practice*. Unpublished doctoral dissertation, New York University.
Sternberg, R. J., Grigorenko, E. L., & Kidd, K. K. (2005). Intelligence, race, and genetics. *The American Psychologist, 60*, 46–59.
Suchet, M. (2007). Unraveling whiteness. *Psychoanalytic Dialogues, 17*(6), 876–886.
Sue, D. (2010). *Microaggressions in everyday life: Race, gender, and sexual orientation*. Hoboken: Wiley.
Sullivan, H. S. (1953). *The interpersonal theory of psychiatry*. New York: Norton.

Relational Social Work and Religious Diversity

Frederick J. Streets

Introduction

The Council on Social Work Education states:

> Given the pervasiveness of religion and spirituality throughout people's lives and cultures, social workers need to understand religion and spirituality to develop a holistic view of the person in environment and to support the professional mission of promoting satisfaction of basic needs, well-being, and justice for all individuals and communities around the world. … Social workers are expected to work ethically and effectively with religion and spirituality as relevant to clients and their communities and to refrain from negative discrimination based on religious or nonreligious beliefs. (www.CSWE.org 2012)

This declaration emerged in 2011 from the CSWE Religion and Spirituality Work Group, on which I served as a member. Its purpose is "to promote social workers' knowledge, values, and skills for ethical and effective practice that takes into account the diverse expressions of religion and spirituality among clients and their communities" (www.CSWE.org 2012). This position statement makes clear the centrality of religious and spiritual considerations in clinical social work practice.

Relational theory's emphasis on discovering and articulating meanings in the immediate clinical process embraces exploration of the religious and spiritual dimensions of what Greenberg and Mitchell (1983) delineated as key intrapsychic structures: self, the other/object, and the unconscious template of self with others. Religion has both conscious and unconscious impact on how these self-structures are defined and enacted. It does not exist in a separate realm from other components

F.J. Streets, M.Div., M.S.W., D.S.W., D.D., LCSW (✉)
Wurzweiler School of Social Work, Yeshiva University, New York, NY, USA

Chaplain of Yale University, New York, NY, USA

Columbia University School of Social Work, New York, NY, USA

Yale University Divinity School, New York, NY, USA
e-mail: frederick.streets@yale.edu

J.B. Rosenberger (ed.), *Relational Social Work Practice with Diverse Populations*,
Essential Clinical Social Work Series, DOI 10.1007/978-1-4614-6681-9_5,
© Springer Science+Business Media New York 2014

of interpersonal experience and functioning that make up the content of clinical social work practice. Being mindful in assessment, treatment planning, and transference and countertransference to religious and spiritual content is essential not only with clients for whom religion and spirituality, or their rejection, are important self-dimensions but also for clinicians' self-awareness of their own religious and spiritual orientations. Cornett (1998) reminds us, "One of the most helpful things that therapy can do with regard to spirituality is not to change the client's view but to amplify it or bring it to sharper focus so that the client may scrutinize it more carefully and decide whether it truly fits the individual circumstance of life and current self-understanding." (p. 41)

Religion and Spirituality in Relational Clinical Social Work Practice

Establishing the kind of engagement and attunement with clients that will facilitate Cornett's goals requires the relational clinician to adopt a posture of letting the client be the teacher about what it means for him or her to be religious or spiritual. The relational principle of mutuality does not require agreement; confirmation that the client's perspective is understood respectfully by the clinician is co-constructed in the "space between" (Bromberg 1998) upon which all interpersonal engagement rests. The client as a teacher is an invaluable role for establishing engagement and identifying core issues that are not to be confused with conflict-free beliefs. For instance, following Cornett's (1998) description of social work and religion, a relational clinician may work with a client struggling with birth control, a concern which is at odds with the doctrine of her religion. The depth of such a struggle cannot be reduced by reducing the role of her religious convictions, but rather by empathizing with her dilemmas and doubts, helping her articulate and be heard about her various thoughts and feelings, including the reality context impinging upon her, and other relational strategies of joining and supporting her as a whole person in a real as well as emotional situation of distress. Religious beliefs and practices can clarify clients' needs and the resources that they rely upon, which emphasizes the relational emphasis on interpersonal and cultural context. The client as a teacher captures the shift from the classic paradigm of treatment by expert clinician to the co-constructed relationship that defines the relational social work perspective. Having content knowledge about the particular history, values and beliefs, and practices of a religion is important, but far more helpful for the relational clinician is to understand the religious client and not just the facts about that client's religion.

We may question whether some of the tenets of a religion as understood by our clients are hurtful or helpful to them, oppressive, or providing a sense of freedom. People who identify themselves as oppressed may interpret their experience of oppression through their religious faith. For instance, many African Americans support a meaning of Christianity that is radically different from the wider Anglo-American Christian community and reflects a religious response to the history of enslavement as a race. Discerning and appreciating such specific distinctions in religious interpretation in the individual client facilitates the professional social work relationship. Self-identification as part of a recognized religious group, be it Islam or Judaism or Buddhism or any other, does not in itself illuminate the intrapsychic meanings and functions of that identification and therefore its role in assessment and intervention. The relational social worker applies the principles of authenticity about what is not yet known and mutuality in developing understanding to deconstruct her own countertransference and explore religious content as she would other aspects of identification like race, gender, sexual orientation, and the like. The central concept is that religion is not extraneous to in-depth assessment, empathic exploration, and inclusion of religious beliefs and memberships as important aspects of client in context.

The Relational Clinician and Religious/Spiritual Content

Apprehension about the relationship between clinical social work and religion is to be appreciated for its value in illuminating the role of this dimension of cultural diversity. Awareness of skepticism or overcompensation to conceal skepticism alerts the relational clinician to engage all the more acutely with the meanings of the client's communications. The same can be said of unexamined assumptions of knowledge based on shared religious affiliation. Both poles represent the relational theory's principle of examining countertransference as the window on the clinician's potential for misapprehension, and thereby redirecting her to empathic listening. It also calls the question of why religious countertransference or transference or religion altogether is so often placed in a special and hands-off category of social work practice.

Some social workers may feel that religion is outside of their professional expertise, and therefore their clients with religious concerns should consult with someone from their own religious tradition. Others worry that the values, principles, and mission of social work as a profession could be compromised and supplanted by religious ideology and evangelical zeal. The perspective long held among some social work educators, implicitly if not consciously, is that the confessional and subjective nature of religious belief does not lend itself to scientific scrutiny, inquiry, and the search for truth. As discussed in chapter "Orientation to and Validation of Relational Diversity Practice", elevation of scientific data as the path to truth not only contradicts the entire interpersonal discovery enterprise but also leaves unanswered the application of such caution when it comes to religion. It reifies a faith/clinical dichotomy. Relational theory allows us to reevaluate this essentially prejudicial and exclusionary position: no meaningful client communication or conviction is extraneous to an attuned clinical social work relationship.

Gender, class, and ethnicity are more present in social work literature as aspects of clients' identity and social context that influence how client and clinician interpret experiences. The relational emphasis on interpersonal attunement has been identified as an important antidote to marginalization in life, and in clinical practice, for many populations (Altman 2010; Berzoff 2011). Our understanding of people and their cultures is incomplete without knowing something about what they consider ultimate in their lives, and religious/spiritual dimensions are not exceptions. An additional feature of religion and spirituality is the understanding that its significance and role may change over time. Relational social workers, along with their clients, live with and negotiate many conflicting, competing, and contradictory values and beliefs in their effort to keep their lives flowing and meaningful. Accounting for the role religion values play in this process adds depth to our knowledge base about diversity and practice as social workers.

Apparent Versus Inherent Tensions Between Religion and Clinical Social Work

Social work supports a client's right to self-determination even when the client's choice may not appear congruent with the clinical social work treatment process. Some religious approaches, for example, direct or proscribe of how the client should handle their problems or concerns. Prayer, for example, rather than self-reflection, may seem to abrogate the clinical function in dealing with a distressing conflict. For the relational practitioner, this tension opens, rather than closes, doors to mutual exploration of how a religiously defined pattern of functioning plays a role in either supporting or obstructing the client's presenting problems. Addressing that mutual exclusivity is not the only question that can set a clinical social work treatment on a course of combined cultural/religious attunement and intrapsychic exploration. The exploration makes conscious but does not judge the impact of religious conviction and fully acknowledges its contributions alongside any discovery of restriction or difficulty it presents in seeking a solution that is self-coherent.

Some clinical social work educators, regardless of their own beliefs, wish to avoid the appearance of promoting religion in any form in their teaching of practices. Concerns about how religious ideologies and practices can be interpreted or used destructively are legitimate, but the answer is not avoidance. For example, the conception of God as the source of behavior and the explanation of feelings is a positivist, cause-and-effect way of thinking that forecloses qualitative inquiry. A more qualitative, constructivist perspective is curious not so much about a specific religion's tenets, but about how those tenets determine ethical discernment, value clarification, approach to conflicts, and pursuit of a meaningful life, which for many define their spiritual quest. For the educator and student, liberation from preconception or avoidance allows authentic interest about how the client makes decisions and assesses outcomes. Psychodynamic thinking is not itself another religion. It is applied in relational practice as a method of becoming attuned to multiple sources of authority and sustaining interpersonal connections.

Relational Appreciation of Religion and Spirituality in Individual Functioning

Relational clinicians are cognizant of how some people more than others seem more aware of living with conflict, ambiguities, and contradictions regarding what they value, believe, and the choices they make. The values people derive from religion give texture to their identity and self-esteem. These values contribute to their sense of cultural continuity and serve as a defense against what they perceive and experience as oppressive. There are those who seem more confident about their convictions than others. The religiosity of a client may be well integrated into their self-understanding, and some dimensions of that religiosity may pose difficulty for the clinician/client relationship regardless of the clinician's own personal or professional view of religion. Relational clinicians are encouraged to show, in a nonjudgmental and authentically inquiring way, interest in the person's religious orientation to life. This approach is one whereby the practitioner asks questions that encourage the client to reflect upon how he or she chooses to live their life and what the sources are that sustain and gives them hope and meaning for living. For example, Smith, in his *The Relational Self: Ethics and Therapy from a Black Church Perspective* (1982), emphasized the importance of helping members of this community see the relationship between personal and social transformation and how this dynamic shapes the way people relate to one another, themselves, and God. Personal identities and ways of relating to one another are socially constructed, and Smith's work explicates the constructed causes and effects of the particular interpretations of religion in a historically oppressed population.

This role of religious beliefs in constructing personal identity and relationship to self, others, society, and God by exploring religious identity is mediated by the context, culture, ethnicity, gender, and sexual orientation of the believer. Relational theories share in common a basic interest in understanding all the factors that influence the development of the sense of self and the capacity to act upon the world and reflect upon how the world impacts us. Not all clients who are religious and who seek the assistance of a clinical practitioner will present that their faith is a problem or concern for them. This does not mean that they are denying that religion might be a part of their clinical needs and desires. Rather, their religious position, whatever it may be, is not apparent, or safe, for them to introduce in the social work process. The relational clinician is alert to what is missing as well as what is presented, especially in the assessment phase of practice. Therefore, omission of something as central to self as religion, including repudiation of religion if that is the case, forecloses a dimension of interpersonal sharing. Maintaining authentic curiosity and not knowing empowers the relational social worker to inquire about religion, along with other ordinary inquiries about a person's central life constructs. Asking, rather than waiting or suggesting, reflects the relational principle of building interpersonal connection itself as a central factor in healing: it establishes the clinical connection as one where no topic is off limits.

Clinical Social Work and Pastoral Counseling

Dittes (1990) offers what I think is an elegant description of pastoral counseling:

> Pastoral counseling aspires to enable people to take their place as responsible citizens of God's world, as agents of God's redemptive hope for that world. But it does not assign them to this mission or instruct them in how to carry it out. It is more effective because it is indirect Pastoral counseling exercises the discipline to be disinterested in the dismaying facts of life just because it takes them so seriously, seriously enough to mobilize people's best resources for contending with them. Pastoral counseling exercises the discipline to disregard the facts of the counselee recounts because it so profoundly regards what transcends these facts; namely, the meaning that they convey to the counselee. The postures of hope or despair, attack or submission, trust or fear, isolation or participation-these makes the difference in how the person lives life. To reclaim commitment and clarity, to beget faith, hope, and love, to find life affirmed-this is the conversation of soul that sometimes happens in pastoral counseling. (p. 61)

In this description of pastoral counseling, Dittes avoids being religiously dogmatic – a position that would not be so liberally stated by more conservative religious counselors. Indeed, many people have an image of religious and pastoral counseling as ideologically narrow, wanting to control and manipulate how people think and live. Other views border on stereotyping all religion as an "opiate of the masses" (Marx 1843). Helping a person to have a relationship with God is not a goal of social work. To the extent such intent is part of the social worker's private motives, corrective supervision is indicated. Relational theory guides the clinician emphatically not to impose upon his or her client, but rather to practice clinical social work in a way that is directed to the client's needs and goals for a meaningful and helpful outcome.

Definition of Terms

Religion is a complex enterprise (Gunn 2003) which one can make an industry. Moving away from organized religion to its key and universal components suggests the common definition as being that which binds or connects us to God (and God, of course, being multiply conceptualized). Definitions of religion are always contextual and provisional as Canda and Furman (1999) observe: *"Our definitions are affected by our life situation, sociocultural conditioning, and self-understanding. Since these change overtime, our personal definitions of spirituality and religion may change as well"* (p. 74). Dow (2007) describes religion by using three categories: (a) cognizer of unobservable agents, (b) sacred category classifier, and (c) motivator of public sacrifice (p. 8). Burton's (1992) description of the interrelationship of spirituality and religion is helpful:

1. Spirituality is grounded in the midst of history where messy life events are being experienced and interpreted.
2. Human beings (a) seek interpersonal connection and (b) at the same time seek safety in/from connection.

3. Spirituality is experienced and expressed in the context of physical structure, social class, ethnicity, gender, age, and sexual orientation.
4. Religion [is] secondary to religion...religion is an organized expression of spirituality, and therefore is more specific and defined in its structure (pp. 14–15).

Canda and Furman (1999) offer five common attributes of the concept of spirituality:

1. An essential or holistic quality of a person that is considered inherently valuable or sacred and irreducible.
2. An aspect of a person or group dealing with a search for meaning, moral frameworks, and relationships with others, including ultimate reality.
3. Particular experience of a transpersonal nature.
4. A developmental process of moving toward a sense of wholeness in oneself and others.
5. Participation in spiritual support groups that may or may not be formally religious (pp. 44–45).

Sheridan (1994) gives this simple definition of religion: "religion refers to a set of belief, practices, and traditions experienced within a specific social institution over time." Every definition or description of religion and spirituality goes wanting. A person is religious, for the purpose of our discussion, when he or she believes in a deity and that belief is informed by a system of beliefs in and adherence to doctrines or dogmas. This is often accompanied by their involvement with rituals and living according to a code of ethics and conduct, all of which influences the believers' view of reality, conceptions of the truth, perspectives on life and its meaning, human nature, and the cosmos. The meaning of these beliefs and actions are filtered through the cultural context and gender of the believer and may include ancestral and other cultural traditions. Matters of religious beliefs shape the believer's way of life and personal and communal identity and influence their actions.

Intrapsychic Functions of Religion and Spirituality: Multicultural Implications

Religious beliefs, values, and practices are among the many characteristics of a client who comes to the social worker seeking assistance. What the client attributes to these aspects of himself is a subject of the discerning work of the helping relationship. A client's religion, spiritual practices, gender, ethnicity, and sexual orientation are not neutral value expressions of a client's being. Any expression of who we are reflects the interplay of the multiple factors that constitute our identity. Religious beliefs, practices, and values are three of the many powerful mediators of the meaning we derive from our interaction with other people and the larger society.

In many places around the world today, the religious beliefs of people cannot be separated from their cultural or national identities (Canda et al. 1999). Old and new immigrant communities in America also reflect this character. Motivated by the growth of these communities and religious convictions, people representing religious institutions and faith based organizations provide significant social support services to many in need living in these communities.

Many ethnic communities such as African American, Hispanic, Native American, Jewish, Middle Eastern, and Asian have strong historical religious traditions and values. The presence of such religious diversity in American society means that we must rethink the value we once placed on the dualistic thinking inherited from the ancient Greeks, that is, mind vs. body, scientific knowledge vs. knowledge from experience, truth vs. falsehood, and feelings vs. reasoning. There is the tendency in Western culture to separate the religious and spiritual aspects of our clients from their other personal attributes. When separated, thus, we run the risk of losing a part of who we are as whole persons. Our understanding of people and their cultures is incomplete without knowing something about what they consider ultimate in their lives.

Our values influence our behavior and the choices we make. Some people derive their values from their religious beliefs. In the effort to keep the dance of their lives going and meaningful, most people live with conflict and negotiate many values that compete with one another. Embedded in their struggle is the challenge that cultural and religious pluralism brings to the values that shape their self-understanding. People who seek the help of a relational clinician may in some way be experiencing a challenge to some of their assumptions about life and the values by which they have made decisions. Their religious worldview may give us additional clues about who they are, their culture, and the nature of their problems.

A Brief Example of Religiously Informed Clinical Practice

Early in my career as a relational clinician and a pastor, a congregation member called to make an appointment. I knew Mrs. Jones from her participation in many of the church's programs. The salient facts of her story she shared with me when we met were that Mrs. Jones is a very nurturing person who is always willing to extend a helping hand to anyone in need. She and her husband were taking care of their teenage niece who had become pregnant, and she found herself feeling a great deal of stress. She also said that she was having difficulty sleeping, was feeling anxious about leaving her home, and had begun to recall a rape experience as a young woman that had caused problems in her relationship with her husband in earlier years. She said what she wanted from me was to pray with her regarding her life situation. She did not link her current distress to caretaking her niece: to her it was inexplicable.

Part of my task when I met with Mrs. Jones was to assess the nature of the issues she was presenting and see how I could be of help. As pastoral counseling, there were areas of convergence with and divergence from essential clinical social work. Engagement by attuned listening and creation of a spirit of exploration by not knowing and striving for mutuality were all relevant skills reflecting relational social work. At the same time, Mrs. Jones was requesting a mode of treatment, prayer, and an implied core problem conceptualization based on her religion. She was unaware of some, not all, of the many emotional, ethical, legal, spiritual, and practical aspects of the experiences about which she was concerned. As the chapters that follow on religious diversity indicate, working within but not being clinically constrained by the client's religious expectations is a challenge in social work and also in pastoral counseling where the counselor is clinically trained. The task is to find a way of introducing dynamics that are active in the client's problem in a way that is congruent with religious convictions. An aspect of pastoral counseling that can broaden clinical social work with diverse populations is this kind of self-relocation to speak from within a client's world view in ways that nonetheless bring necessary awareness to psychodynamic and contextual issues that are converging in their need for help. Listening to Mrs. Jones and asking for clarification gave us both a way to explore how she understood God, her situational reality and her inner world, herself, and her spiritual values. The process and content of our conversations made visible and collaborative a framework to address her feelings and to promote her resilience and capacity to make choices. Our meetings provided the interpersonal recognition and containment that Baker (2012) sites as therapeutic in itself. In addition, recognizing overtly the impact of her choices on herself and her family helped reduce her symptoms: they become understandable as reflecting the complexity of what initially seemed a simple, religiously dictated caretaking obligation. Wise's (1983) description of the pastoral helping process captures the interplay of religion and relational social work:

> Real change comes slowly and with effort at working on those parts of ourselves that are causing us pain. God has placed the potentiality for change within us but we have to accept our responsibility in bringing it about. ... Our past cannot be changed. What can be changed, or rather what we can change, is the character of our inner responses, our feelings and attitudes and patterns of relationship. (p. 191)

Religion and Spirituality in the Secular Clinical Social Work Setting

Clients seem far less confused or concerned about religion than do some social workers and social work educators. Opening the religious door in relational practice often reveals that some form of prayer, meditation, traditional healing, or animistic practice is widely prevalent. When this is the case, the relational clinician begins to uncover the character of what Smith (1982), writing of religion in Black churches, terms *relatingness*, meaning "a way of speaking of the indwelling presence of others in our own concrete reality and of our presence in theirs. Relationality also implies that we can respond not only to the intention and actions of others, but to our own sense of self as well" (p. 51). Smith (1982) adds "Humans need to engage the perspectives of others, especially the oppressed from other cultures and ethnic backgrounds, so that their own understanding of their society and their position in it can evolve beyond where it is presently constituted" (p. 52). These statements, addressed in a designated religious framework, echo the relational theory principle of the social constructions of reality. Religious constructions constitute one way clients filter the meaning of their experiences. Taking this perspective into account, Smith (1982) argues that the "dialogue of therapy" is a form of intervening "into an oppressive situation which seeks to do several things:

1. Bracket the unquestioned and taken-for-granted world of experience and clarify the individual's, the family's, or the group's context.
2. Enable the person or family to reflect upon and reconstruct past events in ways that bring the meaning of the past into working relationship with the present and future. In addition, therapy can help the individual, family or group do something constructive about conditions that oppress them, and thereby they can become agents in the liberation and healing of others.
3. Heighten a person's sense of self as a member of a community (and the community's consciousness of the importance of each member) where perspectives are available for the person's and the community's enlargement, enrichment, and critical reflection.
4. Chart alternative possibilities.
5. Enlarge and free the person's or family's capacity for creative change and meaningful participation in a larger community context in light of a new image and new whole" (p. 111).

These therapeutic actions set goals for clients to assume personal responsibility for their own emotional well-being and not continue their victimization. In the process of our fostering this development, the relational clinician considers the religion of the client as mediating risk, resistance and resilience factors.

Wimberly (2000) offers the concept of "relational refugees," who are "persons not grounded in nurturing and liberating relationships. They are detached and without significant connections with others who promote self-development. They lack a warm relational environment in which to define and nurture their self-identity. As a consequence, they withdraw into destructive relationships that exacerbate rather than alleviate their predicament" (p. 20). While not identifying his ideas as based in relational theory, Wimberly describes the role of the relational clinician as employing skills to assist relational refugees in finding a home in their current context. "Through empathetic listening the mentor provides a safe place for the refugee to risk attempting human connection which is basic if she or he is to come to feel at home in the world. The mentor invites the learner to imitate the mentor's positive attitude and way of being present. This communicates welcoming hospitality. When he or she accepts the mentor's hospitality, the learner is no longer homeless" (Wimberly 2000, p. 35).

Conclusion

I maintain that human actions are more reflective of what we value than what it is we think or believe. Our experiences, gender, sexual orientation, ethnicity, and religious beliefs are all filters through which these values are formed and help form our sense of self and how we relate to others and the world. A relational theory considers the diverse ways that constitute our own being and ways of relating to others and the world, as well as the diversity that is within and among religions. The convergence of relational theory and religious diversity is openness to the content of religious beliefs and values, their context, and how they are processed that leads the believer to feelings and actions in the world. Judgment of religious devotion as fanaticism without understanding the dynamic process of religious conviction and commitment in the life of the believer deprives the social worker of necessary clinical criteria of what we understand as healthy and unhealthy ways of being religious.

Western attitudes toward religion, and particularly its Christian varieties, are often dismissed as offering people a trip to some kind of Garden of Eden or a place free of evil, pain, and death. To the contrary, the relational clinician is attuned to how religious beliefs and practices are not fantastical coping mechanisms but ways people can look realistically at evil, suffering, and death. In Elie Wiesel's novel, *The Fifth Son* (1998), a young son asks his father: "'Since we are Jews, how come we are not dead?' 'Because,' said his father, 'something in us is stronger than the enemy and tries to be stronger than Death itself'" (p. 224). Religious beliefs help to awaken in some people a meaning to their life and guide them in the choices they make. Relational clinicians contribute to this process by helping people realize the choices they have to live responsibly with the consequences of their actions and in a manner that helps them and our society to flourish.

Study Questions

1. Explain how "relationality," described as part of pastoral counseling, reflects the relational theory approach to clinical social work.
2. Discuss how religious beliefs include, rather than substitute for, personal responsibility. Give an example of how a relational clinician can emphasize this concept to develop the therapeutic relationship.
3. Describe how a client's skepticism in the practitioner can be helpful to a relational clinician and illustrate an example from your own practice.
4. Explain why particular attention to religion may be needed when working with ethnic minorities and/or immigrant populations. How might "relatingness" be used in this situation to help to strengthen the connection between the social worker and the client?
5. What initial challenges may a relational clinician face when exploring religion with a client, and what relational steps can be taken to dispel the tension?
6. Write a paragraph about how your perspective on religion as part of the clinical social work process has been affected by this chapter.

References

Altman, N. (2010). *The analyst in the inner city: Race, class and culture through a psychoanalytic lens* (2nd ed.). New York: Routledge.

Baker Miller, J. (2012). *Five good things.* Wellesley: Jean Baker Miller Training Institute at the Wellesley Centers for Women.

Berzoff, J. (Ed.). (2011). *Falling through the cracks: Psychodynamic practice with vulnerable and oppressed populations.* New York: Columbia University Press.

Bromberg, P. (1998). *Standing in the spaces: Essays on clinical process, trauma, and dissociation.* Hillsdale, NJ: Analytic Press.

Burton, L. B. (1992). *Religion and the family: When god helps.* New York: Haworth Pastoral Press.

Canda, E. R., & Furman, L. D. (1999). *Spiritual diversity in social work practice. The heart of helping.* New York: Free Press.

Canda, E. R., Nakashima, M., Burgess, V., & Russell, R. (1999). *Spiritual diversity and social work: A comprehensive bibliography with annotations. Teaching social work: Resources for educators.* Alexandria: Council on Social Work Education.

Cornett, C. (1998). *The soul of Psychotherapy: Recapturing the spiritual dimension in the therapeutic encounter.* New York: Free Press.

Counsel on Social Work Education (2012). www.CSWE.org.

Dittes, J. E. (1990). *Pastoral Counseling. The Basis.* Louisville, KY. Westminster John Knox.

Dow, J. W. (2007). *A Scientific definition of religion.* www.anpere.net/2007/2.

Greenberg, J., & Mitchell, S. A. (1983). *Object relations in psychoanalytic theory.* Cambridge, MA: Harvard University Press.

Gunn, J. T. (2003). The complexity of religion and the definition of "Religion" in international law. *Harvard Human Rights Journal, 16,* 189–215.

Marx, K. (1843). *Marx's critique of Hegel's philosophy of right.* In J. O'Malley (Ed.), (1970). Cambridge: Cambridge University Press.

Sheridan, M.J., Wilmer, C. M., and Atcheson, L. (1994). Inclusion of content on religion and spirituality in the social work curriculum: A study of faculty views. *Journal of Social Work Education, 30*(3), 363–376.

Smith, A., Jr. (1982). *The relational self: Ethics and therapy from a black church perspective.* Nashville: Abingdon.

Wiesel, E. (1998). *The fifth son.* New York: Schocken.

Wimberly, E. P. (2000). *Relational refugees: Alienation and reincorporation in African American churches and communities.* Nashville: Abingdon.

Wise, C. A. (1983). *Pastoral Psychotherapy.* New York, Jason Aronson.

Part II
Racial and Ethnic Diversities

A Relational Approach to Clinical Practice with African-American Clients

Victoria R. Winbush

Introduction

This chapter examines the use of a relational approach to clinical social work practice with African-Americans (DeYoung 2003; Goldstein et al. 2009). Relational social work holds promise for delivering services in a manner that can rebuild trust in the use of formal treatment services (Fontes 2008; Parham 2002; Sanchez-Hucles 2000; Washington 2006). By affirming difficult realities and daily struggles as well as individual suffering (Hopps et al. 1995; Brown and Keith 2003; Germain 1979; Leary 2005), relational theory places social work clinicians in a uniquely applicable position to practice with African-American clients in a way that unifies cultural relevance with clinical expertise.

The term "African-Americans" is used here interchangeably with the term "Blacks" and refers to persons living in the United States who have origins in any of the Black racial groups of Africa (United States Department of Commerce 2007). African-American clients represent a major component of the overall population in the United States who seek clinical social work treatment services. While these clients may share a common racial history, they also reflect vast differences in terms of their individual cultural heritages.

A wealth of literature already describes strategies for increasing the efficacy of service delivery to African-American clients (Altman 2011; Boyd-Franklin 2003; Devore 1991; Green 1982; Harper-Dorton 2007; Johnson 2005; Jones 1991; Locke 1992; Pinderhuges 1989; Sue 2008). Based on the principle of understanding the client's culture as an integrated component of the biopsychosocial assessment

V.R. Winbush, MSSA, LISW, MPH, Ph.D. (✉)
Cleveland State University School of Social Work, Cleveland, OH, USA

Cleveland State University Diversity Management Program, Cleveland, OH, USA

Smith College School for Social Work, Northampton, MA, USA
e-mail: v.winbush@csuohio.edu

J.B. Rosenberger (ed.), *Relational Social Work Practice with Diverse Populations*,
Essential Clinical Social Work Series, DOI 10.1007/978-1-4614-6681-9_6,
© Springer Science+Business Media New York 2014

process, such emphasis on preconditions of culturally competent work requires extension throughout the clinical process. A relational social work approach is complementary: it builds on assessment to provide principles of attunement with unique issues that arise in work with African-American clients.

Many of the historical, social, and political factors that have had an impact on the lives of African-Americans are described. This is followed by a discussion of how African-Americans utilize treatment services to address their mental health needs. The final section uses case illustrations to demonstrate the therapeutic value and impact of using a relational approach to clinical social work practice with African-American clients. It also emphasizes the importance for the social worker to possess a capacity for self-reflection and for genuine empathy as essential ingredients for engaging in relational social work practice.

Understanding the Socio-cultural, Political, and Historical Contexts of African-American Clients

African-Americans are members of a distinct and internally diverse group who share a common history, out of which arises a common vulnerability to social stereotypes. A working knowledge of the historical and contemporary context of persons who identify as African-Americans is critical to clinicians of all races and ethnicities. There are also African-American clinicians with limited personal and professional interactions with other African-Americans whose day-to-day lives are circumscribed by the isolation of poverty and limited access to resources of all types including financial, emotional, and physical (Payne 1996; Pinderhughes 1997). This illustrates the value emphasized in relational theory's approach of using dialogue to support the creation of a codiscovery process between the client and the clinician. This interpersonal authenticity allows client and clinician to fill in gaps of what is yet unknown about the client and the situation, including the multiple meanings of race that apply to African-Americans. Factual understanding of the historical precursors and social composition of African-Americans as a population group will help the relational clinician establish mutuality: authentic not-knowing does not endorse clinician neglect of efforts to gain familiarity with a client's points of reference and world view. An introduction to some key issues is given below.

Complexity, Confusion, and Misunderstanding of What Race Means

Race has been used as political, biological, and social constructs to characterize the differences that exist between groups of people. The focus here will be on race as a social construct, emphasizing how race frames the experiences and perceptions of individuals who identify as African-American and those who interact with them.

According to Hardy (1994), few issues are as "value laden and misunderstood as is race" (p. 5). Taylor (1997) has suggested that the biological dimension of race (Mongoloid, Negroid, Caucasoid, etc.) is invalid as a scientific concept. Reviewing the more than 50 years of research, Taylor (1997) concluded that "...there is no legitimate biological basis for sorting individuals into groups that correspond to races as they are popularly perceived" (p. 279). Taylor (1997) further noted that the recent attempt to correlate race with intelligence (Herrnstein & Murray 1994), with the call to discard the term "race" altogether, is countered by the importance of retaining race as a construct that reflects the "true nature and significance of human diversity" (p. 279). The relational social worker would concur with this last position: obfuscation or denial of individual dimensions of internal and interpersonal experience runs counter to empathic attunement to social work clients' direct experiences.

Taylor (1997) cites Lopez (1996) and Lee (1993) regarding the 1790 United States Census Bureau development of a racial classification system based on political motivations to maintain racial purity during this period of United States' history. The Census Bureau took responsibility for assigning a person's race, based on family heritage and perceived skin color, with the possible choices being White or non-White. The 1890 census included only one category for White and at least seven categories for non-White. To be White meant legal entitlement to the full range of rights and privileges of citizenship, to which non-Whites were not entitled (Taylor 1997, p. 282). In 1977, the United States Office of Management and Budget (OMB) created four race categories (White, Black, Asian, and Pacific Islander), along with two ethnic categories (Hispanic origin and non-Hispanic origin), and prohibited the term non-White (Taylor 1997). This elimination of non-White as a total population did not end the debate about the significance of categorizing individuals based on their heritage. Omi and Winant (1986) introduced the term "racial formation" to underscore how race has become a *central axis* of social relations which cannot be subsumed under or reduced to some broader category or conception" (p. 15). The clinical social worker and her clients, each impacted by racial formation, cannot ignore its impact, conscious or unconscious, in their interpersonal encounters.

Impact of "Racial Formation" on Relational Social Work Practice

Racial formation has created a hierarchy of privilege irrespective of how racial categories are defined and redefined. Increasing ambiguity about a person's position in the social hierarchy based on appearance opens a door to exploration rather than assumption, with both client and clinician benefiting from this need to pursue co-constructed meanings of their individual perspective and experience. To proceed otherwise invites false countertransference enactments. As an example, John Hope Franklin, an internationally acclaimed African-American scholar, who upon the occasion of celebrating his receipt of the Presidential Mental of Freedom in 1995, hosted a party during which a White guest who was attending at different event at the same exclusive club asked him to get her coat. He politely told the woman that any of the uniformed attendants on duty could assist her (Associated Press 2009). Franklin himself being a darker-skinned African-American, and wearing a tuxedo, had provoked the woman to make a social assumption that vividly demonstrated the persistence of the process of racial formation even among the presumably educated.

A case study by Greene (1997) provides another opportunity to consider the process of racial formation from a clinical perspective. A 37-year-old African-American woman entered therapy because she had been bypassed a third time for a promotion in her law firm, in spite of impeccable credentials and outstanding evaluations. The client's belief was that she had faced unfair discrimination, resulting in severe emotional stress. The clinician used the relational approach of co-constructed understanding of meanings to identify the internal and external sources of distress and dysfunction. She struck a balance between overemphasizing or underemphasizing the impact of racial discrimination. Yes, she had faced discrimination, and yes, she realized that staying and continuing to try for promotion in a prejudiced environment would not result in the outcome she sought. At the same time, the clinician guided the client to address deep-seated emotional issues about striving and success in her family of origin, which required denial of a no-win situation and insistence that if she worked hard enough, it would eventually pay off.

This fusion of internal and external exploration sprang from a relational perspective in which the clinical social worker validated reality conditions without abandonment of intrapsychic inquiry. The client eventually left the firm for another position in which her talents and experiences were recognized and valued. When this case was presented to a group of clinical students, there was general disbelief that the client, given her credentials, could *really* (my emphasis) be a "victim of discrimination" (Greene 1997, p. 318). While it may have been contradictory to the conscious values of these clinicians to practice racial discrimination, the teaching point was that they as clinicians could not afford to have their own disappointment and disbelief be used to minimize, refute, or deny the client's experience. In this way, Greene illustrated the central relational theory principle of empathic understanding of the client's interpretation of the problem; this had to precede exploring further dimensions in the treatment process. The social work practitioner's obligation to examine transference and countertransference elements was clarified by Geene's eliciting of the training participants' difficulty validating the client's experience.

The educational preparation of social work clinicians, both clinicians of color as well as white clinicians, requires the adoption of a commitment to include the study and understanding of race, racism, and the social construction of race in the academic curriculum (Basham 1997, 2004). Particularly for the clinical social work student, a basic requirement is to adopt a relational theory perspective that entails critical thinking about the dynamics of dominance and subordination in the delivery of clinical services. Not limited to study *about* populations of diversity, the relational clinical student must process self-reflection for true mutuality in engagement, treatment planning, addressing resistance, transference and countertransference, and co-construction of meanings.

Deconstructing Assumptions/Misconceptions About-African Americans as a Group

A clinical social worker must be prepared to engage African-American clients whose identities include multiple social group memberships, including gender, sexual orientation, and religion, and are rural, urban, and of every social class. In the United States, 12.8 % of households identify as Black (U.S. Department of Commerce 2007). Since this number includes people who identify Black as their only race or Black in combination with other races, being of both Black and White or Black and Hispanic, disparities, social complexities, and psychological dilemmas are baseline expectations (Wijeyesinghe and Jackson 2001). Besides the interpersonal experiences of living in a racially conflicted society, African-American clients of public social service clinicians are apt to represent that portion of the population with economic and social stressors: in the aggregate, Blacks have double or triple unemployment rates, half the income, and three times as many single-mother households (United Stated Department of Commerce 2007). At the same time, it is damaging to assume that every African-American client is living in scarcity or deficit: because middle and upper class Blacks may also be clients. The relational theory position of inquiry rather than assumption guides the social work clinician through authentic discovery.

African-Americans historically have underutilized mental health services (Morris 2001). African-Americans attend fewer mental health sessions than Whites and in general terminate prematurely. Especially low are the statistics for continuation of talk therapy (Lasser 2002), with Blacks showing "…a preference for emergency services over ongoing treatment services, tertiary prevention over secondary prevention, and crisis mode over preventive mode" (Morris 2001, p. 563). Morris (2001) pointed to cultural factors including training deficiencies among therapists, stigma, and culturally inappropriate services, alongside barriers like transportation, inflexible schedules, lack of knowledge about resources, as well as economic constraints. Confirming the bidirectionality of distrust of clinical treatment among African-Americans, Morris (2001) found that among doctoral-level clinicians, less than half felt competent with African-American clients despite their training and exposure to diverse client populations. Richardson (2001) as cited by Winbush (2009) found that African-American parents of child clients reported significantly more negative expectations than did White parents. Their expectations were that providers would be untrustworthy, disrespectful, and would offer poor care. This demonstrable elevation of race over individuality in clinical social work practice points to the urgent need for a relational approach, wherein empathy and responsiveness to each client's reality is necessary and inclusive of the reality of distrust. The relationally oriented clinical social worker follows the principles of attunement, not-knowing, co-construction of meanings, and mutuality in treatment planning during the first visit to acknowledge client fears about what to expect this time around, and helps build trust and confidence in the newly forming relationship.

Case Illustrations of Relational Practice
with African-American Clients

The relational approach to social work practice focuses on using the relationship between the client and the therapist as the "principal vehicle to affect change in the client..." (Tosone 2004, p. 481). This change can encompass all levels of interaction, including intrapsychic, interpersonal, and larger community systems. Tosone (2004) describes that this is done by the clinician making a clear effort to understand the internalized meanings that a client has assigned to the relevant interactions and the mutual influences that client and clinician can have on one another. This can include how interactions are being affected by larger systems in the client's environment. It also can include the impact of the social work practice environment, including social work agency systems as well as the clinician's own internalized configuration of self and of the client as representative of their respective cultural/racial groups.

The following case vignettes demonstrate the value of using a relational approach wherein cultural and racial factors may be different or similar between the client and the clinical social work practitioner. They illustrate the development of the clinical relationship and clarify that all clinicians, regardless of race, can experience significant benefit from the use of a relational approach with Black clients.

Case Illustrations Involving White Clinician and Black Client

A male African-American teenager was being seen by a female White clinical social worker for behavior issues that led to his recent suspension from school. The teenager had already developed a strong alliance with the clinician. He proceeded without hesitation to share his perceptions about the current situation, including his feelings of how Black students in his school were treated differently from White students. He clearly believed that if he had been White, he would not have been suspended.

The focus of the clinical interaction using a relational stance required a shift from the teenager as "client-in-situation" to one of the "client-and-clinician-in-situation." As a therapeutic dyad, the client and the social work practitioner were "recognized as being influenced by complex internal and external forces" (Tosone 2004, p. 483). The focus was on how the clinician would use the dynamics of the therapeutic relationship in service of the client developing a fuller appreciation for his own strengths and capacities and for recognizing how to best make use of the existing supports in his environment. The teen's perceptions and anger regarding differential treatment by school personnel, as well as the clinician's own unresolved feelings about racism and White privilege, could have triggered within the clinician a sense of guilt and/or over-responsibility. Unless the clinician was able to self-reflect and to acknowledge her reactions, the creation of a mutual relationship based on authentic interactions might quickly have been compromised or derailed. In this case, mutuality did not mean that the therapist and the teenager were equals or that the therapist did not have more power than the teenager (Tosone 2004, p. 483). It did mean that the therapist could allow herself to be vulnerable in the presence of the client and to search together for reasonable explanations of what had transpired and what was needed to effectively empower and support the adolescent toward resolution of the issue.

The relational stance in which both are members of a relational dyad is compatible with the collective orientation to which many African-Americans subscribe (Boyd-Franklin 2003). This orientation is in contrast to a more individualistic orientation that characterizes traditional psychodynamic psychotherapy where the clinician is under no obligation and is in fact discouraged from revealing his reaction to the content being discussed by the client. In contrast, the relational social worker cannot relate authentically if attempting to hide her reactions when engaged with a client. In other words if this clinician truly believed that Black and White students were treated equally by the school administration, then it would be important for her to share her doubts and ask how the client had not only different perceptions but experience which supported his different perceptions. This example of clinician and client in context acknowledges that each person's transference and countertransference has roots in direct experience. Practicing from a relational theory base requires the clinician to express genuine curiosity and desire to understand the situation from the client's perspective and to invite the client to assist her in this task. The relational clinician's willingness to acknowledge not-knowing in a respectful way that requests the client's support in teaching understanding of the client's perspective, moves mutuality and co-construction forward. It also reduces risk due to revelation of holding differing perceptions of the same situation.

Another key reason for the compatibility of this approach with the collective orientation held by many African-Americans is its emphasis on the clinician's capacity to demonstrate genuine empathy. The demonstration of empathy suggests to the person in distress that he is not alone and has the companionship and support of someone who is truly interested in his overall well-being. While this is an attribute of a clinician which is important for most clients, its role in the treatment of this Black teenager offered direct contrast to daily instances of brief indignities, racial slights, and insults, intentional or not (Sue et al. 2007). To support her client in his distress, the relational clinician had to be grounded in a clear sense of her own identity, including flaws and vulnerabilities that sometimes may mirror those of the client and her defenses against acknowledging equivalent flaws and vulnerabilities. As described by Tatum (1997), "…in order to empathize one must have a well-differentiated sense of self in addition to an appreciation of and sensitivity to the differences as well as the sameness of another person" (p. 92).

The outcome for this case was one in which the client joined with the clinician in sorting out what had occurred in terms of his suspension. While there was blame on the part of the client related to his acting out behaviors, there was also clear evidence that the disciplinary action taken was more extreme than what had been used with other students. Consequently the clinician and the parent were in a position to advocate for the student to receive a more equitable consequence for his inappropriate behavior. A relational social worker who is not school-affiliated could include in her role consultation with the mother regarding watchfulness of the school's responsiveness to her son as one of very few African-Americans students enrolled. This kind of intervention is in support of the creation of a stronger bond between mother and son particularly in light of the father's absence from the home.

An additional case illustration involved a young White male clinician working in a clinical social service clinic, assigned to work with a college-educated, unemployed Black mother and her teenage daughter. The mother was seeking therapeutic support for her daughter due to her daughter's failing grades and frequent displays of disrespectful behavior in their home. The therapist prided himself on being able to form strong working relationships with Black adolescent clients and for being able to determine which type of treatment might best benefit the teen, even if the treatment might be at odds with what the parent thought was needed.

The clinician consciously chose to meet with the adolescent alone and not to engage the mother's growing anxiety and displeasure with her daughter's treatment. While this decision was rationalized as assisting the teen with separation issues and encouraging a working relationship in which the client could find her own voice, the social worker did not reflect adequately on his countertransference overidentification with adolescents. He was therefore outraged when the mother went directly to the clinician's supervisor to report her dissatisfaction with the care that her daughter was receiving. He also was surprised by this mother's feeling of empowerment to express her opinions. That this mother did not fit the clinician's stereotype of the undereducated Black parent is an example of racial formation.

This scenario demonstrates how the absence of a relational stance can compromise the quality of the therapy provided. This clinician exhibited a lack of self-awareness regarding the potential impact of his presence as a White male authority figure on both mother and daughter. Since self-awareness is core to the success of a relational social work stance, the clinician would need to weigh the implications of the daughter being flattered by his attention and the mother feeling disrespected by his lack of willingness to hear her concerns about her daughter. The absence of self-awareness compromised this social worker's capacity to develop an authentic working alliance with the daughter and an empathetic and supportive relationship with the mother. A relational social work stance had little potential to be cultivated without there being significant adjustments on the clinician's part. There was an opportunity for the supervisor to intervene, redirecting and exploring the clinician's authoritarian and non-collaborative stance. This option was not pursued. As a result the mother terminated her daughter's therapy. Even more significantly, this experience of feeling disrespected may have left the mother more resistant to seeking out clinical services in the future for either herself or her daughter.

Another final case illustration involves a young White female social work clinician who was assigned to work with a middle-aged Black male client. From the beginning the clinician reported that she was keenly aware of the race and age differences between her and her client. She noted that as much as she felt that she and he had created a strong working alliance, she was keenly aware of questioning her own motivations particularly as they related to feeling guilt stemming from her perception of her own White privilege. She knew how easy it was to align with a stereotypic image of her client as the Black man who was uninterested in self-reflection and perhaps dangerous, and the image of herself as a stereotypic White woman who was clinically trained and righteous. She engaged in a lot of reflection about these issues and used her supervisor as a support in this process in order that she might be prepared to respond to these issues as effectively as possible.

The clinician felt challenged because her client often talked of his anger toward Whites while at the same time suggesting that she was different from those Whites with whom he had had negative experiences. While his anger regarding racial discrimination was explicitly not being directed toward her, she wanted to have enough understanding of her own thoughts and feelings about racial differences so as to be able to stay empathic when his anger and hurt about these issues began to surface. By reflecting upon and monitoring her responses to the racial content of the client's life experiences and their implications, internal and interpersonal, in their treatment process, this relationally oriented clinician was able to stay present to the whole of their communications and to seek support and guidance as needed. Although not explicitly spelled out in relational theory, pursuing help to clarify perceptions and misperceptions further reflects the power of not-knowing and continuous self-reflection as a clinical contribution.

This authenticity in the clinician about her own contributions to the co-constructed relationship helped to support the building of a strong working alliance between her and this client. It would have been very destructive and disingenuous if she had bought into the idea that somehow issues of race were not relevant to their interactions. Even though the client wanted to protect her by suggesting that she was "different" from other Whites, it was important that she recognize and own her own participation as a White person in holding a position of privilege. While clearly she would not consciously choose to abuse a position of privilege with this or any client, the fact that she understood its potential impact was inevitably recognizable to the client without it even having to be spoken about directly. This is because the authenticity of a person can often be perceived based on the quality of the interaction and is not reliant on verification through verbal communication. All in all the clinician felt both challenged and pleased with the work she and her client were able to accomplish together.

Case Illustrations Involving Black Clinicians and Black Clients

A 15-year-old African-American female was court-referred for treatment at a public mental health clinic due to an incident of domestic violence against her mother. The client was assigned to work with an African-American clinician in her 50s whose socioeconomic status was middle class. The clinician had not had much previous experience working with adolescents or in a publicly funded treatment facility. During the session the clinician sought to engage the client's trust and attention to help her to better understand what treatment was needed. For her part the client questioned how this treatment could help her: her cousin who had come to the same facility had not been helped. The clinician's response to the client was that she hoped things would be different for her and inquired no further. This non-relational response missed an opportunity to begin the creation of an authentic relationship. The relational social worker would want to learn more about what the client's expectations might be, to demonstrate empathy with the client about being forced to do something that she neither desired to do nor expected to be helpful. The goal in this initial session of creating interpersonal connection through mutuality was compromised.

This failure easily fits into Altman's (2007) description of the risk of attributing resistance to client dynamics rather than to the relational clinician's charge to accept resistance as expectable and valuable starting points for working with diverse, and particularly oppressed, client populations. By the second session, there was no mistaking the client's lack of interest when she flatly asked, "When is this session going to be over?" This is where the relational clinician might have used the client's impatience as an opening to value the client's time and to inquire what the client most wanted or needed from their interactions. This would have been a relational invitation to mutuality and co-construction of a purpose.

Understanding transference and countertransference dynamics are core elements of all clinical work and are active and transparent interactions for a relational social worker. Learning in retrospect is productive for all clinicians. In this case the relational social worker might recognize the strong negative transference reaction by the client at the very first session. That the clinician was similar in age and race to the client's mother could be one element which, for the clinician, engendered a positive countertransference reaction that could have obscured other aspects of the transference and countertransference. She had been responding to the client in ways similar to how she might have responded to her own daughter or how she would have wanted a clinician to respond to her own daughter. This misapprehension of the client's individual story as well as her own reactions to a "mother" countertransference probably intensified the client's negative transference.

This case demonstrates that racial matching of client and clinician does not insure a productive outcome. Without sufficient self-awareness, supported by the use of effective supervision, it is possible for the clinical social worker to miss the developmental as well as present environmental transference and countertransference dynamics or know how to use them relationally to advance clinical alignment. Matching of race as well as other significant dimensions of diversity such as sexual orientation, religion, socioeconomic class, and the like is sometimes requested by clients as necessary for them to engage in clinical work. It is incumbent upon the relational social worker to be vigilant, recalling that there is often more diversity within groups than between groups. The relational social worker must not be lulled into making assumptions about similarities between herself and her client that are ill founded and even more so obscure accurate assessment. Adopting a stance of not-knowing and engaging in a process of co-inquiry to support the creation of realistic goals in the client's real situation are required for effective use of a relational stance.

A second case illustration involved a young African-American woman who was in treatment with an African-American clinician who was slightly older. Both client and clinician had been raised in a religiously conservative households and held similar values. Over time the client and the social worker developed a strong connection that entailed a positive maternal transference/countertransference dynamic, manifestly if not entirely fueled by their similarities in race and religious values. It was well into the treatment that the client finally decided to share with the clinician the secret that she was gay. The clinician was blindsided by this revelation and immediately went silent. The "blind side" was in fact the clinician's overgeneralization of sameness based on her racial and religious assumptions. Her evident emotional retreat from the probably prematurely intimate sense of engagement aroused fear, anger, and tears in the client, and the clinician in response moved to abruptly end the session. This dramatic illustration of unexamined countertransference, including positive feelings of affinity, is a caution to all social workers about maintaining constant self-examination as a relational principle that applies regardless of apparent mutuality. The relational clinical process is always evolving, never complete and permissive of assumptions. The client was looking to the clinician for acknowledgement and supportive empathy about being gay as an aspect of her identity, which she might well have expected given their apparent congruence up to that point. The clinician was unable to provide either because she too had mistaken common features for common understandings and values.

What becomes clear is that clinician and client sharing the same race and background are in and of themselves neither necessary nor sufficient conditions for creating a mutual, authentic relationship. The importance of self-reflection and examination on the part of the clinician cannot be overestimated when the goal is to work from a relational stance. In this particular case after the passage of several months, the relational social worker and client were able to meet again, and the clinician used the relational skills of inquiry and not-knowing to check what had previously been a mistaken attunement: she was able to be authentic in her acknowledgement of misunderstanding, engage in a process of repair and rebuilding of a trusting relationship with the client, and re-engage in actual empathic attunement. Thereafter, all the relational skills, including co-construction and mutuality in building the basis of the treatment contract, were able to be brought into using the "collision" (Bromberg 2011) to introduce issues of sexuality and of sexual orientation that had been hidden in the client's life as well as between her and this client. As the clinician became curious about her own discomfort with inquiring about issues of sexuality and sexual orientation, when appropriate, which was obviously missing with this client in particular and with all of her other clients in general, she came to understand the value of cultural competence as ever expanding. She now had a clear example of the difference between having the intention of being culturally competent and the actual practice of it. She also had a clearer understanding of how an inaccurate or incomplete assessment can lead to a rupture or impasse and potentially to premature termination.

Conclusion

As stated at the beginning of this chapter, relational social work practice with African-Americans presents both challenge and promise. Based on the information and cases reviewed in this chapter, the use of a relational approach (in this case with African-American clients) works for the benefit of both the client and the clinician, but in different ways. For the client there is the opportunity to build an authentic relationship that becomes a safe place to examine and to work out important and often painful emotional concerns. Some of these concerns may evolve from experiences directly related to race and yet may be linked to deeply held individual meanings and internalized relational paradigms related to the client's immediate needs. For some clients this may be the first time where they have been willing to look at their concerns, even though they may have been long standing and the source of significant pain and mental anguish.

For the social work clinician, it is inevitable that her own flaws, conflicts, and vulnerabilities at some point will be triggered in the effort to stay authentically engaged with the client. Attachment and separation are rigorous processes in development; turbulence of the same nature occurs in clinical practice as well. The relational perspective recognizes not only the centrality but also the activity involved in engagement, assessment, co-construction of a meaningful treatment plan, and maintenance of connection through the often turbulent process of personal growth that successful clinical social work practice requires. It is the clinician's ethical responsibility to work through her own unresolved issues so as not to impinge on the work being done with the client. It is the social worker's relational expertise that allows her to accomplish this work as an ever-present aspect of the treatment process. African-American clients, with well-documented skepticism about psychodynamic treatment, intensify these processes when the clinician is not African-American. At the same time, all clinicians benefit from opportunities to be keenly aware of the value of mutuality and co-construction throughout the clinical social work process. In the final analysis, improved treatment outcomes for African-American clients, and a clear sense of professional competence and satisfaction with one's professional work for the clinician, are all worthy accomplishments that honor the investment of time and energy that the relational theory approach requires.

Study Questions

1. What is the significance of the quote "…few issues are as 'value laden and misunderstood as is race' " (Hardy 1994, p. 5)?
2. What key understandings about the social, political, biological, and historical contexts of African-Americans in the United States would be helpful to keep in mind in working with Black clients?
3. Define the term "racial formation" and describe its implications for social work practice with client populations other than African-Americans.

4. Discuss factors that have contributed to the general underutilization of mental health services by African-Americans and how these are instructive about relational contributions to work with oppressed populations.
5. Describe how potential countertransference traps related to race could potentially undermine the treatment process.
6. Describe, using one of the cases above, how the social worker used relational principles. Give a specific example and name the relational principle.

References

Altman, N. (2007). Toward the acceptance of human similarity and difference. In C. J. Muran (Ed.), *Dialogues on difference studies of diversity in the therapeutic relationship* (pp. 15–25). Washington, DC: American Psychological Association.

Altman, N. (2011). *The analyst in the inner city race, class, and culture through a psychoanalytic lens* (2nd ed.). New York: Routledge.

Associated Press. (2009). Obituary John Hope Franklin. *Charlotte Observer.*

Basham, K. (2004). Weaving a tapestry: Anti-racism and the pedagogy of clinical social work practice. *Smith College Studies in Social Work (Haworth), 74*(2), 289–314.

Basham, K. K., Donner, S., Killough, R. M., & Rozas, L. W. (1997). Becoming an anti-racist institution. *Smith College Studies in Social Work (Haworth), 67*(3), 564–585.

Boyd-Franklin, N. (2003). *Black families in therapy understanding the African American experience* (2nd ed.). New York: The Guilford Press.

Bromberg, P. (2011). *The shadow of the tsunami and the growth of the relational mind.* New York: Taylor Francis.

Brown, D. R., & Keith, V. M. (Eds.). (2003). *In and out of our right minds the mental health of African American women.* New York: Columbia University Press.

Devore, W., & Schlesinger, E. G. (1991). *Ethnic-sensitive social work practice* (3rd ed.). New York: Macmillan.

DeYoung, P. A. (2003). *Relational psychotherapy a primer.* New York: Routledge.

Fontes, L. A. (2008). *Interviewing clients across cultures a practitioner's guide.* New York: The Guilford Press.

Germain, C. B. (Ed.). (1979). *Social work practice: People and environments.* New York: Columbia University Press.

Goldstein, E. G., Miehls, D., & Ringel, S. (2009). *Advanced clinical social work practice relational principles and techniques.* New York: Columbia University Press.

Green, J. W. (1982). *Cultural awareness in human services.* Englewood Cliffs: Prentice-Hall.

Greene, B. (1997). Psychotherapy with African American women: Integrating feminist and psychodynamic models. *Smith College Studies in Social Work (Haworth), 67*(3), 300–322.

Hardy, K. L., & Laszloffy, T. A. (1994). Deconstructing race in family therapy. In R. V. Almeida (Ed.), *Expansion of feminist family theory through diversity* (pp. 5–31). New York: The Haworth Press.

Harper-Dorton, K., & Lantz, J. (2007). *Cross-cultural practice social work with diverse populations* (2nd ed.). Chicago: Lyceum Books.

Herrnstein, R. J., & Murray, C. (1994). *The bell curve: Intelligence and class structure in American life.* New York: Free Press.

Hopps, J. G., Pinderhuges, E., & Shankar, R. (1995). *The power to care clinical practice effectiveness with overwhelmed clients.* New York: The Free Press.

Johnson, L. B., & Staples, R. (2005). *Black families at the crossroads challenges and prospects.* San Francisco: Jossey-Bass A Wiley Imprint.

Jones, R. L. (Ed.). (1991). *Black psychology* (3rd ed.). Berkeley: Cobb & Henry.

Lasser, K. E., Himmeistein, D. U., Woolhandler, S. J., McCormick, D., & Bor, D. H. (2002). Do minorities in the United States receive fewer mental health services than whites? *International Journal of Health Services, 32*(3), 567–578.

Leary, J. D. (2005). *Post traumatic slave syndrome: American's legacy of enduring injury and healing*. Milwaukie: Uptone Press.

Lee, S. M. (1993). Racial classifications in the U.S. Census: 1890–1990. *Ethnic and Racial Studies, 16*, 75–93.

Locke, D. C. (1992). *Increasing multicultural understanding a comprehensive model*. Newbury Park: Sage.

Lopez, I. E. (1996). *White by law: The legal construction of race*. New York: New York University Press.

Morris, E. F. (2001). Clinical practices with African Americans: Juxtaposition of standard clinical practices and Africentricism. *Professional Psychology: Research and Practice, 32*(6), 563–572.

Omi, M., & Winant, H. (1986). Racial Formations. In P. S. Rothenberg (Ed.), *Race class and gender in the United States* (6th ed., pp. 12–21). New York: Worth Publishers.

Parham, T. A. (Ed.). (2002). *Counseling persons of African descent raising the bar of practitioner competence*. Thousand Oaks: Sage.

Payne, R. K. (1996). *A framework for understanding poverty* (3rd ed.). Highlands: Aha Process.

Pinderhughes, E. B. (1989). *Understanding race, ethnicity, & Power the key to efficacy in clinical practice*. New York: The Free Press.

Pinderhughes, E. B. (1997). The interaction of difference and power as a basic framework for understanding work with African Americans: Family theory, empowerment and educational approaches. *Smith College Studies in Social Work (Haworth), 67*(3), 323–347.

Richardson, L. A. (2001). Seeking and obtaining metal health services: What do parents expect. *Archives of Psychiatric Nursing, 15*(5), 223–231.

Sanchez-Hucles, J. (2000). *The first session with African Americans a step by step guide*. San Francisco: Jossey-Bass.

Sue, D. W., & Sue, D. (2008). *Counseling the culturally diverse theory and practice* (5th ed.). Hoboken: Wiley.

Sue, D. W., Capodilupo, C. M., Torino, G. C., Bucceri, J. M., Holder, A. M. B., Nadul, K. L., & Esquilin, M. (2007). Racial microaggressions in everyday life implications for clinical practice. *American Psychologist, 67*(4), 271–286.

Tatum, B. D. (1997). Racial identity development and relational theory: The case of black women in white communities. In J. V. Jordan (Ed.), *Women's growth in diversity more writings from the stone center* (pp. 91–106). New York: The Guilford Press.

Taylor, R. L. (1997). The changing meaning of race in the social sciences: Implications for social work practice. *Smith College Studies in Social Work (Haworth), 67*(3), 277–298.

Tosone, C. (2004). Relational social work: Honoring the tradition. *Smith College Studies in Social Work, 74*(3), 475–487.

U.S. Department of Commerce, Economics and Statistics Administration. (2007). *The American community – blacks: 2004 American community survey reports*. U.S. Census Bureau.

Washington, H. A. (2006). *Medical apartheid the dark history of medical experimentation on black Americans from colonial times to the present*. New York: Doubleday.

Wijeyesinghe, C. L., & Jackson, B. W. (Eds.). (2001). *New perspectives on racial identity development a theoretical and practical anthology*. New York: University Press.

Winbush, V. R. (2009*). Parent-created, help-seeking pathways: A narrative explanation of their development and role in facilitating treatment for adolescents with mental illness*. Doctoral Dissertation. Retrieved from UMI Dissertation Publishing (UMI Number 3416172).

Relational Social Work Practice with Hispanic Clients

Manny J. González

Introduction

Hispanics underutilize mental health and clinical services (Fabrega 1990; González and González-Ramos 2005; Mezzich et al. 1999). Numerous obstacles prevent them from successfully navigating the mental health system. These obstacles include language barriers, lack of health insurance and affordable mental health services, limited access to bilingual and bicultural service providers, and inadequate information on accessing mental health services. This underutilization of clinical services is matched by research documentation of increased rates of mental health disorders among Hispanics (Kessler et al. 1994; Malgady and Constantino 1998). Specifically Kessler et al. (1994) and Malgady and Rogler (1993) note that Hispanics, in comparison to other minority ethnic groups and non-Hispanic Whites, present with a higher prevalence of major depression, other mood disorders (including dysthymia and bipolar disorders), and cognitive impairments. In sum, Hispanics are a growing population with disproportionate need of mental health and clinical services. They are most likely, due to economic and access factors, to seek such services in public social service settings, requiring that social work practitioners have the capacity to form a fruitful clinical relationship with a client population that is vulnerable, unaccustomed to clinical treatment, and often unfamiliar to the clinician. The relational model of practice offers the social work clinician a model for culturally and contextually relevant engagement and productive treatment across differences in personal background.

M.J. González, Ph.D., LCSW-R (✉)
Silberman School of Social Work, Hunter College,
City University of New York, New York, USA

Graduate Center, City University of New York, New York, USA
e-mail: manny.gonzalez@hunter.cuny.edu

J.B. Rosenberger (ed.), *Relational Social Work Practice with Diverse Populations*,   95
Essential Clinical Social Work Series, DOI 10.1007/978-1-4614-6681-9_7,
© Springer Science+Business Media New York 2014

The Hispanic Population and Relational Social Work Needs

Hispanics, interchangeably identified as Latinos, are one of the fastest growing ethnic groups in the United States. The Latino population in the United States increased by 43 % between 2000 and 2010, representing 16.3 % of the total population (Pew Hispanic Center 2011). Overall youthfulness, birthrate, and levels of immigration have contributed to this growth. In addition, the diversity of national origin among Latinos has increased. Hispanics can be of any race and from over 20 national origins, with emerging communities of Dominicans, Colombians, Salvadorans, Nicaraguans, and Peruvians, for example, adding to the larger and more established communities of Mexicans, Puerto Ricans, and Cubans. According to the Pew Hispanic Center (2011), Mexicans are by far the largest Latino immigrant group, accounting for more than half of the Hispanic immigrant population, and they are the largest foreign-born group in the nation.

Hispanic immigration has dispersed across the nation, including states, regions, cities, and towns that previously had virtually no Latino residents. The relational clinician in any community, therefore, can expect to work with Hispanic clients. This is especially relevant because the segregation of Hispanic clients to Hispanic practitioners is not only impractical in terms of numbers but is antithetical to the core principles of social work practice which call upon the professional clinician to be adaptive to client needs.

Currently, Hispanics are concentrated in a number of metropolitan areas, including New York City, Los Angeles, Miami-Dade, and Chicago. These traditional destinations for Latino groups (Mexicans, Puerto Ricans, and Cubans) are now the chosen destination of emerging Latino groups (Dominicans, Colombians, Salvadorans, and Guatemalans) (Suro and Singer 2002). However, in the shifting job and housing markets, Hispanic clients are increasingly prevalent throughout the United States, with those in smaller communities being especially vulnerable to stresses of marginalization and a paucity of congruent services.

Hispanics are one of the poorest ethnic groups in the United States, even among full-time workers with intact families. They suffer from economic and benefit less from periods of economic growth (Suro 1998). In their report, *Wealth Gaps Rise to Record Highs Between Whites, Blacks and Hispanics,* Kocharr et al. (2011) found that median household wealth among Hispanics fell 66 % from 2005 to 2009. This is the largest drop among all racial and ethnic groups and underscores the urgent need for models for clinical practice within Latino communities.

Mental health issues associated with the emigration experience are reason enough to justify the need for treatment models of clinical social work practice that are attuned to Hispanics. Compounding the acute stressors of emigration, economic disparity, low educational levels, and social isolation creates an oppressive context of daily life that, unaddressed, erodes the overall mental health and coping strengths. Relational clinical practice, reflecting the core ethical and practice principles on which social work as a profession was founded (Tosone 2004), is responsive in orientation as well as in methodology to address the person-in-situation needs of

Hispanic patients whose mental health is inextricable from severe social circumstances and surrounding attitudes. The relational-cultural model is an extension of core relational theory for clinical social work.

Because the process of individual clinical treatment cannot separate personality structures and issues from the cultural factors that influence emotional health, this chapter underscores key cultural characteristics and issues of Hispanic individuals and families that impact clinical practice. A case vignette illustrates how social work clinicians can apply relational therapy to meet the cultural competency standard (NASW 2001) of treatment of Hispanic clients.

Understanding Relevant Cultural Characteristics of Hispanics

Relational social work is predicated on inclusiveness of the client's social reality, which includes the way specific cultural values or characteristics directly affect effective treatment. Many Hispanic scholars (Sandoval and De la Roza 1986; Gil 1980; González and González-Ramos 2005; Santiago-Rivera et al. 2002) have identified salient cultural characteristics that inform treatment strategies for the amelioration of distressed psychological social functioning among Hispanics. Key values or characteristics are *simpatía*, *personalismo*, *familismo*, *respeto*, and *confianza*. Two gender-specific roles (see Gil 1980; Ruiz 2005), which have acquired common pejorative usage, also influence how the attuned social work clinician approaches her Hispanic client: *marianismo* (female self-sacrifice) and *machismo* (male self-respect and responsibility). *Marianismo* and *machismo* have acquired such common pejorative usage that their actual centrality in the Hispanic maintenance of intrapersonal and interpersonal coherence is obscured. Religion or a sense of spirituality also informs the traditional Hispanic experience and may serve to enhance, or at times challenge, the curative process of clinical social work practice.

Hispanics' level of acculturation, socioeconomic class, family, and gender roles affect their adherence to traditional cultural values or characteristics and their utilization of clinical social work care. Examples of include:

- *Simpatía* relates to *buena gente* (the plural form of a nice person). Hispanics are drawn to individuals who are easygoing, friendly, and fun to be with. Politeness and pleasantness, and avoidance of hostile confrontation, are valued, guiding the social work clinician to demonstrate these qualities in her demeanor and to anticipate the same in her client as the basis of engagement.
- *Personalismo* describes the tendency of Hispanic patients to relate to their service providers personally rather formally or as part of an institution. This serves the relational theory goals of authenticity and mutuality. It may not be reflected in the busy agency culture, requiring an outreach attitude by the clinician as she meets her Hispanic client.
- *Familismo* is a collective loyalty to the nuclear and extended family that outranks the individual (Taylor 1989). The clinician trained in individual techniques needs to extend the relational perspective, in particular not-knowing and co-construction

of meanings, to validate the significance of family. This includes *compadres* (godparents) as vital resources particularly during times of crisis when instrumental and emotional support may be needed. *Familismo* remains strong even among highly acculturated families (Santiago-Rivera et al. 2002).

- *Respeto* (respect) dictates appropriately deferential behavior toward others based on age, gender, social position, economic status, and authority. Clinicians must keep in mind that *respeto* implies mutual and reciprocal deference. The clinician receiving respect as a professional is equally obligated to observe deferential courtesies to the patient based on age, gender, and other sociocultural characteristics.
- *Confianza* (trust) refers to the intimacy and interpersonal comfort in a relationship. The empathic attunement and mutuality of the relational approach are particularly central with Hispanic clients. *Confianza* generates interpersonal resilience overall, based on willingness to engage with the clinician and apply experiential learning.

The clinical social work practitioner is mindful that these Hispanic-specific concepts offer practical guidance in relational work with all populations. Their conscious centrality in work with Hispanic patients may call for more overt demonstration of cultural protocols, particularly where there is diversity between clinician and client in cultural orientation. However, the essential features of sympathy/empathy, respect, individuality, and trust apply across most – if not – all relational lines.

Gender-Specific Roles in Relational Practice with Hispanic Clients

Gender role expectations and values constitute an area where transference and countertransference may create the strongest potential for cultural misalignment. Traditional gender roles within the Hispanic family structure are intrinsically linked to the concepts of *marianismo* and *machismo*. *Marianismo*, the term associated with Hispanic female socialization, implies that girls must grow up to be women and mothers who are pure, long suffering, nurturing, pious, virtuous, and humble, yet spiritually stronger than men (Gil 1980). *Marianismo* is associated with the Virgin Mary and therefore directly tied to the Roman Catholic faith. Although *marianismo* has contributed to a view of Hispanic women as docile, self-sacrificing, and submissive, it is clear that from a family systems viewpoint that women (particularly mothers) are the silent power in the family structure.

Social work clinicians need to be alert to the temptation to view Hispanic female clients' deference to the clinician or submission in gender roles as a deficiency in self-esteem or self-assertiveness. Deconstructing and co-constructing the ways the client's posture toward others are the relational approach to seeing what is or is not inherent to the problem for clinical attention. In his seminal paper, *Masochism, Submission, and Surrender,* Ghent (1990) clearly distinguishes deference from powerlessness or self-devaluation. The relational practitioner, seeking empathic attunement to the client's meanings and methods rather than superficial evaluation of manifest behavior, is well advised regarding surrender of dominance as a legitimate relational paradigm when matched by reciprocal protection and provision for the *machismo* role.

This observation underscores the value of diversity practice in clarifying the value of the relational practice model: surrendering to the cultural and individual attributions of meaning and worth of the client is not submission as a professional but rather a cornerstone of the constructivist, non-positivist, and clinical practice (Tosone 2004). Similarly, clinical authority does not require dominance.

Hispanic *machismo,* contrary to being a cult of the gender role socialization of Hispanic males, has centered on the construct of *machismo.* Machismo has been defined in the general social science literature as the cult of virility, arrogance, and sexual aggressiveness (Santiago-Rivera 2002), and it refers to a man's responsibility of loyalty to friends, family, and community. He must provide for, protect, and defend his family (Sandoval and De la Roza 1986) and in turn commands respect from others. If the relational clinician is to succeed with Hispanic males, she must be skilled at proffering respect as a means of engagement, addressing any resistance in herself as a countertransference phenomenon. This applies to male and female clinicians alike. Acculturation may conceal the degree to which Hispanic males and females adhere to *machismo* and *marianismo*, but the relational clinician's attunement and acceptance of such important dimensions of self are needed to offset disruptions and impasses in clinical services with Hispanics (Sandoval and De la Roza 1986).

The Role of Religion and Spirituality with Hispanic Clients

Comas-Diaz (1989) has observed that, for Hispanics, religion not only affects their conception of mental illness and treatment but also influences their behaviors in the clinical social work process. Religious value placed on suffering and self-denial can be misinterpreted as another source of resistance (Acosta et al. 1982). The relational social work practitioner might anticipate culturally normative ambivalence and confusion about how to use the clinical process without violating religious tenets. The relational practice principles prescribe open and co-constructed exploration at all times to determine how a problem can be approached in ways congruent with the client's outlook. The Hispanic client presents arenas wherein a collision of clinical assumptions, absent relational openness, can defeat willingness to forego help to preserve internal cohesion (Flores and Carey 2000; González and González-Ramos 2005; Santiago-Rivera et al. 2002; Sue and Sue 1999).

Religion and clinical social work often are separated by the theoretical models of psychoanalytic history. Fortunately, relational theory's nonjudgmental embrace of all contents, seeking only to identify its utility in the maintenance of self-fulfillment and functioning, poses no barrier to religious or spiritual beliefs as they serve the client. Urrabazo (2000) has noted the curative potential of faith and religion in therapeutically assisting undocumented Hispanic immigrants who have been robbed, raped, and beaten while crossing the border into the United States. Religion appears to emotionally sustain Hispanics who are continuously subjected to the realities of racism, discrimination, and social injustice. During times of psychological crisis or environmental distress, the religious belief systems of Hispanics may be used as a complementary adjunct to conventional clinical social work practice, providing a healing community where self-validation, connection to others, guidance, and social support may be found. In fact, the pursuit of relatedness and community are present in most clinical social work treatment goals.

Mutual Empathy in Practice with Hispanic Clients

Empathic attunement as a familiar principle of relational practice takes on an emphasis on mutuality in work with Hispanic clients. Recalling that core Hispanic values and characteristics are steeped in reciprocity, the social work clinician is alerted to the establishment of mutuality as an explicit as well as implicit element of the practice structure. For example, concern and attention by the clinician is culturally alien to the Hispanic client unless there is a means of expressing and being acknowledged for her value to the practitioner in the treatment effort. Similarly, disconnection to protect vulnerability from an unfamiliar other can be a coping strategy that is understandable given a Hispanic client's larger social experience, including with Hispanics of other subgroups or who feel themselves more acculturated (Comstock 2005; Jordan 2010; Miller and Stiver 1997).

The "complex affective-cognitive skill that allows [clinicians] to 'know' another person's experience" (Jordan 2010, p. 103) that is empathy traditionally has been viewed as a one-way, professional ability (Fox 2001). In contrast, Miller and Stiver (1997) have described mutual empathy as co-created in the treatment relationship, and as a major component of a healing, curative process. The relational social worker establishes this two-way process by inquiring about and being receptive to client feedback about the clinician's empathic efforts (Freedberg 2009). In mutual empathy, both patient and therapist are moved by the experience of the other. Interaction between two or more people that is mutually empathic is mutually empowering (Jordan 2010; Miller and Stiver 1997). The creation of this connection in the clinical encounter becomes an internalized working model for the client's life with others (Comstock et al. 2002).

In contrast, disconnection is marked by decreased energy, inability to act, lack of clarity or confusion regarding self and other, decreased self-worth, and a turning-away from relationships (Jordan et al. 2004). Jordan (2010) has noted that disconnections are often the by-product of unresolved feelings of disappointment, humiliation, interpersonal injuries, misunderstandings or empathic failures, boundary violations, or a sense of danger within a relationship. These life antecedents become accessible in the relational therapeutic process through the social work clinician's posture of mutuality and co-construction: empathic attunement alone may not suffice if the content of the client's history is too unfamiliar for the clinician to have ways of symbolizing for herself the nature of the client's self-experience.

This exemplifies the contribution of diversity practice in learning relational social work: the clinician is willing to ask, the client feels the power of knowing and informing, and the new shared knowledge expands both. The Hispanic client brings not only individual but also cultural disconnection in the sociopolitical arena due to being a minority and a disempowered minority whose contributions are unacknowledged. Transference and countertransference dimensions of work with Hispanic patients are inevitably suffused with clinician concerns about power and client concerns about *respeto*. It is helpful for the clinician to remember that power and dominance are not synonymous for Hispanic patients. Scrupulous relational monitoring of the state of mutuality, co-constructed meanings, and collaborative goal setting empower the relational clinical process.

Relational Images

In their monograph, *Relational images and their meanings in psychotherapy*, Miller and Stiver (1995) state that relational images are expressions of our expectations and fears of how others will respond to us within the context of any given relational matrix. In the clinical matrix, the social work practitioner must titrate the client's presentation of her images through culturally determined unconscious frameworks. Distortions, idealizations, or omissions may reflect, for example, *familismo* for a Hispanic client; she may feel disloyal as a member of an oppressed minority if her personal images are incongruent with that representation. Especially when the clinician represents a dominant cultural group, the client will be alert to "disaffirming stimuli" (Hill Collins 2000; Walker 2005). Periods of struggle and conflict build connection and vitalize the interpersonal field and therefore are comfortably uncomfortable for the relational social worker.

Case Example

Ricardo is a 35-year-old Cuban man who lives alone in a studio apartment and is currently employed as a mechanic. His father and paternal aunt have been living in South Florida for many years. Ricardo left Cuba through the visa-granting lottery system with the expectation that he would be able to rely on their assistance as he made a new life for himself in the United States. Upon his arrival to Miami, however, he reports that he was rejected both by his father and his aunt. His father is now remarried and his new wife wasn't even aware that he existed.

Ricardo became extremely depressed as a result of his family situation. Recently his sister exited Cuba, also through the visa lottery, and joined him in Miami. Although the sibling reunion was a joyful occasion for Ricardo, the sister has been of minimal support to him. His depressive symptoms increased, leading to his first suicide attempt and subsequently to his first psychiatric hospitalization. He was discharged without a solidified outpatient treatment plan, remaining unemployed for 6 months. A cousin, who entered the United States in the Mariel exodus, then offered Ricardo a job in a small restaurant that he owned. Ricardo later discovered that this venture was funded with "fast money" made through illegal drug dealing and that he was involved as a delivery man. A drug raid closed the restaurant, leaving Ricardo without a job. Once again he became severely depressed, leading to a second suicide attempt and psychiatric hospitalization. He was discharged from this second hospitalization with a diagnosis of major mood disorder. After 2 months he got the mechanic job.

Ricardo reports feeling tremendous emotional pain at being shunned and rejected by his father and aunt, who expect him "to make something out of himself," but do not give him support. The father does not approve of his employment. Ricardo tries to please his father by visiting frequently and doing chores for him despite receiving no recognition in return. To try to cope with his emotional distress, Ricardo is beginning to attend mass at a nearby Catholic church a few times a week. He has adopted the daily praying of the rosary and firmly believes that through divine intervention "life will take a turn for the better."

Application of the Relational-Cultural Treatment Approach

Ricardo's presenting problem and symptoms must be examined through a framework that includes race, ethnicity, culture, gender, and sociopolitical factors as well as interpersonal dynamics. Hispanic cultural values in Ricardo's past and current psychosocial functioning, as well as sociopolitical factors, affect his interactions in relationships where mutual empathy and mutual empowerment do not occur. *Familismo, confianza*, and *respeto* are pursued but thwarted in his relations with his father. His *machismo* also is thwarted by his isolation and powerlessness to feel worthily productive. Shame, a psychological state or affect in which the individual feels disconnected from others, unworthy of empathy or love, and unable to experience a sense of efficacy (Jordan 2010), which has propelled Ricardo's suicide attempts and clinical depression, must be addressed within the context of a supportive and mutually empathic therapeutic relationship wherein his strengths (self-sufficient earner, caring son and brother, spiritual seeker, continuing striver) as well as his suffering can be acknowledged.

A central part of Ricardo's treatment is helping him connect to others in more mutually satisfying ways. Mourning his relationship to his father, and attempting to rework his methods of pursuing other family members, is vital; it would be culturally incongruent for these pivotal connections to be dismissed. At the same time, "realigning supports, creating a spiral of positive feelings and an increased sense of strength in the agential self" (Freedberg 2009, p. 73) is a potential therapeutic goal which the culturally attuned relational clinician can support as supplemental, not antagonistic, to *familismo*. Connections to others in the service of self-esteem regulation, support, increased sense of self-worth, and zest for life do not, however, come without tension, notably for men (Kimmel 2004). Bergman (1991, 1996) argues that the masculine need for connection has been denied and made invisible by complex societal structures and dominant cultural expectations that impel men to pursue the goals of independence, power, autonomy, and competitive achievement at the expense of intimacy, reciprocal relationships, and the expression of emotional vulnerability. For Ricardo this socio-relational conundrum is exacerbated further by the traditional Hispanic value of *machismo*. As a first-generation Cuban male, Ricardo is expected to demonstrate virility, courage, and manliness; to be in full control of his life; and to never be emotionally vulnerable. His suicide attempts reflect his hopelessness about reconciling his personal needs with the cultural standards he can neither meet nor discard. Treatment that is informed by a relational-cultural perspective is necessary for Ricardo to own his Hispanic sense of manhood while working through his yearning and possible fear of engaging with others.

The clinical social work process itself, following relational therapy principles, must offer Ricardo the opportunity to learn experientially about his relational strategies and to test out his capacity for authentic and growth-producing connection. Concurrent with this goal, Ricardo will also need to explore, and thereby potentially modify, his internal and external patterns of connection with his father. The relational therapist will need to create a climate of mutual exploration about his current maladaptive relationship, based on concurrent empathic attunement to his desires relational images of the past, alongside inquiry and authentic reflection about present reality. The Hispanic value of *familismo* is in contradiction to the disconnection he experiences with his father. In the treatment relationship, he can find *simpatia* and *respeto* and hopefully thereby counter an "escalating and ongoing dynamic in which the less powerful person in a relationship is prevented from representing the hurt or disconnection to the more powerful person and learns that she or he cannot bring this aspect of her or his experience into the relationship" (Jordan 2010, p. 102).

Ricardo's emerging participation in his faith tradition is an adaptive mechanism that may facilitate his emotional healing process. The relational clinician will welcome this resource as an alternate view to the sufferings and pain of life, simultaneously addressing other adaptive coping strategies. The faith community can offer access to relationships that may be responsive to him as an individual. The social work clinician would explore this potential, realistically, rather than relying on transference and countertransference alone to be the arena of relational healing.

These adjustments may give rise to individual or family disintegration and loss, psychological distress, trauma, and even suicide. Despite these noted challenges and vulnerabilities, many immigrants are able to adjust well to the demands of a host country. Ricardo's treatment must be guided by a framework of resilience (see Hartling 2008) that underscores his noted capacities – such as maintaining employment and his desire to have a relationship with his father – and risk factors (e.g., major mood disorder diagnosis, history of suicide attempts).

A relationally informed therapist must be attuned to the connections and disconnections within the therapeutic process and in Ricardo's life that promote or impede his ability to overcome adversity. Certainly entrance into his current social context as a refugee presents an extraordinarily complex array of social and psychological challenges, transitions, and adaptations that, while common, are unique for each individual (González and González-Ramos 2005; Sue and Sue 1999). In the relational social work process, Ricardo's resilience as well as his defeats are weighed in the dialogue, giving them symbolized representation in his thinking as well as interpersonal support in his struggles. Moments of disconnection or conflict in the clinical process may be used to show Ricardo that disagreements or disappointments can be opportunities to enhance relational authenticity and resilience within a relational context.

Conclusion

This chapter highlights how relational theory and a relational-cultural framework provide a context through which Hispanic clients can heal from the effects of complex psychosocial challenges and non-mutual relational and sociocultural experiences. The theoretical underpinnings are consistent with the cultural characteristics and traditional value base of the Hispanic population. Relational theory aims to find ways to promote growth-fostering relationships between individuals *and* between the individual and society and to lessen the psychic suffering that is caused by chronic disconnection and social isolation. These aims are in harmony with a relational psychotherapy approach to clinical practice with all clients that view problems in living as a by-product of interlocking internal and external forces. Consistent with the principles of multicultural practice and social justice, relational-cultural concepts draw attention to the experiences of isolation, shame, relational violations, and micro-aggressions that many marginalized and oppressed groups, such as Hispanics, confront on a day-to-day basis. Within this theoretical and treatment framework, the centrality of relationship, the pain of isolation, and the power of mutually empathic attunement and mutually empowering connections to others are viewed as key ingredients for understanding complexity and healing in the human being. Using relational theory, social work clinicians can effectively meet the psychosocial needs of one of the fastest growing diverse populations in the United States.

Study Questions

1. What makes relational-cultural theory and therapy particularly well suited for Hispanic clients?
2. How do the core tenets of relational practice mesh with the cultural characteristics of Hispanics? Give an example.
3. Provide a brief explanation of the differences between empathy, mutual empathy, and relational resilience. Cite examples of how have you used these skills to build the treatment relationship.
4. From relational-cultural perspective, how might religion and spirituality contribute to the healing process of Hispanic patients who may suffer from chronic disconnection?

5. How might the core cultural values of *familismo* and *personalismo* inform therapeutic interventions aimed at increasing the relational resilience of Hispanic patients? Discuss similarities or differences in application of these values with non-Hispanic clients.
6. In what way do controlling images contribute to the maladaptive disconnection and sense of disempowerment that may be experienced by Hispanic patients who are attempting to cope with psychosocial distress?

References

Acosta, F. X., Yamamoto, J., & Evans, L. A. (1982). *Effective psychotherapy for low-income and minority patients*. New York: Plenum Press.

Bergman, S. J. (1991). *Men's psychological development: A relational perspective* (work in progress, no. 48). Wellesley: Stone Center Working Paper Series.

Bergman, S. J. (1996). Male relational dread. *Psychiatric Annals, 26*(1), 24–28.

Comas-Diaz, L. (1989). Culturally relevant issues and treatment implications for Hispanics. In D. R. Koslow & E. P. Salett (Eds.), *Crossing cultures in mental health* (pp. 31–48). Washington, DC: SIETAR International.

Comstock, D. L. (Ed.). (2005). *Diversity and development: Critical contexts that shape our lives and relationships*. Belmont: Brooks/Cole.

Comstock, D. L., Duffey, T., & St. George, H. (2002). The relational-cultural model: A framework for group process. *Journal for Specialists in Group Work, 27*(3), 254–272.

Fabrega, H. (1990). Hispanic mental health research: A case for cultural psychiatry. *Hispanic Journal of Behavioral Sciences, 12*, 339–365.

Flores, M. T., & Carey, G. (Eds.). (2000). *Family therapy with Hispanics: Toward appreciating diversity*. Boston: Allyn and Bacon.

Fox, R. (2001). *Elements of the helping process: A guide for clinicians*. New York: Haworth.

Freedberg, S. (2009). *Relational theory for social work practice: A feminist perspective*. New York: Routledge.

Ghent, E. (1990). Masochism, submission, surrender–Masochism as a perversion of surrender. *Contemporary Psychoanalysis, 26*, 108–136.

Gil, R. M. (1980). *Cultural attitudes toward mental illness among Puerto Rican migrant women and their relationship to the utilization of outpatient mental health services*. Unpublished doctoral dissertation, Adelphi University, New York.

González, M. J., & González-Ramos, G. (Eds.). (2005). *Mental health care for new Hispanic immigrants: Innovations in contemporary clinical practice*. New York: Haworth.

Hartling, L. (2008). Strengthening resilience in a risky world: It's all about relationships. *Women and Therapy, 31*(2/3/4), 51–70.

Hill Collins, P. (2000). *Black feminist thought: Knowledge, consciousness, and the politics of empowerment*. New York: Routledge.

Jordan, J. V. (2010). *Relational-cultural therapy*. Washington, DC: American Psychological Association.

Jordan, J. V., Walker, M., & Hartling, L. (2004). *The complexity of connection*. New York: Guilford Press.

Kessler, R. C., McGonagle, K. A., Zhao, S., & Nelson, C. B. (1994). Lifetime and 12 month prevalence of DSM-III-R psychiatric disorders in the United States: Results from the National Comorbidity Study. *Archives of General Psychiatry, 51*, 8–19.

Kimmel, M. (Ed.). (2004). *The gendered society*. New York: Oxford University Press.

Kocharr, R., Fry, R., & Taylor, P. (2011). *Wealth gaps rise to record highs between whites, blacks, Hispanics* (Per social and demographic trends). Washington, DC: Pew Research Center.

Malgady, R. G., & Costantino, G. (1998). Symptom severity in bilingual Hispanics as a function of clinician ethnicity and language of interview. *Psychological Assessment, 10*(2), 120–127.

Malgady, R. G., & Rogler, L. H. (1993). Mental health status among Puerto Ricans, Mexican Americans, and non-Hispanic Whites: The case of the misbegotten hypothesis. *American Journal of Community Psychology, 21*, 383–388.

Mezzich, J. E., Ruiz, P., & Munoz, R. A. (1999). Mental health care for Hispanic Americans: A current perspective. *Cultural Diversity and Ethnic Minority Psychology, 5*(2), 91–102.

Miller, J. B., & Stiver, I. P. (1995). *Relational images and their meanings in psychotherapy* (work in progress, no. 74). Wellesley: Stone Center Working Paper Series.

Miller, J. B., & Stiver, I. P. (1997). *The healing connection: How women form relationships in therapy and life*. Boston: Beacon.

National Association of Social Work. (2001). *NASW standards for cultural competence*. New York: NASW.

Pew Hispanic Center. (2011). *Census 2010: 50 million Latinos*. Washington, DC: Author.

Ruiz, E. (2005). Hispanic culture and relational cultural theory. *Journal of Creativity in Mental Health, 1*(1), 33–55.

Sandoval, M. C., & De la Roza, M. (1986). A cultural perspective for serving the Hispanic client. In H. P. Lefley & P. B. Pedersen (Eds.), *Cross-cultural training for mental health professionals* (pp. 151–181). Springfield: Charles C. Thomas.

Santiago-Rivera, A. L., Arredondo, P., & Cooper-Gallardo, M. (2002). *Counseling Latinos and la familia: A practical guide*. Thousand Oaks: Sage.

Sue, D. W., & Sue, D. (1999). *Counseling the culturally different: Theory and practice*. New York: Wiley.

Suro, R. (1998). *Strangers among us: Latino lives in a changing America*. New York: Vintage.

Suro, R., & Singer, A. (2002). *Latino growth in metropolitan America: Changing patterns, new locations*. Washington, DC: Brookings Institution.

Taylor, O. (1989). The effects of cultural assumptions on cross-cultural communication. In D. R. Koslow & E. P. Salett (Eds.), *Crossing cultures in mental health* (pp. 18–30). Washington, DC: SIETAR International.

Tosone, C. (2004). Relational social work: Honoring the tradition. *Smith College Studies in Social Work, 74*(3), 475–487.

Urrabazo, R. (2000). Therapeutic sensitivity to the Latino Spiritual soul. In M. T. Flores & G. Carey (Eds.), *Family therapy with Hispanics: Toward appreciating diversity* (pp. 205–227). Boston: Allyn and Bacon.

Walker, M. (2005). Critical thinking: Challenging developmental myths, stigmas and stereotypes. In D. Comstock (Ed.), *Diversity and development: Critical contexts that shape our lives and relationships* (pp. 47–66). Belmont: Brooks/Cole.

Relational Social Work Practice with Asian American Populations

Monit Cheung and Carol A. Leung

Introduction

This chapter describes the essentials of relational social work practice with Asian Americans by establishing the connection between the relational framework and cross-cultural practice. The terms Asian Americans and Asian are used interchangeably, emphasizing that they are a heterogeneous group (Leong and Lau 2001) and have acquired cultural roots from many of the world (Hines et al. 1992). The Asian population, including Asians alone and in combination with another race, represents 5.6 % of the United States total population. The top ten Asian ethnic groups in 2009 were Chinese (3.8 million), Filipinos (3.2 million), Asian Indians (2.8 million), Vietnamese (1.7 million), Koreans (1.6 million), and Japanese (1.3 million) (US Census Bureau 2011). The 2010 census reported that the Asian population grew at a faster rate than any other race (US Census Bureau 2011). Knowledge of relational social work practice with Asian Americans is, therefore, increasingly important (Gamst et al. 2001; Lyons 2006; Wright 2009) for reasons of numbers and also for reasons of relevance to specific cross-cultural needs of this population.

Relational Social Work Principles with Asian Americans

Relational theory's attention to the client's connections with her/his cultural and social context helps to express attunement and mutuality in the helping process, a precondition to experiential learning as a means of identifying issues and enhancing

M. Cheung, Ph.D., LCSW (✉)
Graduate College of Social Work, University of Houston, Houston, TX, USA
e-mail: mcheung@uh.edu

C.A. Leung, LMSW
Flushing Hospital Medical Center, New York, USA

J.B. Rosenberger (ed.), *Relational Social Work Practice with Diverse Populations*,
Essential Clinical Social Work Series, DOI 10.1007/978-1-4614-6681-9_8,
© Springer Science+Business Media New York 2014

client strengths (Tosone 2004). Internal issues, interpersonal relationships, and patterns of connection encountered within the relational co-construction of meaning and inquiry with the clinician are explored as replications, or not, within the larger environment. Using relational theory as a base for work with Asian clients, the social work clinician identifies the cross-cultural factors in their own relationship-building process that may affect the clients' beliefs concerning these environmental connections.

Certainly the similarity in backgrounds between client and clinician plays a role: resistance, through overcompliance (more culturally congruent for most Asians), or outright rejection of the relational practitioner's reflection of understanding becomes the road to more robust collaborative planning as the two parties discuss perceptions and misperceptions. Resistance may stem from transference and countertransference and/or be a reflection of straightforward cultural lack of attunement. In any of these cases, resistance allows authentic not knowing and inquiry by the relational clinician that validates the mutuality of the clinical endeavor.

The relational social work practitioner working with an Asian clients begins with a practice hypothesis that the client may not represent only one cultural, racial, or ethnic background. The amalgamation of internalized models and expectations demonstrates that relational work with any population, and particularly as complex a population as that identified as Asian, requires special attention to distilling the individual client's interpretation of her/his worldviews, context of change, goals, and use of a therapeutic relationship itself. From a cross-cultural perspective, the clinician confirms or disconfirms with the client a hypothesis of the core problem for therapeutic attention. One theme for inquiry is an analysis of the client's cross-cultural interactions with significant individuals and surrounding environments. The aim is to identify knowledge, skills, and values for working with Asian clients and specifically Asian clients who are affected by their multiple roles and diverse cultural experiences and expectations. This relational theoretical framework provides a bridge to connect the clinician with knowledge of the client's personal subjectivity in order to align practice principles for effective work with Asian clients.

When seeking help, most Asian American clients, regardless of their ethnic background, look up to the clinician as an expert (Leung et al. 2012). Recent Chinese immigrants, for example, respect scholars and clinicians with a strong academic background (Cheung 2009). In most contexts, when the clients view the clinician as an expert, their resistance level will be reduced, and their participation in the therapeutic process significantly increased (Sodowsky 1991). Because of this "expert-is-best" view, it is essential for the social work clinician to help clients understand that this expertise can be passed on to them by receiving the most up-to-date information to resolve current difficulties. Even if the clinician is new to working with Asian clients, he/she[1] can increase competence by asking culturally relevant questions to gain the trust of clients, such as asking about the cultural

---

[1]The pronoun "she" has been used in the chapter to include both genders.

meaning of their ethnic names. Trust also can be built when the clinician does not attempt to display a thorough knowledge about the culture and instead asks questions to understand from the client's unique perspective (Chu 2007).

While relational practice emphasizes the interpersonal exchange as the vital ingredient in engendering a client's capacity to reflect and discover hidden aspects of self that affect presenting problems, the manner of that exchange must be culturally acceptable. Asking about feelings, for instance, can be threatening to Asian American clients who are not inclined to be guided by or share emotional experience. When such a line of inquiry is bracketed by purpose clarification, it is more tolerable. It is fair to say that relational practice that is culturally competent uses the principles of emotional attunement and mutuality to downplay direct emotional exploration with Asian American clients until the collaborative goals and treatment planning are confirmed.

Current research literature addresses ten practice principles that relational social work clinicians can implement in order to build culturally competent expertise. As the case material will demonstrate, the straightforward organization of how these principles are connected to clinical practice is particularly germane to work with Asian Americans, who value clarity and road maps for work (Chu 2007). The acronym "COMPETENCE" is used to represent these ten guiding principles:

1. Composing assessments and treatment plans that draw upon relational thinking and concrete outcomes (Silverstein et al. 2006)

This principle highlights the importance of connectedness between the clinician and the clients, through which the client participates in establishing a concrete plan of action to deal with the presenting issue. Mutual respect when first engaging the client is an important practice component to help connect with Asian American clients. Generally speaking, Asian Americans would prefer to engage in activities that achieve concrete outcomes rather than merely sharing feelings (Gutiérrez 1990). It is essential to show professional readiness through mutual goal setting in which the clinician demonstrates professional confidence. First, the clinician should conduct an assessment to become more knowledgeable about the client's cultural background and language preference. Then, the clinician should ask what outcome the client would like to accomplish. Being humble while at the same time demonstrating expertise through proper assessment procedures can help the clinician project a co-constructivist image throughout the helping process.

Since many Asian American clients are recent immigrants, an important component of this principle is to identify language proficiency (Spencer et al. 2010). If the clinician does not know the client's native language, it does not make her/him less of an expert. The priority is not fluency, but appropriate not knowing and guided inquiry. Asian American clients value the use of nonverbal language to convey messages, rather than directly talking about the content (Ino and Glicken 2002), which is congruent with the relational emphasis on interpersonal process. Specific tools such as drawing, collage building, or storytelling are alternative ways of symbolizing collaborative exploration and empathic attunement.

Many Asian immigrants understand English but cannot express their feelings in English. Encouraging clients to express emotions or issues in their preferred language is an empowering method, and the relational social worker's willingness to struggle with understanding underscores co-construction of meaning both literally and emotionally. Referral or use of a translator may be necessary, but must arise out of mutual agreement and the clarification of the importance that the client is able to feel understood. In most social work settings in the United States, particularly in rural counties, cultural translators are not readily available (de Anda 1984), and their use challenges the relational practitioner to concentrate on body language and eye contact as the primary bond with the clients. In Asian cultures, using a child (regardless of age) or a family member as the interpreter is not culturally sensitive, since it demeans the authority image of the speaker (Ngo-Metzger et al. 2003) and violates the importance of privacy and relational intimacy in the clinical social work exchange (Ino and Glicken 2002).

As a relational outcome, enhancing the client's ability to locate and utilize culturally congruent resources is an extension of the relational clinician's attunement to clients needs. This adaptation of collaborative treatment planning extends the clinician's role as an important interpersonal relational partner, allowing the clients to feel excited that they can speak their native language to express worries or disclose challenges that are difficult to share in a second language. This also allows them to have concrete demonstration of the relational clinician's concern for them and to their families. Generally speaking, Asian Americans prefer to engage in activities that achieve concrete outcomes; they do not naturally tend toward sharing feelings (Gutiérrez 1990). Asking what outcome the client would like to accomplish establishes mutuality by being humble, while at the same time demonstrating expertise projects a secure relational bond.

2. **O**bserving the cultural construction of self and its relationships with one's own definition of relational dynamics (Duffey 2006)

Beyond immigration or citizenship status and age, other factors may influence cultural definitions of self, such as gender, ethnicity, marital status, generation in the United States, household members, and financial position. All of these factors are compounded by past experiences that may have spurred immigration, such as wars or other traumatic events (Leung et al. 2010). Using concrete steps to deal with unresolved problems is an important service expectation for the Asian client (Gutiérrez 1990). Through a relational assessment, the clinician can identify relational outcomes as defined by the client's ability to disclose self-identity or the use of self as affected or altered by both current and previous cultural experiences. This assessment can be evaluated by the concrete use of techniques such as verbally valuing the client's input; using creative arts, homework assignments, or exercises to help the client visualize tangible outcomes; charting progress; praising courage to tap into interpersonal relationships as a source of strength; or identifying family support.

3. **M**aximizing the importance of interconnections between mental health factors and the client's social and cultural context that may affect the choice of coping mechanisms (Danner et al. 2007)

Many Asian American clients believe that seeking help means showing deficiency in their coping abilities (Leung et al. 2010). Furthermore, they may feel ashamed and uncomfortable when people have any concerns about their family member's behavior (Ino and Glicken 2002). As a result, clients may use a coping method that saves "face" and avoid sharing their true emotions to others outside of the family. By withholding these emotions and concerns, the root of the problem cannot be addressed (Ino and Glicken 2002; Tsui et al. 2010). The clinician's assessment which may include normalization or universalization techniques, focuses on the fact that many Asian immigrants or families face similar problems (Ka'opua et al. 2005). If clients understand how others typically react to the same problems, they may feel less intimidated by their situations and start disclosing their own reactions. This normalization process helps clients accept their problems as part of life rather than a source of shame. When clients are able to admit their struggles without indignity, they will be less reluctant to find possible solutions (Ahmad et al. 2004). During the assessment phase, coping is reframed as using resources to change the situation, not as a way to hide the problem or escape from it (Tsui et al. 2010). The clients will then become aware of ways to resolve these issues in order to prevent further damage to the family.

A relational outcome from this principle is a feeling of personal acceptance. It is important to help the Asian client accept who she is and not to lose hope in a positive future (Cook and Hayes 2010). When the client knows the cultural meaning of a relational choice to maintain a positive image with the family and others, she will find meaning to support a future action or plan.

4. **P**rioritizing the interconnection between heritage/tradition and personal perceptions (Oyserman and Sakamoto 1997; Wachtel 2008)

The clients can often find a harmonious connection between traditional beliefs and the societal values relevant to her/his current tradition by sharing about her cultural adjustment. Cook and Hayes (2010) call this "acceptance-based coping styles" (p. 186). In this situation, the client will perceive cultural tradition as a helpful tool for finding solutions or ways to reduce psychological distress. However, in the event that there is disharmony between these two elements, the clinician may need to explore the possible ways that traditional values and beliefs may have negatively affected the client's emotions and help the client analyze how to reverse these negative feelings. By asking a client about the most memorable cultural learning or most daunting cultural barrier, the clinician may learn more about how this upbringing may have caused a tendency for the client to stick to only one perspective that may not be helpful.

A relational outcome from maintaining this principle may include the use of symbolism to represent a personal struggle. Using cultural proverbs and metaphors with meaningful elements tends to instill hope in the client's thinking; then, she/he can clearly identify her present contributions to the future solution-seeking process. Employing familiar cultural symbols to represent their adaptability can bring the clients to a higher level of self-acceptance. This mindfulness outcome is not about hiding or resignation, but about the connectedness between self and others (Cook and Hayes 2010).

5. Exploring the power of healing which takes place in the context of mutually empathic growth-fostering relationships (Shibusawa and Chung 2009)

Asian cultural backgrounds usually contain healing traditions and practices. Even when physicians have provided them with referrals, many Asian American clients do not access mental health services when needed (Ino and Glicken 2002). Often, these clients hold strong beliefs that mental troubles are caused by evil spirits or wrongdoings in a previous life. As a result, they may also believe that their problems will be dissolved only by good deeds and being spiritually enriched (Chhean 2007). Many also practice the self-administration of alternative medicine such as herbal supplements (Nguyen et al. 2011).

Sometimes these strong beliefs can increase the psychological motivation to build inner strength to fight against adversities (Tyson and Flaskerud 2009); however, if these treatment alternatives have been incorrectly applied, the client's problems can become worse and result in medical neglect. The social work clinician who respects the importance of different healing methods may help the client analyze the benefits of different treatment methods using available evidence. Instead of strongly opposing the use of an alternative, the relationally informed social work practitioner uses educational information to help the client make the best combination of treatment choices. Most Asian American clients will appreciate a clinician's input so long as evidence is provided to support (or not support) the use of certain healing methods (Simpson and Long 2007).

One example of an alternative healing method is the practice of coining. Traditionally, this method involves using a coin to massage the patient's pressure points in order to chase *bad wind* out of the body for the purpose of healing headaches or body aches. It is not appropriate for the social work clinician to outright reject such a method without knowing much about it. Rather than minimizing or overexerting expertise, the relational clinician can acknowledge the significance of the method a client suggests and advise the client to consult with trusted traditional healers to learn more about this method and possibilities of selecting alternative methods.

A relational outcome that results from this principle is that the client will grow to appreciate the clinician's authentic interest, especially when the clinician can recommend different treatment outcomes as well as be open to the client's viewpoint about traditional methods of treatment. The use of concrete evidence when supporting a treatment decision is the key to achieving this outcome (Cheung et al. 2011). Once a connection has been established between the client's culture and concept of healing, the clinician might want to use questions to evaluate the safety and efficiency of the client's healing methods and gauge her receptivity to clinician input.

6. Taking a partnership role with clients by establishing a working alliance (Shonfeld-Ringel 2001)

A healthy partnership relationship requires the establishment of a working alliance for helping clients appreciate the meaning of life (Meyer et al. 2011). It emphasizes that there are many ways to resolve a difficulty, but a willingness to communicate with others is essential for all of them (Atkinson et al. 1995). The treatment focus is, therefore, to free clients from their perceived *cultural barriers* to allow working alliances with the social work clinician and others to develop. A positive initial contact often determines the success of such interaction (Meyer et al. 2011).

In addition to identifying cross-cultural factors, a second key to relational practice with Asian Americans lies in the social work practitioner's ability to reference her/his own role. This clear introduction can help Asian clients understand the importance of working together with the social worker when connecting their troubles to the surrounding environments. One potential environment is the client's own family. First, the client must acknowledge the fact that she/he is part of this powerful system in which she/he is embedded. Once the immediate environment is connected, the client would perceive the social worker's assistance to be helpful, particularly when therapeutic activities are planned to enable the client to experience the importance of the worker-client linkage. To most Asian clients, establishing a relationship with a mental health professional may mean risking their "model minority" image (Chou 2008). Therefore, it is culturally more acceptable to reframe the helping relationship as one concerned about mutual support and community health (Leung et al. 2011).

The therapeutic relationship can be facilitated when the *wholeness* concept is used, taking into account the client's concept of the body-mind-spirit connections to healing. This healing process is initiated from within the client's own definition of her /his culture. Since the definition is culturally relevant to the client, the client will work toward achieving the goal of connecting her/his concept of holistic health to the promotion of physical and psychological well-being (Chan et al. 2006). For instance, when working with Asian American clients with depressive symptoms, clinicians may want to consider linking their mental health needs to healthcare concerns (Kim and Keefe 2009; Leung et al. 2012).

A relational outcome from this principle is a minimization of the client's resistance to trying methods that otherwise would be interpreted as negative cultural experiences. Many times a reframing method helps place the problem in the background and place the positive intent to improve in the forefront (Roesch et al. 2006). Should a client have difficulty engaging in a working alliance, the clinician may reframe seeking healthcare as a method for emotional healing to help the client overcome cultural or personal barriers and enhance emotional coping.

7. Expanding the meaning of culture, cultural ideologies, and social networks (Comstock et al. 2008)

A "growth-fostering" strategy that focuses on the client's future development is advised in the treatment process (Shibusawa and Chung 2009). This strategy not only utilizes the cultural contexts of the client's past experiences but also addresses the future aspect of the ever-changing environment in which the client functions. For immigrants and visitors, this means that growth may rapidly result in expanding friendships, taking advantage of learning opportunities, assuming leadership roles, and building occupational or professional networks.

One relational outcome from applying this principle to practice is an understanding of the importance of connecting with social networks that are available in the client's culture and immediate environment. Linking Asian Americans to resources through which they can show pride in their cultural heritage may help clients feel a sense of belonging in a community.

8. Navigating through and connecting clients with local, national, and/or global resources that can affect change (Folgheraiter 2004)

Many Asian American clients still have family connections in their country of origin. These relatives may be able to provide additional support or connect clients with other relatives and friends in the local community (Gunnings 1997). It is also important to find out if a client knows how to access local cultural centers that provide social and educational services such as English as a second language, citizenship preparation, job training, and knowledge of cultural events in the client's location. The linguistically competent staff in these cultural centers can assist clients with finding resources, overcoming language difficulties, and identifying ways to deal with cultural adjustment issues (Cheung et al. 2011). One relational outcome the client may gain from this "resource" principle is a sense of gaining community support that results in a renewed appreciation of her cultural heritage (Kim et al. 2006).

9. Conducting evaluations to support the effectiveness of practice within the client's environment (Saari 2005)

One initial evaluative option often used in clinical social work practice is to design an exercise for the client to focus on her strengths in dealing with stress or crises. For the Asian American client, it is especially important for the clinician to assess the client's ability to turn a problem situation into a positive learning experience and design a measure for the client to report progress and success.

A cultural identity crisis is common to many Asian American clients. When the client is adjusting to a new or culturally different environment, she/he may feel torn between the two cultural identities and challenged by two sets of cultural values. When an Asian American client cannot express well in English, the clinician can encourage the client to write down a few words in each session and then use these words to start journal writing as a tool to record concerns, needs, and intense feelings. Journaling in a native language may allow clients to think through issues before attempting to dialogue about them. By assisting the client to interpret and discuss the content within the journal, the clinician may discover the client's view of the environment, particularly regarding the new culture and the people surrounding the client. The clinician can then assess the client's ability to deal with adversity. If the clinician identifies areas still in need of growth or change, she/he can use this evaluative data to plan new therapeutic assignments to engage the client.

A possible relational outcome could be a record of successful changes. Although journaling is a technique used in teaching students how to reflect their learning in a concrete measure (Gursansky et al. 2010), it has been found to be applicable to engage nonverbal clients or clients from a different culture to reflect on their unsolved feelings through writing (Taylor and Cheung 2010). When Asian clients are encouraged to use a short 1-min writing (such as word association) in a session using the language of their choice, they will be able to further address their overwhelming feelings before trying out different methods of cultural adjustment or family communication. These methods may then serve as a bridge for clients to express their feelings.

10. Enhancing knowledge and updating psychoeducational information for clients to process a culturally relevant definition of mental health (Mijung 2007)

Most Asian clients consider learning as a lifelong process (Lee 2004). When the client is feeling doubtful about the effectiveness of clinical social work services, it may be an opportunity to draw upon the client's motivation to learn. Reframing therapy as a search for knowledge will help Asian clients feel comfortable with evidence that defies cultural myths about mental health (Cheung et al. 2011).

A relational outcome from the psychoeducational principle is that clients will be better informed about mental health and thus better able to think about how their culture may affect their families' understanding of mental issues. In most Asian cultures, when the clinician is enhancing the client's knowledge about treatment options, the client feels better about the treatment being provided (Nguyen et al. 2011).

Unique Clinical Social Work Skills with Asians: Case Studies

Although the clients come from different Asian populations, the clinician can extrapolate major principles for working with Asian clients from the case studies described below. Clients from any ethnic background can struggle with similar cultural adjustment issues. Diverse client populations can include international émigrés, those who relocate for work, school, or marriage, as well as other versions of dislocation that apply beyond Asian American populations. Nonetheless, a more authoritative tone, posture, and activity of input are congruent applications of relational concepts to clinical work with Asian American clients. These shifts reflect the adaptability of the relational approach, in which the way the client can use the clinical social work process illustrates reciprocity as a key principle. Three short cases are offered to describe typical Asian American scenarios and some specific adaptations; a fourth case is explored to illustrate the specific application of relational social work with an Asian American client.

Case 1: A Korean International Student's Suicidal Thoughts

Seo, a graduate student (age 26) from Korea, was admitted to an inpatient psychiatric unit because of suicidal ideations. Her husband, Min, stated that Seo has been acting differently, and he is afraid she might kill herself. During the psychosocial assessment with Seo, the relational clinician inquired about Seo's family background. As an Asian American, family membership is critical irrespective of years and miles of separation. She is the firstborn, living with her parents and younger sister before she immigrated to the United States. During her childhood, her father was extremely strict and verbally abusive to her and her sister. Describing this, Seo became depressed and briefly mentioned that her sister was disowned and not allowed to attend Seo's wedding, giving no explanation about why and how her sister was disowned.

Before coming to the United States, Seo was extremely nervous about her parents' expectations that she complete doctoral studies, even though she had always loved school. After 4 months in the United States, Seo began feeling sad because adjusting to school and speaking English were difficult. She felt like a failure because classmates tended to ignore her and not include her in group activities. Before the end of the first semester was over, Seo took sick leave from the university. She called Min constantly, urging him to come to the United States. He came immediately, and they have been married 1 year.

When the relational clinician noticed that Seo could not express herself well particularly when talking about her family, she noted the apparent impact of stress on her language skills. While Seo attributed this to language barriers overall, the clinician determined that talking about feelings and relationships was creating distance rather than attunement in the clinical process. Asking Seo more about her own perceptions of dealing with distress, the clinician learned that Seo believes in "qi" (meaning "air within") breathing exercises. The social worker encouraged Seo to show her how to do "qi," and they did it together. After the third session, Seo stated that suicidal thoughts were no longer a part of her thinking. Although all the meanings of this shift are not known, it is apparent that co-construction of a meaningful approach to the presenting problem and mutuality of its pursuit were sustaining for this client.

Case 2: A New Immigrant's Troubles

Ai is a 38-year-old woman and a new immigrant from Vietnam. She sought help from a social service agency specializing in domestic violence. Ai appeared sad and frustrated as she spoke of her experience in the United States, a place she called the "foreign land." As she described her journey to the United States, she began to sob and said, "I was a successful business woman in Ho Chi Minh City and saved $100,000 to come to join my husband in the United States. After I gave my money to my husband, I became nobody and lost everything." Ai's husband promised her the money would be used for building their future. However, her husband deposited the money in his individual account, saying that Ai did not have any bank credit to open her own account.

Two months ago, Ai discovered that her husband had a mistress. Ai was deeply shocked by the situation. To make the matter worse, the mistress came to look for Ai and physically assaulted her. Ai called the police, but no report was filed because they could not find injuries.

Ai stated that she was not allowed to leave the house without her husband and the only time she interactions with others was when she worked at her husband's grocery store. One day she decided to leave her husband after being yelled at, pushed, and slapped. She asked for help by calling the agency's hotline and then moved to an emergency shelter. The hotline staff asked a bilingual social worker to accompany Ai when she arrived as she could not understand English. She cried because she had no friends or family in this country. She had family back in Vietnam, but she was afraid to tell them about her troubles. Ai stated that she was well liked in her community and was known to be successful. If people in her hometown discovered what had happened, Ai stated that she would lose her sense of pride and dignity.

The social worker informed Ai that she could stay at the shelter for at least a month. During the stay at the shelter, the social worker helped Ai look for affordable housing and a job so that Ai could become self-sufficient. Furthermore, Ai decided to register for a class to improve her English.

Case 3: Concerns About Being a Refugee

San (age 12) came from Burma 2 years ago with his parents, Pha and Suu. Last year upon arrival to the United States, San entered Grade 4 because he did not perform well in his language and math proficiency tests. His close schoolmates were primarily of Latino descent. San was always mistakenly identified as Latino because of his skin complexion and large eyes. He disliked being called "Asian" because his Asian peers never seemed to welcome him.

San was referred to a school-based social worker after being involved in a group fight at school. He said he did not hit anybody; his friends simply asked him to help when they were verbally assaulted by another group of students. San did not want the social worker to see his parents. When asked about the reason, he said his parents do not speak English and that they always ask San to be their "language helper." San always felt embarrassed by his parents because they look like refugees, and he hated being called a "refugee." When asked about his definition of a refugee, San said the word "refugee" reminds him of killings. He is afraid of seeing these bloody images again.

San preferred to speak like his peers and only wanted to hang out with his Latino friends. At home, he hated to speak Burmese, but he could understand the language. When school started, he always got into trouble because he decided his teachers were biased against him. He failed English and Math in his first 9-week school report (Grade 5), and the teachers wanted him to retake the tests after school this week. He said he could not concentrate well enough to take the tests. His teacher assessed that San lacked writing skills and did not cooperate in class. He said he always felt depressed at home because he could not see any possibilities for his future. He said he felt invisible and ignored as an older student.

Reflections from the Cases: Assessment

Relational assessment focuses on both internal and external evaluations of the connection between self and others. Major assessment components include external realities like the client's socioeconomic and environmental contexts, including immigration-related issues, but also require psychodynamic attunement through relational recognition, assessment of self-states of client and clinician as they interact, and context management in terms of culturally meaningful methods of intervention (O'Connor 2006; Shonfeld-Ringel 2001; Toasland 2007; Tosone 2005). Using Case 3 (San) as example, these three components will be analyzed to help the client resolve interpersonal issues and identify context-based solutions.

Relational recognition. During the relational recognition component of assessment, the clinician must first make primary appraisals of the client's problem from the perspective of a social worker or clinician. This may be done by inquiring about the client's initially presented concerns. In the case of San, the relational clinician should ask about his problems with his schoolmates, his difficulty identifying himself as a refugee, or any other concerns he would personally identify.

Once the primary appraisal is complete and the client has begun to work toward resolving her concerns, it is important that the clinician complete a secondary appraisal. At this point, the clinician not only identifies the continued presence of ongoing difficulties but also evaluates the effectiveness of treatment, including any barriers the client may be coming against. The clinician must remember to keep the client's background in the forefront when identifying and attempting to remove barriers in a culturally sensitive way. For instance, San's relational clinician would want to know if his relationships with his peers were improving and, if not, what obstacles were getting in his way. Once San has identified his role in the problem, the clinician might also ask San what he has done differently in his relationship with his parents, including both the actions that were helpful and those that were not helpful. The clinician would also want to pay particular attention to San's willingness or unwillingness to identify himself as a Burmese refugee and how that is affecting his ability or inability to improve his relationships.

Finally, the last step of relational recognition is to identify the client's emotional responses to healing plans. During the healing process, clients often encounter upsetting and fearful emotions as well as feelings of hope and accomplishment. For San, this may mean facing the difficulty of the killings he witnessed or accepting his identity as a refugee. The clinician needs to be empathic to the emotional difficulty of these tasks. On the other hand, San may experience an increase in motivation at school or a sense of hope about his future which he once thought was bleak. The social worker may also ask San about these emotions and validate his new feelings of self-efficacy.

Relational assessment of self. During this part of the assessment, the clinician may initially help San understand his personal construction of self, how he sees himself functioning in relation to others, and what risk and protective factors are regarding the client's feelings of safety. The relational clinician includes her own self-assessment: transference and countertransference are identified but may not be pointed to directly; the clinician's direct self-experience with the client and sense or alignment or misalignment with the client's prevailing self-state are methods of seeking more open interpersonal connection.

In San's situation, the clinician should ask him about the events and experiences in his past that he believes most affected him. As the clinician moves San into thinking about how his construction of self relates to others, she may want to ask about the roles of his parents and friends. For instance, the clinician could ask how his parents reacted to the killings the client witnessed or how others, including peers and teachers, have made him feel about being older and behind in school. Then, the clinician could identify areas that affect San's feelings of personal safety, taking into account his culture and previous traumatic experiences. The clinician could ask how he felt during the fight with his peers or what it means to feel like his teachers are always biased against him. The clinician could also ask San about how he coped with being in danger in the past and identify his priorities for selecting sources of support, including what it is about his Latino friends that make him feel safe and accepted.

Context management. Once the clinician has helped San identify areas of protection and safety, she may guide the client in keeping and expanding these protective factors and locating further environmental support. For instance, San's clinician would want to know which people San most likes talking to because they listen and understand his background. San might be guided with solution-focused questions to evaluate the support he has received or the actions he has taken that have helped him grow or identify ways for him to help others. It could also be helpful for San to think about how his difficult relationships, like with his parents and teachers, may be transformed into supportive ones. In other words, what would San need for this to happen? The clinician may then guide San to imagine a solution by saying "*I think this would happen when I...,*" with San completing the statement in his own way.

Reflections from the Cases: Evaluating Practice

Professional clinical social work requires the practitioner to monitor her own practice in ways that reflect her capacity to develop an interpersonal attunement and relationally devised steps of problem definition and treatment. This evaluation framework includes cultural comparisons, relationship-building successes and failures, and the client's growth toward mutually constructed goals that are evidenced by both practical change and capacity for self-reflection. As a mental health professional, the clinician identifies skills and understanding of the relational framework that are learned through study and practice with real-world case interaction. For diversity practice, the cases must cover areas that are unfamiliar and challenge the clinician to apply the relational theory steps that invite discovery of common alliance within cultural differences. Using holistic methods that embrace the client's context and culture is accomplished by evaluating the client's background, his/her definition of self, and the strengths as well as limitations presented by the client's culture. The relational clinician focuses on the skills necessary to carry out activities that accomplish the client's life objectives in his/her cultural context, setting aside a priori definitions of a singular model of health. Core components of practice are expanded from a problem-solving model to include relationship-building skills from a dual perspective for self-development. Finally, the clinician integrates *lessons learned* into an overall treatment plan. This involves helping the client turn real-life situations into positive lessons or outcomes. The clinician may ask the client solution-focused questions to suggest ways to incorporate this learning and to measure the client's accomplishments.

Asian American clients, particularly those who face cultural adjustment issues, need time to digest suggestions from the clinician. It would be helpful to bring attention to their strengths so that their thinking will not be connected to a negative self-image or necessarily be about their coping with a past trauma. In order to help Asian clients deal with adversity, clinicians may use questions (or statements) that focus on positivity, strengths, relationship building, solution-focused thinking, and mutual respect. These statements and questions should highlight plans that draw upon relational thinking and concrete outcomes. When Asian clients are informed that the purpose of a program or service is for their future planning, they tend to respond positively (Lee et al. 2011).

The clinician may ask the client to examine her cultural construction of self and her relationship with the client's own definition of successful functioning in relationships with others. Questions should aim at maximizing the importance of the interconnections between mental health factors and the client's social and cultural context that may affect her choice of coping mechanisms. It is also important to emphasize the interconnection between heritage/tradition and personal perceptions. In exploring the power of healing which takes place in the context of mutually empathic growth-fostering relationships, the clinician can also identify the partnership role with the client by establishing a working alliance. Helping the client navigate through and connect with local, national, and/or global resources can effect change as well as expand the meaning of culture, cultural ideologies, and social networks. In this process, the clinician can assist the client to use knowledge and update psychoeducational information to process a culturally relevant definition of mental health. The use of the solution-based questioning technique aims to empower clients to appreciate their strengths and relational connections so that they can move in a positive direction based on their learning through therapy. These questions should be used with the clients' cultural and social contexts in mind.

Conclusion

In this chapter, three major relational components in practice were demonstrated as therapeutic steps as clinical examples with the diverse Asian client populations. In the first step, the social work clinician establishes mutuality and attunement that invites client reflection. Second, the clinician identifies the client's internal and external strengths to create an empowering treatment plan. Third, the clinician encourages the client to collaborate on evaluating outcomes to demonstrate mutual respect as a relational thinking tool in interpersonal relating.

Relational social work connects the client with internal and external resources. Seeking help from a professional is a way to gain emotional support. The client may share difficulties with an expert because she wants to hear an echo of support for her decisions or solutions. Mutually constructing and reflecting on self-empowerment enables the clinician to assist the client in thinking beyond original and often deferential expectations by identifying boundaries, realistic goals, and both intrapsychic and social barriers to be addressed.

When Asian clients positively and constructively look for support, they would like to hear praises from their clinician that confirm that they are making a sound decision in help seeking. Internally, the clinician encourages the clients to commit to continuous learning. Once the clients can find internal peace in their thinking patterns and maintain positive values, they will be able to develop social competencies and connect to their cultural identity in a positive way. When the clients are able to find meaning in their cultural background or heritage, the clinician can help them reframe their strengths and form positive relationships.

To say clinicians must be patient and culturally sensitive is a summary of the complex psychodynamic processes that go into creating any interpersonal connection. When obvious points of disconnection are most visible, such as in the cases that involve cross-ethnic communications, in many ways the process is more evident. Relational social work directs the practitioner to assume a state of not knowing, empathic attunement to establish an intent and invitation to know, exploratory inquiry to test understanding and allow mutual work, and co-constructed meanings of client communications to emerge. Identifying issues so that the client can relate her/his thinking to the clinician's explanation and thereby expand self-awareness must precede the collaborative pursuit of possible solutions. The complexities in clinical practice with culturally diverse clients require the clinician to connect with the client's perspective, parameters of action, and strengths that have constituted coping thus far. The quality of the interpersonal exchange is itself a therapeutic element that engages the client in self-reflection rather than automatic reactivity. Alongside treatment planning for direct changes in behavior, which Asian American clients particularly seek, the culturally sensitive clinician attends to the relational matrix so positivity and hope can be instilled.

Study Questions

1. When considering the steps that are necessary when working with Asian American clients, which cultural factors are the most important as a relational clinician?
2. Describe two ways that "being culturally sensitive" would be demonstrated by a relational clinician who is working cross-culturally with an Asian American client or family. How would those ways differ, or not, for a relational clinician working within her own Asian American population?

3. Describe the stereotypic Asian identity and ways that stereotype affects the client's self-perception. What skills would a relational clinician use to explore self-image?
4. How does a clinician use relational-based strategies to address concerns a client expresses about another family member?
5. Explain how the social work clinician uses self-reflection to help an Asian American client realize both the existence of inner strengths and the importance of an external support system.
6. Choose one case from the chapter and write an additional therapeutic question or statement for each of the ten COMPETENCE areas with a focus on working with Asian American clients. Your questions should demonstrate how to address:

   (a) Mutual empathy in relationship building
   (b) Co-construction of treatment planning
   (c) The balance between being humble and demonstrating professional expertise

References

Ahmad, F., Shik, A., Vanza, R., Cheung, A. M., George, U., & Stewart, D. E. (2004). Voices of South Asian women: Immigration and mental health. *Women & Health, 40*(4), 113–130. doi:10.1300/J013v40n0407.

Atkinson, D. R., Lowe, S., & Matthews, L. (1995). Asian-American acculturation, gender, and willingness to seek counseling. *Journal of Multicultural Counseling & Development, 23*(3), 130–138.

Chan, C. L. W., Ng, S. M., Ho, R. T. H., & Chow, A. Y. M. (2006). East meets west: Applying eastern spirituality in clinical practice. *Journal of Clinical Nursing, 15*(7), 822–832. doi:10.1111/j.1365-2702.2006.01649.x.

Cheung, M. (2009). Mental health issues expressed by the Cantonese-Chinese radio listeners. *Hong Kong Journal of Social Work, 43*(2), 147–155. doi:10.1142/S021924620900014X.

Cheung, M., Leung, P., & Cheung, A. (2011). Depression symptoms and help-seeking behaviors among Korean Americans. *International Journal of Social Welfare, 20*(4), 421–429. doi:10.1111/j.1468-2397.2010.00764.x.

Chhean, V. K. (2007). A Buddhist perspective on coping with catastrophe. *Southern Medical Journal, 100*(9), 952–953.

Chou, C.-C. (2008). Critique on the notion of model minority: An alternative racism to Asian American? *Asian Ethnicity, 9*(3), 219–229. doi:10.1080/14631360802349239.

Chu, B. C. (2007). Considering culture one client at a time: Maximizing the cultural exchange. *Pragmatic Case Studies in Psychotherapy, 3*(3), 34–43.

Comstock, D., Hammer, T., Strentzsch, J., Cannon, K., Parsons, J., & Salazar, G. (2008). Relational-cultural theory: A framework for bridging relational, multicultural, and social justice competencies. *Journal of Counseling and Development, 86*(3), 279–287.

Cook, D., & Hayes, S. C. (2010). Acceptance-based coping and the psychological adjustment of Asian and Caucasian Americans. *International Journal of Behavioral Consultation & Therapy, 6*(3), 186–197.

Danner, C. C., Robinson, B. E., Striepe, M. I., & Yang Rhodes, P. F. (2007). Running from the demon: Culturally specific group therapy for depressed Hmong women in a family medicine residency clinic. *Women & Therapy, 30*(1/2), 151–176.

de Anda, D. (1984). Bicultural socialization: Factors affecting the minority experience. *Social Work, 29*(2), 101–107.

Duffey, T. (2006). Promoting relational competencies in counselor education through creativity and relational-cultural theory. *Journal of Creativity in Mental Health, 2*(1), 47–59.

Folgheraiter, F. (2004). *Relational social work: Toward networking and societal practices.* London: Jessica Kingsley Publishers.

Gamst, G., Dana, R. H., Der-Karabetian, A., & Kramer, T. (2001). Asian American mental health clients: Effects of ethnic match and age on global assessment and visitation. *Journal of Mental Health Counseling, 23*(1), 57–72.

Gunnings, T. S. (1997). Editorial. *Journal of Multicultural Counseling & Development, 25*(1), 3–4.

Gursansky, D., Quinn, D., & Le Sueur, E. (2010). Authenticity in reflection: Building reflective skills for social work. *Social Work Education, 29*(7), 778–791. doi:10.1080/02615471003650062.

Gutiérrez, L. M. (1990). Working with women of color: An empowerment perspective. *Social Work, 35*(2), 149–154.

Hines, P. M., Garcia-Preto, N., McGoldrick, M., Almeida, R., & Weltman, S. (1992). Intergenerational relationships across cultures. *Families in Society, 73*(6), 323–338.

Ino, S. M., & Glicken, M. D. (2002). Understanding and treating the ethnically Asian client: A collectivist approach. *Journal of Health & Social Policy, 14*(4), 37–49.

Ka'opua, L. S. I., Gotay, C. C., Hannum, M., & Bunghanoy, G. (2005). Adaptation to long-term prostate cancer survival: The perspective of elderly Asian/Pacific Islander wives. *Health and Social Work, 30*(2), 145–154.

Kim, W., & Keefe, R. H. (2009). Examining health-related factors among an ethnically diverse group of Asian-American mental health clients. *Journal of Evidence-Based Social Work, 6*(1), 17–28. doi:10.1080/15433710802633288.

Kim, I. J., Kim, L. I. C., & Kelly, J. G. (2006). Developing cultural competence in working with Korean immigrant families. *Journal of Community Psychology, 34*(2), 149–165. doi:10.1002/jcop.20093.

Lee, E. (2004). The way of being a social worker: Implications for Confucianism to social work education and clinical practice. *Smith College Studies in Social Work, 74*(2), 393–408.

Lee, S., Ma, G., Juon, H.-S., Martinez, G., Hsu, C., & Bawa, J. (2011). Assessing the needs and guiding the future: Findings from the health needs assessment in 13 Asian American communities of Maryland in the United States. *Journal of Immigrant and Minority Health, 13*(2), 395–401. doi:10.1007/s10903-009-9310-3.

Leong, F., & Lau, A. (2001). Barriers to providing effective mental health services to Asian Americans. *Mental Health Services Research, 3*(4), 201–214. doi:10.1023/A:1013177014788.

Leung, P., Cheung, M., & Cheung, A. (2010). Vietnamese Americans and depression: A health and mental health concern. *Social Work in Mental Health, 8*(6), 526–542. doi:10.1080/15332985.2010.485092.

Leung, P., Cheung, M., & Cheung, A. (2011). Developing help-seeking strategies for Pakistani clients with depressive symptoms. *Asian Pacific Journal of Social Work and Development, 21*(2), 21–33. doi:10.1111/j.1468-2397.2010.00764.x

Leung, P., Cheung, M., & Tsui, V. (2012). Asian Indians and depressive symptoms: Reframing mental health help-seeking behavior. *International Social Work, 55*(1), 53–70. doi:10.1177/0020872811407940.

Lyons, K. (2006). Editorial. *International Social Work, 49*(1), 5–8. doi:10.1177/0020872806059396.

Meyer, O., Zane, N., & Young, I. C. (2011). Understanding the psychological processes of the racial match effect in Asian Americans. *Journal of Counseling Psychology, 58*(3), 335–345. doi:10.1037/a0023605.

Mijung, P. (2007). *Working with culture: Psychiatric and mental health care providers' perspectives on practice with Asian American families.* San Francisco: University of California.

Ngo-Metzger, Q., Massagli, M. P., Clarridge, B. R., Manocchia, M., Davis, R. B., Iezzoni, L. I., & Phillips, R. S. (2003). Linguistic and cultural barriers to care. *Journal of General Internal Medicine, 18*(1), 44–52. doi:10.1046/j.1525-1497.2003.20205.x.

Nguyen, P., Leung, P., & Cheung, M. (2011). Bridging help-seeking options to Vietnamese Americans with parent-child conflict and depressive symptoms. *Child & Youth Services Review,* 33(2011), 1842–1846. doi:10.1016/j.childyouth.2011.05.009.

O'Connor, H. (2006). Primary care mental health workers: A narrative of the search for identity. *Primary Care Mental Health, 4*(2), 93–98.

Oyserman, D., & Sakamoto, I. (1997). Being Asian American: Identity, cultural constructs, and stereotype perception. *The Journal of Applied Behavioral Science, 33*(4), 435–453.

Roesch, S. C., Wee, C., & Vaughn, A. A. (2006). Relations between the big five personality traits and dispositional coping in Korean Americans: Acculturation as a moderating factor. *International Journal of Psychology, 41*(2), 85–96. doi:10.1080/00207590544000112.

Saari, C. (2005). The contribution of relational theory to social work practice. *Smith College Studies in Social Work, 75*(3), 3–14.

Shibusawa, T., & Chung, I. W. (2009). Wrapping and unwrapping emotions: Clinical practice with East Asian immigrant elders. *Clinical Social Work Journal, 37*(4), 312–319.

Shonfeld-Ringel, S. (2001). A re-conceptualization of the working alliance in cross-cultural practice with non-western clients: Integrating relational perspectives and multicultural theories. *Clinical Social Work Journal, 29*(1), 53–63.

Silverstein, R., Bass, L. B., Tuttle, A., Knudson-Martin, C., & Huenergardt, D. (2006). What does it mean to be relational? A framework for assessment and practice. *Family Process, 45*(4), 391–405.

Simpson, S. A., & Long, J. A. (2007). Medical student-run health clinics: Important contributors to patient care and medical education. *Journal of General Internal Medicine, 22*(3), 352–356. doi:10.1007/s11606-006-0073-4.

Sodowsky, G. R. (1991). Effects of culturally consistent counseling tasks on American and international student observers' perception of counselor credibility: A preliminary investigation. *Journal of Counseling and Development, 69*(3), 253–257.

Spencer, M. S., Chen, J., Gee, G. C., Fabian, C. G., & Takeuchi, D. T. (2010). Discrimination and mental health-related service use in a national study of Asian Americans. *American Journal of Public Health, 100*(12), 2410–2417. doi:10.2105/AJPH.2009.176321.

Taylor, P., & Cheung, M. (2010). Integration of Personal/Professional Self (IPPS) through reflective/experiential learning. *Journal of Teaching in Social Work, 30*(2), 159–174. doi:10.1080/08841231003705248.

Toasland, J. (2007). Containing the container: An exploration of the containing role of management in a social work context. *Journal of Social Work Practice, 21*(2), 197–202. doi:10.1080/02650530701371903.

Tosone, C. (2004). Relational social work: Honoring the tradition. *Smith College Studies in Social Work, 74*(3), 475–487.

Tosone, C. (2005). The Guijin therapist and the nature of therapeutic truth: A relational perspective. *Clinical Social Work Journal, 33*(1), 9–19.

Tsui, V., Cheung, M., & Leung, P. (2010). Help-seeking among male victims of partner abuse: Men's hard times. *Journal of Community Psychology, 38*(6), 769–780.

Tyson, S., & Flaskerud, J. H. (2009). Cultural explanations of mental health and illness. *Issues in Mental Health Nursing, 30*(10), 650–651. doi:10.1080/01612840902838587.

U.S. Census Bureau. (2011, April 29). Asian American Heritage Month: May 2011. Washington, DC: U.S. Census Bureau Public Information Office. Retrieved from http://www.census.gov/newsroom/releases/archives/facts_for_features_special_editions/cb11-ff06.html.

Wachtel, P. L. (2008). *Relational theory and the practice of psychotherapy*. New York: Guilford.

Wright, J. (January 22, 2009). Burmese refugees fearful of new life in USA. *USA Today*. McLean, VA: Gannett Company. http://www.usatoday.com/news/world/2009-01-22-burmarefugees_N.htm.

Co-creating Culture Through Relationship with Individuals of Asian Indian Origin

Mohan Krishna Vinjamuri

Introduction

This chapter discusses potential applications of relational theory to clinical social work practice with individuals in the United States of Asian Indian origin. Social workers may come into contact with Asian Indians for many reasons, such as parent–child conflicts, stresses created by taking care of aging family members, couple difficulties, work-related difficulties, family violence, and challenges related to sexual orientation, immigration, death, or illness (Almeida 2005). Second-generation Asian Indian immigrants in particular may be struggling with issues of identity and separation and individuation from their families of origin. A relational framework helps practitioners recognize the emotional and interpersonal needs that may be encoded in their client's presenting problems and respond to these needs in ways that make aspects of the client's culture amenable for exploration in the clinical social work process. As Tosone (2004), Berzoff (2011), Goldstein (2001), and other social work clinicians have pointed out, attention to the manifest and pragmatic concerns of clients must be matched with a deeper understanding of the internal dynamics that guide their capacities to adapt and their ways of using the practice process.

This chapter reviews findings about experiences of Asian Indians in the United States and clinical literature on therapeutic work with this population. Application in direct practice is presented in the case example of Naresh, a client of Asian Indian origin, and his social worker Jessica, who is Caucasian (English and German). Naresh is a gay-identified Asian Indian legal immigrant from a Hindu family who moved to the United States voluntarily with significant educational and meager economic resources. His case illustrates how the practitioner can use a relational framework to co-construct with the client a space of curiosity, mutuality,

M.K.Vinjamuri, Ph.D., LMSW (✉)
Department of Social Work, Lehman College, City University of New York, New York, USA
e-mail: mohanvinjamuri@gmail.com

J.B. Rosenberger (ed.), *Relational Social Work Practice with Diverse Populations*,
Essential Clinical Social Work Series, DOI 10.1007/978-1-4614-6681-9_9,
© Springer Science+Business Media New York 2014

and possibility. In this space, the client can unlock his potential for transforming his relationship to self, his family of origin, and his cultural identities and thereby live more fully in the world.

Clinical Work with Asian Indian Immigrants

The Term "Asian Indian": Illuminating and Obscuring

"Asian Indian" refers to individuals whose country of origin is India. More than 20 million South Asians – that is, people whose country of origin is India, Pakistan, Bangladesh, Sri Lanka, Nepal, or Bhutan – have migrated throughout the world, some for several generations (Guzder and Krishna 2005). Most South Asian immigrants in the United States are Asian Indians. They are the fourth largest immigrant community in the United States (Khanna et al. 2009) and are one of the fastest-growing immigrant groups (Baptiste 2005).

Discussion of a particular population always must acknowledge its diversity within diversity. Homogenizing people's experiences by group not recognizing intragroup differences can run "the risk of flattening out complexity and…in doing so, [increase] the potential for reproducing wider forms of essentialism, stereotyping and racism" (Gunaratnam 2003 as cited in Singh 2009, p. 363). "Asian Indian," for example, includes multiple religious traditions (Hindu, Muslim, Buddhist, Christian, Jain, and Sikh) and any of the 22 official languages of India (Almeida 2005; Baptiste 2005). Akhtar (1995) suggests caution about "essentializing" immigration: differences in immigrants' experiences include the circumstances (voluntary, under duress, legal, or not) and reasons (economic, familial, educational) they immigrated to the United States (Guzder and Krishna 2005; Baptiste 2005). Additionally, immigrants come to the United States with a variety of social, economic, and occupational resources (Baptiste 2005). Practicing within a relational framework helps the practitioner with this tension by applying the principle of not knowing and thereby using mutuality and co-construction of meanings to illuminate how presenting problems and symptoms may reflect vastly different internal experiences.

Fortunately for both the clinician and the client, human relationships, by their very nature, are creative spaces. In speaking about the origins of the therapeutic alliance, Bollas (1998) poignantly describes the clinical therapeutic process as one that

> evoke[s] some of the mysteries of human life…[and] could evoke the transfer of so many different if interconnected alliances: of fetus inside womb, infant inside maternal world, child inside the law of the father, child inside family complexity, self inside the dream, addressee inside the textures of the "I's" discourses. (p. 29)

The evolving relationship between clinician and client, by reproducing aspects of these past relationships, gives the client and clinician opportunities to see how her definitions of "me" and "not me" have been constructed and can be re-envisioned.

In these spaces for exploration, the clinical social work practitioner can become empathically attuned to culturally specific experiences while continually letting go of assumptions about the meanings of these experiences. Relational practice puts the clinical social worker into the heart of this dialectic of knowing and not knowing. In order to accomplish this engagement, the practitioner must encounter the transferences and countertransferences evoked by the very concept of a relationally engaged clinical social work relationship.

Barriers to Help Seeking

Asian Indians may be reluctant to seek services from providers whom they see as culturally alien from them, anticipating dissonance between basic cultural positions (Baptiste 2005). Western clinicians may view personal problems and responses in diagnostic terms (APA 1994). An example being what Western thinking classifies as depression (Leung et al. 2011) found that Asian Indians experience the hallmarks of what is called depression, like loss of motivation, concentration, appetite changes, and loss of hope, but not see these conditions as psychological in nature. The relational clinician's assessment is focused less on symptoms and categories and more on mutual articulation of the client's explanation of suffering and dysfunction. McWilliams (2011) stresses understanding the key dynamics in the client's distress, and relational social work stresses inquiry and dialogue to co-construct this understanding (Greenberg and Mitchell 1983). To do so, the practitioner must be aware of the lens through which she is viewing the experiences of the client and how holding on to this paradigm can impede the therapeutic process (Bromberg 2011).

Seeking clinical services is controversial for Asian Indians (Almeida 2005) who are averse to speaking to strangers, and thus seek advice from friends or relatives. Stigma is attached to people with mental health problems (Leung et al. 2011), so professional consultation is especially threatening because it is a sign of failure (Almeida 2005). Issues such as domestic abuse and homosexuality evoke denial, shame, and social anxiety (Guzder and Krishna 2005). The relational social worker can express understanding through mutual empathy with these sentiments, incorporating this understanding into constructing a mutually viable representation of the problem that includes psychodynamic aspects in a form that is congruent with cultural imperatives. For example, a client's avoidance of feelings about a shamefully experienced problem can be introduced in terms of expressed empathic attunement about this difficulty and its role in engaging possible remedies. Another example is that Asian Indian clients may express somatic complaints that mask challenges related to racial and cultural identity (Almeida 2005), or, conversely, use "cultural camouflage" (Guzder and Krishna 2005, p. 135), blaming their cultural background to mask emotional processes and avoid personal agency or responsibility for change. In keeping with relational theory, these authors ask the clinician to "widen the bedrock questions of counter transference, neutrality, identity, and psychotherapy processes to accommodate cross-cultural realities" (Guzder and Krishna 2005, p. 121).

Immigration and Acculturation Experiences

The not-knowing stance for creating a more open and inviting space of mutuality wherein the therapeutic relationship can grow (Tosone 2004) nonetheless requires the practitioner to be aware of the cultural imperatives that may be impinging on the client's individual process of handling difficulties and relieving suffering. Not knowing is individual; a clinical awareness that there is much cultural knowledge *to know* spurs the mutual exploration and co-construction of meanings at the heart of relational social work practice. Many constructs of Asian Indians, particularly those brought up in India, are in stark contrast to dominant individualistic Western values (Baptiste 2005) about identity, family, community, life meaning, and personal growth. Acknowledging these contrasts requires surfacing and challenging norms and values clinicians themselves may take for granted and perpetuate in the culture of the dominant society. Authenticity as a relational principle invites open communication about perceptions in order to explore in direct interpersonal dialogue what would constitute healthy change. This may take a non-Western form, requiring the relational clinician to embrace the potential of "a collective psychology [in which] the social and familial contexts are central to individual development" (Almeida 2005, p. 389). Intergenerational fealty and the role of religious and spiritual beliefs are equally significant, as will be illustrated in the case example. Oyserman and Lee (2008) explain:

> Within individualism, the core unit is the individual; societies exist to promote the well-being of individuals. Individuals are seen as separate from one another and as the basic unit of analysis. Within collectivism, the core unit is the group; societies exist, and individuals must fit into them. Individuals are seen as fundamentally connected and related through relationships and group memberships. (p. 311)

Kakar (2006) posits that "[t]he high value placed on connection does not mean that [Asian] Indians are incapable of functioning by themselves or that they do not have a sense of their own agency" (p. 34). Rather, the yearning for autonomy and the yearning for relationships coexist, which in fact confirms the relational theory emphasis on connection as the primary human drive (Greenberg and Mitchell 1983).

Viewing the experiences of Asian Indians through the lens of transitions can be useful (Rastogi 2007). Migration, immigration, and acculturation bring transitions and losses which may include lowered social class and status and loss of economic power (Khanna et al. 2009). Less visible but more psychologically painful are losses of moving away from families of origin. Many immigrant Asian Indians lived very closely and were continuously involved with their families of origin. They may prioritize maintaining and strengthening these ties by bringing family members to this country and being vigilant in keeping their cultural values front and center in everyday life (Inman et al. 2007). Asian Indian immigrants tend to idealize their culture, which makes it possible to distinguish themselves from and within a racist mainstream society (Patel 2007; Almeida 2005). Women may preserve gendered roles and hierarchies (Patel 2007). Children and adolescents being reared in this country may, in particular, experience conflicts with elder generations (Farver et al. 2002; Khanna et al. 2009).

Intergenerational Conflicts

A common presenting problem of Asian Indians in clinical social work practice is intergenerational conflicts (Inman et al. 2007). Normative life cycle transitions including separation–individuation of adolescents occur in "an unfamiliar context under different cultural rules" (Baptiste 2005, p. 364). Asian Indian families are often referred for clinical social work services because of mental health and behavioral concerns about their children (Almeida 2005). Parents fear losing their children to mainstream American culture, losing parental authority, and losing face within their Asian Indian communities because of their child's behaviors (Baptiste 2005). The children speak about the stress and strain brought about by their parents' focus on educational and financial success as a model minority syndrome (Lee et al. 2009). This is a classic example of where relational social work practice can help reach for the deeper emotional pain about change and transition presenting as a behavioral issue. The empathic attunement to emotional challenges, the "me" and "not-me" dilemma, does not require discrediting of cultural representations. Rather, the relational practitioner enlarges the culturally explicated problem, validating its diversity roots and reaching for mutual exploration of more deeply felt individual experience of the client. Opening up a singular cultural explanation in an interpersonally respectful exploration requires the social work clinician to monitor her own reductive tendencies; resolution in the individual of conflict between cultural preservation and individual needs and goals requires "standing in spaces" (Bromberg 1996) where mutual validation can occur.

Case Example: Naresh and Jessica

Naresh is a 34-year-old male of Asian Indian origin who was being seen by Jessica, a 28-year-old clinical social worker in a small outpatient mental health clinic. Jessica is Caucasian (English and German) and was brought up in the United States in a Protestant family. When Naresh began seeing Jessica, he had a boyfriend of 2 years who was 36 years old, Caucasian (Irish), and brought up in the United States in a Catholic family. He and his boyfriend did not live together. Naresh came voluntarily to this clinic seeking help for what he described as relationship difficulties with his boyfriend and recurring anxiety. His difficulties getting emotionally and sexually closer to his boyfriend reflected experiences in previous relationships with both men and women. In the work described below, Jessica had been seeing Naresh once a week for approximately 4 months.

Many Mothers

Naresh, an only child, came to the United States from India with his parents when he was 3 years old. The traditions of extended family and Mother India remained central. Expressing feelings, particularly difficult ones like sadness, anger, and being hurt, was actively discouraged as self-indulgent and threatening family unity. Naresh either suppressed or became dissociated (Bromberg 2011) from emotional experience, leading to functional adequacy but internal dissatisfaction. This reserve and remoteness was apparent among his small United States circle of friends, who encouraged Naresh to, like them, work on personal issues with a professional clinician, despite its incongruence with family and cultural norms. Harlem (2009) notes a special benefit of addressing diversity practice in clinical social work is that it "serves as an intimate point of contact" (p. 274) between host country realities and the fixed idealization or denigration of a culture of origin. In the same way, the relational clinician is a potential point of contact between disparate self-aspects: her tolerance of ambiguity and ambivalence, as well as facility in bringing dissociated self-states together (Bromberg 1996, 2011). Naresh's need to feel connected to his mother country, as well as his mother herself, required a space in which to formulate and relate intimately with the values of both present and past environments (Akhtar 1995).

The relational model, stressing process of connection over implications of specific content, embraces all forms of diversity as ultimately aspects of individuality in search of coherence. When Naresh came out as gay at age 30 years, and told his parents shortly thereafter, he was not surprised, but was distressed, by their visceral negative reactions to him. Shame, guilt, behavioral demands, invoking extended family pressure, and the like were their tools to try to "fix" him. Naresh felt great affection for and had a profound need to please and be close to his parents, in keeping with his Asian Indian identity. Their emphatic refusal to know about his personal life was wounding. At the same time, they said that they would be there for him if he ever needed help financially or fell ill. Overtly less abandoned than might be the case for other homosexual Asian Indians, Naresh nonetheless struggled with the disconnection between demonstrated care and emotional connection. This problem, a state of mixed signals, shows the importance of understanding diversity in clinical social work practice: clients bring all kinds of variations of divided self-identities, with powerful organizing self-experiences in primary relationships being incongruent with prevailing social messages. The relational practitioner is especially well equipped to engage this confusion: the relationship of practice itself is the forum for reconciliation of these kinds of conflicts. Through exploration, mutuality, attunement, collaboration, and all the relational practice skills, the social work practitioner guides the self-integration process, the specific contents of which fuse individual characteristics with cultural values and expectations.

Engagement, Assessment, and Core Problem

Self-differentiation from the "mother" country, particularly for Indians, invariably leads to internal and interpersonal conflict. For Naresh, recognizing and eventually being open to his parents about his homosexuality was a catalyst for accepting himself as an individual while striving to preserve the collectivist values of his family and culture of origin. Jessica, his clinical social worker, was familiar with homosexuality as a family conflict issue and had resolved her initial Protestant, Anglo countertransference to homosexuality. Thus prepared for mutually empathic engagement with Naresh's core conflict of how to reconcile personal and familial/community differences, her assessment included co-created appraisal of how this interpersonal conflict was causing him intrapsychic pain. On another level, however, the culturally specific meanings that interpersonal relations had for Naresh were beyond Jessica's experience. Therefore, she was mindful of invoking the stance of not knowing, inquiry, and pursuing mutual definitions of issues rather than translating Naresh's core problem into her familiar constructs. Taking time to read about Asian Indian culture was part of her charge, but the engagement with her client as a clinical social work practitioner rested most heavily on her authenticity as a learner of cultural meanings as she reflected on how to relate her understanding of individual experience with the turbulence her client experienced.

The Treatment Process: Reflective Listening and Functional Exploration

Naresh practiced his Hindu faith until age 28. By the time he began seeing Jessica, he did not subscribe to any organized religion but described himself as spiritual. Nevertheless, Naresh understood deeply and identified strongly with the worldview he grew up with in a Hindu household, particularly family lineage and children's duties to their parents. He explained to Jessica that he did not see himself as a good son. While he was feeling freer and happier overall after having come out and beginning to have intimate relationships with men, he felt guilty that he did not perform his duty to get married and provide grandchildren. He was failing in his duty to give them pleasure in this life and to passing on to the next life his father's family name, which represented continuity in lineage proudly traced back to Hindu saints and scholars. This sense of continuity was becoming increasingly important to Naresh's father as he aged and reflected on his own mortality and the cycle of birth, death, and rebirth that is central to Hindu beliefs.

Naresh's parents felt embarrassed in their extended families about their son being gay, which caused them to withdraw from various social activities. This was a crisis, as continuous involvement with extended family was both culturally expected and personally very meaningful for his parents. Naresh felt responsible for this problem. Nevertheless, Naresh came out to several relatives, which posed another threat to his parents' sense of being part of a stable and respectable family. Some relatives tried to pressure him, telling him that he was being selfish, and others who did not know he was gay said that he needed to fulfill his duties as a son. Though Naresh was living life as an openly gay man, he knew that his sexuality was shameful and disgraceful to his family.

For the relational practitioner, the treatment process involved helping Naresh express his grief about his family's disapproval and deal with the conflicted internal feelings this engendered. Jessica was stymied about a remedy, based on her limited cultural understanding of the Asian Indian complexity of family, so different from her own nuclear family experience. Her relational technique required forthright authenticity about not knowing, seeking clarification for herself and facilitating conscious explication for Naresh to assist in his own reflective process. Try as he might, Naresh was focused on feelings of failure and inadequacy, could not see his own beauty and strengths, and easily felt criticized and diminished. He had great difficulties feeling good enough and often equated what he did and what he experienced as either right or wrong. Jessica could help Naresh recognize the repercussions of his conflict in terms of his own self-state and his disrupted functioning, but a resolution required an internal reconciliation of self-states that was demonstrable, not just psychological.

A Critical Clinical Moment

A pivotal moment in the clinical process and its impact on Naresh's striving for resolution arrived when Naresh told Jessica that he had decided to travel back to India with his parents to participate in a ceremony to initiate him as a Brahmin male, which is the highest caste in the Hindu caste system. His parents had indicated that they would like him to have this ceremony, even though he had stopped practicing as a Hindu and in many ways opposed the hierarchies of the caste system. This affirmation of cultural identity was important to Naresh's parents independent of their dismay about his avowed homosexuality. Deciding to fulfill their wishes so that he would be allowed to perform the prescribed and required religious rituals as a Brahmin son upon the death of his parents, Naresh felt he could provide a compromise between his individuality and his affiliation with his culture in a way that did not constitute a violation of his personal identity.

Jessica's response was to be annoyed and angry with Naresh, protective of his partner, and in competition with his parents. Jessica's countertransference, rooted in Western individuality, was to pathologize Naresh's need to satisfy his parents' wishes as a failure of individuation. As a Caucasian, she struggled to grasp the cultural significance of Naresh's relationship to his shared familial bond to Mother India. Holding to her relational theory convictions, Jessica recognized the issue might be her own inability to fully understand the nuances of the issues Naresh was presenting from his population's perspective and that it was she who was constricted by a parent/child conflict point of view.

In their interpersonal linkage, Naresh recognized Jessica's struggle. He often downplayed how hurt he felt by his parent's behaviors toward him out of fear of being misunderstood and blamed Jessica for trying to turn him against them. This was challenging for Jessica who did not want to "enable Naresh in buying into the shame and guilt that his parents were projecting onto him," assuming that these emotions were somehow psychologically universal. Reducing a client's individual struggle to terms with which the clinician is familiar, rather than using the relational skills of co-construction of meaning and acknowledgement of not knowing, represents the clinical social worker's challenge in working with a culturally different population: misunderstanding can arise from trying to understand on the clinician's experiential terms that are unconsciously assigned universal validity. Harlem (2009) suggests, instead, that emotional life is culturally constructed. Rosaldo (1984), as cited in Harlem (2009), writes that "feelings are not substances to be discovered in our blood but social practices organized by stories that…are structured by our forms of understanding" (p. 143). Therefore, although Jessica was not incorrect in understanding Naresh's core issues as expressing separation and attachment conflicts, she was out of alignment with the culturally specific dimensions of how separation and attachment can be negotiated in a different cultural context.

Jessica projected her own beliefs about religion as controlling and judgmental onto how she thought his Hindu upbringing was contributing to Naresh's struggles, even though she knew very little about Hinduism and was apprehensive about asking Naresh religious questions. This apprehension may have stemmed from the fact that the clinical social work literature has virtually ignored, at least until very recently, the impact of Eastern spirituality or religious influences on clients' lives (Kakar 2003; Streets 2009). Because of the lack of openness about religion as part of the clinical discourse, when Jessica occasionally suggested to Naresh that his Hindu upbringing could be contributing to his current conflictual feelings, he responded by avoiding the topic and diverting the conversation to other matters. Though he did not practice the Hindu faith anymore, Naresh was proud of his religious upbringing, saying it gave him a sense of belonging, identity, and stability.

When Naresh told Jessica that he had decided to have his caste initiation ceremony, she felt taken aback, because Naresh had not brought up this topic in previous sessions. She was surprised and angry that he did not involve her in making this decision. She felt protective and worried that Naresh would be "pulled back into his parents' vortex of shame and guilt." She could not understand why he would want to go through with this ceremony when he had expressed such strong philosophical, moral, and emotional objections to what it represents. Looking at the familial relationship with Western ideas of parity, Jessica did not feel Naresh's parents had earned his respect since they did not show respect toward his own life choices. She also saw his parents' continual focus on what will happen after they die as a way of manipulating Naresh to remain enmeshed with them, again displaying cultural myopia about death and its aftermath. Self-awareness of feelings such as anger, surprise, confusion, disapproval, protectiveness, and the like is a valuable signpost of countertransference. For a relational clinician, they signal the need for active inquiry and openness to not understanding, as a version of not knowing. The achievement of relational connection thus reflects mutual regard and tolerance for uncertainty, rather than all-knowing clinical expertise. In this manner, Jessica could use this opportunity to engender greater compassion for herself and for Naresh by reaffirming the core value of the client's subjective experience (Bean and Titus 2009).

Leaning into Uncertainty: The Need for Constant Self-Reflection

One of the key tenets of relational social work (Tosone 2004) is that the therapeutic relationship is a primary catalyst for client change. A nurturing therapeutic relationship enlists the powers of client and clinician as individuals, with individual histories, and the in-the-moment transformative powers of the therapeutic dyad. Tosone (2004) describes these elements as the aspects of the actual relationship, the working alliance, and the "transference-countertransference matrix as it operates in the intersubjective field" (p. 482). The intersubjective field encompasses both empathic attunement and the role of mentalization through the dialogic exchange (Allen et al. 2008).

Seeking the guidance of a supervisor or peer is a natural step in relational practice. It confirms the unending process of experiential learning and the centrality of interpersonal exploration as sources of growth in client and clinician alike (Baker Miller 2012). "Starting where the client is" (Woods and Hollis 1999) should be replaced by starting where the client and clinician are (Jordan 2004). Urdang (2010) notes that social workers, motivated to find the best solutions for their clients or to empower them to improve their lives, can feel pressured to apply time-limited and outcome-focused treatments and may "tend to reinforce [workers'] own tendencies towards 'omniscience, benevolence, and omnipotence', without a need to reflect upon or alter them" (Urdang 2010, p. 524). A relationally informed clinical practice stance could allow a social work clinician like Jessica to see her countertransference not as something problematic or to be avoided, but rather as something vital for engaging more deeply with Naresh. Countertransference "result[s] from dynamics with a client that are both inevitable and essential for meaningful change to occur…[and] is a way to feel in one's bones that which the client cannot convey through language alone" (Berzoff and Kita 2010, p. 342). In her strong desire to have the therapeutic relationship of her fantasy, however, Jessica unwittingly engaged in a power struggle with Naresh and his cultural legacy. She was bringing into her work European American notions of personal agency, pride, and parent–child relationships, concepts that may be the product of her own personal experiences and reinforced through Western psychological, psychoanalytic, and psychosocial theories. The relational perspective of individual agency (Bennet and Nelson 2011; Berzoff et al. 2008) recognizes rather than disregards the unique culturally congruent features of individuality. Perhaps reflecting the invisibility of culture as an aspect of self due to membership in a dominant population, Jessica attributed her own experiences of being overwhelmed or pressured to intra-familial conflicts with her nuclear family. Thus her preconceived notions reproduced the power struggle that existed between Naresh and his parents and that played out within Naresh himself. Jessica felt that as she was trying to build a relationship with Naresh, she was in competition with his parents. This competition may have paralleled the competing forces in Naresh – one urging him toward greater autonomy and individuality and another pulling him toward familiar patterns of relationship in his family of origin. The struggle between developing autonomy and maintaining interpersonal relatedness can be a central theme for some clients, particularly those who came from family environments that did not encourage expressing one's emerging competency or one's desire and need for connection (Safyer et al. 1997).

Co-creating Culture and Connection Through Relationship

Just as Naresh was creating splits between right and wrong, or choosing his own life versus choosing his parents/family, Jessica also was making a sharp distinction between Naresh's culture and his presenting problems. His presenting problems were his relationship with his boyfriend and anxiety. His former troubles with intimacy were linked to feeling withdrawn and defensive about being truly understood. In this way, there was a parallel process between Naresh's struggles in connecting with his partner and family and his ability to form an open and authentic dialogue with his clinical social worker. The relationally attuned practitioner needs to recognize, embrace, and work with this parallel process as a here-and-now modification of what is a reality-based struggle for the client to exist authentically in the present in a culturally divergent and uncomprehending society.

In addition to trying to view the presenting problem within the client's cultural context, the practitioner needs to attune herself to how aspects of his culture get *enacted* through the presenting problem. In this way, "the problem contextualizes the relationship between clients and [clinician] and organizes possibilities and limitations for counseling" (Bean and Titus 2009, p. 42). Aspects of Naresh's culture (relationships with parents and extended family, religious upbringing, caste, etc.) and his presenting problems (anxiety, struggles with intimacy, conflictual relationships, feelings about himself/his own sexuality, etc.) shape and transform each other. Neither is static. The reported presenting problem may allow the client the opportunity to acknowledge and face struggles that are either downplayed or silenced in his culture and/or family.

Often, culture is seen as already existing properties residing in the individual; the individual brings these qualities into the clinical encounter and the clinical social worker must then orient her work so as to understand, become aware of, and respond to these properties as they get revealed. Rather than seeing her reactions as stemming from something inside Naresh that she needs to understand but is avoiding for her own defensive reasons, Jessica can "question whether or not there is ever anything objective of the client's that the [clinical social worker] can grasp" (Berzoff and Kita 2010, p. 343). This more dynamic relational perspective suggests that the client's culture and the presenting problem get enacted by and through each other in the vessel that is the therapeutic relationship. Berzoff and Kita (2010) describe the possibilities for growth that these enactments present:

> The hope is that by getting *into* an enactment, the [clinician] can then *get out* and, in the process of doing so, make the enacted material available for conscious reflection. This requires that the [clinician] get emotionally involved with the client…From this perspective, [clinicians] and their clients will inevitably enact parts of the patient's mental life and parts of the [clinician's] mental life, creating what Ogden (1994) has called the "third space" in which something new can be understood between them. (p. 342)

Both the clinician and the client then have an opportunity to participate and construct this enactment in ways that can shift the client's views of both the presenting problem and his experiences of his own culture. This is the essence of applying constructivist theory to clinical social work practice through the relational model. Instead of relying on gaining detailed knowledge of a client's culture, which can be a form of maintaining the dominant control of the narrative by becoming more expert rather than by valuing the client's expertise, the clinician can see this pressure as a signal to "becom[e] aware of [her own] culture's fundamental propositions about human nature, human experience, and the fulfilled human life and….then [see] them as cultural products, embedded in a particular place and time" (Kakar 2006, p. 41). In doing this, Jessica could join with Naresh around these life journeys and thereby co-construct with her client what Winnicott (1967) has called "the potential space between baby and mother, between child and family, between individual and society or the world…[which is] sacred to the individual in that it is here that the individual experiences creative living" (p. 372). This is the space, according to Winnicott (1967), where "cultural experience" (p. 371) is located and is also what he called "the place where we live" (Winnicott 1971, p. 104). Thus, culture in the clinical encounter is a location of creative experiences that gives the person a sense of his past, present, and future as a human being living in this world, a space where he can discover or rediscover himself in relation to his cultural and familial history.

What Separates Us Joins Us

In describing the possibility and impossibility of communicating human experience in the therapeutic alliance, Bollas (1998) writes that "there is a 'strangeness' between people, an 'interruption escaping all measure' (Blanchot 1993, p. 68), an infinite separation, that is the outcome of that difference between any two persons" (p. 33). Both the clinician and the client may become starkly aware of this strangeness at any moment in the clinical encounter. In sharing with her his decision to have his caste initiation ceremony, a ritual that is rich with cultural, familial, and historical meaning, Naresh took an important step to let Jessica further into his world, a world to which she feels she cannot relate. Jessica has an opportunity to invite, rather than shut out, her feelings of disconnection with Naresh as he speaks with her about his decision to perform a very important rite in his life. In fact, her feeling shut out presented an opportunity to empathize with how shut out Naresh may feel from her and from others in his life, as well as how shut out he and his parents may feel from each other. Difference between the clinician and the client can thereby become not an obstacle to engagement but a catalyst for growing a trusting, more open relationship. Cultural dissimilarities need not be barriers and, in fact, may be openings for identifying with our clients' pain (Lobban 2011).

Engaging with one's feelings and experiences of disconnection is the very vehicle for healing, as well as individual and societal change (Comstock et al. 2008). Opening herself up to the pain of disconnection and being misunderstood may allow

Jessica to genuinely respect Naresh's need and wish to fulfill certain cultural and familial obligations. Engaging with Naresh around all of his thoughts and feelings about having his caste initiation ceremony, be they of social, familial, cultural, or developmental origins, can open the door to expand how he thinks about his own and his parents' happiness, norms which may have been passed down through generations. Perhaps Naresh's decision to go to India for the ceremony was his attempt to connect more with himself and his parents and develop what Akhtar (1995) has called a "good-humored ambivalence" (p. 1060) toward himself, his parents, his country of origin, and the country he grew up in and adopted for his adult life.

Recognizing that while there will always be an unbridgeable separation between them, Jessica may find new ways to engage with Naresh around the many meanings religion and spirituality may have for him. His disavowal of the importance of reflecting on his Hindu upbringing illustrates that the inquiry process for the social work clinician who is bold enough to pursue it may not always be met with ready acceptance. Beginning clinicians often struggle with what they perceive as negative reactions from their clients, such as clients not appreciating or accepting their help in the ways they may have envisioned or wished (Urdang 2010). Clients from populations labeled as diverse, and therefore marginalized, may be reluctant, as was Naresh, to be open with clinicians who are diverse from themselves about their deepest cultural convictions.

Conclusion

Dharma is an unwritten and often unexpressed code or law in Hindu thought that helps one know if one is acting in accordance with right action and the truth of things (Kakar 2006). Dharma, however, is not a prescriptive code and may lead to what may seem incongruent actions. The right action depends on the context in which this action is taking place. Thus, contained within the concept and enactments of dharma in people's lives is the realization that truth is all encompassing, not by limiting or predetermining but by creating a space where multiple potentialities can emerge. Dharma, like co-constructing meaning through relationship with one another, is constantly creative and evolving. This Asian Indian (Hindu) construct can be understood as a version of the relational space that can cradle what Winnicott (1967) describes as paradoxes between separateness and union, between originality and tradition, and between the individual and the shared (communal). In the potential space where cultural experience is located (Winnicott 1967), all of these exist and, in fact, are necessary for one another. Allowing for these paradoxes is important in working with Asian Indian clients, particularly second-generation immigrants like Naresh, who want to connect even more deeply with their familial and cultural histories while transforming them and adopting new ways of living in the world.

Kakar (2006) states, "the relativism of dharma supports both tradition and modernity, innovation and conformity" (p. 30). In the realm of relational theory's endorsement of construction and found meaning rather than prescription and validated meaning, dharma is a useful principle that may be central to working with Asian Indian clients and more broadly with clients who are culturally different. Transformation requires being able to hold multiple truths, to let oneself be pulled toward the past while reaching for the future, and to embrace new ways of being while honoring the collective wisdom of tradition. To embark on such a journey can be frightening and unsettling. Transformation cannot happen in isolation, but rather in relationship with others. Clinical social workers have the precious opportunity to build these relationships, and doing so requires both knowing and not knowing how to be with another human being.

Study Questions

1. Discuss the impact of immigration on the lives of Asian Indian families and individuals. How might these impacts be similar and/or different for other immigrant groups in the United States with whom you are familiar?
2. How might the concepts – collectivism and individualism – be useful to you in working with an Asian Indian client? How might these concepts be limiting?
3. What are some of the reasons Asian Indian clients may be reluctant to seek services or engage in therapy? Choose one of these reasons and discuss whether this is a common theme when it comes to hesitations that clients may have when reaching out?
4. Choose one of the following terms: family, identity, community, self-determination. Discuss any countertransference this concept evokes that may influence relational work with an Asian Indian client.
5. Earlier in this chapter, it was stated that "a relational framework can help practitioners recognize the emotional and interpersonal needs that may be encoded in their client's presenting problems and then respond to these needs in ways that make aspects of the client's culture amenable for exploration in the therapeutic process." Discuss this statement using an example from your own practice.
6. Reflect on a core idea or value from any religious or spiritual tradition, not limited to Asian Americans. Discuss how this core idea might inform your practice as you explore presenting issues in their daily life.

References

Akhtar, S. (1995). A third individuation: Immigration, identity, and the psychoanalytic process. *Journal of the American Psychoanalytic Association, 43*, 1051–1084.

Allen, J. G., Fonagy, P., & Bateman, A. (2008). *Mentalizing in clinical practice*. Washington, DC: American Psychiatric Publishing.

Almeida, R. (2005). Asian Indian families. In M. McGoldrick, J. Giardano, & N. Garcia-Preto (Eds.), *Ethnicity and family therapy* (pp. 377–394). New York: Guilford Press.

American Psychiatric Association. (1994). *Diagnostic and statistical manual of mental disorders* (4th ed.). Arlington, VA: American Psychiatric Association.

Baker Miller, J. (2012). *Five good things. Jean Baker Miller Training Institute at the Wellesley Centers for Women*. New Hampshire: Wellesley.

Baptiste, D. A. (2005). Family therapy with East Indian immigrant parents rearing children in the United States: Parental concerns, therapeutic issues, and recommendations. *Contemporary Family Therapy, 27*(3), 345–366.

Bean, R. A., & Titus, G. (2009). Cultural intersection of Asian Indian ethnicity and presenting problem: Adapting multicultural competence for clinical accessibility. *Journal of Multicultural Counseling and Development, 37*, 40–51.

Bennett, S., & Nelson, J. (2011). *Adult attachment in clinical social work*. New York: Springer.

Berzoff, J. (2011). *Falling through the cracks: Psychodynamic practice with at risk and vulnerable clients*. New York: Columbia Press.

Berzoff, J., & Kita, E. (2010). Compassion fatigue and countertransference: Two different concepts. *Clinical Social Work Journal, 38*, 341–349.

Berzoff, J., Flanagan, L., & Hertz, P. (2008). *Inside out and outside in: Psychodynamic clinical theory and psychopathology in contemporary multicultural contexts* (2nd ed.). New York: Jason Aronson.

Blanchot, M. (1993). *The infinite conversation*. Minneapolis: University of Minnesota Press.

Bollas, C. (1998). Origins of the therapeutic alliance. *Scandinavian Psychoanalytic Review, 21*, 24–36.

Bromberg, P. (1996). Standing in the spaces: The multiplicity of self and the psychoanalytic relationship. *Contemporary Psychoanalysis, 32*, 509–535.

Bromberg, P. (2011). *The shadow of the tsunami and growth of the relational mind*. New York: Taylor and Francis.

Comstock, D. L., Hammer, T. R., Strentzsch, J., Cannon, K., Parsons, J., & Salazar, G., II. (2008). Relational-cultural theory: A framework for bridging relational, multicultural, and social justice competencies. *Journal of Counseling and Development, 86*, 279–287.

Farver, J. M., Narang, S. K., & Bhadha, B. R. (2002). East meets west: Ethnic identity, acculturation, and conflict in Asian Indian families. *Journal of Family Psychology, 16*(3), 338–350.

Goldstein, E. (2001). *Object relations theory and self psychology in social work practice*. New York: The Free Press.

Greenberg, J., & Mitchell, S. A. (1983). *Object relations in psychoanalytic theory*. Cambridge: Harvard University Press.

Gunaratnam, Y. (2003). *Researching 'race' and ethnicity: Methods, knowledge, and power*. London: Sage.

Guzder, J., & Krishna, M. (2005). Mind the gap: Diaspora issues of Indian origin women in psychotherapy. *Psychology and Developing Societies, 17*(2), 121–138.

Harlem, A. (2009). Thinking through others: Cultural psychology and the psychoanalytic treatment of immigrants. *Psychoanalysis, Culture and Society, 14*(3), 273–288.

Inman, A. G., Howard, E. E., Beaumont, R. L., & Walker, J. A. (2007). Cultural transmission: Influence of contextual factors in Asian Indian immigrant parents' experiences. *Journal of Counseling Psychology, 54*(1), 93–100.

Jordan, J. V. (2004). Toward competence and connection. In J. V. Jordan, M. Walker, & L. M. Hartling (Eds.), *The complexity of connection* (pp. 11–27). New York: The Guilford Press.

Kakar, S. (2003). Psychoanalysis and Eastern spiritual healing traditions. *Journal of Analytic Psychology, 48*, 659–678.

Kakar, S. (2006). Culture and psychoanalysis. *Social Analysis, 50*(2), 25–44.

Khanna, A., McDowell, T., Perumbilly, S., & Titus, G. (2009). Working with Asian Indian American families: A Delphi study. *Journal of Systemic Therapies, 28*(1), 52–71.

Lee, S., Juon, H.-S., Martinez, G., Hsu, C. E., Robinson, E. S., Bawa, J., & Ma, G. X. (2009). Model minority at risk: Expressed needs of mental health by Asian American young adults. *Journal of Community Health, 34*, 144–152.

Leung, P., Cheung, M., & Tsui, V. (2011). Asian Indians and depressive symptoms: Reframing mental health help-seeking behavior. *International Social Work*, 1–18. doi:10.1177/0020872811407940.

Lobban, G. (2011). Li-an: Wounded by war. In M. Dimen (Ed.), *With culture in mind: Psychoanalytic stories* (pp. 25–30). New York: Routledge.

McWilliams, N. (2011). The psychodynamic diagnostic manual: An effort to compensate for the limitations of descriptive psychiatric diagnosis. *Journal of Personality Assessment, 93*(2), 112–122.

Ogden, T. H. (1994). The analytic third: Working with intersubjective clinical facts. In B. Rothschild & M. Rand (Eds.), *Help for the helper: The psychophysiology of compassion fatigue, vicarious traumatization, and self care*. New York: W.W. Norton.

Oyserman, D., & Lee, S. W. S. (2008). Does culture influence what and how we think? Effects of priming individualism and collectivism. *Psychological Bulletin, 134*(2), 311–342.

Patel, N. R. (2007). The construction of South-Asian-American womanhood: Implications for counseling and psychotherapy. *Women and Therapy, 30*(3/4), 51–61.

Rastogi, M. (2007). Coping with transitions in Asian Indian families: Systemic clinical interventions with immigrants. *Journal of Systemic Therapies, 26*(2), 55–67.

Rosaldo, M. Z. (1984). Toward an anthropology of self and feeling. In R. A. Schweder & R. Levine (Eds.), *Culture theory: Essays on mind, self, and emotion* (pp. 137–157). Cambridge: Cambridge University Press.

Safyer, A. W., Brandell, J. R., & Atwood, R. (1997). The autonomous self versus the relational self: A developmental perspective. *Smith College Studies in Social Work, 67*(2), 137–158.

Singh, R. (2009). Constructing 'the family' across culture. *Journal of Family Therapy, 31*, 359–383.

Streets, F. (2009). Overcoming a fear of religion in social work education and practice. *Journal of Religion and Spirituality in Social Work: Social Thought, 28*(1/2), 185–199.

Tosone, C. (2004). Relational social work: Honoring the tradition. *Smith College Studies in Social Work, 74*(3), 475–487.

Urdang, E. (2010). Awareness of self – A critical tool. *Social Work Education, 29*(5), 523–538.

Winnicott, D. W. (1967). The location of cultural experience. *The International Journal of Psychoanalysis, 48*, 368–372.

Winnicott, D. W. (1971). *Playing and reality*. London: Tavistock Publications.

Woods, M., & Hollis, F. (1999). *Casework: A psychosocial therapy*. New York: McGraw-Hill.

Part III
Religious Diversities

Relational Social Work Practice with Evangelical Christian Clients

David P. Cecil and Kenneth M. Stoltzfus

Introduction

Practice with Evangelical Christians requires an authentic relationship and a close examination of the diversity and relational aspects within this group. Relational theory, as an approach to relational social work, provides valuable methods for working with this group for all practitioners, regardless of their own religious affiliations. This chapter begins with an overview of the defining beliefs and practices of Evangelical Christianity and a discussion of the types of presenting problems and clinical issues that are common among Evangelical Christian clients. The discussion addresses relational clinical principles in work with Evangelical Christians from the perspectives of the relational clinician as a non-Evangelical Christian and as an Evangelical Christian. A case study of Kelly, a 29-year-old Caucasian woman who grew up in a nondenominational Christian Church, demonstrates the use of the clinical relationship in addressing issues between the social worker and client, the client and her family, and, for the purpose of this case, the client and God. The client's presenting problems and treatment are analyzed in light of attunement that contains authenticity and not knowing, mutuality and the co-construction of meaning and treatment goals, and the balance of reflective exploration with affirmation of strengths. The chapter includes recommendations for direct relational social work practice with Evangelical Christian clients, as well as discussion questions.

D.P. Cecil, Ph.D., LCSW (✉)
Master of Social Work Program, Asbury University, Wilmore, KY, USA
e-mail: David.cecil@asbury.edu

K.M. Stoltzfus, Ph.D., LISW-S
Department of Social Sciences, LCC International University, Klaipeda, Lithuania

J.B. Rosenberger (ed.), *Relational Social Work Practice with Diverse Populations*,
Essential Clinical Social Work Series, DOI 10.1007/978-1-4614-6681-9_10,
© Springer Science+Business Media New York 2014

Overview of Evangelical Beliefs

Evangelical Christians currently make up about a third of the population across the United States (Bader et al. 2006). Inevitably all relational clinicians will encounter Evangelical clients and need to attain a basic understanding of the religious beliefs and cultural attributes of this group. Despite shared characteristics, a specific definition of "Evangelical Christian" is difficult given multiple dimensions of diversity within this group. The term *evangelical* derives from the Greek word *evangelion* and literally means "good news." Evangelical Christians are one of many subgroups within the larger Christian community that, Evangelical or not, believe that God came to earth in the form of Jesus Christ, lived a perfect life, was wrongfully executed by crucifixion, and was resurrected through the power of God. These beliefs are based in Bible passages such as John 3:16 and Philippians 2:5–8 (New International Version [NIV]). The nearly universal belief among Christians, including Evangelical Christians, is the "good news" that Jesus' life, death, and resurrection allow humans to be reconciled with God and to escape from the burden of their sins (Romans 5:10, New International Version). In addition to sharing these beliefs with the larger Christian faith community, Evangelical Christians emphasize a number of unique convictions.

Bebbington (1989) suggests that Evangelical faith can be defined by the presence of four core beliefs: *activism, Biblicism, conversionism,* and *crucicentrism. Activism* is activity focused on telling the story and promulgating the Christian faith. Evangelical Christians place a high value on "witnessing" or "testifying" to their faith in hopes of converting others. Although such activity may seem presumptuous or judgmental to others, Evangelical Christians view such "evangelism" as the sharing of their most prized possession, the "good news" of their faith. *Biblicism* reflects regard for the Bible as the divinely inspired, irrefutable word of God. While there is debate within the Evangelical community regarding how properly to utilize and understand the Bible, most groups agree that the Bible should be considered a guide for life and religious practices. Some groups require a literal adherence to all aspects of the Bible, while others tolerate a considerable amount of nuance and ambiguity in terms of Biblical interpretation (Olsen 2004).

Conversionism refers to the importance that Evangelical groups ascribe to having a conversion experience (Bebbington 1989). Christians may refer to such a conversion experience as being "born again" or "saved." *Crucicentrism* refers to the centrality of the crucifixion of Jesus of Nazareth to Evangelical Christian theology. Again, there are varying views among Evangelical Christians regarding the crucifixion, but in general there is common agreement that Jesus' crucifixion frees humans from the bondage of sin and restores a relationship to God (Eddy and Beilby 2006). Some scholars utilize additional elements to define Evangelical Christian belief. McGrath (1995) emphasizes "controlling convictions," including "[t]he majesty of Jesus Christ," "[t]he lordship of the Holy Spirit," and "[t]he importance of the Christian community" (pp. 55–56). Olsen (2008) adds assent to traditional Christian doctrine (i.e., the nearly universal beliefs of the larger Christian community).

Intra-group Diversity

Relational clinicians' effectiveness relies upon a deep and nuanced understanding of diversity, including relational dynamics, within all groups. There are specific diversities among Evangelical Christians (Olsen 2004). For example, Evangelicals differ widely in terms of sacraments, such as baptism and communion, and eschatology, or beliefs about the end of time/history (Olsen 2004). There also is political diversity. Chaves (2011) reports that while a majority and dramatically increasing percentage of Evangelical Christians are politically conservative, there remains a noteworthy "Christian left." The intentionally multiracial *Sojourners* community makes the case that Christians should promote social justice and environmental care (Swartz 2012). The political views of Evangelical Christians may be complicated by a sense that faith transcends party affiliation and eschews voting or other political activity. Alternatively, they may be extremely conservative on some social issues (such as abortion), while liberal or progressive on other issues (such as health-care reform). It cannot be assumed, therefore, that Evangelical Christians are homogenous. Nonetheless, they do share the primacy of faith as a determinant of their thinking and behavior.

Constructivist Relational Practice with a Positivist Client

For the relational clinician, the essential understanding is the individual's submission to a religious doctrine that prescribes beliefs, secure attachment through membership, and the path to ultimate salvation. This positivism is at odds with the constructivism of relational theory. The fusion of self and religious convictions, even if those convictions are explicated differently in subgroups, establishes the Evangelical Christian client as a particular challenge to cultural competence in relational social work. Not as definitely self-identified as a marginalized United States population as Orthodox Jews or Muslims, for instance, Evangelical Christians may find reflection on their religious beliefs less evident as aspects of clinical treatment. While no social worker would consider reflection on any religious beliefs in the sense of questioning them, the exploratory nature of relational practice requires special attunement with clients for whom exploration itself is religiously threatening.

How can the clinician establish accepted empathy, authenticity, mutual goal setting, co-construction of meaning, and the like to become interpersonally valuable to her client when a lack of confirmation of the client's religious convictions places her among the unsaved? How can the clinician work with the entanglement of religious beliefs and personal problems (illustrated in the case study) while supporting convictions that are irreducible? This dilemma is a striking example of relational social work with diverse populations altogether: shared and unshared realities must meet in an interpersonal relationship. With religious diversities and especially a religious belief system striving for conversion of the nonbeliever, the shared and unshared aspects take on implications that call for exceptional empathic attunement, and willingness to not know and be educated, at every step. Personal conflicts and suffering are universal; the relational model reaches for the healing power of interpersonal connection (Baker Miller 2012; Bromberg 1998; Greenberg and Mitchell 1983) without falling into ideational power struggles? Evangelical clients' struggles with their personal conflicts and doubts can be understood by the relational clinician as part of their pursuit of greater connection, with their faith or with the relational social work process. In the article "Jesus and Object-Use: A Winnicottian Account of the Resurrection Myth," Hopkins (1989) states that "believers can acknowledge their own destructiveness while at the same time enabling them to live life more fully in 'a world of objects…a world of shared reality.' The sacrament of the Eucharist is seen as partly reenacting this process" (p. 93).

Clinical Issues in the Relational Social Work Process with Evangelicals

Evangelicals seek relational social work services for essentially the same reasons as others, but there also are a number of presenting problems that are unique to Evangelicals and may manifest in unique ways. After describing the unique formulations of the problem definition, the remainder of the chapter will utilize a relational theory perspective to suggest ways that relational clinicians can address these presenting problems in their work with Evangelical Christian clients.

Unique Presenting Problems

Religiously based denial and resistance. Evangelical faith can sometimes serve to undergird relationally challenging defenses of denial and resistance among Evangelical clients. This is especially true when the client, or the clinician, does not connect her/his faith to the treatment process. In such cases, individual clients may believe they are immune to certain types of problems because of their faith or they may resist involvement with a relational clinician if that worker is not coming from an overtly Biblical perspective. For the clinician, recognition of denial and resistance stemming from religious conviction can expand the perspective on transference and countertransference. The relational practitioner perceives the parameters of establishing a mutually determined and strength-enhancing course of treatment requiring a "space" where their goals can be sufficiently aligned to have a dialogue. This requires the clinician to search for, and inquire about, a form of interpersonal joining that may take the clinician far into not knowing.

Stoltzfus (2006) reported working with an Evangelical client who, while on parole and court-mandated to attend substance abuse counseling, informed his therapist that he had injected heroin but that due to the power of God, the drug no longer had any effect on him. The client believed his faith eliminated the impact of his continued chemical dependency, and therefore, there was no sense that the relational clinician could offer help. Using the Bible, the relational clinician should explore the consistencies of pursuing faith in God with the truth-seeking process of psychotherapy (i.e., 2 Timothy 3:16; 2 Peter 1:21, NIV). For the less Biblically informed clinician, the process might be how to affirm the client's comfort in his interpretation of truth yet authentically question how the clinician should make sense of it in the face of legal processes that require other truths. Pointing to this disjuncture can open the dialogue to personal consequences and feelings they engender. The relational principle of mutual definition of the problem thereby shifts the focus from substance abuse per se to his life situation, about which the relational clinician is concerned.

Decision paralysis. Many Evangelical faith communities believe that God has a preordained plan for the lives of individuals, and instruct their members to attempt to discern God's will for their lives, especially prior to making major life decisions. For some individuals, such injunctions may be extremely troubling, as they may not have a sense of God's will. Such individuals may find themselves "paralyzed" and unable to make decisions, due to their fear that they may be acting outside the will of God. The relational clinician should work to ensure that relational exploration is seen as an acceptable aid to the discovery of a sense of God's will. The collaborative goal is the client's resolution of conflict. The clinician cannot resolve this by authority about God's will but can collaborate with the client in her search clarity. The relational clinician's role in this search is to broaden the parameters, including intrapsychic as well as interpersonal experiences that have added to paralysis.

Duality. Psychodynamic and relational perspectives provide a way to understand and address how Evangelicals sometimes embrace a dualistic view of human life and functioning that places a unique filter on the issues that relational clinicians deal with on a daily basis (Aron 1996; Freud 1977; Narramore 1994). Within the Evangelical view, spiritual needs are prioritized as eternal concerns, but temporal concerns (such as health, relationships, and mental health) are de-emphasized because such concerns belong only to the present, earthly life. Such belief systems can lead to the neglect of medical care, nutrition, mental health, and personal relationships, to the detriment of the overall functioning of the individual. Evangelical clients may also believe that their faith should lead to mental and physical health. This belief that requires careful navigation by the relational clinician so as to avoid conflict and support a process of mutual searching for health through inquiry about understanding health deficits of the moment and affirming the collaborative search as religiously congruent. In other words, the relational practice emphasis on process does not have to run aground about content; the healing impact of interpersonal joining and authentic acceptance of unique individual versions of a solution reduces duality as a state.

It could also be asserted that Evangelicals may feel safer keeping their problems between them and God rather than exposing themselves to the vulnerability of an open relationship with another person. It is therefore a complex process to determine when there are psychodynamic issues such as unconscious use of defense mechanisms that prevent the client from addressing disturbances (Freud 1977). For example, resistance in the form of denial, repression, and projection leads to decisional paralysis and neglect of physical health for all clients. Practice based in relational theory is a powerful way to address these issues (Aron 1996). Given the confluence of religious and psychodynamic processes, the informed relational clinician is mindfully open to the specific practice processes accessible to this population. The remainder of this chapter will utilize relational theory to suggest ways in which relational clinicians can be of assistance to Evangelical Christian clients.

The Relational Clinician-Client Relationship

Of the many factors that may affect the social worker-client relationship during the course of clinical work with Evangelical Christians, some issues are more likely to arise when non-Evangelical social workers provide services to Evangelical clients. A different set of issues is likely to occur when Evangelical social workers practice with Evangelical clients. These differences are illuminated as the relational clinician learns to apply relational solutions to Evangelical Christian client issues. A core concept from relational theory that applies overall comes from Winnicott's (1971) explanation of the necessity of the object (the mother/the clinician) to withstand destructiveness in order to become "useful." By "useful," Winnicott means trustworthy and of value. The Evangelical client's resistance to and even repudiation of clinical intervention can be seen, in this light, as necessary to this nonreligious process of engagement becoming useful.

Non-Evangelical relational clinician-Evangelical client. Research suggests that social workers are least likely to self-identify as Christian than the general United States population and most likely to self-identify as atheist or agnostic (Canda and Furman 1999). Jewish, Muslim, Hindu, and other faith traditions also populate the relational social work profession. This means there is a high potential for Evangelical clients to be treated by relational clinicians who are unfamiliar with, and perhaps inwardly skeptical of, their belief systems. Even if the relational clinician and client share other aspects of cultural backgrounds (e.g., racial, ethnic, geographic, and socioeconomic identities), Evangelical clients may distrust the secular social work profession and any intervention that is not based in their own belief system. Some conservative Evangelical groups are opposed to any counseling or therapy that is not based solely and explicitly on the Bible (Johnson 2010). Other groups may prefer to utilize "Christian counseling" conducted by individuals who are trained both in pastoral ministry and psychotherapeutic techniques, rather than secular social work services. At the same time, circumstances may necessitate service despite religious beliefs. The relational clinician therefore must be prepared to work effectively with all clients, including those who are resistant based on distrust due to religious difference.

Political views also are likely to differ between the relational clinician and Evangelical client (Rosenwald and Hyde 2006), as relational clinicians are more likely to be politically liberal or progressive and Evangelical Christians are more likely to be politically conservative (Chaves 2011). The *Code of Ethics of the National Association of Social Workers* (National Association of Social Workers 1999) states that social workers should always be respectful of differing cultural and political views. Rosenwald and Hyde (2006) reported positive findings about social workers' ability to be respectful of differing views. Respect, however, is a term that may or may not accompany interpersonal distance, which is contrary to the relational practice stance. The relational clinician must be aware of these potential issues in the transference and countertransference but even more must invoke her "belief" in the apolitical and a-religious clinical process as a professional obligation and a professional solution.

For example, errors of assumption are a consistent subject for the practitioner to bear in mind, irrespective of identified sameness and differences with the client. The relational clinician is attuned to errors she may make by empathic assessment of the interpersonal process. This assessment is continuous, applying not only to problem definition but to how practice is unfolding. The authenticity principle allows the relational clinician to inquire about or observe, at any time, a disjuncture between herself and her client. The openness of her intent to cocreate meaning, not impose or falsely agree, may be slow to penetrate suspicion and may not always succeed. The relational stance is inherently respectful but also inquiring; patience for the invitation to inquire is maintained by sincere interest and willingness to not know or even to understand rejection as a statement of the client's need for self-preservation.

Despite the likelihood of divergent religious and political views, it is possible for non-Evangelical relational clinicians to work effectively with Evangelical Christian clients. The relational clinician must be able to empathically understand and explore belief systems that may be radically different from their own. Exploration may easily become challenging if the relational clinician encounters an ideology that she finds to be offensive or incomprehensible according to her own views. Evangelical clients may educate the relational clinician as no other diverse group can about the suspension of an a priori perspective on problem definitions, their components, and the order and timing of relational outreach to establish interpersonal connection. An emphasis on collaborating with the client in defining the presenting problem and developing the treatment plan, utilizing the relational principle of co-constructivism, will allow the relational clinician to enter the world of the client and to partner with him in problem resolution.

Evangelical relational clinician-Evangelical client. Relational clinicians who identify as Evangelical Christians may face a different set of issues when attempting to establish a therapeutic relationship with an Evangelical Christian client. Narramore (1994) describes a dilemma for Christian therapists wherein Evangelical therapists may have difficulty confronting manifestations of Evangelical faith that appear to have been unhealthily distorted or utilized as a means of resistance. For example, a client who is abused by a spouse may believe God is testing her and it is therefore God's will that she stay in the marriage. The dilemma occurs when Evangelical therapists must confront such possible distortions of faith with their clients, which can lead clients to question the faith and therefore the utility of the relational clinician. The relational theory principle of authenticity guides the clinician to present her hypotheses of a different interpretation of events as hers alone, not as official judgment. Her hypotheses are provisional, seeking confirmation, and, if rejected, seeking deeper clarification of her misunderstanding. This demonstration of nondefensive pursuit of collaborative structuring of viewpoint as well as intervention is in itself a relational therapy action: it clarifies the absence of an agenda of control or professional dominance.

The relational clinician may also struggle with feelings of guilt if her comments lead the client to confusion or questioning of faith. Building on the prior example of the abused spouse, the client begins to look at the relational clinician as a worldly tempter or, conversely, becomes distressed at the prospect of misinterpreting God's will. Such an encounter is potentially troubling to both parties and may interfere with the functioning of the therapeutic relationship. However, relational approaches to relational social work allow both the relational clinician and the client to explore their concerns via authentic, open dialogue. The construction of a safe, supportive relationship requires the occurrence and the survival of conflict (Winnicott 1971). The work of the relational practitioner, then, is to encourage exploration and non-hierarchical definitions of truth as a basis in all practice and a basis particularly useful in the complex intersection of religion and interpersonal and intrapsychic work.

Toward Mutuality

Tosone (2004) suggests that mutuality is a defining characteristic of relational social work. Building on the work of Aron (1996), Tosone further states that mutuality "implies that both parties are impacted by their interaction, but not necessarily in an equal or symmetrical way. Instead, mutuality reflects that the participants have been open to and touched by the authenticity and genuineness of another" (p. 484). Relational techniques such as active listening, open-ended questioning, and allowing the client to be the "expert" on his situation are concrete ways of promoting mutuality when working with Evangelical Christians.

Striving for an authentic, genuine, and mutual relationship, the relational clinician may begin to bridge the gap created by divergent religious and philosophical worldviews. Mutuality should be viewed as a respectful understanding and appreciation for the client's views and is especially important if the client's Evangelical faith is undergirding unhealthy emotional, relational, or behavioral patterns. In such cases, the therapeutic relationship must be strong enough to allow the relational practitioner to help the client confront unhealthy distortions of faith without losing the trust of the client. Such trust will be heightened if the relational clinician expresses an appreciative understanding of the client's faith while also exploring distortions that prevent growth. It is especially important for the skeptical clinician not to imply the client's faith is simplistic or anachronistic. This judgmental position violates the constructivist principles of relational therapy.

In order to work toward mutuality in therapeutic relationships with Evangelical Christian clients, it is important for relational clinicians not only to show respect for the belief systems of their clients but also to seek to understand how these beliefs influence the client's cognition, relationships, and behavior. Delving into the client's understanding of the four key Evangelical beliefs (activism, Biblicism, conversionism, and crucicentrism) may be helpful for clinicians who are attempting to understand the belief systems of their Evangelical clients. For example, asking about a client's view of the Bible or understanding of the crucifixion will show some familiarity with Evangelical faith and also convey a desire to better understand the client's situation. The relational clinician can also explore how these beliefs inform the client's issues.

Postmodernism and social constructionism. Relational clinicians who have been trained in postmodern social work practice models (such as constructivism) may struggle with the rigidity of Evangelical faith, which posits a connection to, and limited understanding of, absolute truth as divinely revealed. In fact, the postmodern impulse to deconstruct traditional narratives and critique traditional forms of authority may lead relational clinicians to instinctively feel critical of people who subscribe to traditional beliefs. In light of the apparent conflict between postmodernity and religious faith, it is important to remember that postmodern perspectives allow for multiple sources of authority and validate multiple perspectives simultaneously. In their openness to multiple, overlapping constructions of reality, postmodern social work practice models "leave room" for the belief systems of the client, even if these are significantly different from those of the clinician herself.

Postmodern perspectives have begun to influence Evangelical theology more recently, which may be helpful in clinical practice with Evangelical clients. One such development is the impact of narrative theology, which emphasizes the importance of understanding the Biblical narrative as a unified story, rather than focusing on rigid interpretation of short scriptural passages as rules for belief and behavior (Frei 1974). Another development is the emergent church, which seeks to understand the Christian faith story by incorporating many overlapping and contrasting understandings of Christian doctrine (McLaren 2004). The incursion of a more constructivist perspective may be helpful in working with some Evangelical Christians, especially those for whom extremely rigid understandings of faith have become problematic. For example, some Evangelical women have been reluctant to leave abusive spouses because of a rigid interpretation of Biblical injunctions against divorce. In such cases, a relational clinician can seek authorization to explore the underlying themes of the Biblical narrative, which are usually summarized in terms of God's love for humanity and God's desire for reconciliation and peace among the created order. Cocreation of meaning as a relational principle does not mean finding agreement; it means illuminating more aspects of a belief through dialogue to look at other options which were not "on the table" when the focus was on developing rules based on a few select Biblical passages.

Case Analysis and Discussion: Kelly

Kelly is a 29-year-old Caucasian woman who grew up the daughter of a minister at a nondenominational Evangelical Christian Church. (Such churches tend to interpret the Bible literally and believe it should be the ultimate authority for religious life and practice.) Kelly continues as a member of this church to present day. She states emphatically that her relationship with God is "everything" to her. Kelly demonstrates how Evangelical Christian clients will often present with the same types of issues we see in our non-Evangelical clients. Her case further illustrates that Evangelical Christianity, along with other religious belief systems, is not inherently exclusive from the kinds of thinking that inform psychotherapeutic practices of many schools such as relational theory. Though they will not be the focus of this analysis, approaches that bridge a perceived divide between the psychotherapeutic process and issues of faith, including Carl Jung's work on the collective unconscious and spirituality (Jung 1961) and the 12-step program as suggested by Alcoholics Anonymous (Alcoholics Anonymous 2001), draw widely on spirituality along with psychotherapeutic processes.

Kelly works as a bank teller, has four children, and is in her second marriage. Her reason for seeking treatment is that she is "completely overwhelmed and ashamed and cannot believe what I am doing to my husband and I just want to run away from it all." Kelly's church and family held strong beliefs regarding the sinfulness of extramarital sex. She became pregnant prior to each of her marriages, and marriage in both cases legitimized her behavior. She states she was a "model Christian" through high school but went through a "rebellious phase" when she went to college. She states, "I love the Lord, but when I got to college I fell in with some girls who were smoking pot and having sex. I was like their mom for a while until I was like, hey, I can have some fun, too!"

Kelly became pregnant the next semester, had a very hard time staying away from marijuana even during her pregnancy, dropped out of college, and married the father of her child. Divorced at 23, Kelly started seeing Eddie and was soon pregnant again. They married and had two more children shortly thereafter. She states that Eddie is a much better person than her first husband, but she is not sure she loves him: "There is just not much that is exciting and we do not have much to talk about." Kelly is anxious, depressed, and restless. The most current and acute issue is anxiety bordering on panic-type symptoms related to recent intimate contact with another man while at a conference for work. Here is part of that interview:

SW: So tell me about your current anxieties and what has you so overwhelmed?

Kelly: Well, you know I am an idiot. I have everything to live for, but I have days that I just can't stand it.

SW: What is it you cannot stand?

Kelly: Just the pressure, the life, you know, of being a mommy and a wife. It is so not me! And now I've really gone and messed up. I've had an inappropriate relationship with another man. We crossed some lines.

SW: You feel you are living the wrong kind of life and that now you have done something inappropriate?

Kelly: No! I am right where God wants me! It's me; it's not my life. I am just such a fool.

SW: You feel foolish.

Kelly: I am foolish.

SW: You are saying that you cannot stand the pressure of your life but that you feel God wants you right here. Is that right?

Kelly: Yeah, it's spiritual warfare. Satan is attacking me everywhere right now.

Kelly is struggling with ambivalence, feeling torn between being a good Christian and having natural desires for independence and excitement. The psychodynamic assessment suggests Kelly did not resolve adolescent conflicts related to identity and intimacy (Erikson and Erikson 1997), but Kelly's view is that sinfulness leads her into temptation. Since the relational clinician must establish mutual conceptualization, she must be oriented by the religious explanation and strive for co-construction of a more complex interplay of Kelly's individuality with her Evangelical convictions. Authenticity is demonstrated by not knowing and inquiry about how Kelly reconciles, or doesn't, these two states of self. The "not-me" restless sinner is dissociated from the "me" compliant believer, and the clinician's collaborative goal setting needs to demonstrate the value of bringing these states into communication. In the following section, the relational clinician draws on his relationship with Kelly to begin to challenge some potentially distorted aspects of her beliefs:

SW: Kelly, can you help me more clearly understand some of your concerns? I get the impression that you feel your relationship with God has not been strong enough, that you have not believed enough in God or you have not been good enough to receive God's blessings. And the choices you have made and regret are because of this?

Kelly: Well, that could be part of what is going on.

SW: Yes. But on the other hand you say that it will be God who delivers you from these problems.

Kelly: Yes! Without God, none of this is possible.

SW: Right, you count on God to provide you with what you need to get through this.

Kelly: Yeah, I really believe he would be able to give me what I need, if I could only really lean on him.

SW: I think I understand. You feel that you have just not been able to trust God
        enough.
Kelly: You don't think I am a freak and a failure?
SW: Absolutely not! On the contrary, you seem very bright and gifted.
Kelly: Well, that's nice to hear.
SW: But you are very disturbed with where you are now and you wish it could
        have been different.
Kelly: No kidding. If I had it all to do over again.
SW: Yes, what would that look like?
Kelly: Well, I would not have fallen into Satan's traps; that's for sure!
SW: So you would not want to have any of the experiences you had. They were
        all Satan's traps.
Kelly: Well, I mean. Here's the thing. I was looking forward to college. I wanted
        to get away. I needed to get away. My brother and sisters could just hang in
        there at home and church; they never seemed to want more or anything dif-
        ferent. It wasn't that I could not stand my family or being a Christian. I was
        just ready to see some new things and let my hair down and relax some.

This was a critical moment to engage with Kelly: she apparently had not been
able to tell this part of her story before. The relational clinician amplifies this
authentic disclosure to begin the co-construction of a space where her ambivalence
is acknowledged but remains within the religiously informed narrative of her
identification.

SW: Ok, so part of your plan was to get away from home and try some things
        you could not do at home. To go where there was not so much pressure?
Kelly: Well, I don't just mean go off and smoke pot and have sex. But to be some-
        where it would not matter so much if I did these things. At least I would
        have the choice. At least I wouldn't feel I was letting everyone down; it
        would be a normal thing to do in that situation.
SW: Sure, it was important for you to test the boundaries a bit, to make some
        decisions for yourself.
Kelly: Absolutely! I actually like that part of me. But here I am now.
SW: But here you are now.
Kelly: Yeah, things didn't go as planned. I was immediately punished.
SW: But I can see this great part of you that wants to get out and explore and try
        new things. That really is a part of your personality that you love and want
        to embrace. But you feel that you were punished the moment you tried
        anything different.
Kelly: Well, I don't really believe in a God who punishes me. But I guess I feel he
        did let me fall down right away. And disappointing my family was incred-
        ible punishment!
SW: Yes, these would be very disturbing and painful things, I imagine. You feel
        that you have been a disappointment. But you also feel that God and your
        family have let you down in some ways.
Kelly: Yes, that's it.

The relational clinician affirms the disparate parts of the client. Empathic inquiry creates an interpersonal space where conflicting self-aspects can converge. The relationship thereby becomes the active therapeutic action.

Kelly: Well, I must say that I am confused about why things had to go so wrong and I cannot say I have not questioned my faith…. Every second of every day (smiling).

SW: So ultimately, you feel as though you have let down many people and also feel that God, even though he loves you, has taken a pretty harsh position with you?

Kelly: Yeah, and I cannot do anything about that. I cannot recreate history.

SW: I suppose not. You speak of your love and trust of God but you also seem confused and even a bit hurt by what you see Him doing in your life.

Kelly: I would never question God's will, but yes, I am definitely confused.

SW: You would never question God's will, but if you thought of God like another person, what would you say?

Kelly: Gosh, I don't know. Kind of like, hey, where ya been? Was I really so bad? Sorry I disappointed you.

SW: In a way you wonder where He's been, but you are also sorry for things you've done.

Kelly: (tearful) It has been so hard. I am so tired. I think I have been more unfair with myself than He has.

SW: In what way?

Kelly: I guess I can't really expect God to go easy on me when I can't stop punishing myself.

Kelly had high hopes for herself and feels strongly that the way she values her faith should have kept her from making mistakes. The relational clinician may wonder if Kelly blocks her own path to resolution because her behavior is outside the bounds of her perception of acceptable behavior, but she focuses on God and her family expressing disappointment. Inquiry that accepts the content of her religious beliefs but addresses the affect state of confusion for an empathically attuned exploration process can reduce resistance to her own reflections as worthy content. Kelly wonders if she is also punishing herself. Posing this as an interesting question and inquiring about its foundation, the clinician opens the door to exploration about issues with the family, from which she learned how her religious beliefs should be expressed.

SW: So Kelly, can you tell me more about your relationships in your family?

Kelly: Well, my family is everything to me, but they are very disappointed I am sure. Now there is all of this weird tension. I don't know if it is them or me, but I know that I made things difficult.

SW: You love them deeply but are pretty sure they are not happy with you?

Kelly: Well, it's not that they are unhappy. They are always there for me, but there is a strange competition in my family, I mean with my brother and sisters.

SW: You feel they are there for you, but that you are in competition at the same time. So they are support and competition?

Kelly: Yes, you could say it that way. I never thought of it that way, but it's true.

SW: And what about your parents?

Kelly: Well, I know I am a huge disappointment to them! You should have heard some of the fights that my Mom and I had. But my Dad is like my siblings; he is there for me, but I sense he is none too happy with my choices.

SW: But wait a minute; here you are, living back in your hometown, going to church, married with children. Did these things not satisfy them? Was there pressure even before you and Eddie started having problems with your marriage?

Kelly: Oh yeah. The pressure is always there. It's hard to describe. And it's not just pressure from my family. Really, they are okay. But everything changes at church. My Dad is the pastor; I know he has a reputation to uphold. I just feel that I bring shame on them, that everyone sees me that way.

SW: Wow, that would be a lot of pressure indeed! You are simultaneously involved and helping in the church but also feeling that you are a source of… what? Embarrassment, shame?

Kelly: I don't know how embarrassed I am. I mean, if these people are going to judge me… believe me, I could tell some stories on them, too! But I love my church and I know they love me. But I could tell some stories.

Several important things are occurring at this juncture in the relational social work process. First, Kelly recognizes troubling themes of disappointment and competition. Second, she acknowledges that these are her perceptions. By following, rather than presenting, this line of thought, the relational clinician invites self-reflection. Finally, Kelly begins to normalize her behavior by acknowledging how common it is for her fellow church members to fall short of the high ideals of their faith. All of these indicate levels of socially constructed beliefs, which are explored in the following dialogue.

Kelly: Well, I am clearly the black sheep of the family.

SW: I am curious to know how someone becomes a black sheep; this has something to do with disappointment?

Kelly: Yeah, you just repeat mistakes and get down and after a while, people just expect you to fail.

SW: Is this you or your family that expects you to fail?

Kelly: In a way it's a self-fulfilling prophecy, I guess.

SW: And what of marriage?

Kelly: Oh, the Bible is very clear about marriage. One man, one woman, forever, that's the way it is meant to be.

SW: And most Christians get this right? They pick out a life partner, get married, and that is the end of the story?

Kelly: I highly doubt that. But I knew better than to make the mistake I did.

SW: Oh, so you say the Bible is clear, but you are confused?

Kelly: Huh, well, yes. Clearly I have been confused. I mean, I knew better, didn't I?

SW: Okay, I see. You have a clear definition and you have clearly not lived up to that definition.

Kelly: Right, I am way off of the path.

SW: You are off the path because of your recent behavior (intimate contact with another man)?

Kelly: I've been off track from the beginning! I haven't done any of this right. I keep getting it backwards.

SW: You got off track years ago and it has never been right since?

Kelly: Right, you make one bad choice and it is like you are stuck in those decisions forever!

SW: Okay, so this is something that you have to get right from the beginning or else it can never be right?

Kelly: Wait, what?

SW: I thought I understood you to say that since you did not do marriage correctly from the beginning, you could basically never get it right; somehow it was doomed from the start. Was I wrong about that?

Kelly: Well, no. Did I say that?

SW: I do not mean to put words in your mouth.

Kelly: No, I think that is exactly what I was saying. I cannot get right because it was never right to begin with.

SW: Well, is there anything in the teaching of the Bible about situations like that? Or does the Bible basically tell you to get it right from the beginning or else you will never have it right.

Kelly: I can't believe I am saying this. Of course not. The Bible is filled with stories of people who never got anything right and God's grace and power helped them transcend their problems. (Pause, smiling) But I doubt their dads were pastors!

This passage illustrates the presentation to the client of the clinician's understanding of what is being said. The dialogue extends the tolerance for ambivalence by keeping conflicting beliefs in view. For example, the clinician emphasizes relational issues alongside religious ones and self-criticism alongside the redemptive aspects of Christian faith. Inquiry about Biblical understandings can reveal multiple dimensions that build a more complex picture within which complex self-states can be contained. In this case, Kelly references Biblical passages on marriage (1 Colossians 7:2, NIV) and adultery (Ephesians 5:3, NIV) that mandate levels of morality and purity, but she does not refer to passages on grace and forgiveness (Roman 3:23–24, NIV). It is psychodynamically tempting to point out the convergence of her struggles against excessive expectations from father/pastor, but the more relationally attuned path is to keep the resolution focused on her individual religious beliefs and their flexibility compared to her own rigidity. The following discussion occurs after some time, during which social worker and client have concurred on the treatment goal of Kelly solving her confusion, rather than Kelly becoming a better Christian.

SW: So Kelly, you identified real differences between your definition of marriage and morality and what you have actually done in your life. You attribute this to the fact that you are human and prone to making mistakes. You view this as part of your sinful nature?

Kelly: Yes, I am so short-sighted as a human being and cannot see the forest through the trees.

SW: So where do you go from here?

Kelly: I can see how a lot of my pain comes from my own definitions. I am sure there is some truth to God's disapproval and my family's disappointment. But honestly, I have just not been able to let God or my family in. Maybe this was my pride, but I did not want all of my defects to be on display. I just could not stand that.

SW: Sure, nobody wants to feel like they have disappointed everyone. But what is it that makes it so difficult to open yourself to God's or your family's understanding?

Kelly: Like I said, I guess it is my pride. But I think it is also that my definitions of a Christian life were just much more simple and constricting and it is time to open my mind to a broader and more accurate viewpoint. But I think it is also that I have not seen much value in forgiveness when it doesn't change my circumstances.

SW: You felt that if you are going to be forced to live with your mistakes, what good is forgiveness, from God, your family, or you?

Kelly: Yeah, nothing can give me a fresh start. But now I see how that puts me in an impossible situation. No wonder I am such a mess!

SW: You are seeing how you subconsciously developed expectations that could never be met. And how will these definitions change moving forward?

Kelly: Well, I have to realize first and foremost that I have all of the love and support I will ever need. I also need a constant reminder that I am just like anyone else. I get to make mistakes, too. And all of this new understanding is consistent with what I have learned in church. I just never realized how much I would need love and understanding or how hard it would be to accept that.

This case illustrates the utility of a relational approach to relational social work practice with Evangelical Christian clients: Kelly and her clinician established an exploratory dialogue marked by trust and mutuality. The relational clinician uses Kelly's spiritual and ontological frameworks without pathologizing her belief systems. Kelly begins to assert that her original views of herself and behavior require modification, but not the impossible rejection of her Evangelical values. She seems interested in developing new constructions that will accommodate imperfection and an ability to allow others to love and support her in spite of her mistakes. She also seems to recognize there may even be things to value about her experiences in terms of deepening her self-worth and her sense of faith.

Practice recommendations that emerge from this illustration include the development of the authentic and genuine relationship, an intentional openness to client's beliefs, utilization of established literature on the integration of faith and practice, and a continued effort to help the client to see the consistencies between therapeutic help and their faith (Freedberg 2008). In Kelly's case, we see the social worker and client stumble a few times in developing shared understanding. This vital part of relationship building fosters growth that encompasses ruptures.

If the relational clinician in fact does not share the religious beliefs of the client, she can validate, by an open and inquisitive demeanor, how Kelly can help her better understand; removing the pressure to get it right the first time, as the case demonstrated, empowers the client's sense of personal authority and valuable resources. Diversity does pose risks of transference and countertransference oversimplification. Although the relational clinician may not oppose, disrespect, or discriminate against the client, differences can subtly influence interactions with clients. The relational model of relational social work practice is steeped in empathic attunement, not only to the client but also to the nuances of interpersonal alignment in the treatment process.

Important developments are bringing the secular psychotherapeutic domain together with faith-related issues. The North American Association of Christians in Social Work (NACSW 2011) is working to equip Christians in social work to ethically integrate their faith and practice and may be helpful by providing written material and/or individual consultation related to understanding and treating Evangelical Christian clients. Also, Evangelical colleges and universities are increasingly adding academic programs in social work, counseling, and psychology and are accredited by secular agencies, such as the Council on Social Work Education. Such developments speak to a healthy discourse on blending social work and faith-related issues. They also encourage the relational clinician to place herself in the process of inquiry, mutuality, cocreation of understanding, and professional enhancement as a parallel to treatment goals.

Conclusion

This chapter illustrates important ground in considering how to practice with Evangelical Christian clients from a relational theoretical perspective. Definitions and meanings of terms like *evangelical* were explored with discussion of how meaning has evolved in our culture. Bebbington (1989) provided a framework for a deeper understanding of the client's Evangelical background. Clinical issues, including problem presentation and relationship building, were also explored. Next, a case analysis based on Kelly demonstrated how a relational clinician could apply relational theory, emphasizing relatedness, strengths perspective, and social construction of meaning. Focusing on relational aspects and social constructions of meaning, the relational clinician built on the client's understanding rather than tearing it down and starting over. Kelly described both a sense of great love and commitment to God as well as feelings of restriction and harsh judgment. Before seeking help, Kelly was unaware of these beliefs, yet they caused significant emotional disturbance. These discussions and analyses yielded recommendations for the relational clinician to foster an authentic relationship, learn from the client, bridge the gap between social work practice and Evangelical beliefs, and carefully explore her own beliefs in order to manage countertransference.

Study Questions

1. Give a brief overview of the definition of "Evangelical Christian." What are some of the variations that make defining this term complex?
2. How do the areas of diversity within the Evangelical group impact practice?
3. Give a specific example of how a relational clinician would avoid assumptions about religious beliefs regarding a problem area introduced by the client.
4. What are the strengths you can identify in the Evangelical Christian group? (What are the strengths you can identify within the Evangelical Christian group? How would a relational clinician emphasize and utilize those strengths to inform their practice?
5. Give an example of a constructed view that Evangelical Christians might have. What are some of the challenges a relational clinician may have when it comes to understanding and working with a client with this view?
6. How might social and political differences influence the relationship between the social worker and the client? Focus specifically on the differences in values that are tied to these ideas.

References

Alcoholics, A. (2001). *Alcoholics Anonymous* (Vol. 4). New York: Alcoholics Anonymous World Services.

Aron, L. (1996). *A meeting of minds: Mutuality in psychoanalysis*. Hillsdale: The Analytic Press.

Bader, C., Dougherty, K., Froese, P., Johnson, B., Mencken, F. C., Park, J., & Stark, R. (2006). *American piety in the 21st century: New insights to the depth and complexity of religion in the US: Selected findings from The Baylor Religion Survey*. Waco: Baylor Institute for Studies of Religion. Retrieved from http://www.baylor.edu/content/services/document.php/33304.pdf

Baker Miller, J. (2012). *Five good things. Jean Baker Miller Training Institute at the Wellesley Centers for Women*. New Hampshire: Wellesley.

Bebbington, D. W. (1989). *Evangelicalism in modern Britain: A history from the 1730's to the 1980's*. London: Unwin Hyman.

Bromberg, P. M. (1998). *Standing in the spaces: Essays on clinical process, trauma, and dissociation*. Hillsdale: Analytic Press.

Canda, E. R., & Furman, L. D. (1999). *Spiritual diversity in social work practice: The heart of helping*. New York: The Free Press.

Chaves, M. (2011). Religious trends in America. *Social Work and Christianity, 38*, 119–132.

Eddy, P. R., & Beilby, J. (2006). The atonement: An introduction. In P. R. Eddy & J. Beilby (Eds.), *The nature of the atonement: Four views* (pp. 9–21). Downers Grove: IVP Academic.

Erikson, E. H., & Erikson, J. M. (1997). *The life cycle completed*. New York: W. W. Norton.

Freedberg, S. (2008). *Relational theory for social work practice: A feminist perspective*. London: Routledge.

Frei, H. W. (1974). *The eclipse of the Biblical narrative: A study in eighteenth and nineteenth century hermeneutics*. New Haven: Yale University Press.

Freud, A. (1977). *The writings of Anna Freud, Volume II, 1936: The ego and mechanisms of defense* (Rev. ed.). Madison: International Universities Press.

Greenberg, J., & Mitchell, S. A. (1983). *Object relations in psychoanalytic theory*. Cambridge: Harvard University Press.

Hopkins, B. (1989). Jesus and object-use: A Winnicottian account of the resurrection myth. *International Review of Psycho-Analysis, 16*, 93–100.

Johnson, E. L. (2010). A brief history of Christians in psychology. In E. L. Johnson (Ed.), *Psychology and Christianity: Five views* (pp. 9–47). Downers Grove: IVP Academic.

Jung, C. G. (1961). *Memories, dreams, reflections*. New York: Random House.

McGrath, A. (1995). *Evangelicalism and the future of Christianity*. Downers Grove: IVP Academic.

McLaren, B. (2004). *A generous orthodoxy: Why I am a missional, evangelical, post/protestant, liberal/conservative, mystical/poetic, Biblical, charismatic/contemplative, fundamentalist/calvinist, anabaptist/anglican, methodist, catholic, green, incarnational, depressed-yet-hopeful, emergent, unfinished Christian*. Grand Rapids: Zondervan.

Narramore, B. (1994). Dealing with religious resistances in psychotherapy. *Journal of Psychology and Theology, 22*(4), 249–258.

National Association of Social Workers. (1999). *The code of ethics of the National Association of Social Workers*. Washington: NASW Press.

North American Association of Christians in Social Work (2011). Retrieved Aug 1, 2011, from http://www.nacsw.org/index.shtml

Olsen, R. E. (2004). *The Westminster handbook to Evangelical theology*. Louisville: Westminster John Knox Press.

Olsen, R. E. (2008). *How to be Evangelical without being conservative*. Grand Rapids: Zondervan.

Rosenwald, M., & Hyde, C. A. (2006). Political ideologies of social workers: An under explored dimension of practice. *Advances in Social Work, 7*(2), 12–22.

Stoltzfus, K. M. (2006). An elephant in the sanctuary: Denial and resistance in addicted Christians and their churches. *Social Work and Christianity, 33*, 141–163.

Swartz, D. R. (2012). *Moral minority: the evangelical left in an age of conservatism (politics and culture in modern America)*. Philadelphia, PA: University of Pennsylvania Press.

Tosone, C. (2004). Relational social work: Honoring the tradition. *Smith College Studies in Social Work, 74*(3), 475–487.

Winnicott, D. (1971). The use of an object and relating through identifications. In *Playing and reality* (pp. 86–94). London: Tavistock.

Clinical Social Work Practice with Muslim Clients: A Relational Approach

Cheryl El-Amin and Aneesah Nadir

Introduction

Engaging the Muslim client is dependent on active use of the relational principles of creating mutuality in the interaction, affirmation of the strengths within the Islamic worldview for the client, inquiry and not knowing to arrive at a shared understanding of the meaningful elements of the client's problems and perspective, and collaboration in the course of treatment. Religiously prescriptive faiths, especially when the prescribed religious practices are associated in the wider society with an alien and perhaps, for Muslims today, threatening identity, invariably pose challenges in the transference and countertransference: a clinical process that entails exploration, however benignly introduced, requires all the skills of relational therapy in creating a contract for clinical social work. The client would not be present if significant problems were not prompting or requiring clinical social work intervention. Circumstances bring Muslim clients to clinical attention, often on a mandatory basis, which may already be tainted by conflict with Western social standards. The clinical social work orientation, as opposed to concrete services on demand, can be experienced as hostile. The nonauthoritarian, interpersonal-validation emphases

C. El-Amin, Ph.D. LMSW (✉)
Islamic Social Services Association - USA, Tempe, AZ, USA

Detroit Public Schools Social Worker, Detroit, MI, USA
e-mail: cze46@hotmail.com

A. Nadir, Ph.D. MSW
Islamic Social Services Association - USA, Tempe, AZ, USA

Retired Professor-Arizona State University, Phoenix, AZ, USA
e-mail: draneesah@hotmail.com

J.B. Rosenberger (ed.), *Relational Social Work Practice with Diverse Populations*,
Essential Clinical Social Work Series, DOI 10.1007/978-1-4614-6681-9_11,
© Springer Science+Business Media New York 2014

of relational clinical practice therefore stand the best chance of engaging the Muslim client in problem solving.

In relational theory, diversity is considered a given in any two-person encounter, and the principles of the theory are specifically directed to broadening the scope of clinical social work practice to eradicate theory-induced obstacles (Tosone 2004; Berzoff 2011). Minimization of distance-creating distinctions based on clients' cultural incongruence with insight-focused or blank screen models was not the well spring of relational theory (Greenberg and Mitchell 1983), but is a natural application of the shift from content analysis to interpersonal process as the therapeutic action. The social work clinician's personal identity, level of training and experience, and humility to not know even with apparently similar client populations are all pivotal in engagement and the ongoing phases of the treatment process. Certainly, clients' worldviews, beliefs, and traditions impact their level of comfort within the clinical social work relationship. These characteristics also affect decision-making, self-disclosure, incorporation of relevant of members of the client's support system, and construction of the problem at hand. The relational practitioner is attuned not only to the client's intrapsychic state but to the salience of cultural identity or religious tradition. While this is always necessary, it is especially the case when establishing a therapeutic relationship with the marginalized and even demonized population of American Muslims.

Islamophobia and Relational Social Work Practice

Ten years after the tragedy of September 11, 2001, Muslim Americans continue to be among the most misunderstood community in American society. They are significantly represented in hate crime statistics (CAIR 2011). Islamophobia is a term referencing an unfounded fear of Muslims and Islam (Hopkins and Kahani-Hopkins 2006) which, like all phobias, evokes exaggerated anxiety about exposure or anticipated contact to a the phobic object or situation (American Psychiatric Association 2000). Panagopoulos (2006) observed irony in the fact that the same persons claiming to fear Islam and Muslims admitted to having little or no knowledge about either. Social workers and other helping professionals have not been immune to popular negative stereotypes of Muslims, and most have had little experience or training to prepare them for their work with the growing Muslim community in the United States (Hodge 2005). Recent searches of academic databases (ProQuest, Academic Search Premier) using key words *Muslim/Islam* and *social work* brought up links to *terrorism* (El-Amin 2009). Clinical social work practice, with its emphasis on the individual, needs to be especially attuned to collective transference and countertransference, including unconscious stereotypes, because the clinical presentation of Muslim clients typically does not reveal sociopolitical concerns. This in fact may demonstrate the degree of uncertainty or suspicion Muslim clients feel in an intimate process with a Westerner. Muslims in need of mental health services may be reluctant not only to seek services but to express fears and complications in their lives created by Islamophobia (Abu-Ras et al. 2008). Unfortunately, this reluctance parallels a significant amount of perceived abuse and discrimination and an increase in psychological and physical distress within Muslim and Arab American families and communities post 9/11 (Padela and Heisler 2010; Rippy and Newman 2006).

This chapter provides the student practitioner with background information about the beliefs and traditions of Muslims and guidance on effective clinical social work practice with this population. The information and discussion also may be valuable to advanced practitioners without experience in relational practice especially with Muslim clients. The authors paint a picture for the practitioner of the socio/historic context in which American Muslims live. Discussion about the intergroup diversity of the community, as well as the intrapersonal diversity of each American Muslim, will facilitate practitioners' broader understanding of their Muslim client, the client family, and their representative community. The case of Ali and Sandra, and Sandra's daughter, Sarah, provides an understanding of the relational therapeutic experience of a clinical practitioner in her work with an Muslim family and how challenges can be negotiated in the helping relationship.

Muslim Clients: Orientation for the Relational Social Worker

Literature on social work with Muslims has expanded over the past 10 years (Graham et al. 2010; Hodge 2005; Hodge and Nadir 2008; Nadir 2003), but in general little content on Islam is included in social work education (Canda and Furman 1999; Hodge and Nadir 2008). Clinical practice guidance in particular has been lacking. Most of what practitioners *do* know is based on media stereotypes of Islam and Muslims. As relational clinical practitioners, it is important to become familiar with the worldview of the Muslim client in order to understand the role the client's faith plays in his or her life, as well as in the resolution of the challenges he or she may be facing (Graham et al. 2010).

Islamic Beliefs and Practices

Islam is the third of the three Abrahamic traditions, along with Christianity and Judaism. The language of Islam is Arabic; it was introduced to the people of Arabia 1,400 years ago. A monotheistic religion, the faith is based on the core tenet of *Tawheed,* the belief in Allah (Arabic word for God). Muslims believe in Angels; the Prophets and Messengers of God including Abraham, Moses, Jesus, and Muhammad; and in the revealed scriptures, including the Psalms of David, the Gospel of Jesus, the Torah of Moses, and the Qur'an. The Islamic worldview also includes the belief in Divine Destiny (everything is predetermined by God), in the Hereafter (life after death), and the Day of Judgment (Nadir and Dziegielewski 2001). Social justice, equity, and compassion are core Islamic values (Armstrong 2000). The primary sources of Islamic values and teachings are the Qur'an, the Holy Scripture of Islam, and the Hadith, the compilation of the traditions of the Prophet Muhammad (Hodge and Nadir 2008).

The social work clinician will discover, or know, that her clients are guided by obligatory duties and regular practices known as the Five Pillars of Islam. These include affirmation that there is one God and Muhammad is His messenger; the performance of ritual prayers five times a day; obligatory charity (giving of 2.5 % of assets annually after expenses and debts have been paid); the annual fasting from food, water and other drink, and sex during the Islamic calendar month of Ramadan; and the Hajj (pilgrimage to Mecca) (Nadir and Dziegielewski 2001; Hodge and Nadir 2008). Specific circumstances may vary a Muslim client's practices of these beliefs, so the clinical social worker needs to discover how they structure the individual's life. The relational principles of empathic communication and co-construction of acceptable and meaningful definitions of core problems and plans for intervention require this knowledge if their interaction is going to be collaborative. Errors in interpretation of each other's intentions and parameters of solution finding can derail the most well-motivated client or clinician if a priori assumptions and interpersonal templates develop interpersonal field. This goes beyond transference and countertransference, which of course are rampant given the portrayal of Muslims to Western models and vice versa (Abu-Ras et al. 2008). The content of diversity is to be shared as material with which the relational interconnection process is built. One of the "cracks" which Berzoff (2011) identifies in *Falling through the Cracks* is hasty problem definition and treatment planning that does not reflect mutuality as the foundation of relational practice. The relational practitioner is alert to the centrality of co-constructed understandings through empathic attunement to the nuances, often unannounced and requiring inquiry, of Islamic perspective as she strives for interpersonal congruence. Contrary to the concept of working alliance as articulated in earlier psychodynamic theories (Greenson 1967), the interpersonal approach of relational social work clinician does not independently assess the client's capacity for self-reflection, but rather seeks to engender it through her close listening, checking for clarification, and willingness to not know and be informed (Tosone 2004; Brandell 2004; Greenberg and Mitchell 1983).

Social Etiquette Considerations in Practice with Muslims

While the key relational theory feature of mutuality may imply parity, in fact it falls to the clinical social worker to set aside preconceptions and demonstrate the desire to comprehend the client's perspective. As Baker Miller (2012) describes, this sets the stage for experiential learning (Bromberg 2011) that stimulates motivation to engage, change, and feel valued. This posture also leads the clinician, through her own experiential learning, to observe the etiquette of formality, appropriate physical distance, gender roles, and other protocols of Muslim culture.

Gender. Professional accommodation may be required in the Islamic tradition of not having an unrelated male or female alone with the opposite gender. Clients may be accommodated by allowing a close friend or family member into the session, or by having an assistant practitioner be present. While including others may raise clinician's concerns about confidentiality, the Muslim client's faith-based imperative of gender etiquette may make this accommodation necessary at least at the start. The relational clinician can note that this is done in recognition of the client's religious requirements, thus demonstrating her willingness to co-create a viable treatment arrangement as well as her attunement to client needs.

Greetings. A common and familiar greeting for Muslims is "AsSalaamuAlaikum", which means "may God's peace be with you." Extending this greeting or an abbreviated version of "salaam" (peace) may be an icebreaker between the practitioner and client. The handshake or direct eye contact customary in Western society may engender distress and distance. The authenticity of relational practice does not suggest the clinician pretend to knowledge she does not have, but taking cues from the client and some knowledge of simple courtesies go a long way toward showing willingness to try to meet the client where he is. Lowered gaze between opposite genders is a sign of respect for both self and others in Muslim tradition (Nadir and El-Amin 2012). The relational model's encouragement of alertness to the many signals and formative power embedded in simple greetings are worthy of careful forethought on the threshold of assessment.

Physical Distance. As noted regarding handshaking and lowered gaze, the theme of Muslim etiquette is deference and not presuming intimacy. Adapting Bromberg's (1996) *Standing in the Spaces,* the actual physical space becomes a matter of negotiation with Muslim clients showing the social work clinician's readiness for co-creation of meaning and mutuality in a concrete form.

Home-Based Practice Etiquette. Student practitioners providing home-based social services should be aware of the Muslim practice of removing shoes before entering the home; its meaning is to prevent impurities and keep the designated prayer space clean. Anticipating this preference, the clinician can inquire and even bring shoe covers to the home visit (Nadir and El-Amin 2012). Hospitality in Islamic tradition requires anyone to be treated as a guest in the home and be offered food or other refreshment. The relational clinician, seeking an authentic relationship, cannot differentiate herself as a professional from this basic etiquette. Some believe it is shameful for a Muslim to omit the offer, despite any financial hardship, and if the offer is refused, a rupture in engagement is likely to result (Nadir and El-Amin 2012). The relational clinician should discuss this potential mishap, if it goes against agency policy or there are other barriers, and communicate the issues with her Muslim client in advance. This clarifies thoughtfulness about the client's needs, and the clinician's parameters, without inviting awkwardness or offense.

A Continuum of Religiosity

While Muslims follow the tenets of Islam to varying degrees, the relational clinician should assume an adherence to the fundamental principles of the five pillars of Islam (Graham et al. 2010). Religious identity and expression will be dictated by level of practice. Fundamentalist Muslims are concerned with how their actions will be judged by God in the Hereafter as an immutable boundary of conduct. The Qur'an, prayer, respected community members, the Imam, or a Muslim professional is more likely to be consulted than a social work clinician in help seeking (Abu-Ras and Abu-Bader 2008; Ahmed 2012). Khan (2006) noted a preferred strategy of prayer as a means of coping for Muslims. Therefore, the social work clinician is most apt to see these strongly practicing Muslims only in mandated conditions.

Muslims who identify themselves as nonreligious, having a primarily secular worldview based on cultural nonreligious values, cannot be assumed to dismiss core beliefs that shape acceptable and unacceptable behaviors. This group would be the more likely clients of clinical services but still bear the stamp of culturally traditional modes of interacting. The social work practitioner may be presented with a family whose parents are very religious, strongly practicing, while the youth or young adults of the same family seem nonreligious (El-Amin Naeem 2008). Conversely, it might be noted that the youth in a family devoutly practice, while their parents' practice is marginal (Nadir and Dziegielewski 2001). In any of these cases, the following considerations may come into play in the relational social work process:

1. Rule for interaction with persons of opposite gender.
2. Scheduling of appointments to observe religious holidays and prayer.
3. Dietary laws affecting sharing of food at the agency or home.
4. Restrictions on playing music, viewing movies, television, etc. The agency or office setting must not violate these prohibitions.
5. Islamic funeral services requiring shrouding and burial within 48 h.
6. Religious scripture and texts as sources of authority may be cited in discussion.

All these aspects of Islamic observance will enter into the clinical social work process to some degree. The relational principles prepare the clinician to listen for content or, even more importantly, to note discord in the interaction that may reflect collision with religious convictions. Frank acknowledgment of insufficient information or familiarity is part of building a collaborative atmosphere. Similarly, appreciation of these structures as providing strengths, in the form of guidance and restrictions that give order to the Muslim's life, calls for validation, even when their exploration in terms of impact on presenting problems will be the subject of further conversations.

Clinical Social Work Practice with Muslim Clients

Berzoff (2011) identified power and privilege as common components in treatment that generate enactments and reenactments on both the client and clinician's parts. The Muslim client may reject or revive attempts at acculturation/assimilation to

American society. The clinician may unconsciously assume defensive or rescuing roles, reflecting sociopolitical views and countertransference. Both client and clinician individuality is diminished in either case. The circular impact of projection and projective identification can derail clinical practice if the social work practitioner is unprepared to embrace the coexistence of conflict and connection as inherent in practice with all clients and especially with clients of diverse populations (Berzoff 2011).

Reticence in help seeking among Muslim Americans has already been mentioned as a barrier to treatment. Besides reluctance to seek professional help in general, particularly from those of other faith traditions, Muslim men in particular eschew help seeking and may go so far as to bar others from seeking clinical social work services (Ali et al. 2004; Khan 2006; Rippy and Newman 2006). In addition to concerns about looking beyond scripture and community, some Muslims are concerned about the generalization of their issues onto the religion of Islam. Ahmed (2012) noted that Muslim converts in particular fear the clinician will attribute the presenting problem to conversion. Professional clinical treatment with a non-Muslim has been ranked as the least acceptable choice for services (Carolan et al. 2000).

Despite these barriers, the Muslim client may be in a service situation where a relationally viable treatment connection must be forged. Aware of the extra measure of resistance likely with Muslim clients, as well as countertransference struggles, the relational clinician can allow extra time for therapeutic engagement when initiating treatment with Muslim clients. Relational theory is promoted through a proactive stance by the practitioner that concedes limited knowledge and/or the presence of reasonable reticence in the client. A shared dissociative process whereby an effort to establish a working relationship disregards Muslim/Western disconnect violates the relational principle of authenticity and attunement for the clinician with herself and with the client. Achieving congruence as whole people, allowing for inevitable mistakes, lack of awareness, resistance, and all the ways a truly interpersonal connection is generated, is the goal of the relational model and requires patience (Jordan 2000; McWilliams 2000). The outcome is enhanced when the therapist has the strength and intention to be present, open, and willing to be impacted in the treatment process. Empathic listening, selective sharing, inquiry, and continuous pursuit of confirmation of understanding must be balanced with demonstrable relevance to the pressing problems the client brings.

Present-oriented and strengths-based treatment is preferred by Muslim clients (Hodge and Nadir 2008). This means the relational clinician must validate the client's effort and search for relevance of Islamic concepts as a means of formulating a collaborative treatment plan. The emphasis on the emerging interpersonal dialogue keeps the focus on the here and now, while the empathic attunement inevitably evokes historically relevant precursors to better understand the presenting problem. For example, "we have worth because we are created by Allah. We are created with strengths and weaknesses," may be preferred by the Muslim as a self-statement, rather than the more Western, "I am a worthwhile person, with positive and negative traits" (Hodge and Nadir 2008, pp. 34–37). A solution focused and brief therapy orientation can be relationally congruent in that it is responsive to the client's mode of perceiving appropriate boundaries (Chaudhry and Li 2011). In all relational therapy, adoption of the client's frame of reference for speaking and hearing about new ways of approaching problem definition and solution strategies reflects the centrality of dialogue and mutual understanding.

When the family or significant others are included as part of the Muslim client's approach to professional consultation, Daneshpour (1998) suggests that the relational clinician consider the constellation as a holistic unit. Tosone (2004) notes that including the meaning of family and larger community, here not just abstractly but concretely, can strengthen alignment and strategies for change, which will involve all parties. A variation is inclusion of an Imam or other Muslim community leader (Nakhaima and Dicks 1995). The clinical social work practitioner who embraces the relational perspective will not be threatened by an adjunctive role with religious consultants. Because forwarding the process of mutual aims and acceptable intervention, including collaboration, undergirds the relational approach, variants that make clinical social work accessible to Muslim clients are within practice reach.

Case Example: Relational Approach that Incorporate Faith and Cultural Modality

Muslim clients in therapy may present with issues having all or nothing to do with their religious tradition. In the case of Ali (African American) and Sandra (White American), both converts to Islam, individual histories and present practices converged. Sandra, raised Catholic, found both her parents and ex-husband objected when she married Ali. A focus was the 10-year-old daughter, Sarah, of whom Sandra was custodial parent.

Ali converted to Islam in college, changing his name from Stanley Johnson III to Ali Abdur-Rahman. The name change upset his parents; they felt he was abandoning his legacy of being named after his grandfather and father. An angry exchange resulted in his no longer being welcome in their home and subsequent estrangement from his extended family. He was unwilling to talk to or about his parents, Sandra's parents, the ex-husband's concerns, or Sandra's daughter's resistance to accepting him. All these topics were disallowed. At the time of the first clinical social work meeting, they were expecting their first child.

As an example of Muslim clients entering clinical social work treatment by force, Child Protective Services was a catalyst. Issues had come to a breaking point when Ali and Sarah got into an argument about what she wanted to wear to school: she wanted to wear jeans and a tee shirt like her classmates, but Ali wanted her to wear a tunic top and head scarf. Sandra was taking a shower and did not hear the argument. Ali grabbed Sarah's arm and thrust her into her room demanding that she not come out until she was properly dressed. When Sandra got to Sarah, she was crying uncontrollably and describing the situation to her father over the phone. Sandra tried to comfort her daughter and told her "there's no compulsion in Islam, we're just trying to guide you toward a more modest dress style." Sandra had previously decided that given Sarah's resistance, it would be better not to force the issue of dress and introduce changes more gradually. Feeling undermined regarding his Islamic observances, angry and frustrated, Ali left the house to cool off.

Before Sandra and her daughter could finish their conversation, Sarah's father came to the house and picked up his daughter and called Child Protective Services, which determined that Ali had physically abused Sarah, as evidenced by her bruised arm. The court ordered the couple take parenting classes and to participate in therapy. Sarah was placed temporarily with her biological father pending the court hearing.

The clinical social worker assigned to the case met with Ali and Sarah and was put off by Ali's demeanor. He looked at her warily, refused to shake hands, and seemed to be in total denial of any culpability. Having heard that Black Muslims disdained White people in general, the White social worker wondered if race was the reason for his behavior. She knew the risks of allowing her feelings of intimidation and distrust to grow and therefore the need to orient herself proactively to the client family, pursuing some traction of interpersonal alignment.

Sandra expressed readiness to do anything to get Sarah back. She was not sleeping well and often had little appetite. The potential negative effects of these stressors on her pregnancy spurred the worker's empathy to Sandra's plight. The worker began to prejudge Ali as cruel and oppressive and most likely the cause of the problem. Ali echoed these thoughts, saying "Everyone, the system, always blames Blacks and Muslims. I didn't do anything wrong!" He left the room and waited outside for Sandra. The worker pointed out that the sessions were mandatory if their daughter was to return to the home, and it really had nothing to do with Ali's ethnicity or their religion. She stated that the real issue was the alleged abuse and finding out what would be required to make a case for Sarah to return to a safe home. The mandatory status gave the social worker leverage in directly confronting Ali's resistance, yet she was aware that her own religious/ethnic judgments needed bracketing and self-reflection. The relational social work model helped her accept her countertransference as requiring bracketing and self-reflection, at the same time it instructed her that this was part of the interpersonal disjuncture that informed the presenting problem. She was able to use her distrust, fear, anger, and rush to judgment as a beginning empathic attunement to Ali's experience as someone rejected for his religious identity by family, in-laws, and now in his nuclear family. She wondered if Ali sensed her feelings. Feeling uncertain of her ability to facilitate resolution, she told her supervisor that Sarah and Ali could be better served by a different clinician because "Ali doesn't like the White system and thinks we are against Muslims."

Bringing her feelings of inadequacy to her supervisor was a relational therapy step: the acceptance of insecurity and pursuit of an interpersonal relationship for processing the dilemma parallel the clinical practice itself. Admitting she was angry at Ali's accusations and that Sandra seemed to have no real voice helped her recognize her identification as victim and confirmation of Ali's perceptions of the bias. She further acknowledged that she felt Islam was influencing Ali to make unreasonable demands on the family, and she felt it necessary to speak up and advocate for Sarah and Sandra. The supervisor noted the transference and countertransference stating, "Do you think he picked up on your thoughts about him? How do you know his behavior had anything to do with Islam?" To her admission that her opinion about Muslims was media-informed, the supervisor responded that "Clinical practice extends beyond the manner in which we intervene; it can also apply to our sources and resources when we gather the information that determines our treatment plan." In this case, then, the information was gathered not from the client himself and, interestingly, not from Sandra who also was Muslim. In other words, lack of self-reflection, including in preparing for a clinical encounter, violated the relational principles of inquiry and not knowing and substituted a version of the judgmental position of "right" behavior or interpretation of resistances as the client's issue.

The clinical social worker was surprised to realize that she too had not allowed Sandra's voice to be heard. Her questions had been directed at Ali about the alleged abuse. Of course a Child Protective Custody case skews the interaction to address this manifest problem. Nonetheless, attempting to engender a relational process of mutual understanding and co-created treatment planning, the disregard of the interpersonal exchange at the outset is decidedly not empathic attunement. The clinician had said the situation had nothing to do with Ali's being Black or Muslim, yet her prejudgment was based on angry Black men, Black Muslims, and female oppression under Islam. In short, the clinician had undermined the relational process by imposing suppositions rather than seeking clarification, education, reactions, and other input from her clients.

The supervisor suggested that the transferences and countertransferences with Ali and Sandra suggested that this revelation could be used to make a positive connection with the couple. She also offered the *Muslim Culture and Faith Guide for Social Service Providers* as a reference (ISSA 2003). Noting that the bio/psycho/social/spiritual assessment had not been completed, she suggested applying a spiritual genogram as a tool to get a picture of the spiritual structure of the family (Hodge et al. 2006). The worker felt ashamed that she had let her resentment and anger interfere with her professionalism in handling the situation. She called to schedule another meeting with the couple, this time at their home.

Sandra was reluctant about a home visit but gave in when the social worker explained that it was required by the court. Sandra asked that the meeting be held after her afternoon prayer (Asr) because Ali would be home from work at that time. The worker, more cautious now not to offend and proactively indicated her wish to be accessible to the couple, asked if there was any special preparation or considerations regarding the visit. Sandra remarked, "We don't wear shoes inside the home. I have some footies if you need them." The meeting was set for the following day.

In an effort to reconcile the discord of the previous session, the worker asked to meet with Ali and Sandra separately and get to know them as individuals. She spoke first to Ali and extended her hand for a handshake. Ali indicated that he did not shake women's hands outside of family members. The worker conceded to Ali that she did not know much about Muslims but what she had heard had led to an assumption that Black Muslims hated White people and Western society. She acknowledged that her assumptions most likely had contributed to them getting off to a rocky start but expressed her desire and her belief that they could learn from each other and work together to see if Sarah could return to the home. She expressed appreciation (affirming strengths) that their interaction had prompted her to read the *Muslim Culture and Faith Guide* (ISSA 2003). Ali seemed to soften with this awareness that the worker was willing to work to gain understanding of their religion and lifestyle.

Ali seemed totally different from the angry young man that had stormed out of the agency office. He said his love and marriage to Sandra was evidence that he didn't hate White people. Ali admitted that he didn't totally agree with American society and United States government policies, but added, "I'm not anti-American." He stated that he felt family issues should be solved "in house" because outsiders "just don't understand." The worker admitted her general lack of knowledge about Muslims and Islam. She expressed a willingness to learn and asked that Ali in turn allow her to inform him about parenting practices and court expectations. Ali shared how he met Sandra and his apprehension of being thrust into stepfatherhood and the impact of Islam on parenting and marriage in a Western society. The social worker noted a dramatic shift in tone and degree of connection. She attributed it to her acknowledgement of her own prejudgments, her awareness of a lack of knowledge about Islam, and her making an effort to learn about him, all within the understanding that there was a clinical problem to be solved which would require mutual effort.

Ali indicated that as a convert he too was still learning about Islamic practice, marriage, and fatherhood and often consulted the Imam. Thinking of this as an opportunity to clarify a potential conflation of professional authority and religion, the clinician asked if he always agreed with the Imam if he left sessions abruptly when he didn't. He stated that he did not leave in those instances out of respect for the Imam and that usually the issue would be resolved by the time the end of meeting. Capitalizing on that point, the social worker noted that premature endings prevented anyone from hearing Ali's views and stopped the communication, making it impossible to resolve the problem. She included her own experience, indicating transparency of the professional process, by admitting that after their first encounter she was ready to leave and let another practitioner take the case. She shared her reflective decision that this would have confirmed everyone's conviction of irreconcilable differences – a parallel process in what both she and the clients were undertaking – that was especially risky given the accusations against Ali and Sandra. Their exchange and reactions revealed the projections and conflicts that had led to the legal process and the perceptions of the extended families, making important clinical assessment use of the interactive process for psychodynamic clarification. They confirmed a common goal of reconciling the family, which would entail difficult aspects; this treatment plan acknowledgment of a potential rough road ahead meets the criterion of authenticity (McWilliams 1999).

Ali admitted that the stress was having a negative impact on Sandra's pregnancy and it was really about getting Sarah home. He wanted his family back together, including Sarah. He said the initial rupture wasn't about the clinician's Whiteness; it was the way she had looked at and spoken to him. He said it reminded him of his parents making him wrong without hearing his side of things. It became apparent that the core problem for Ali really was not a Black, White, Muslim, or even an American system issue, but more about his estrangement from his family of origin and his new stepdaughter. As the conversation deepened, the additional principles of relational theory allowed the problem definition, core dynamic exploration, and treatment strategies to unfold.

As an example of diversity practice, this case illustrates how preconceived ideas, here about Muslims and African Americans and males, feed resistance bidirectionally. Both client and clinician enter the social work practice setting with intact individual and sociopolitical histories, and it behooves the relational clinician to mindfully reflect upon and acknowledge the impact of on all concerned. This includes authenticity about the reality stressors on the family as part of a marginalized group, which may implicate the clinician as oppressor. Processing the initial session with the supervisor was relationally sound practice for the clinician in order to understand and explore the nature of the client/practitioner disconnect as co-created. The negative aspects of the transference and countertransference were de-escalated and transformed as both the client(s) and the clinical social work practitioner began to relate more authentically in terms of their mutual resistances. The therapist's honest disclosure of her initial thoughts and feelings opened the door to a more honest and equal client/therapist interaction. The deleterious effects of acting on previous "knowledge" without validation, and the positive effect of deconstructing erroneous viewpoints, were exemplified in this case vignette. The constructivist principles of relational theory therefore applied not only in the case conduct but also in the clinician's self-reflective work.

The practitioner could have capitalized on the strengths of this family's religious practice by exploring the possibility of consulting their Imam and asking the couple to consult their religious texts for answers regarding relationships between parents, children, and extended family (Hodge and Nadir 2008). These familiar resources and reflection upon them can parallel the clinical interview practice of deconstructing rigid assumptions, learned behaviors, and personal histories of conflict that have distorted larger meanings. It should be noted that although this case vignette described an American Muslim convert couple, it could just as easily have been an immigrant family grappling with differing levels of Islamic religiosity or unresolved family conflicts having little or no root in religious expression.

Conclusion

Relational social work practice with Muslim clients requires awareness of the diversity within the community, the context in which it exists today, as well as an understanding of religious traditions and practices. Inquiry and not knowing but instead acknowledging limitations and asking for clarification are part of culturally competent practice. It is important that practitioners, be they neophytes or experienced clinicians first encountering Islamic clients, perceive and monitor the role their own beliefs about Muslims play in their work. The inclusion of the supervisory process was cited to underscore the ongoing value of consultation and dialogue as part of maintaining balance and self-awareness as a professional social work clinician. The relational principle of mutual discovery of meanings and collaborative problem solving is exemplified in the pursuit of open communication with professional colleagues. It further demonstrated, and reminded, that clinicians as well as clients are subject to transferences and counter transferences and that their discovery and resolution is developmentally supportive. Clinical practice with Muslims provides fertile teaching ground because of the potential for misalignment based on prevailing beliefs and anxieties for both client and clinician. The additional value is for both parties to be changed for the better in the process.

Study Questions

1. Prior to reading this chapter, what were the major influences on your view of Muslims? Discuss how your preconceptions might have influenced your practice.
2. What relational practices did you identify in the chapter that the clinician applied in the work with her Muslim clients? Explain how these skills can be transferred to practice with clients of other backgrounds.
3. Discuss the potential benefits of collaborating with a local community leader in your work with a client. Give an example of how you might go about this process.
4. Transference and countertransference issues are not limited to non-Muslim relational clinicians with Muslim clients. Give an example of such issues that may arise from something other than religious differences.
5. Clinical social workers encounter challenges to mutuality and co-creation of problem definition with Muslim clients based on professional role versus religious authority. Explain relational therapy principles that can help resolve these challenges.
6. How can a relational practice perspective help address resistance arising from beliefs and practices that a client may have? Identify a specific belief or practice that you have encountered with a client and explain how it may have changed your approach to the therapeutic process.

References

Abu-Ras, W., & Abu-Bader, S. (2008). The impact of the September 11, 2001, attacks on the well-being of Arab Americans in New York City. *Journal of Muslim Mental Health, 3*(2), 217–239. doi:10.1080/15564900802487634.

Abu-Ras, W., Gheith, A., & Cournos, F. (2008). The Imam's role in mental health promotion: A study at 22 mosques in New York City's Muslim community. *Journal of Muslim Mental Health, 3*(2), 155–176.

Ahmed, S. (2012). Converts to Islam. In S. Ahmed & M. M. Amer (Eds.), *Counseling Muslims* (pp. 229–250). New York: Routledge/Taylor & Francis Group.

Ali, S., Liu, W., & Humedian, M. (2004). Islam 101: Understanding the religion and therapy implications. *Professional Psychology: Research and Practice, 35*(6), 635–642. doi:10.1037/0735_7028.35.6.635.

American Psychiatric Association. (2000). *Diagnostic and statistical manual of mental disorders* (Fourth ed., Text Revision). Washington, DC: American Psychiatric Association.

Armstrong, K. (2000). *Islam: A short history*. New York: The Modern Library.

Baker Miller, J. (2012). Five good things. Wellesley: Jean Baker Miller Training Institute at the Wellesley Centers for Women.

Berzoff, J. (2011). Why we need a biopsychosocial perspective with vulnerable, oppressed, and at-risk clients. *Smith College Studies in Social Work, 81*(2–3), 132–166. doi:10.1080/0037732 17.2011.590768.

Brandell, J. (2004). *Psychodynamic social work*. New York: Columbia University Press.

Bromberg, P. (1996). Standing in the spaces: The multiplicity of self and the psychoanalytic relationship. *Contemporary Psychoanalysis, 32*, 509–535.

Bromberg, P. (2011). The shadow of the tsunami and growth of the relational mind. New York: Taylor and Francis.

Canda, E., & Furman, L. (1999). *Spiritual diversity in social work practice*. New York: The Free Press.

Carolan, M., Bagherina, G., Juhari, R., Himelright, J., & Mouton-Sanders, M. (2000). Contemporary Muslim families: Research and practice. *Contemporary Family Therapy, 22*(1), 67–79. Retrieved from Academic Search Premier database.

Chaudhry, S., & Li, C. (2011). Is solution-focused brief therapy culturally appropriate for Muslim American counselees? *Journal of Contemporary Psychotherapy, 41*, 109–113. doi:10.1007/s 10879-010-9153-1.

Council of American Islamic Relations (CAIR). (2011). *The status of Muslim civil rights in the United States 2009: Seeking full inclusion*. Retrieved July, 2011 from www.cair.com/civilrightsreports.aspx.

Daneshpour, M. (1998). Muslim families and family therapy. *Journal of Marital and Family Therapy, 24*(3), 355–368.

El-Amin, C. (2009). *Personal and professional spirituality: Muslim social workers' perspectives*. Unpublished dissertation, Walden University.

El-Amin Naeem, Z. (2008). *Jihad of the soul*. New York: The Niyah Company.

Graham, J., Bradshaw, C., & Trew, J. (2010). Cultural considerations for social service agencies working with Muslim clients. *Social Work, 55*(4), 337–347.

Greenberg, J., & Mitchell, S. A. (1983). *Object relations in psychoanalytic theory*. Cambridge: Harvard University Press.

Greenson, R. (1967). *The technique and practice of psychoanalysis* (Vol. 1). New York: International Universities Press.

Hodge, D. (2005). Social work and the house of Islam: Orienting practitioners to the beliefs and values of Muslims in the United States. *Social Work, 50*(2), 162–173. Retrieved from Academic Search Premier database.

Hodge, D., & Nadir, A. (2008). Moving toward culturally competent practice with Muslims: Modifying cognitive therapy with Islamic tenets. *Social Work, 53*(1), 31–42.

Hodge, D., Boughman, L., & Cummings, J. (2006). Moving toward spiritual competency: Deconstructing religious stereotypes and spiritual prejudices in social work literature. *Journal of Social Service Research, 32*(4), 211–231. Retrieved from Academic Search Premier database.

Hopkins, N., & Kahni-Hopkins, V. (2006). Minority group members' theories of intergroup contact: A case study of British Muslim's conceptualizations of "Islamophobia" and social change. *British Journal of Social Psychology, 45*, 245–264.

Islamic Social Services Association. (2003). *Muslim culture and faith: A guide for social service providers*. Tempe, AZ: Islamic Social Services Association. Revised Edition.

Jordan, J. (2000). The role of mutual empathy in relational/cultural therapy. *JCLP/In Session: Psychotherapy in Practice, 56*(8), 1005–1016. doi:10.1002/1097-4679(200008).

Khan, Z. (2006). Attitudes toward counseling and alternative support among Muslims in Toledo, Ohio. *Journal of Muslim Mental Health, 1*(1), 21–42.

McWilliams, N. (1999). *Psychoanalytic case formulation*. New York: Guilford Press.

McWilliams, N. (2000). On teaching psychoanalysis in anti-analytic times: A polemic. *The American Journal of Psycho Analysis, 60*(4), 371–390. doi:doi: 10.1023/A: 1002046915249.

Nadir, P. (2003). *An act of faith: Voices of young Muslim women in America.* Unpublished doctoral dissertation, Arizona State University.

Nadir, A., & Dziegielewski, S. F. (2001). Islam. In M. Van Hook, B. Hugen, & M. A. Aguilar (Eds.), *Spirituality with religious traditions in social work practice* (pp. 146–162). Pacific Grove: Brooks/Cole.

Nadir, A., & El-Amin, C. (2012). Home-based social services. In S. Ahmed & M. M. Amer (Eds.), *Counseling Muslims: Handbook of mental health issues and interventions* (pp. 197–211). New York: Routledge/Taylor & Francis Group.

Nakhaima, J. M., & Dicks, B. H. (1995). Social work practice with religious families. *Families in Society, 76*(6), 360–369. Retrieved from ProQuest database.

Padela, A., & Heisler, M. (2010). The association of perceived abuse & discrimination after September 11, 2001, with psychological distress, and health status among Arab Americans. *American Journal of Public Health, 100,* 284–291. doi:10.2105/ajph.2009.164954.

Panagopoulos, C. (2006). The polls – Trends: Arab and Muslim Americans and Islam in the aftermath of 9/11. *Public Opinion Quarterly, 70*(4), 608–624.

Rippy, A. E., & Newman, E. (2006). Perceived religious discrimination and its relationship to anxiety and paranoia among Muslim Americans. *Journal of Muslim Mental Health, 1*(1), 5–20.

Tosone, C. (2004). Relational social work: Honoring the tradition. *Smith College Studies in Social Work, 74*(3), 475–487.

Clinical Social Work with Orthodox Jews: A Relational Approach

Renée Schlesinger

Introduction

Relational theory is an update and integration of the various psychoanalytic approaches to clinical theory and practice. As initially developed and elaborated by Greenberg and Mitchell (1983), relational theory addresses the centrality of the interpersonal exchange as the therapeutic medium and the co-construction of meaning as the means of pursuing in-depth understanding across the individual differences that inform interpersonal relating. This position of mutual discovery and problem definition in the treatment process reflects the stance of clinical social work both historically and contemporaneously (Tosone 2004). The social work clinician in today's complex practice environment finds special relevance for the application of relational theory principles as he or she encounters the diverse racial, ethnic, religious, sexual, and other self-defining dimensions of client populations. This chapter applies relational theory to direct clinical practice with Orthodox Jews, a population that brings the challenges of interpersonal connection across differences to many clinical social work practitioners. The specific features, needs, transference and countertransference evocations, and parameters of effective treatment of Orthodox Jews are explored both to inform the worker of unique issues and to illustrate their solutions through the relational application of established clinical social work practice models.

The subject of religion has a long and controversial history among theorists beginning with Freud, who considered religion a form of obsessional neurosis (Freud 1907, 1913). His contemporary, Jung, saw religion as a universal need (Jung 1954). Relational theorists, who are by definition less dogmatic and are at odds with a priori

R. Schlesinger, LCSW (✉)
Wurzweiler School of Social Work, Yeshiva University, New York, NY, USA
e-mail: rschlesingernyc@aol.com

J.B. Rosenberger (ed.), *Relational Social Work Practice with Diverse Populations*,
Essential Clinical Social Work Series, DOI 10.1007/978-1-4614-6681-9_12,
© Springer Science+Business Media New York 2014

assessments, focus on the individual and his or her unique experience, thereby approaching religion as a dimension of the clinical social work client's worldview. The role of religion for the social work clinician who encounters a client for whom religion plays a dominant role in their daily life is the subject of this chapter. In particular, I will look at the factors influencing the relationally oriented treatment of the Orthodox and of the ultra-Orthodox Jewish client.

This chapter provides background about the kinds of issues that may arise in clinical work with Orthodox Jews and the way the relational model can guide the clinician by applying the principles of mutually co-constructed clinical social work practice. It will provide a necessarily limited introduction to the belief system and practices of Orthodox Judaism and be followed by a discussion of how relational theory has evolved and interfaces with Jewish traditions. Principles of engagement and practice for practitioners and supervisors dealing with Orthodox Jews in their practice are illustrated by a number of clinical examples that demonstrate the application of these principles. Finally, it will demonstrate how relational concepts can be functionally applied in clinical social work with this population, as well as identifying areas of theoretical incompatibility that need to be acknowledged and addressed in the theoretical field.

Relational theory, which provides an orientation to engagement, assessment, and treatment planning that allows the practitioner to recognize, respond to, and demonstrate meaningful cultural competence with the client and his or her immediate service needs, serves the practice guidance needs of all clinicians. This includes the clinician who is not identified as Orthodox, who represents a different sect within Judaism, or who may himself or herself be Orthodox. Those less familiar with the Orthodox may experience concern about understanding the detailed teachings that shape the lives of the Orthodox. Conversely, the Orthodox clinician who can identify with and understand this client population may over-identify, develop countertransference responses, and fail empathically in other dimensions of his or her clinical work. Clinical social work clients are, after all, seeking help with problems of living. A religious context of practice determines perspective, treatment options, and relational parameters but may also require culturally sensitive deconstruction of its interaction with human struggles of all kinds.

Judaism and Relational Social Work

The history of Judaism and relational practice captures the often conflicted relationship between the individualism of a psychodynamically informed theory of experience and functioning and the tradition of hierarchical and collective perspectives on living that define membership in a defined population. The relationship between clinical theory and Judaism begins with Freud himself, with his intense rejection, first of his own Orthodox Jewish background, and then with rejection of all religions. The early practitioner, following Freud's drive theory, considered religion a type of pathological defense mechanism (Jones 1957). While there were prominent early defectors from this psychoanalytic orthodoxy, notably Jung and Adler, the hostility to religious practice as opposed to the Freudian "scientific" model continued well into the 1950s (Greenberg and Witztum 1991, 2001; Rubin 2004).

The emergence of object relations theories introduced by Fairbairn (1952); Guntrip, Winnicott (1958), and Klein in Europe and the interpersonal theories of Sullivan, Horney (1942), and Fromm in the United States emphasized the importance of relationship as a fundamental human motivation and thus challenged the primacy of drive theory and infantile sexuality as drivers of behavior with a model based on interpersonally co-constructed relationships (Greenberg and Mitchell 1983).

This broadening perspective provided a new realm for consideration of religious motivation. Indeed, "spirituality" has become increasingly recognized as an aspect of mental health. The desire for spiritual connectedness (Welwood 1996; Rubin 1999, 2004) is now viewed as a legitimate and valuable aspiration. The religious orientation that has gained the most acceptability is Eastern spirituality, which emphasizes meditative practices and is decidedly not monotheistic (Rubin 2004). Nevertheless, clinical social workers still encounter a wide range of clients who are members of faith-based communities. Like others affiliated with faith-based communities, followers of Orthodox Judaism are highly sensitive to perceived criticisms of their customs, which lie outside the frame of mainstream American culture, which are linked with political turmoil past and present, and which may be unfamiliar to most clinical social work practitioners.

Just as the relational theory privileges relationships, particularly parent–child relations, over drive theory's emphasis on instincts as the root of psychological development, it also reclaims the important role of social relationships in contrast to Freud's disdain of sociological explanations. Relational theory reminds us of social work's original emphasis on the bio–psycho–social framework and the person-in-situation framework for understanding self experience and current functioning (Tosone 2004). While the movement toward inclusion of cultural factors has been met with resistance in psychoanalytic theory, clinical social work has readily embraced relational theory as an outgrowth of psychoanalytic thinking. With its constructivist roots, relational theory unifies in-depth individual dynamic understanding with the sociocultural forces surrounding and shaping the past, present, and future contexts for that individual (Goldstein 1995; Hollis 2000; Berzoff et al. 2008).

The notions of relationship seeking as a primary driver of behavior, and the importance of being part of an interpersonal group giving meaning to and organizing the thoughts, feelings, and values that guide the individual's behavior, are congruent with relational theory and with the roots of clinical social work (Tosone 2004). Even Winnicott (1945, 1948), among the psychoanalytic theoreticians, emphasized the power of membership as an interpersonal holding environment. Following this paradigm, the individual's connection to his or her God can be understood as a meaningful relationship that is part of the internal object relation world (Meissner 1984). This would similarly be true for a member of a Christian or Muslim believer who interprets their sacred text literally and bases their daily activities on a relationship with the God of their understanding.

Clinical social work practice with a person for whom religion plays a prominent role requires an acceptance of and sensitivity to how that person lives his or her religion and how it affects his or her relationship to others. McWilliams (1994) observes that "a deeply religious person of any personality type will need first for the therapist to demonstrate respect for his or her depth of conviction" (p. 17). While there are many ways to become familiar with a specific population, it is important to introduce this group descriptively, to cognitively prepare for engagement with Orthodoxy. The challenge is to conduct clinical practice with Orthodox Jews without making assumptions based on shared religious beliefs or to impose their beliefs on clients in the guise of clinical advice. To the non-Orthodox practitioner, ritual observances of Orthodox Jews may seem mystifying and atavistic and thereby entwined with the pathological. This intersection of the community and individual becomes a dominant factor particularly when working with members of ultra-Orthodox groups. The natural extension of the relational orientation includes the importance to observant Jews of being part of a community as well as the seeking of God as an object that meets the legitimate needs of individuals.

Orthodox Judaism: Some Central Practices and Beliefs

Judaism is the oldest monotheistic religion. There are currently 14,824,000 Jews worldwide and 5,720,000 Jews in North America (World Almanac 2012, p. 699). American Judaism is divided into four primary branches – Orthodox, Conservative, Reform, and Reconstructionist. These branches vary in degree of liberalism in interpretation of the guiding texts of Judaism. Orthodox Judaism is the most strict and traditional branch, encompassing those who interact with the larger community and those who stay apart. The "modern Orthodox" wear ordinary clothing, generally go to college, and work in many professions. By contrast, the "ultra-Orthodox" generally keep themselves separate from the influences of outside culture, avoiding television, movies, and the Internet. For the men in this group, study of Torah is considered a legitimate full-time professional pursuit. Although many Orthodox find the "modern" and "ultra" categorizations culturally insensitive, they are commonly used to describe real differences.

Key Observances

The most traditionalist ultra-religious group is called *haredim*, which include Hassidim. The majority of this group migrated to the United States after World War II and is the most easily identifiable, insular, and segregated. They have recognizable differences in customs and clothing, maintained since the mid-1700s, and continue to use Yiddish as their language. Their communities are organized around the leadership of a rabbi, or *rebbe*, who is the final arbiter of all issues, religious and nonreligious. They consider their goal in life to be the perpetuation of Jewish laws, practices, and observance, and conduct is defined by extreme religious dogma and principle (Poll 1962). Orthodox Judaism maintains sharp gender-role distinctions (Levine 2003). Males and females who are not related cannot touch each other, even to shake hands, and gender-specific religious rituals shape daily life. Their world is often full of drama, intensity, and, for some, a craving to break the rules (Levine 2003). Such clients therefore present a rigid yet often conflicted picture for the social work clinician, who must help the client sort out the individual from the group expectations without violating religious imperatives.

Most Jewish observance is outlined in numerous holy texts beginning with and extending from the Torah (the Old Testament) and other texts, including the Talmud (a codification of laws) and various responses. These codify for Jews how and what to eat, rules regarding sex and procreation, rituals around death and mourning, and how generally to behave in relationship to others, including family, strangers, and even animals. The genesis of these laws is the bargain God offers the Jews that He will care for them if they obey His commandments. Rules of daily living are spelled out with great specificity and are strict and binding, with severe punishments, including ostracism from the community, for noncompliance. One example of this is the set of instructions in the bibllcal book of Deuteronomy that deal with food and food preparation. Orthodox Jews are only permitted to eat kosher food (Hertz 1981). They do not mix meat and milk products or eat "unclean" animals, such as pig, and are constrained from involvement with people who do not follow these laws. Thus familial, social, and professional experiences are impacted, and the most observant would not go outside the Orthodox community, including to seek professional clinical help. When social realities (access, fees, presenting problem) do cause the Orthodox to make compromises, awareness of these issues requires the relationally attuned clinician to take care to avoid deviations from prescribed practices as much as possible. For example, patterns of greeting would not include a handshake, and assessment might include such questions as, "What might your rabbi say about…?"

Clinical practice of any kind is forbidden on the Sabbath. The Ten Commandments state: "Remember the Sabbath day and keep it holy. Six days shall you labor and do all your work, but the seventh is a Sabbath of the Lord your God" (Exodus 20:8, Hertz Second Edition). Orthodox Jews do no work of any kind on this day, and work is defined broadly, including earning of wages, traveling, pushing an elevator button, cooking food, or even tearing toilet paper. Asking another Jew to violate the Sabbath by any such actions is equivalent to violating the law personally. Similarly, suggesting an appointment on a Friday night, when the Sabbath begins, through Saturday night would be a significant breach, demonstrating insensitivity to the most important of all religious practices. This would not necessarily be the case for many Conservative or Reform Jews, who have more liberal practices, but the clinician needs to assume observance applies unless informed otherwise. While it is unreasonable for every clinical social worker to have expert knowledge in all dimensions and variations of any population of diversity, it is not unreasonable for his or her to have a method of discovery and connection with his or her client that includes the client's freedom to express and adhere to specific belief constraints. The relational principles of inquiry, not knowing, and mutuality in establishing practice orientation serve this purpose well.

Gender, Sexuality, and Family Life

Another aspect of Orthodox Jewish practice has to do with laws relating to sexuality, sexual purity, and sexual modesty. There are extensive rules relating to purity and modesty. One example is the instruction for married women to wear a head covering, a cap or wig, after marriage. Orthodox rules of modesty also can affect open and frank discussion and even problem solving in couples. Guilt and shame, recurring religious motifs, can create resistances to self-disclosure which the relational clinician will be able to understand not as unconscious conflict per se, but as reflections of internalized identifications with a religious reference group.

The Orthodox Jew as Client

In some communities, specifically including Hassidic, the rabbi is consulted on all matters, not only religious. In other Orthodox communities, the rabbi is consulted on religious issues and sometimes about crises not pertaining to religion, such as marital and sexual problems, addiction, violence and abuse, and severe psychopathology. The social work clinician, working relationally, can be open to collaboration or referral to rabbinic counsel. The client's preference for addressing different problems with different professionals can effect positive connections to clinical experiences.

Orthodox Jews come to the attention of clinical social work practitioners in a wide variety of settings, from mental health clinics to domestic violence services to all forms of medical and health-care centers and every other arena of social services. For an Orthodox Jew, seeking clinical or other social work services outside of his or her sect may represent a break from traditional modes, and a bridge must be built through respect for religious observances as well as the emotional quality of the relationship, so highly correlated with positive outcome of treatment (Strupp 1989).

Engagement, from the outset, requires reference to Jewish law. For example, while it is unusual for an ultra-Orthodox man to be in treatment with a female clinician, the female clinician should not extend a handshake and may need to accommodate the prohibition of being alone with a female, and vice versa, by leaving a door ajar. Speaking ill of others and all forms of gossip is considered sinful, so telling a clinician about specific relational problems is violating this restriction. Assuring a client that these problems are confidential and their conveyance is for no other purpose than alleviating pain helps clients understand that this is not "idle gossip." This is an ideal opportunity for the clinical social worker to demonstrate the principles of openness about his or her own knowledge or lack thereof, mutuality of problem definition, and exploration of resistances as instances of conflict that contain critical religious and personal information. Since the Orthodox client accepts constraint on personal choice by religious doctrine as a value in itself, a clinician must not confuse defensive structures with religiously determined rigidity. In this person-in-situation perspective, religious aspects of the situation are largely immutable, and the area of clinical focus must be on the individual client's experiences and range of options within that situation.

A particularly complex exception to the social worker's acceptance of Orthodox rules is the Orthodox client who is struggling with his or her religious convictions. This delicate issue, often implicit rather than stated, must be allowed room to emerge, in the spirit of "potential space" (Winnicott 1967; Bollas 1987), constructed of the clinician's empathic attunement to and reflection of the client's communications. This is particularly true when the individual questions how an all-powerful God can permit seemingly needless suffering and tragic natural disasters. Whether the social work clinician is Orthodox or not may shape discussion of such questions of conviction. This is one reason that non-Orthodox social workers need preparation to work relationally with the Orthodox: their outsider status may facilitate potential space if they can demonstrate respect and understanding of what is at stake, including membership in a closed community as well as religious observance.

For example, a gifted supervisee reported a first meeting with a potential Orthodox client who initially asked, "Are you religious?" "No," she answered authentically, adding "I was never able to have that experience but I do believe that I am a spiritual person." A successful clinical experience followed from that meeting of the Orthodox client and nominally Catholic clinician based on this opening of shared space. The Orthodox clinician, likewise, must demonstrate respect for the client's individual relationship to his or her religious membership, even if deviating from the group rules in some ways. The relational stance of constructing the client's meanings and feelings by interactive search for clarity will offer assurance that judgment or ignorance of the issues will not interfere with a commitment to the client's trajectory of clinical exploration. The utilization of mirroring (Winnicott 1967) by the relational clinician can help the client to see the role religion plays in his or her life and how it shapes the way he or she relates, including the way he or she relates to the clinician.

Individuals seeking clinical social work services may be struggling with conflicts about religious adherence and subsequently go beyond the traditional system of seeking rabbinic counsel. Some Orthodox rabbis will refer their congregants to trusted clinicians who they feel confident will support religious practices. Conflict with a too strict or abusive parent, for example, would be a difficult subject for a rabbinic authority, but could be handled in the holding environment with a relational clinician. Orthodox clients do develop strong attachments to non-Orthodox clinicians who are empathic and do not pathologize or undermine religious practice. An Orthodox colleague once shared, "I will only work with my Italian Catholic analyst because he does not pathologize my religion."

One arena of clinical practice that is particularly complex for Orthodox and non-Orthodox practitioners alike is that of Orthodoxy and homosexuality. A 2007 National Survey of American Jews reported by Ariel (2007) shows that 7% of American Jews are lesbian, gay, or bisexual. Orthodox homosexuals, particularly the youth, feel shame and fear of exposure and often suffer severe ostracism if they reveal their homosexuality (Ariel 2007; Davis 2008). Disclosure of homosexuality, as well as many other issues, affects marital prospects of siblings and casts shame on the entire family.

In 1973 the American Psychiatric Association voted to remove homosexuality from their list of sexual pathologies, and this was included in the revised Diagnostic and Statistical Manual (American Psychiatric Association 1980). While this opened the door for all homosexual men and women to seek clinical services to deal openly with issues in living rather than to change or conceal their sexual orientation, Orthodox clients report catastrophic experiences of rejection by family and community, feelings of alienation and marginalization, and continued wishes for inclusion. A still current explicit Orthodox position states that homosexuality is a choice and can be either suppressed or "cured" using conversion therapies (Ariel 2007). Relational theoreticians reject "cure" out of hand, along with the Freudian definition of maturity as mature heterosexuality. Rather, in the relational perspective maturation is reflected in self-cohesion that includes sexual identification (Mitchell 1988; Kohut 1984; Berzoff et al. 2008). Still, acceptance by the clinical world does not translate into acceptance by Orthodoxy.

Judaism and Relational Theory

Judaism, while prescriptive and laden with consequences for transgressions, is nonetheless a religion that contains teachings about tolerance and higher-order principles of righteous living. In few other religions does one find a God portrayed as so punitive, exacting, and jealous as the God of the Jews. Jews see themselves as having an authority-driven relationship with a God who offers the ultimate reward, punishes severely for transgressions, yet commands the people to live justly, have mercy, and to show compassion. Sorting this out is an individual process and occurs in a relational matrix. Buber (1937) asserts that man's relationship to God is a personal one. He stated that God, who is presumably both spirit and personal, is clearly and unequivocally object seeking and has both direct and indirect relationships with His people. They, in turn, are always seeking expressions of their relationship with Him.

The whole conceptualization of good self-development and the sources of personal happiness or suffering are defined, for Jews, as the products of being in the right or wrong relationship with God. There are no intermediating factors or abstractions: healthy self must be a self without conflict with God's rules, and rabbis function to interpret situations according to those rules. The clinician should stay attuned to this representation of the core relationship: mutual construction of meaning and behavioral adaptation supports the validity of the client's quest for a unique solution to problems that align the client with his or her religious convictions.

Eigen (1981), in *The Area of Faith in Winnicott, Lacan and Bion*, introduced religion into the relational sphere, stating that "By the area of faith I mean to point to a way of experiencing which is undertaken with one's whole being, all out, with all one's heart, with all one's soul, and with all one's might" (p. 3). Here, even partially quoting words from the Sh'ma, the central prayer of the Jews, Eigen admits religious faith into the fabric of relational theorizing: "In transitional experiencing, the infant lives through a faith that is proof to clear realization of self and other differences...." (Eigen 1981, p. 4). Fromm (1950) developed his own position that some obsessional rituals can be viewed as a private religion, but he clearly added that religious belief does not need to be "cured." Eigen's position can help doubtful clinicians sort through some of their own religious questions in preparation for challenging clinical situations.

Relational Theory and Practice: Congruence with Orthodox Judaism

What does working within relational theoretical frameworks offer the clinician working with Orthodox Jews and the clients themselves over more traditional schools of social work theory or psychoanalytic thought? Freud himself was an atheist who communicated often his understanding that religious belief was an illusion and that belief in God was a projection of early wishes for protection by an omnipotent parent figure (Freud 1927). This bias affects many traditional psychoanalysts and psychoanalytically oriented clinicians who also see themselves as grounded in "science" and view science as antithetical to religious belief and faith. Applying a relational theoretical model offers Orthodox Jews a framework which does not, out of hand, reject basic belief. A number of relational theoreticians offer a view of religious belief and a bridge between traditional psychoanalytic positions and social work positions that favor adaptation and behavior over internal self-cohesion.

According to McWilliams (1994), "Longings for the omnipotent caregiver naturally appear in people's religious convictions" (p. 106). Goldman (1993) cites Winnicott as speaking of the therapist in the transference as an omnipotent holding object, but not rejecting a belief in a supernatural God. He also quotes Winnicott (1985) as stating "Psychotherapy does not prescribe for a patient's religion, his cultural interests or his private life, but a patient who keeps part of himself completely defended is avoiding the dependence that is inherent in the process" (Goldman 1993, p. 75).

Emmanuel Ghent (1990) develops another position, viz., that there is a universal need or wish for an experience of surrender that takes multiple forms, including religious surrender. He supports the religious position without interpreting belief in God as a wishful myth. Relational social workers, embracing their understanding both of early transference manifestations and other early archaic experiences of the infant and child, are in a good clinical position to understand and truly empathize with an "I–Thou moment" and its importance for Orthodox Jews. In understanding the earliest interpersonal encounters, the clinician can demonstrate his or her attunement to the power of religious force and its place in human experience.

Engagement: Starting Where the Orthodox Client Is

A question for clinical consideration in working with Orthodox clients begins with the impetus for seeking clinical help. What change is desired and how can change be achieved? The immediate client/clinician relationship offers a nonjudgmental arena for the client to explore deeper layers of meaning about his or her presenting problems so long as the framing of conflicts is congruent with the religiously informed definition of self-in-relation. Is he or she struggling with relationship problems or what Sullivan (1954) called problems of living in the present or with issues reemerging from and complicated by early childhood struggles? The question of why the client is seeking out a social work clinician rather than a rabbi is a fruitful point of engagement. If a clinician works in a Jewish social service agency, the client population may receive a variety of services from that agency in a venue that would be acceptable to the community. In other settings, the question may have particular salience. Receptivity to an interest in the patient's religion as well as the circumstances of religious conviction that surround the clinical encounter must be accomplished lest the client reject the treatment and perhaps internalize or reenact discriminatory relationships from his or her own life.

The religious orientation and self-presentation of the social worker and of the client are often obvious in their first encounter, by the dress or other physical presentation, evoking transference and countertransference reactions from the outset. Active work with this nexus is a relational theory expectation and contrasts with the classical psychoanalytic position of the blank screen clinician onto which the client projects. Silence about points of apparent similarity and difference is not constructive with most Orthodox clients. The clinician needs to be more accessible as a real person interested in two people coming together in a shared therapeutic encounter (Greenberg and Mitchell 1983). Bowlby's (1969) formulation that good clinicians use the language of feeling and emotion to communicate with clients is germane: it utilizes common ground for the relational social worker's proactive inquiry and pursuit of mutual understandings and treatment goals.

Emphasis on the real relationship illuminates transference concerns and is a significant departure from the non-relational models that emphasize more distance, abstinence, and neutrality. The aim of such openness is to establish a positive working alliance as well as a positive transference and countertransference relationship, seeking to illuminate and dispel any earlier negative experiences, including clinical experiences that would affect the establishment of a beginning bond for the work. A stance of openness to listen and understand, rather than to evaluate and interpret, is a proactive one for the relational clinician. Once a bond has been established, transference issues beyond those relating to Orthodoxy can be investigated or revisited.

The role of the supervisor is crucial for clinical social work practitioners working with Orthodox clients. Ideally the supervisor would be at least somewhat familiar with the practices, beliefs, and customs of the Orthodox community in order to educate supervisees accurately. The supervisor is charged with encouraging the worker to be as frank as possible regarding their reactions, thoughts, and feelings. In supervision, the social work clinician can be invited to acknowledge areas of uncertainty of understanding, responses, confusions about how to work with religiosity in connection with presenting problems of daily life, and the like. The relational aspects of the supervisor/supervisee are the model for the work and require the supervisor to have a real relationship with the supervisee. This can include a tactful exploration of the clinician and supervisor's religious orientation and its relationship to treatment.

A Case of Relational Social Work Practice with a Female Orthodox Client

An Orthodox female, Amy, presented for treatment wearing a snood, the traditional headscarf worn by ultra-Orthodox women. While she seemed easily identifiable in this way, I had to resist quick assumptions about her, knowing that assumptions, even if they prove correct, are relationally counterproductive. Though I had expected that I was meeting an Orthodox client, based upon the source of the referral, I had worn a sleeveless top rather than more modest dress. It was one of those steamy summers, but nonetheless I was giving a message about my position on Orthodox rules of dress. I quickly felt self-conscious about being sleeveless and wearing dramatic nail polish. I was intensely aware of how I appeared. Following the relational principle of ongoing self-reflection in the treatment setting, I asked myself why I was inviting assumptions by the client that I knew could be provocative.

As is the case when beginning with all clients, mutual scrutiny was occurring. With Orthodox clients, this scrutiny reflects the expectation of relational misalignment that they live with in daily life as a visible minority. In the earliest part of our meeting, the client asked if I understood her background. I responded authentically but with neutral affect, offering information without persuasion: I said that I was familiar with traditional Jewish practice. I also said that I wanted to be able to understand her experiences. Despite this overt exchange about whether I was sufficiently attuned to the Orthodox culture, her noticeable reaction to my manner of dress, indicating I was not as observant a Jew as she was, was a transference and countertransference moment not to be wasted. While this unspoken "collision" (Bromberg 2011) no doubt contained developmental precursors (Why had I chosen not to dress according to Orthodox rules? Why had she chosen to maintain her dress observance?), an interpersonal exchange was occurring in the present and shaping the mutual exchange process, where relational practice directs its primary focus. I contained any tendency to be defensive and tested the capacity to have open and authentic exploration of religiously prescribed matters. I stated that I sensed her reacting to my way of dressing. She responded with "I noticed your green nail polish; I wore that once and my mother objected." I continued the here-and-now relational exchange, inquiring what my deviations from the strict rules meant in terms of our working together on her concerns. She stated, "I do sense that you are sympathetic and sincere." I did not pursue this response except to nod in acknowledgement, seeing it as an example of co-constructing a shared space in the client-with-clinician relationship where variation could exist (from Orthodoxy, from mother's authority) without it being a violation that led to flight. She had asked, rather than judging silently, about my capacity to be informed about her orientation, and she responded to my question about our differences with reflection on her own experience. As Bromberg (2011) notes, the "collisions" that bring dissociated material into conscious interaction are key relational treatment elements in themselves: creating in the interpersonal exchange a shared space that contains variations expands tolerance for internal dissonance.

The client's response added to my assessment that, despite a physical presentation of hesitant uncertainty, this woman possessed an intact self, adequate to be expressive and assertive about her concerns. She also communicated an emotional intuitiveness, attentiveness to relational issues, and an ability to discriminate between people on the basis of human rather than solely religious criteria. The practice knowledge gained in this simple exchange, preliminary but highly informative, demonstrates the strategic and relationship-building self-disclosure that is one of the distinctive principles of relational approaches (Aron 1991). It also demonstrates how this kind of openness addresses the sensitivity of Orthodox clients, and other marginalized clients, to having a real need to know about safety in the clinical social work process.

While this client and I were not both Orthodox Jews, we were co-participants in this sharing of perceptions of ourselves as mutually engaged, working on the edge of intimacy (Mitchell and Aron 1999) as we established other areas of similarity. We communicated a considerable amount in this exchange. She talked about her mother, about awareness of the impingement of her Orthodoxy on her choices, about her attunement to differences as raising valid questions of understanding. By airing those questions about encompassing diversity in traditional Jewish background, we were able to create a mutual exploration process. The exploration is not a questioning of the centrality of cultural identity for the client's well-being. Rather, it is an entry into discussion of how the client's cultural identity informs her thinking about the many issues that may arise. Many Jews "return" to Judaism, especially to Orthodoxy, after being raised in less religious or nonreligious families. Some of these *baal teshuva* (returnees) do so for spiritual reasons; others make this choice unconsciously as expressions of difficulty in the family of origin. At this point, with Amy, the relevance of her Orthodoxy to the core problem that brought her to treatment was not yet spelled out. However, the need to establish an interpersonal connection wherein problems or concerns could be examined in context of religious observance had been established.

This greater degree of self-disclosure is consistent with most relational approaches and is generally indicated with Orthodox clients, who need to know that you understand, or wish to understand, the rules by which they live. The relational stance is one that can include the sharing of relevant information, as compared to a client giving information to a more traditional clinician, who receives manifest and latent details, lying in wait to interpret unconscious motivations. As Goldstein (1995) states, "In ego-oriented intervention the worker generally permits his or her personal qualities to enter the client-worker relationship in a disciplined way based on his or her determination of the client's need and therapeutic goals" (p. 201).

A Case of Sexual Issues with a Male Orthodox Client

Ari, a highly sexual Orthodox male, adhered to the religious requirement to have sex for only two "clean" weeks of the month, when his wife was not menstruating and only after she returned from the ritual cleansing bath. Ari came to treatment with a particular struggle: it was both an internal conflict and one between him and his wife. He was beset and disturbed by his sexual preoccupations, with a sex drive he felt demanded gratification by having sex "off schedule" or alternatively by masturbating. Though conflicted about these alternate routes to gratification, they were for him stopgap measures. Ari reported craving regular sexual encounters in order to feel emotionally reassured by and connected to his wife. At times he spent hours negotiating with himself before masturbating, feeling intense shame and weakness about his inability to control this behavior which had been expressly religiously forbidden and pathologized by his rabbinic teachers. Sometimes he pressured his wife for sex during her unclean weeks. Living in this constant bind led to frustration, anger, and bargaining with himself and others, including many debates with God. Ari even sought loopholes to express or to get around his "bestial impulses." Simultaneously, he seemingly self-righteously, perhaps defensively, justified these urges that competed with his mostly pious, religious observance.

In this clinical example, employing both a Darwinian and Freudian perspective, Ari could be viewed as a man plagued by normal impulses that strive for gratification to achieve his own satisfaction. To live in civilization, Freud (1930) posited that man, through the internalization of the superego, in this case religiously defined, must force himself to resist natural, understandable sexual urges. This theoretical model fits neatly if problematically with Ari's conception of self-regulation by religious laws. The Talmud states that man has two opposing inclinations, a good inclination (*yetzer hatov*) and an evil inclination (*yetzer hara*), and mastering and balancing these two inclinations is ongoing through life. Freud's drive theory bases civilization on requiring repression and suppression of sexual and aggressive drives for the survival of the social group. Jewish law attempts to solve the same problem by codifying and prescribing sexual behavior.

As Ari requested, I consulted first with an ordained Hasidic rabbi who was also a social work professional, asking him to research any possible exceptions to the laws of sexual abstinence, which provisionally would allow Ari to masturbate or to have sex with his wife during her unclean weeks. The rabbi moved around the question respectfully but deftly, saying that there were some obscure references to the possibility of masturbation under special circumstances. However, he related, interpretations relating to these abstinent periods had to do with the importance of creating space to enhance a couple's nonphysical intimacy.

This emphasis on the interpersonal ramifications moved the issue back into the clinical social work practice sphere, placing sexual expression in a relational perspective. The social work clinician can validate the client's attention to his urges as a good dynamism, worth holding, but simultaneously underscore the significance of his relational needs. The relational model communicates the formative impact of early childhood experience as the source of disconnection between the biological and relational drives. In this larger clinical context, Ari's dilemma was created not only by his basic maleness but by how he internalized complex parental, rabbinic, and scriptural messages. If parents and rabbis communicated many complex messages about his phallus and his sexuality, his urges have not only pressure but also meaning, perhaps aimed at reassuring him, diminishing his anxiety, and otherwise being compensatory for relational longings. Ari could be helped to delay gratification and sustain connection by expanding his understanding of himself as a person who was not solely infantile in nature, but rather moving progressively through stages of development toward integration of primitive and more mature forms of meeting his needs. In this symbolic way, the relational model unified Ari's struggle religiously and clinically, one shoring up the other. Specifically, it moved Ari from viewing himself as less primitively constructed and significantly impacted his marital relationship.

Conclusion

In groups classically under siege, as has historically been the experience of Jews, the probability of developing a bunker mentality is high. This mentality leads naturally to an "us against them" position and a "we will take care of our own problems" stance. This self-protective orientation can lead to insularity and repetitive experiences where pathological scenarios are repeated and reenacted without transformation. An empathic attunement to the complex experience, including the outsider status of such a group, promotes a respect for the stress created by being a stranger in a strange land. The clinician can potentially utilize this knowledge in clinical engagement by assuming and dealing with a position of mistrust and by creating levels of safety. The relational clinician employs distance as well as self-disclosure, maintenance of a positive transference relationship, and expressions of affirmation and approval to reinforce the mutuality of the task of therapy. "Mutuality involves being engaged in a growing connection with another person. As the relationship unfolds, honoring the uniqueness of each other becomes integral to the growth of mutual respect" (Freedberg 2009, p. 87).

In revisiting and comparing relational theory to clinical social work and traditional casework theory, we see that there are few differences. Both employ a generally accepting relationship with the client, working within a person–situation and environmental fit and informed by a bio–psycho–social matrix without being limited to, or excluding, an explanation based on infantile sexuality. Working with Orthodoxy parallels working with familiar concepts of family hierarchies and models of relationship. The social work clinician is not pursuing changing religious convictions, but instead decoupling them from residual familial conflicts. Ultimately, the issue for clinicians is the stance of co-construction that focuses on the person-in-situation matrix, a bio–psycho–social history, and the existential facts of each person's life. The clinician's empathic response, rather than their theoretical orientation, is the crucial factor in helping the individual find their way out of the pain that brought them to treatment in the first place. The crucial dimension of cultural competence in dealing with clients from various backgrounds highlights the importance of being in a relationship with the client that honors their lived experience. Relational theory is where traditional social work has always been.

Study Questions

1. What have you learned about Orthodox Jews that alters preconceived notions about what a relational clinician would need to bear in mind in practice?
2. How does a secular bias in psychotherapy impact on working with religious Jews? Give an example and generalize about ways in which secular bias can have an impact on practice.
3. How might a relational clinician approach a client who ascribes to the authority of a religious figure, such as a rabbi? What role may this person play, and how could it affect the role of the clinician?
4. What part does countertransference play when working with clients who have strict customs to which they adhere? Give an example of a time when you have had such a reaction and what relational skills you used to manage the situation.
5. What relational social work principles were illustrated in the cases of Amy and Ari? Identify one in each case, and explain how the case material demonstrated the principle.
6. What might you begin to do to prepare for work with Orthodox Jews? As a relational clinician, what are your feelings about needing to incorporate previously unfamiliar cultural information into your practice?

References

American Psychiatric Association. (1980). *Diagnostic and statistical manual of mental disorders* (3rd ed.). Washington, DC: American Psychiatric Association.

Ariel, Y. (2007). Gay, orthodox and trembling: The rise of orthodox gay consciousness, 1970s-2000s. *Journal of Homosexuality, 52*(3/4), 91–109.

Aron, L. (1991). The patient's experience of the analyst's subjectivity. In S. Mitchell & L. Aron (Eds.), *Relational psychoanalysis: The emergence of a tradition* (pp. 245–268). New Jersey: The Analytic Press.

Berzoff, J., Flanagan, L. M., & Heretz, P. (2008). *Inside out and outside in: Psychodynamic clinical theory and psychopathology in contemporary multicultural contexts.* New York: Jason Aronson.

Bollas, C. (1987). Loving hate. In *The Shadow of the object* (pp. 117–134). New York: Columbia University Press.

Bowlby, J. (1969). *Attachment.* New York: Basic Books.

Bromberg, P. (2011). *The shadow of the tsunami and growth of the relational mind.* New York: Taylor and Francis.

Buber, M. (1937). I & Thou. (Smith, R. G. Trans.). Edinburgh/New York: T. and T. Clark/Charles Scribner's Sons.

Davis, D. S. (2008). Religion, genetics and sexual orientation: The Jewish tradition. *Kennedy Institute of Ethics Journal, 18*(2), 125–148. doi:10.1353/ken.0.0008.

Eigen, M. (1981). The area of faith in Winnicott, Lacan and Bion. In S. Mitchell & L. Aron (Eds.), *Relational psychoanalysis: The emergence of a tradition* (pp. 3–37). New Jersey: The Analytic Press.

Fairbairn, W. R. D. (1952). *An object relations theory of the personality.* New York: Viking.

Freedberg, S. (2009). *Relational theory for social work practice: A feminist perspective.* New York: Routledge Press.

Freud, S. (1907). Obsessive actions and religious practices. The completely psychological works of Sigmund Freud Vol. 9 (The standard ed., 115–128).

Freud, S. (1913). The standard edition of the complete psychological works of Sigmund Freud. London: Hogarth Press. The claims of psycho-analysis to scientific interest. SE, 13: 165–200.

Freud, S. (1927). The future of an illusion. In: *The complete psychological works of Sigmund Freud Vol. 21* (The Standard ed. , pp. 1–56). London: Hogarth Press.

Freud, S. (1930). Civilization and its discontents. In: *The complete psychological works of Sigmund Freud Vol. 21* (The Standard ed., pp. 57–145). London: Hogarth Press.

Fromm, E. (1950). *Psychoanalysis and religion*. New Haven: Yale University Press.

Ghent, E. (1990). Masochism, submission, surrender – Masochism as a perversion of surrender. *Contemporary Psychoanalysis, 26*, 108–136.

Goldman, D. (1993). *In one's bones: The clinical genius of Winnicott*. New Jersey: Jason Aronson.

Goldstein, E. (1995). *Ego psychology and social work practice* (2nd ed.). New York: The Free Press.

Greenberg, J., & Mitchell, S. A. (1983). *Object relations in psychoanalytic theory*. Cambridge: Harvard University Press.

Greenberg, D., & Witztum, E. (1991). Problems in the treatment of religious patients. *American Journal of Psychotherapy, 15*(4), 554–565.

Greenberg, D., & Witztum, E. (2001). *Sanity and sanctity*. New Haven: Yale University Press.

Hertz, J. H. (Ed.). (1981). *The Pentateuch and Haftorahs*. London: Soncino Press.

Hollis, F. (2000). *Casework: A psychosocial therapy* (5th ed.). New York: McGraw-Hill.

Horney, K. (1942). *Self analysis*. New York: W.W. Norton.

Jones, E. (1957). *The life and work of Sigmund Freud: Vols. 2 and 3*. New York: Basic Books.

Jung, C. J. (1954). *Collected works* (Vol. 11). New York: Bollingen Foundation.

Kohut, H. (1984). In A. Goldberg & P. Stepansky (Eds.), *How does analysis cure?* Chicago: University of Chicago Press.

Levine, S. W. (2003). *Mystics, mavericks, and merrymakers: An intimate journey among Hasidic girls*. New York: New York University Press.

McWilliams, N. (1994). *Psychoanalytic diagnosis: Understanding personality structure in the clinical process*. New York: Guilford Press.

Meissner, W. (1984). *Psychoanalysis and religious experience*. New Haven: Yale University Press.

Miller, A. (1969). *God of Daniel S: In search of the American Jew*. London: Macmillan Press.

Mitchell, S. (1988). *Relational concepts in psychoanalysis: An integration*. Cambridge: Harvard University Press.

Mitchell, S., & Aron, L. (Eds.). (1999). *Relational psychoanalysis: The emergence of a tradition*. New Jersey: The Analytic Press.

Poll, S. (1962). *The Hasidic Community of Williamsburg: A study in the sociology of religion*. New York: Schocken Books.

Rubin, J. (1999). Religion, Freud and women. *Gender and Psychoanalysis, 4*(4), 333–365.

Rubin, J. (2004). *The good life: Psychoanalytic reflections on love, ethics, creativity, and spirituality*. Albany: State University of New York Press.

Strupp, H. H. (1989). Psychotherapy: Can the practitioner learn from the researcher? *American Psychologist, 44*, 717–724.

Sullivan, H. S. (1954). *The psychiatric interview*. New York: W.W. Norton.

Tosone, C. (2004). Relational social work: Honoring the tradition. *Smith College Studies in Social Work, 74*(3), 475–487.

Welwood, J. (1996). *Love and awakening: Discovering the sacred path of intimate relationship*. New York: Harper Collins.

Winnicott, D.W. (1945). Primitive emotional development in the Collected Papers: Through Pediatrics to Psychoanalysis. New York: Basic Books.

Winnicott, D. W. (1948). Pediatrics and psychiatry in the Collected Papers: Through Pediatrics to Psychoanalysis. New York: Basic Books.

Winnicott, D. W. (1958). *Collected papers: Through paediatrics to psychoanalysis*. New York: Basic Books.

Winnicott, D. W. (1967). Mirror-role of mother and family in child development. In *Playing and reality* (pp. 111–118). New York: Basic Books.

World Almanac. (2012). New York: World Almanac Books.

Part IV
Diversities of Sexual Identity

Working Relationally with LGBT Clients in Clinical Practice: Client and Clinician in Context

Griffin Hansbury and John L. Bennett

Introduction

"Since this is a gay clinic, you probably want me to be gay, out, and proud," said Tom in our first session. Conflicted about his sexual orientation, recently diagnosed with HIV, still living in the closet at 40 years old, and suspicious of my motives, Tom spoke volumes with that one statement. He also brought us right into the fact that we were already in a relationship, one filled with expectation, hope, and dread. He further illustrated, as will be discussed, the clinical challenges and necessary relational theory elements for effective clinical social work practice.

Relational social work is particularly suited for intervention with oppressed populations, such as lesbian, gay, bisexual, and transgender (LGBT) clients, who are vulnerable to pathological labeling (Glassgold 1995; Lewes 2005). Relational therapy directs the clinician away from unidirectional diagnostic labeling and toward a mutual articulation of problems and goal setting for clinical work (Orange et al. 1997). Deconstruction of pathogenic narratives applied to any population is a core clinical element of relational theory's basis in constructivism and its techniques of mutual exploration and co-created strategies of addressing problems that are both individual and generic for marginalized or maligned groups (Berzoff 2011). The relational social worker strives to normalize and thereby depathologize

G. Hansbury, M.A., LCSW (✉)
National Psychological Association for Psychoanalysis, New York, NY, USA

J.L. Bennett, LCSW
Callen-Lorde Community Health Center, New York, NY, USA

Silver School of Social Work, New York University, New York, NY, USA

J.B. Rosenberger (ed.), *Relational Social Work Practice with Diverse Populations*,
Essential Clinical Social Work Series, DOI 10.1007/978-1-4614-6681-9_13,
© Springer Science+Business Media New York 2014

the client's experience. In this way the worker helps to alleviate the experience of shame and the stigmatization inflicted by hegemony of a homophobic and hetero-sexist society (Glassgold 2004). The relational social worker does not pursue try-ing to know the etiology of the client's sexual orientation or gender identity. Instead of asking "why?" the relational clinician is more interested in the "how" of the client's present lived experience. She is curious about the many ways that the cli-ent's sexual orientation and gender identity have had an impact on his relationships with others and the self.

Unlike some earlier, psychoanalytically informed models of practice, relational theory does not have a tradition that seeks to find the origin of sexual orientation and gender identity in the client's developmental history (Drescher 1998). The focus is on the individual's particular subjectivity and not upon the etiology of sexual orientation or gender identity. Subjective experience is the departure point for clinical exploration (Ganzer 2007). This can include an examination of the impact of sexual orientation and gender expression upon personality development across the lifespan.

LGBT Identity and the Mental Health Professions

Historically, within the mental health professions, LGBT orientations have been deemed pathological and diagnosed as mental illnesses and perversions. In American psychiatry, which has shaped American clinical practice in general, homosexuality was considered a mental illness to be cured. Clinical social work was heavily impacted by the diagnostic categories and descriptions of mental illnesses, being in most public service sectors required to legitimize clinical treatment based on an approved diagnosis. In 1973, through the lobbying efforts of the LGBT community, the American Psychiatric Association (APA) removed homosexuality as a diagnosis from the Diagnostic and Statistical Manual (DSM) III (Drescher 2010). From 1980 to 1986, a new diagnosis appeared in the DSM-III, viz., ego-dystonic homosexual-ity (American Psychiatric Association 1980). Some argue that this was a compro-mise to appease prominent segments of the APA who persisted in conceptualizing homosexuality as the result of pathological personality development and that this diagnosis perpetuated the homophobic treatment of gays and lesbians by the mental health professions (Bayer 1987), including clinical social workers as primary pro-viders of public mental health care.

The pathologizing of transgender experience in particular remains entrenched in the current version of the diagnostic manual, *DSM-IV-TR* (APA 2000). Gender iden-tity disorder (GID) is routinely assigned as a diagnosis to transgender clients seek-ing help from the mental health professions (Sennott 2011). Medical practitioners often require a psychiatrically assigned diagnosis of GID as a prerequisite for access to gender-confirming medical treatments such as hormone therapy or surgery (Drescher 2010). The planned fifth edition of the DSM strikes GID from its list of disorders; however, it contains a diagnostic compromise similar to one used by the APA in the 1980s – gender incongruence. While sidestepping the issue of individual pathology and the etiology of transgender experience, this diagnosis persists in labeling persons of transgender experience as prone to dysphoria in ways in which no other identity is described in the DSM (Bennett 2010). Activists, including many prominent providers of transgender health-care services, have decried this addition to the DSM-5 (Davis et al. 2010).

The long-held notion that lesbian, gay, bisexual, and transgender subjectivities are inherently pathological reflects our society's tendency to segment human diversity into "good" and "bad," "us" and "them" (Berreby 2005). This dichotomous thinking about sexuality has been the case among many mental health professionals for more than a century (Carlson 2005), even though the founder of psychodynamic thinking and practice, Sigmund Freud, wrote explicitly that psychoanalysis "is decidedly opposed to any attempt at separating off homosexuals from the rest of mankind as a group of special character" (Freud 1949). While Freud supported gay rights and believed that homosexuals were fit to be trained as psychoanalysts, his theories on sexuality, which generally held up heterosexuality as the norm, provided a basis for anti-LGBT bias in the mental health field (Drescher 2008).

Prominent LGB theorists (transgender-identified theorists were not publishing until very recently) have left their mark on relational theory, affecting more than just the relationship between psychoanalysis and sexuality. In addition to changes in the DSM, in the 1990s, there was a convergence of relational psychoanalysis, feminism, and queer theory. Queer theory, which emerged from feminism and LGBT studies, is the analysis of text and theory from an LGBT perspective. This convergence of these theories led to the depathologizing of homosexuality (Kassoff 2004) and created a path by which openly gay, lesbian, and bisexual people could enter psychoanalytic training, previously forbidden to them (Drescher 2008). While psychoanalytic training per se was not the central issue, its influence pervaded the perspectives on mental health and qualifications for providers. The end of the twentieth century saw more and more lesbian, gay, and bisexual (LGB) people enter into the fields of social work, psychology, and psychiatry, doing research and publishing in those professional capacities, which has furthered the de-stigmatization of LGB people (transgender people remain stigmatized by the mental health professions) and broadened the focus of psychoanalytic thinking.

Most recently, relational theory has taken up the question of transgender subjectivity, positioning transgender identity not as pathology but as variance (Goldner 2011), just as was done previously with homosexuality. Transgender clinicians, in social work and other health arenas, are entering the field, publishing their clinical experiences and theories on this topic (Hansbury 2011). As relational theory continues to integrate LGBT orientations into the framework of normal variation, rather than pathology, thereby altering the thinking in the field, the relational approach can do the same work between clinician and client, altering the way LGBT clients think and feel about themselves in relation to others and the world around them.

Clinical Social Work Understanding of Homophobia, Transphobia, and Biphobia

LGBT clients seek the assistance of clinical social workers with the usual goals and problems common to non-LGBT clients. They want to find meaningful and stable work, improve their relationships, feel less depressed and anxious, increase their self-esteem, etc. In a mutual working alliance, client and clinician collaborate to work on the interpersonal and developmental issues that can underlie many presenting issues. The piece that complicates clinical social work with LGBT clients is accurate apprehension of the experience of growing up and continuing to be a diverse individual in an environment marked by the oppression and marginalization of homophobia, transphobia, and biphobia. Homophobia refers to the hatred and fear of homosexuals, transphobia to the hatred and fear of transgender people, and, similarly, biphobia is the hatred and fear of bisexuals (Elze 2006). However, many transgender people are the victims of homophobia, and many gay, lesbian, and bisexual people experience a kind of transphobia if we recognize the word to include the fear and hatred of gender-nonconforming individuals. Just as diversity of all kinds challenges the clinician, and thereby potentially evokes powerful countertransference reactions, understanding the issues and relational social work practice solutions with the LGBT population enhances all clinical social work practice.

It is important to note that sexual orientation, gender identity, and biological sex are three different aspects of the self (Morrow 2006). Sexual orientation refers to one's preference in sexual and/or romantic partners. Gender identity refers to a person's sense of self as a man, woman, both, or neither. And biological sex refers to physiological aspects of maleness, femaleness, and combinations of the two, including gonads, genitals, and chromosomes. Keeping these differences in mind, a transgender man, who began life as female, may be primarily attracted to men and identify as gay. He would experience both transphobia and homophobia. A butch lesbian experiences homophobia, but she also may be subject to a kind of transphobia due to her masculine appearance and demeanor. Bisexual people experience homophobia when expressing their same-sex desires and relationships, and they also experience biphobia.

Despite much of Western culture's advancements, these LGBT phobias have not gone away. In their grip, LGBT clients continue to come into therapy with related presenting problems. For example, gay male clients may seek treatment for deep shame about sex and the "feminine" aspects of their gender identities (Shelby 2000). Many lesbian clients continue to struggle in intimate partnerships where they subjugate their own needs and desires to those of their partner (Buloff and Osterman 1995). Many transgender women clients suffer anxiety and depression due to daily harassment in the streets, and the loss of family, friends, and jobs (Sánchez and Vilain 2009), while many transgender men clients struggle with the pressures of being male in the world and may often hold themselves back from realizing life goals (Hansbury 2011). Bisexual and genderqueer clients often find they are getting lost in the shuffle, rejected by gay and trans groups, without adequate social support (Weiss 2003). These are generalizations, but they are included here to alert the relational clinician to the diversity of presenting problems with which LGBT clients struggle and to the likely transference stance to clinical services that may represent the problems that stem from heteronormative society's pressure on the LGBT person to conform to rigid ways of being.

Whether or not the client is being seen in an LGBT-specific setting, with an LGBT clinician or the most liberal-minded straight social worker, homophobia and transphobia are in the room, in both members of the dyad. In a homophobic society, all persons harbor homophobia to one extent or another, just as racism exists in any member of a racist society, regardless of background, politics, personal intention, and the like. As feminist psychoanalyst Young-Bruehl (1997) writes, "Homophobes hate acts that they themselves can and usually do engage in, so, to repudiate these acts they must assign them clearly to another category of people. The category is all that stands between them and those acts" (p. 143). Homophobia, whether internalized or externalized, is repudiation, a splitting off, of the homosexual parts of the self. We could say the same for transphobia, since all human beings are a combination of masculine and feminine, male and female aspects (Knights and Kerfoot 2004). It is this split, in LGBT clients, which relational therapy can help to heal. To do so requires that the clinician be aware of her own sex and gender splits and that she be willing to work through them. A clinician who is unwilling to confront her own homophobia and transphobia, who believes that homosexuality, bisexuality, or transgender identity is a curable disease, must get ample supervision from an LGBT-affirmative clinician. If these issues cannot be worked through, then it would be unethical for the clinician to continue working with LGBT clients (Rosik 2003), and she must refer them to more qualified colleagues or risk retraumatizing the clients with her own unprocessed fear, envy, and hate.

Clinician Sameness and Difference

In clinical social work practice with diverse client populations, the sameness or difference of the clinician's population of identification comes into play overtly and covertly. Two primary issues need to be in the forefront of the social work practitioner's awareness as she engages, assesses, and constructs a working treatment plan with any client. First, to designate as "diverse," only those peoples who are from marginalized and oppressed groups, privileges the dominant group in insidious ways which may cloak transference and countertransference elements, among other clinical elements. Second, identification with one's own group, be it dominant or oppressed, when meeting a client of the same group, can equally obscure individual assessment and treatment option considerations. While sameness and difference may not be readily apparent, being a member of any population of identification is a strong force in the self-experience of both client and clinician. In relational theory thinking, discovery of such forces is a central feature of both client assessment and clinician self-regulation, including most significantly factors that can rupture the attunement process.

LGBT clinicians are not immune to homophobia, transphobia, and biphobia. For example, a gay male therapist who had been working with gay and lesbian clients for many years found himself face to face with his own transphobia when he began working with his first transgender client. He had difficulty accepting that the client, a transwoman, was not a man, and he continually referred to the client inappropriately with male pronouns, unwittingly shaming and erasing her each time. In supervision, he discovered his own deep feelings of shame and rage around thwarted childhood longings to express his femininity. Unable to work quickly through his envy of the client, he rightly referred her to a colleague. Another example might be a feminine-presenting lesbian therapist who is prejudiced against lesbian clients whom she perceives as being too masculine. A transgender therapist might be prejudiced against a genderqueer client, a transgender person whose gender expression challenges the boundaries between male and female. There are many hypothetical clinician and client pairings that, due to apparent sameness, could appear on the surface to be a good match but underneath reveal entrenched prejudices that could have the potential to deeply impair clinical work.

These examples of internal barriers to successful clinical social work practice are not the norm and are offered as cautions to point up the need for clinical social workers to master the methods that allow such barriers to become integrated and useful in the treatment process. While similar biases exist in all people and all clinicians to some extent, use of the relational approach can foster open dialogue and self-examination, and they can use these biases in a productive way to help LGBT clients work through the traumas of both internalized and external homophobia and transphobia. Some key techniques, reflecting the relational model, are essential in this work and are described here to provide clinical social work students with tools to orient their practice with LGBT clients.

The Clinical Process: A Case Example

Beginning with Transference and Countertransference

While clinical social workers typically are not introduced to clinical process starting with transference and countertransference, work with diverse populations elevates the significance of this dimension of the relationship to a primary position. As noted in the introductory chapter of this book, the very designation of diversity population creates an anticipatory separation of the client group from an implicit norm. Therefore, the clinical social worker needs to reflect on the implications of a population's diversity identification in the service of distinguishing collective expectations in the transference and especially the countertransference from her readiness to meet the client as an individual.

Regarding assessment, it is important to remember that this is a process in which both clinician and client engage. Before the clinician can begin to assess the client, the client has already begun assessing the clinician. This is assumed in the two-way dynamics of intersubjectivity that is the hallmark of relational therapy (Goldstein et al. 2009). The client's and clinician's own diversity identifications also are among many factors at play in the preliminary development of the intersubjectivity between client and clinician. In our current Information Age, the client has access not only to impressionistic information and predictions based on agency context; he also has access to powerful information sources, such as agency websites. These sources frequently contain information about services as well as service provider photographs and professional profiles. Additionally, the client will often identify the clinician with qualities inherent in the agency environment, such as the tidiness of the facility, or the professionalism and client-centeredness of agency administrative staff. A clinician in private practice might also have a professional website, online published papers, or other caches of information, personal and professional, available to anyone who knows how to use Google.

The client, Tom, cited at the beginning of this chapter, offers a good example of the power of predictive transference based on the client's first impressions of the clinical encounter. His first relational statement of "you probably want me to be gay, out, and proud," in which he imagined that I wanted something for him, quickly conveyed that Tom was expecting coercion from me, a kind of brainwashing in which my desires would attempt to wipe out his own. His worry, and perhaps also his hope, about what I might want came from the setting in which we met. We were meeting at the Callen-Lorde Community Health Center, an agency in New York City with the specific mission to meet the medical and mental health needs of the LGBT and HIV-affected populations. To reach my office, Tom had walked through a lobby decorated with rainbow flags, flyers offering transgender name-change workshops, and posters about safer sex between men. He was in a setting that clearly valued being "out and proud," and he understandably assumed that his clinician's values would be in line with those of the clinic. Tom's transference was not just to me but also to the agency as a whole.

This illustrates how, in the two-person psychology of the relational approach, the social services agency acts as a third entity, co-creating the clinical relationship along with client and clinician. This further demonstrates how a relationship takes shape before client and clinical social worker even meet face to face. Each agency setting and client pairing will elicit a different sort of predictive transference. It is neither advantageous nor possible for an agency setting to be completely neutral. Relational theory posits that it is equally impossible and not by definition advantageous for the clinician to be free of transference triggers. Instead, awareness of the messages conveyed and received provides a wealth of clinical material regarding client attitudes, internalizations, and experiences to be explored in relationship with the relational social work practitioner.

LGBT clients in smaller cities and rural settings across the country receive treatment in settings not designated as LGBT focused (Foster 1997). This has practice implications for the social worker in such settings, who must create a relationship of trust where the absence of LGBT service identification reflects the broader society in which sexual and gender diversity is unwelcome. In the absence of overt recognition, a population of diversity might be expected to predict lack of recognition, ignorance, or, even worse, intolerance. The clinical social worker cannot know in advance how the client will forecast the agency climate and the clinician's perspective. His presence in a generically identified service setting calls for special alertness to how a client of a diverse population configures the relational baseline.

These are examples of how transference and countertransference elements merit clinical reflection from the outset. The clinician in a generic practice setting is not less influenced by the agency culture than one in a population-identified setting. From a relational practice viewpoint, the clinical social worker needs to be mindful of what communications are taking place and what their influences are on her and on the clients entering the practice setting. In agencies where LGBT clients don't see obvious reflections of themselves in the waiting room, they may well believe that the agency does not employ persons like themselves, and expectations that LGBT prohibitions exist are predictable. Therefore, an absence of open LGBT presence surrounding the clinical encounter places the onus of trust building more completely on the clinician. All populations, where diversity is fused with rejection or marginalization, identify social work services with the dominant and therefore negating social order (Ferguson and Woodward 2009).

As the transference relationship has already begun, the client waiting to meet the clinical social worker may wonder, "How will my sexuality be received? How will the social worker respond to my gender presentation? Will I be judged? Will I be shamed? Can I be understood?" Of course, similar worries are typical of any client beginning work with a new clinician and come up throughout the treatment. However, LGBT clients are entering the relationship having endured a history of homophobia and transphobia imposed by family and culture, and thereby, internalization may be anticipated at conscious and unconscious levels. As Cabaj (2000) states "All gay people have internalized homophobia, having been brought up in a homophobic society that either tends to promote prejudicial myths about gay people or negates the existence of gay people in general" (p. 9). To this should be added that all bisexual and transgender people have internalized bi- and transphobia for the same reasons. No matter what the setting, the LGBT client can be expected, at least preliminarily, to enter the clinician's office with a lack of trust, expecting the same negative treatment from the clinician that he has received from the world at large and that he might continue to receive from inside himself.

Assessment with LGBT Clients

Assessment is an ongoing process, one that continually unfolds during the course of treatment. The clinician thinks about the person as a whole and from within the context of the individual in their particular social environment. The DSM should be used with careful reflection. In a clinic setting and in the current age of managed care, a diagnosis code is often required. The relational clinician should consider diagnoses that address the underlying psychological situation of the whole person, such as dysthymia or anxiety, rather than diagnoses that are based upon identity.

For transgender clients, clinicians must keep in mind that the DSM's gender identity disorder diagnosis is controversial. Similar to earlier diagnostic categories related to homosexuality, long since removed from the DSM, the gender identity disorder diagnosis stigmatizes the individual's identity, rather than describing the individual's particular emotional or psychological distress (Sennott 2011). Indeed, in recognition of the perils of diagnosis by identity, gender identity disorder is slated to be removed in the next revision of the DSM (Lawrence 2010).

While the clinician's assessment continues throughout the entire treatment, the first session often sets the tone for the qualities of the transference that the client brings in. While any first session with a clinician is intensified by anticipation of confronting the presenting problem, and does not therefore reflect the client's highest level of functioning, it nonetheless reveals patterns of relating, problem conceptualization, hopes for clinical assistance, and the like. In the first session, the clinician should also pay attention to her own countertransferential responses. These can provide the clinician with plentiful information about the client's relational world. Transference often explains how he experienced his early caregivers and how they experienced him. Its thread continues through his current relationships today.

The social worker is well schooled in starting where the client is, and the clinical social worker is additionally alerted to the relational meaning in all of the initial transactions. The clinician pays attention to body language. How does the client walk into the office? Does he give a deferential greeting and sit stiffly in the chair, waiting silently for the clinician to begin? Or, does he robustly shake the clinician's hand, then scatter his coat, gloves, and bag, flop down in the chair and launch into it? What are the client's first words? Does he answer the question, "What brings you here?" with a list of specific and concrete goals (to get a new job, to stop using drugs, to improve his relationship with his husband) or with a shrug and a mumbled, "I don't know. I just want to feel better." These opening remarks may be along the lines of "Nobody listens to me," or "Everybody wants me to take care of them," or "I just want everyone to leave me alone." The relational clinician wonders how the dominant themes in that first session might shape the contours of the entire treatment. One client might feel that the clinician never listens, the next might take care of the clinician's feelings, and another might continually present as withdrawn. Each of these situations not only describes what is happening in a session but provides the clinician a summary of the experience that the client brings to the relationship with the clinician, often foreshadowing the course of explorations, resistances, interpersonal exchanges, and other elements of the treatment relationship.

Simultaneously, the relational social worker is listening to her countertransference. Maybe the clinician notices her attention is wandering or else feels riveted to every word the client is saying, as if watching a thrilling blockbuster movie. Maybe the clinician feels something in her body, a flush of sexual heat, a discomfort that sends her fidgeting, or a heavy tiredness that threatens to come out in a yawn. This information sets in motion a means of problem analysis, in that the relational expectations and reactions reflect the worldview that the client is bringing to his overall functioning. All of this countertransferential information provides an overview to the clinician of how a relational matrix is being co-created by client and clinician.

Tom's case provides an example of how this initial and open-ended assessment process creates a dialogue wherein conflicts, strengths and liabilities, and patterns that may pertain to the core problem can emerge.

The Course of Treatment

Remembering that assessment spans the entire treatment, from initial intake to termination, the relational social worker constantly interrogates her internal response to the client and her participation in the relationship that emerges between client and clinician. Specifically in the model of relational treatment, she does not view the client's statements about her as mere projections but as part of the mutually created field of interaction. The client who perceives the clinician with suspicion and guardedness may evoke a parallel carefulness in the clinician. The relational clinician is observant of this interactive pattern and may proactively comment on it and ask the client's observations as a means of promoting mutuality in the working process (McWilliams 1999). Therefore, I had to wonder aloud about Tom's statement in our first meeting and invite him to join in this exploration. I noted that he stated that I wanted him to be "gay, out and proud." On the manifest level, this was his expectation. On the interpersonal level, he was declaring his expectation of our interactional hierarchy, including who was in charge of what he should be. On an intrapsychic level, this topic was clearly on his mind and therefore a target of clinical attention. Was this also a statement of his ambivalence and perhaps confusion about what I should want for him? Did he want me to replicate the shaming he had received from important figures in his life such as family, friends, Church, and State, or was he daring me to push him toward self-acceptance? These were questions, which, with tact and timing, would form a central part of our clinical practice dialogue.

Relational theory recognizes that meaning is co-created (Mitchell 1988). Both perception and expression contain material from the client and clinician. Tom, as is often the case and recognized as such in relational practice, was partially right about me. While I did not imagine him marching in gay pride parades or becoming an HIV activist, I did harbor the hope that he could eventually live without internalized homophobia. I did hope that he could stop blunting his emotions with, as I came to learn, drugs and dangerous sex. I did hope that he could feel less shame about his sexuality and his longing for intimacy with men. It was, as revealed as the clinical practice proceeded, a hope that Tom and I shared, and that would, over the course of our relationship, develop into a reality. In relational work, the trajectory of the client's hope is elicited and shared. Its specific content and the real-life ramifications are first lived out in the dialogue of the clinical social work relationship. The client then can begin to bring this orientation of hopefulness to his daily life (Mitchell 1993).

The process of relational assessment would be the same with non-LGBT clients. From the first moments of the first encounter with a client, the clinician is assessing defenses and resistances, ego strengths, attachment style, and the like (McWilliams 1999). With LGBT clients, however, it is key that the clinician listen especially for two things: (1) the reverberations of gender trauma from early experiences when the client's gender presentation was corrected or punished, a common experience for LGBT persons (Bailey and Zucker 1995; Hiestand and Levitt 2005), and (2) internalized homophobia or transphobia and its impact on the client's psychosocial functioning (Elze 2006). Both of these phenomena can manifest at any point in the clinical relationship.

Mirroring. LGBT clients often grow up without adequate mirroring. The LGBT child typically has heterosexual, cisgender (non-transgender) parents, teachers, and friends. Unlike the offspring of other marginalized and oppressed minorities, such as the African-American or Hispanic child and the Muslim or Orthodox Jewish child, all of whom typically have some opportunity to see themselves reflected in important others, the LGBT child is an outsider from early life. The LGBT child is typically un-mirrored in his identity formation (Beard and Glickauf-Hughes 1994; Gair 2004) and must make meaning out of a selfhood that is more likely to experience shame and censorship, even assault, than it is to be supported. In adolescence, when the LGBT client is first expressing his sexuality and gender identity, the lack of mirroring often comes from peers and society, as he moves outward from the sphere of family. The most prevalent problem faced by lesbian and gay adolescents, especially those with nonconforming gender expressions, is isolation, which Hetrick and Martin (1987) break down into three types: (1) cognitive isolation, "the almost total lack of accurate information"; (2) social isolation, "the negative self-view enforced by the denial of accurate information"; and (3) emotional isolation, "feelings of being alone, of being the only who feels this way" (pp. 165–171). In a time when peer identifications are so crucial, the gay, lesbian, and/or non-gender-normative adolescent may find him or herself without the opportunity to develop a group identity, a sense of the "we." Without self-sustaining models and mirrors, this cognitive isolation may lead to a "cognitive dissonance that will radically affect the young person's sense of self" (Hetrick and Martin 1987, p. 167).

What is the impact of a lack of mirroring on the developing self? Relational theory, drawing on the key interpersonal precepts of many psychodynamic bodies of theory, describes several powerful repercussions of mirroring failures that must be addressed in the treatment process. Without adequate empathic responses from early caregivers, the individual may develop narcissistic traits and relational dynamics. According to self psychology, the lack may also lead to what is called a vertical split in the psyche, "the side-by-side, conscious existence of otherwise incompatible psychological attitudes" (Kohut 2009, p. 177). A client with a vertical split alternates between grandiose feelings and states of low self-esteem. He may feel like a superstar 1 day and a miserable wretch the next, an oscillation that generates, and is generated by, deeply unbearable shame and rage. Lack of mirroring may also lead to the child's development of a formidable false self. As Winnicott (1956) explained throughout much of his work, the false self is a defensive structure the child uses to comply with external demands and to get basic needs met by caregivers and the environment. It is like a mask used to protect the true self, which remains hidden. These and other concepts from Kohut and Winnicott, though they predated the development of relational theory as the basis of clinical social work practice, focus on the relational matrix and are often used by clinicians who follow this approach to working with clients. They are useful when working with LGBT clients who, due to the lack of mirroring discussed here, often keep their true selves hidden for fear of being shunned or shamed. Inviting those hidden parts out into the light, where they can be seen and mirrored without judgment, is part of the relational clinician's task.

Active Attunement. As Buloff and Osterman (1995) write in *Lesbians and Psychoanalysis*, "Peering into the face of society, much as a child looks into the face of her parent, the lesbian looks for a reflection of her self" (p. 95). The young lesbian searches to find mirrors that reflect her emerging self; she sees instead "grotesque and distorted images reflected back in words like: perverse, sinful, immoral, infantile, arrested, inadequate, or she sees no reflection at all – a peculiar silence – an invisibility" (Buloff and Osterman 1995, p. 95). This idea can be expanded to include all LGBT expressions of selfhood in relation to others. The mother of a young female child who will grow up to be a transgender man might look with distaste or turn her gaze away from a "daughter" with more masculine expressions, sending a message to the child that her/his self and strivings are not loveable. A gay male's mother, worrying that her son might be socially punished for having more feminine characteristics, might hold the child close, smothering him with protectiveness, sending the message that it is not safe to be himself. These and other unstated relational messages resulting from distorted or absent attunement to the reality of the growing self are often internalized and frequently emerge in the relational matrix of the clinical situation.

The clinical social work practitioner is well aware that events of the past may not be directly remembered but present themselves as derivatives in the client's struggles with problems in treatment (Goldstein 2001). In adulthood, the client may exhibit conflicted attachment styles bred from such earliest maternal interactions (Ainsworth 1989; Hazan and Shaver 1987). For the LGBT-aware clinician, it is important to explore these attachment issues in themselves and determine how, if so, they are connected to the client's gender identity and sexual orientation (Mohr 2008). Recognizing with the client the impact of attachment anxieties in his relationships to self and others, including the clinician, allows the clinical social worker to reflect back to the client the presented material in a manner that confirms its emotional significance. A client, for example, who presents distress, not about developmental misinterpretation or disapproval but about present reactivity to misinterpretation or disapproval by others, can be helped by the relational clinician to address the emotional depth of experience, not only its factual profile.

Pursuing active attunement with previously unrecognized suffering and conflict can be the crux of the therapeutic process. I have invited transgender clients preparing to transition from male to female, who have been ambivalent about their gender expression, to come to their sessions dressed in women's clothing or to bring photographs of themselves in women's clothing. The clinical intention of these sessions was to actively engage and affirm the gender identity the client wishes to express in the greater world. In this way the client can begin to share this aspect of self with another and experience doing so without the shaming received from earlier objects. In addition to the direct relational interchange of being present with another person in the new form, the client and clinician talk about the details of this identity expression experience. In inviting direct practice and interaction with identity expression, the clinician and client collaborate in the creation of a corrective emotional experience. The corrective emotional experience, a concept first proposed by Franz Alexander (McCarthy 2010), was an early relational innovation in psychoanalytic theory and persists in contemporary relational theory (McWilliams 1999). The clinician fosters this correction in creating a favorable emotional environment in which previously distressing material, such as shamed or thwarted attempts at female gender expression, is validated and the traumatic influence is diminished.

Self-Disclosure as an Aspect of Relational Treatment. Self-disclosure is a broad topic. It can mean any revelation about the clinician, verbal or nonverbal. The clinician who blushes when the client talks about sex is self-disclosing. So is the clinician who decorates her office with expensive art. Deliberate self-disclosure for therapeutic purposes, however, includes the revelation of the clinician's affects, conflicts, and thought processes about the client and the work (Hanson 2005). What is revealed, ultimately, is a clinician who is a human being with human feelings, rather than a robot or a computer that spits out data analyses. McWilliams (1999) encourages inclusion of self-disclosure of the clinician's experiences or observations, particularly for clients who lack reference points for alternative perspectives; her caveat is that the clinical social worker scrupulously determines if the disclosure is targeted to a client's needs and interests.

Although controversial in relational work (Sparks 2009), judicious disclosure of the clinician's countertransference is another hallmark of relational therapy and can be useful in mitigating shame. Morrison (2007) writes, "I consider self-disclosure generally to be a useful antidote to shame, both as part of our acceptance and soothing of personal shame, and as a potent procedure from clinician to client as a means to 'level the playing field' and humanize the shame experience" (pp. 106–107). Many LGBT clinicians today routinely disclose their sexual orientation and/or gender identity to their LGBT clients for the purpose of providing a model and to detoxify the client's shame. In addition, HIV-positive clinicians sometimes disclose their serostatus to HIV-positive clients for the same reasons (Cole 2001).

Rupture and Repair. Ruptures in empathy, also known as empathic failures, and their repair through mutual exploration by client and clinician are a significant aspect of relational social work practice. The clinician's empathic failure is inevitable, although never intentional, and profoundly important to the work. Kohut (2009) was among the first to underscore the significance of rupture and repair as a therapeutic element. The erasure, shaming, and punishment LGBT clients have endured often make them exquisitely sensitive to empathic failure from the therapist. The relational clinician should realize that although these ruptures are inevitable, they also represent clinical opportunities to not only repair the clinical relationship but also mitigate the effects of previous empathic failures by significant figures in the client's past.

Regarding my client Tom's early statement "you probably want me to be gay, out, and proud," his words "you probably want me to be" reveal a parental order: Be this; don't be that. We can imagine that this order, to be and not to be, generated shame, as well as rage, in Tom from a young age. LGBT clients have been ordered to be silent throughout life, keeping parts of their true selves hidden from the homophobia and transphobia of the environment. This internalized homophobia and transphobia become part of the ego or self where, as Malyon (1981) explains, "it influences identity formation, self-esteem, the elaboration of defenses, patterns of cognition, psychological integrity and object relations" (p. 60). It is hardly unexpected that LGBT clients enter therapy with the expectation that they will be bullied, coerced, and judged by the clinician. They expect rupture to happen, but they expect the outcome to be without repair. Unfortunately, in too many cases, the client's expectations turn out to be correct. It is the clinical social worker's role, and opportunity, to allow voice for the client's narcissistic wounding of rupture to be met with empathy, open exploration, and reparative attunement to the sequelae of the original rupture in the any ongoing relational issues the client may bring.

Gair (2004) calls attachment ruptures for LGBT children a "silent traumatization." "Narcissistic rage" is a term coined by Kohut (1972) as arising "when self or object fail to live up to the absolutarian expectations which are directed at their function" (p. 386). It is often provoked in response to psychological injuries such as "ridicule, contempt, and conspicuous defeat" (Kohut 1972, p. 380). It is important for the clinical social worker to not only explore this rage as a reaction to environmental oppression but also to explore ways in which this rage continues to shape relational as well as internal functioning.

Termination. Shelby (2000) reminds us that "If we focus on gays and lesbians as the 'victims' of social prejudice, we tend to minimize narcissistic rage" (p. 278). Helping the client to work through his narcissistic rage related to repeated empathic failures by important figures across his lifetime, including through ruptures in the clinical practice process, is often a key component of relational work with LGBT persons. The decision to terminate in a clinical case such as Tom's is reached through a mutually agreed-upon decision that the difficulties that brought him into treatment, known and unknown at the time, were adequately addressed in the clinical social work process. Adequacy in the face of inevitably ongoing conflict means having sufficient tools to handle interpersonal misunderstandings without their triggering dysfunction or disproportionate internal distress. Not insignificant among these tools is the internal representation of his relational experience with an empathic social work clinician who has offered respect and understanding of his struggle.

Conclusion

LGBT persons represent a community of diversity that intersects all segments of society. As such, LGBT persons can be expected to present at almost any setting in which clinical social workers are engaged. It is important that the relational social worker be prepared to engage in a mutual dialogue, informed in part by the clinician's attempts to grapple with her own countertransference, toward opening pathways of remedy with the client.

Relational clinical practice is an approach of choice when working with LGBT clients because it provides an empathic and open exchange in which clinician and client can collaborate, using the here-and-now relationship to work through relational difficulties from the past and outside of the treatment. Due to homophobia and transphobia in society, and a lack or mirroring in the immediate environment, LGBT clients come to therapy with traumas large and small, an abundance of shame, and rage. Using relational techniques, highlighting mirroring, listening for transference, monitoring countertransference, self-disclosure, the repair of empathic ruptures, and the exploration of narcissistic rage, the clinician can provide a corrective emotional experience that can help the client work through these issues and improve self-esteem, intimate relationships, and overall psychosocial functioning.

Study Questions

1. What makes relational social work particularly well suited for LGBT clients?
2. How does stigmatization within the mental health profession affect the treatment relationship? Discuss how stigmatization illustrates client and clinician in context and how relational social work might address this when working with a client.
3. Provide a brief explanation of the differences between sexual orientation, gender identity, and biological sex. Write a paragraph illustrating encounters with confusion about these distinctions and how clarification would improve your practice.
4. Give an example of how lack of affirmative mirroring in early development of LGBT adults can be addressed through relational practices to enhance coherent sense of self.
5. Identify two strategies of relational social work that can provide a corrective emotional experience for LGBT clients. Describe how these strategies can pertain to other marginalized populations.
6. Identify a personal quality that impacts your work with LGBT clients. Give an example from your own practice in which this quality played a role.

References

Ainsworth, M. (1989). Attachments beyond infancy. *The American Psychologist, 44*(4), 709–716.

American Psychiatric Association. (1980). *Diagnostic and statistical manual of mental disorders* (3rd ed.). Washington, DC: Author.

American Psychiatric Association. (2000). *Diagnostic and statistical manual of mental disorders* (4th ed., Text Rev.). Washington, DC: Author.

Bailey, J. M., & Zucker, K. J. (1995). Childhood sex-typed behavior and sexual orientation: A conceptual analysis and quantitative review. *Developmental Psychology. Special Issue: Sexual Orientation and Human Development, 31*(1), 43–55. doi:10.1037/0012-1649.31.1.43.

Bayer, R. (1987). *Homosexuality and American psychiatry: The politics of diagnosis.* Princeton: Princeton University Press.

Beard, J., & Glickauf-Hughes, C. (1994). Gay identity and sense of self: Rethinking male homosexuality. *Journal of Gay and Lesbian Psychotherapy, 2*, 21–37. doi:10.1300/J236v02n02_02.

Bennett, J. B. (2010). 'Inocencia': Case study of a transgender woman preparing for gender reassignment surgery without gender dysphoria. *British Gestalt Journal, 19*(2), 16–27.

Berreby, D. (2005). *Us and them: Understanding your tribal mind.* New York: Little, Brown and Co.

Berzoff, J. (Ed.). (2011). *Falling through the cracks: Psychodynamic practice with vulnerable and oppressed populations.* New York: Columbia University Press.

Buloff, B., & Osterman, M. (1995). Queer reflections: Mirroring and the lesbian experience of self. In J. M. Glassgold & S. Iasenza (Eds.), *Lesbians and psychoanalysis: Revolutions in theory and practice* (pp. 93–106). New York: Free Press.

Cabaj, R. (2000). Substance abuse, internalized homophobia, and gay men and lesbians: Psychodynamic issues and clinical impression. *Psychotherapy, 3*(3/4), 5–24.

Carlson, H. M. (2005). Psychoanalysis meets postmodern queer theory. *PsycCRITIQUES, 50*(48). US: American Psychological Association. doi:10.1037/05206311.

Cole, G. W. (2001). The HIV-positive analyst: Identifying the other. *Contemporary Psychoanalysis, 37*(1), 113–132.

Davis, C., Ben-Israel, A., Herrera, C., Henderson, A., Douglass, K. E., Bennett, J. B. (2010). *DSM-5 gender identity disorder reform.* Retrieved Nov 14, 2011, from http://www.gaycenter.org/node/5268

Drescher, J. (1998). *Psychoanalytic therapy and the gay man.* Mahwah: Analytic Press.

Drescher, J. (2008). A history of homosexuality and organized psychoanalysis. *Journal of the American Academy of Psychoanalysis and Dynamic Psychiatry, 36*(3), 443–460. doi:10.1521/jaap.2008.36.3.443.

Drescher, J. (2010). Queer diagnoses: Parallels and contrasts in the history of homosexuality, gender variance, and the diagnostic and statistical manual. *Archives of Sexual Behavior, 39*(2), 427–460. doi:10.1007/s10508-009-9531-5.

Elze, D. E. (2006). Oppression, prejudice, and discrimination. In D. F. Morrow & L. Messinger (Eds.), *Sexual orientation and gender expression in social work practice: Working with gay, lesbian, bisexual, and transgender people* (pp. 43–77). New York: Columbia University Press.

Ferguson, I., & Woodward, R. (2009). *Radical social work in practice: Making a difference.* Bristol: Policy Press.

Foster, S. J. (1997). Rural lesbians and gays: Public perceptions, worker perceptions, and service delivery. In J. D. Smith, R. J. Mancoske, J. D. Smith, & R. J. Mancoske (Eds.), *Rural gays and lesbians: Building on the strengths of communities* (pp. 23–35). Binghamton: Harrington Park Press/The Haworth Press.

Freud, S. (1949). *Three essays on the theory of sexuality.* Oxford: Imago Publishing.

Gair, S. (2004). It takes a community. *Journal of Lesbian Studies, 8*, 45–56. doi:10.1300/J155v08n01_03.

Ganzer, C. (2007). The use of self from a relational perspective. *Clinical Social Work Journal, 35*(2), 117–123.

Glassgold, J. M. (1995). Coming out of the frame: Lesbian feminism and psychoanalytic theory. In J. M. Glassgold & S. Iasenza (Eds.), *Lesbians and psychoanalysis: Revolutions in theory and practice* (pp. 203–228). New York: Free Press.

Glassgold, J. M. (2004). *From deviance to diversity: Psychoanalytic approaches to gay men and lesbians.* US: American Psychological Association. doi:10.1037/04019S.

Goldner, V. (2011). Trans: Gender in free fall. *Psychoanalytic Dialogues, 21*(2), 159–171. doi:10.1080/10481885.2011.562836.

Goldstein, E. (2001). *Object relations theory and self psychology in social work practice.* New York: The Free Press.

Goldstein, E. G., Miehls, D., & Ringel, S. (2009). *Advanced clinical social work practice: Relational principles and techniques.* New York: Columbia University Press.

Hansbury, G. (2011). King Kong & Goldilocks: Imagining transmasculinities through the trans-trans dyad. *Psychoanalytic Dialogues, 21*(2), 210–220. doi:10.1080/10481885.2011.562846.

Hanson, J. (2005). Should your lips be zipped? how therapist self-disclosure and non-disclosure affects clients. *Counseling and Psychotherapy Research, 5*(2), 96–104. doi:10.1080/17441690500226658.

Hazan, C., & Shaver, P. (1987). Romantic love conceptualized as an attachment process. *Journal of Personality and Social Psychology, 52*(3), 511–524. doi:10.1037/0022-3514.52.3.511.

Hetrick, E. S., & Martin, A. D. (1987). Developmental issues and their resolution for gay and lesbian adolescents. *Journal of Homosexuality, 14*(1–2), 25–43. doi:10.1300/J082v14n01_03.

Hiestand, K. R., & Levitt, H. M. (2005). Butch identity development: The formation of an authentic gender. *Feminism and Psychology, 15*(1), 61–85. doi:10.1177/0959353505049709.

Kassoff, B. (2004). The queering of relational psychoanalysis: Who's topping whom? In J. M. Glassgold, S. Iasenza, J. M. Glassgold, & S. Iasenza (Eds.), *Lesbians, feminism, and psychoanalysis: The second wave* (pp. 159–176). Binghamton: Harrington Park Press/The Haworth Press.

Knights, D., & Kerfoot, D. (2004). Between representations and subjectivity: Gender binaries and the politics of organizational transformation. *Gender, Work and Organization, 11*(4), 430–454. doi:10.1111/j.1468-0432.2004.00241.x.

Kohut, H. (1972). Thoughts on narcissism and narcissistic rage. *The Psychoanalytic Study of the Child, 27*, 360–400.

Kohut, H. (2009). *The analysis of the self: A systematic approach to the psychoanalytic treatment of narcissistic personality disorders.* Chicago: University of Chicago Press. Original work published in 1971.

Lawrence, A. A. (2010). Proposed revisions to gender identity disorder diagnoses in the DSM-5. *Archives of Sexual Behavior, 39*(6), 1253–1260. doi:10.1007/s10508-010-9660-x.

Lewes, K. (2005). Homosexuality, homophobia, and gay-friendly psychoanalysis. *Fort Da, 11*, 13–34.

Malyon, A. (1981). Psychotherapeutic implications of internalized homophobia in gay men. *Journal of Homosexuality, 7*(2/3), 59.

McCarthy, M. E. (2010). Corrective emotional experience revisited. *The International Journal of Psychoanalysis, 91*(5), 1272–1275. doi:10.1111/j.1745-8315.2010.00345.x.

McWilliams, N. (1999). *Psychoanalytic case formulation.* New York: Guilford Press.

Mitchell, S. A. (1988). *Relational concepts in psychoanalysis: An integration.* Cambridge: Harvard University Press.

Mitchell, S. (1993). *Hope and dread in psychoanalysis.* New York: BasicBooks.

Mohr, J. J. (2008). *Same-sex romantic attachment.* New York: Guilford Press.

Morrison, A. P. (2007). Shame–considerations and revisions: Discussion of papers by Sandra Buechler and Donna Orange. *Contemporary Psychoanalysis, 44*(1), 105–109.

Morrow, D. F. (2006). Gay, lesbian, and bisexual identity development. In D. F. Morrow & L. Messinger (Eds.), *Sexual orientation and gender expression in social work practice: Working with gay, lesbian, bisexual, and transgender people* (pp. 81–104). New York: Columbia University Press.

Orange, D. M., Atwood, G. E., & Stolorow, R. D. (1997). *Working intersubjectively: Contextualism in psychoanalytic practice.* Mahwah: Analytic Press.

Rosik, C. H. (2003). When therapists do not acknowledge their moral values: Green's response as a case study. *Journal of Marital and Family Therapy, 29*(1), 39–45. doi:10.1111/j.1752-0606.2003.tb00381.x.

Sánchez, F. J., & Vilain, E. (2009). Collective self-esteem as a coping resource for male-to-female transsexuals. *Journal of Counseling Psychology, 56*(1), 202–209. doi:10.1037/a0014573.

Sennott, S. L. (2011). Gender disorder as gender oppression: A transfeminist approach to rethinking the pathologization of gender non-conformity. *Women and Therapy, 34*(1–2), 93–113. doi:10.1080/02703149.2010.532683.

Shelby, R. D. (2000). Narcissistic injury, humiliation, rage, and the desire for revenge: Thoughts on Drescher's psychoanalytic therapy and the gay man. *Gender and Psychoanalysis, 5*(3), 275–289.

Sparks, E. (2009). Learning to be authentic with clients: The untold journey of a relational practitioner. In A. Bloomgarden & R. B. Mennuti (Eds.), *Psychotherapist revealed: Therapists speak about self-disclosure in psychotherapy* (pp. 163–179). New York: Routledge/Taylor & Francis Group.

Weiss, J. T. (2003). GL vs. BT: The archaeology of biphobia and transphobia within the U.S. gay and lesbian community. *Journal of Bisexuality, 3*, 25–55. doi:10.1300/J159v03n03_02.

Winnicott, D. W. (1956). On transference. *The International Journal of Psychoanalysis, 37*, 386–388.

Young-Bruehl, E. (1997). The anatomy of prejudices. *Journal for the Psychoanalysis of Culture and Society, 2*(2), 13–21.

Part V
Diversities Founded on Life-Altering Experience

Relational Social Work Practice with Combat Veterans

Jeni Tyson

Introduction

Relational social work is a practice model rich in social constructivist, relational-cultural, feminist, and interpersonal theories born out of the psychoanalytic object relations and self-psychology schools of thought (Tosone 2004). Despite theoretical variations, all these orientations share the foundational construct that human beings are inextricably embedded in their social environments and cannot be understood apart from the relational context in which they are immersed in (Aron 1996; DeYoung 2003; Jordan 2010; Miller and Stiver 1997; Wachtel 2007; Watts 2003). The context of combat powerfully and enduringly impacts the survivors who become clinical social work clients and therefore calls for the contextual sensitivity of relational practice.

Contemporary neuroscience, psychological, and social work research findings confirm that human beings are hardwired to form social attachments (Cozolino 2002; Fosha et al. 2009; Porges 2011; Shore 2001). Clinicians observe how desire for human bonding, connection, and mutuality fuels many of our strivings (Adler 1992; Aron 1996; Bowlby 1983; Mitchell 2000); Stern 2000). Many of these strivings also fuel the promotion of human welfare within our social and subcultural groups. In total, human beings make meaning, and create and maintain their sense of self through the context of their social relationships (Wrenn 2003). The dramatic change in the meanings and sense of self between combat and post-combat contexts creates an urgent need for a relationally attuned process to reestablish the combat veteran's sense of cohesion and relevance.

J. Tyson, LCSW (✉)
Maplewood, NJ, USA
e-mail: jenityson@hotmail.com

J.B. Rosenberger (ed.), *Relational Social Work Practice with Diverse Populations*,
Essential Clinical Social Work Series, DOI 10.1007/978-1-4614-6681-9_14,
© Springer Science+Business Media New York 2014

Individuals learn to cope in the world by assigning rules, attitudes, and values to self and other. They develop plans for action through images of what relationships should be as well as for the ideal self (Adler 1992; Stolorow 2007; Watts 2003). Relational social work focuses on the healing nature of relationships through connection and co-creation of narratives and meanings (Aron 1996). This is the heart of relational social work, which adopts a client-centered non-pathological stance. The focus is not merely on symptoms catalogued in the Diagnostic Statistical Manual of Mental Disorders 4th Ed. (DSM-IV) (American Psychiatric Association 1994) but on difficulties arising from conflicts caused by disconnection, ruptures, and misattunements, in an individual's relational environment (Mitchell and Aron 1999). This relational environment includes group membership, which can be a product of shared heritage and/or shared significant life experiences.

Combat Veterans and the Social Work Perspective

Combat veterans, like members of other diverse subcultures, present with complex cultural layers derived from their war experience that impact all phases of clinical work. While clinical social work, embracing client in context, is especially suited to the required cultural competency and sensitivity in working with any group that is socially constructed, unique features of the military context, and combat in particular, are central to practice with this population. This is even more the case when, as is common, the clinician himself/herself is or has been a member of the military. The relational clinician is actively engaged in monitoring her own as well as her client's interaction of military socialization with experience in the civilian world. Attunement is specifically necessary to the veteran's symptoms, issues, and personal narrative, as an adaptation of that person to the environment of war (Goldstein et al. 2009). Awareness of the adaptations that are necessary to survive the culture of combat, coupled with the specific social work value of taking into account a person's present and past context (Tosone 2004), reframes events and helps redevelop new growth to promote optimism, hopefulness, and successful reintegration with a prewar, and perhaps enhanced, identity. The literature review and case illustration presented below support the importance of a relational social work perspective for this population.

Recent studies note that many veterans go outside of the Veterans Administration and military mental health settings in order to receive care (Hoge et al. 2006, 2004). Therefore, clinical social workers will encounter this population in settings that provide individual, family, and child treatment. Indeed, presenting problems and even initial assessments often do not directly reveal combat experience or link that experience to the problems for which help is sought. This is particularly true in when a veteran or his/her family member presents for clinical services that are not combat related; such as marital, child or substance abuse issues. The veteran may be attempting to compartmentalize that history in his/her life. Therefore the social work practitioner should routinely ask about military history in the initial assessment phase.

The Department of Defense estimates that 2.2 million men and women have served in the wars in Iraq and Afghanistan (Watson 2009). To simplify the reading of this material, the words combat veteran, soldier, or combatant will be used synonymously and are not meant to exclude marines, airmen, or seamen. Military culture remains steeped in masculine language, and it is impossible to avoid when trying to give the reader a sense of cultural competency (Sherman 2010). The use of him/his for the veteran and she/her for clinician also is used here to simplify the writing and is not intended to minimize the role women serve in the military or diminish their war experiences or to disregard the increasing number of male clinical social workers. It is beyond the scope of this chapter to discuss in detail military values and norms in each branch of service or issues related to gender, sexual orientation, or ethnicity. The focus is on competency in dealing with a client who has undergone adaptations in identity, values, and behaviors to survive deployment to a combat zone.

The material presented is also relevant to deployments to a noncombat zone. Peacekeeping and Homeland Security missions are similar to combat deployments. Soldiers typically will spend a long time away from family and friends, the conditions of the field are generally uncertain or harsh, there is a lack of privacy and unpredictable level of boredom mixed with threat, and a high chance of bearing witness to interpersonal violence (Adler et al. 2005; Castro 2004). While it is beyond the scope of this volume to address the clinical practice with family and children in reunification with their deployed family member, a social work perspective that focuses on the person's entire family system can recognize and assess issues related to family anxiety, anger, and resentment due to a combat deployment. These issues if remain unacknowledged or treated can create further isolation and disconnection for the combat survivor upon return home. Roles also undergo change, as does the power structure in the family regarding making decisions, which may further create relational and feelings of failure in combat survivor (Laser and Stephens 2011).

Cultural Adaptations to Survival in War

Hoge (2010) asserts that during the phases of engagement and assessment, it is more helpful to view any altered meanings and schemas as adaptive solutions to surviving combat, rather than focusing on the DSM-IV (APA 2000) framework of dissociation, arousal, hypervigilance, numbing, and avoidance as posttraumatic stress disorder (PTSD) symptoms. Viewing the symptoms merely as a disorder can create stigma and interfere with the veteran's ability to reintegrate with his prewar identity. Failing to understand the individual's personal adaptive strategies, however imperfectly they serve at the moment, will limit the clinician's ability to know the combat veteran's experience or to form a therapeutic alliance (Hoge 2010; Shay 2002). Such misalignment between clinician and client violates the mutual pursuit of understanding of relational social work practice and in turn may lead to impairment in psychological, social, and occupational functioning, risking inviting chronic complex posttraumatic stress disorder (PTSD) and other comorbid disorders

(Figley 1978; Van der Kolk et al. 1996). Within the relational principles of collaboration and co-construction of the therapeutic alliance, the clinician can proactively normalize, validate, and affirm to the client that they have had to develop new constructs for self-protection that cannot be easily switched off (Adler 1931/1992; Hoge 2010; Watts 2003). Of course there are veterans who do exhibit symptomatology beyond their combat adaptations; the caution here is against presumptively classifying all phenomena presented as evidence of psychopathological makeup.

The following adaptations should be understood in the context of the combat environment and the difficulty in adjusting upon return to civilian culture due to physiological changes that occur upon exposure to trauma (Castro 2004).

Normal adaptation to combat vs. symptoms in civilian context	
Tactical awareness of environment	Hypervigilance
Trust only in combat buddies	Emotional withdrawal from family, friends
Personal accountability	Over-controlling behaviors
Targeted aggression	Difficulty assessing appropriate level of threat
Armed for battle	Perceived need to be armed for danger
Emotional control	Anger/detachment
Mission operational security	Secretiveness
Individual responsibility	Guilt
Combat driving	Aggressive driving
Discipline	Ordering others/inflexibility

Military Culture and the Subculture of Combat

The military is a social construction formed for the purpose of protecting the dominant culture it represents (Shay 2002). All branches of the military share the same core value of commitment to serve the greater good of its society. This commitment requires the soldier to serve the prevailing government's ideological beliefs and unquestioningly carry out orders given by superiors. Technology, tactics, and demographics have changed over time, but what remains unchanged is the fundamental organizing principle that "one must do what's right, honorably and courageously" for self, comrade, and fellow Americans (Shay 1994, p. 5). These individuals enter into a social contract to secure and protect against the aggression of others. The social work clinician must set aside opinions of the military and of war in order to create the mutuality and co-constructive process of the therapeutic alliance. Transference by the veteran himself to a civilian or Veterans Administration social work practitioner also is active and powerful in the determination of the therapeutic engagement. The relational stance may need more explicit articulation and pursuit of the client's expectations than is typical of the initial clinical social work encounter. Many individuals called to serve in war do not always agree with the mission at hand, but do what is ordered because they took an oath to do so (Sherman 2010; Wachtel 2007).

Early in training, the military individual is re-socialized through the rigid rules of moral order, conventions, normative expectations, ethics, and social values. This acculturation intentionally and forcefully strips away the personal identity, so that the individual can become a member of a military cadre. The new service person undergoes a conversion experience, where the previous focus of life shifts to new collective organizing principles and relational schemas (Sherman 2010). These organizing principles and schemas focus on mission objectives, survival of self and other, and a sense of meaning in purpose derived from the oath to serve.

To assimilate into military culture, one must abandon the social construction of the concept of "I" for the collective good (Grossman and Christensen 2008). Modern military is structured so that each individual is dependent on the chain of command to provide for all their needs, supplies, and orders/responsibilities. This emphasizes that each person's survival is dependent on the others in the group (Shay 1994; Watson 2009). These men and women must suspend many beliefs of their ethno-cultural and social groups of origin in order to commit government sanctioned actions, including killing or being killed, on behalf of their fellow Americans (Lifton 1973). This realignment of self-identity requires the construction of a personal meaning that they are doing what is right for the greater good. The construction of personal meaning to serve in combat may be further complicated if the person disagrees with the fundamental objective of the mission. In this case, attempts at meaning will be derived from the commitment they made to serve and the value they find in protecting their comrades in arms (Hoge 2010; Shay 2002; Sherman 2010). Failure to do so might result in rejection of support from the unit they are serving with or psychological decompensation when they are confronted with the realities of combat. The new constructions of relational schemas and meanings that emerge serve not only to acculturate the individual but as a necessary adaptation for survival once deployed to a war zone. Mitchell's (1988) statement that "I become the person I am in interaction with specific others…" (p. 276) is particularly reinforced for combat veterans who need to be aligned with the group to secure mutual survival. As a result, a combatant's newly formed view of the world may feel incommensurable with others outside of military culture (Shatan 1978).

Many men and women join the military due to a sense of patriotism and want to serve and protect others. However, many also join in the hopes of improving their life condition with education, employment, a family tradition, or a lack of alternative life plans. Some desire the structure and discipline, may seek to have basic needs met, experience a sense of belonging, or as a vehicle to gain citizenship (Sherman 2010). This may result in further inner conflicts over participating in, or witnessing, the horrors of interpersonal violence (Lifton 1973). These complex motivations are further arenas of relational exploration and clarification rather than presumption of meanings of which the clinical social worker needs to be aware of.

Training is an unconditional submission to the hierarchy of command for the maintenance of order occurs in other cultural groups where deference and respect to those deemed in authority is a primary value (Berzoff et al. 2008). As is the case in any rigid and closed cultural group, some soldiers may experience inner conflict about betrayal by civilian authority, politicians, or commanders while trying not to break existing rules, norms, or standard operating procedures (Hoge 2010; Shay 1994). In other words, conscious submission does not quell all unconscious conflicts, even as it is endorsed as the means of survival.

The Intersubjective Context of War: Rationale for a Relational Social Work

Combat trauma originates in an intersubjective cultural context: interpersonal violence of one human is pitted against another (Janoff-Bulman 1992). Combat is personal in comparison to an act of nature: instead of fleeing from the threat of injury or possible death, a soldier is required to face down interpersonal aggression. In this extreme context, disconnection from others and self-identity after military service may be and inevitable by product. The experience of war breaks down the individual's attunement to previously shared meanings with people outside of the combat experience. It also derails previous systems of mutual regulation of self and self with other (Grossman and Christensen 2008; Janoff-Bulman 1992).

Combat trauma is the experience of "unbearable affect" and results in changes in meaning, purpose, values, beliefs, and worldview (Stolorow and Atwood 2002, p. 52). It destroys social trust, which is a key resource to healing (Shay 2002). Herman (1992) asserts that healing from war trauma depends on "communalization." Shay (1994) further clarifies that communilization, which is the reconnection to community membership post-combat, can only happen in an inter subjective context. Freud (1918) in Totem and Taboo, wrote about the communal social purification rituals performed for returning warriors to heal the taint of war Absolution was given not just through acknowledgment of the warrior's experience, but by the community not disavowing the violence and aggression that is endemic to any war so the returning soldier could be reconnected to society, without judgment (Bragin, 2010). In the current social context, the opportunity for this communalization and social purification occurs frequently in the clinical social work process where incorporation of context, past and future, is central. The relational social worker can help the veteran make explicit the words and affect of fragmented, disavowed, and intolerable parts of the combat experience in order to create a whole narrative (Bromberg 1998; Wrenn 2003). Disassociating memories and disavowing affects result in what Saari (2002) described as events that are unconstructed (without meaning), uninterpreted (without words), and unintegrated (without affect). The combat veteran needs to be able to tell his story safely to an empathic compassionate listener, who can be trusted to assist in authentically cocreating a narrative of his experience that is interwoven with pre-combat narratives surrounding self and community identity (Bragin 2010; Shay 1994).

Herman (1992) noted that combat veterans are experts in coping in a society that rejects its injured members, while they struggle with spiritual pain and personal loss. This is confounding to the returning combat veteran because emphasis during tours of duty on protecting injured members is not replicated in the civilian community. Especially when such injury is not visible, failures of support or appropriate response takes on particularly virulent meaning. Bonanno (2004) underscores the importance of focusing on the individual's resilience and capacity to thrive after traumatic events, which expresses the clinical social work value of empowerment.

Relational theory focuses on the positive psychology of prevention, optimism, resilience, social conscious, meaning making, and a sense of community within relationships (Jordan 2010; Tosone 2004). Restorative application of these principles is a central relational clinical practice. Watts (2003), in discussing relational constructivist theories, noted that human beings are driven by the desire to share with and contribute as individuals to others. The veteran is emerging from a specific culture of prescribed ways of contributing and protecting others into a very different configuration of community. Relational social work emphasizes the core value of healing in context and with veterans must include disjuncture in context. Deconstruction as well as reconstruction of an individual's narrative is bidirectional; the relational clinical relationship's emphasis on mutuality in problem definition and context-embedded attunement to past and future allows interpersonal recognition, a primary self organizer, to be a vehicle for self-healing to occur (Aron 1999; Schamess 2011; Teicholz 2009). The military value of interdependence for survival and growth is in keeping with a relational social work perspective and can be emphasized to counteract infantilization in help receiving (Grossman and Christenson 2008; Herman 1992; Hoge 2010). Working in collaboration with this shared value, the relational social worker, generally embedded in the veteran's civilian social environment, can help the veteran relay, or translate, his new narrative and meanings to his family and community (Figley 1978; Janoff-Bulman 1992; Stolorow 2007). This value assists the clinician in focusing on a representation of what's wrong as not being something inside the combat survivor but rather being how he feels about his trauma experience and what it is like for him to be in the world afterward (Goldstein et al. 2009; Jordan 2010). A relational social work approach can be the fertile intersubjective ground, drenched with shared meanings, not only to create new future based narratives but also to reclaim mourned aspects of a prewar identity (Mitchell 2000; Stolorow and Atwood 2002).

Shattered Assumptions and Altered Schemas of Meaning: Barriers to Treatment

After the overwhelming experience of war, the combat veteran experiences a shattering of his assumptive world regarding safety, trust, and meaning (Janoff-Bulman 1992). Existential issues arise such as traumatic rage and grief, annihilation anxiety, a foreshortened sense of future, external locus of control, guilt and survivor guilt, suspiciousness that the universe is counterfeit, and a loss of meaning and purpose (Frankl 1996; Southwick et al. 2006). These worldviews serve as barriers to treatment, with their isolative and constrictive nature blocking a deepening of the clinical alliance (Lifton 1973; Shay 2002). The double problem of adapting to the new community ethos while maintaining a sense of good self for his combat experience creates and invitation to fractures self-cohesion and a depletion of original meaning.

The combat veteran faced with chronic disconnection, which in turn creates negative, fixed, and painful relational images, can create a state Miller (1989) describes as "condemned isolation." This state decreases energy, creating immobilization, confusion, and a negative self-image, causing his focus to be limited to regulating emotions, avoiding negative outcomes, and/or controlling interactions with others (Wilson et al. 2001). Life projects and meaningful pursuits take a back seat to self-regulating strategies designed to avoid reminders of his combat trauma (Tedeschi and Calhoun 2004). A combat veteran often constricts emotional experience so as not to show that which might be unacceptable or dangerous to others outside of his combat buddies, who he feels understand him (Van der Kolk et al. 1996). Disavowed affects may feel like inner defectiveness or badness if they emerge. This sense of defectiveness may further self-loathing, isolation, and shame that may be perceived as, or is real rejection of the veteran by his social group of origin (Janoff-Bulman 1992; Lifton 1973; Stolorow 2007).

Jordan (2010) discusses how society has the power to create and control images of shame in the prevailing culture. These images become a part of a person's relational images for self and others. In the Vietnam War, veterans, who for the most part were adolescents when drafted, were called "baby killers," marginalized and reviled, due to the sociopolitical atmosphere among the general public. They reported that they felt shunned by the World War II and Korean War veterans. Had this not been their experience, the social rupture could have been alleviated by being socially aligned with the groups that were welcomed and reintegrated in the larger societal context (Shay 2002). Fontana and Rosenheck (2005) noted that Vietnam veterans most often sought help due to existential issues, feeling not so much injured or subject to PTSD, but more as having lost a core sense of self or meaning. Finding a pathway to reintegration is a social work principle fused with clinical treatment: healing isolation and building trust must occur before deeper trauma work can begin (Stolorow 2007).

The strengths perspective of relational social work that seeks to locate and empower the functional value of defensive and coping strategies can assist the veteran in viewing himself as an expert in survival and agent of change in his life, but not a victim (Herman 1992). A veteran experiencing a foreshortened sense of future can be moved to act, rather than to fall into immobilization. New meanings can be created through support in encouraging redemptive acts, newly discovered competencies, and altruism (Fontana and Rosenheck 2005; Southwick et al. 2006). Clinical social work practice that underscores the importance of the encounter with an empathic other will help shift the emphasis from problems, symptoms, failures, and deficits toward strengths, goals, solutions, and possibilities (Goldstein et al. 2009).

Cultural Competence in Clinical Assessment and Treatment of Combat Veterans

The engagement phase is critical in clinical work with combat veterans. Many will not report difficulties during the phase called demobilization, upon when they are preparing for release and return home from a deployment. Many may come into social work clinical services voluntarily, or be mandated to treatment in community mental health settings, due to marital or child problems, legal problems from substance abuse, or occupational problems (Laser and Stephens 2011). When initially seen, the clinical social worker should be cautious not to pathologize behaviors but rather focus on engagement with the individual around the nature of the presenting problem. Behaviors within any subculture may be seen as abnormal if the clinical practitioner is unaware of applicable cultural norms (Berzoff et al. 2008). In this case, combat training emphasizes the constriction of emotional expression and the value of limited self-disclosure. An equally cautious countertransference is expectable. This is the relational clinician's cultural context in the work with combat veterans and like all transference and countertransference is to be understood, not characterized as treatment resistance or problematic.

In the initial engagement process, seeking specific information rather than generalizing about the military or combat is crucial. For example, the clinician should try to find out what position, or Military Occupational Specialty (MOS), the veteran held. Rank structures (Enlisted, Warrant Officer, and Commissioned Officer) are important self-identifiers. The National Center for PTSD (www.ptsd.va.gov) is an excellent clinical resource for information regarding this population. A brief Internet search of the branch of service, unit, and combat theater the veteran served in helps the clinician conceptualize the deployment, without having to be too intrusive during the initial phase of contact. Familiarity with geographic or regions of the veteran's deployment will go a long way in the engagement process with a veteran (Watson 2009). Applying authenticity, the relational clinician does not pretend to have expert knowledge she does not have or to comparability of her own military experience with that of her client. At the same time, an effort to understand the "language" of the client can avert innocent mistakes like referring to a marine as a soldier or a navy seal or member of the air force. Specific designations are especially powerful in the military (Watson 2009), and clinician errors need to be acknowledged and corrections requested, which can be part of the mutual construction process.

The clinician needs to convey that power in the relationship is shared and that the veteran can be helped even if the clinician is not a member of the group (Goldstein et al. 2009). The empathic and not-knowing stances of relational practice let the veteran know the social worker is interested in learning, through the veteran's privileged knowledge, about the combat experience. Granting expertise to the client conveys reciprocity and tolerance for learning from someone else's experience. Authenticity of the inquiring stance dissipates suspiciousness and may reduce shame about asking for help. It is not unusual for a combat veteran to want to know he has positively impacted the clinician. The relational model endorses not over-interpreting countertransference: in the clinical context, in this case the military, interpersonal responsibility means difficulty accepting help without offering something of value in return (Figley 1978).

Sherman (2010) also underscores clinician in context, calling attention to how the returning soldier constantly must struggle with macro-level forces (prevailing social culture), mezzo-level forces (military culture), and micro-level forces (how he experiences of himself). The clinician represents the dominant group, be she military or civilian. When a veteran is experiencing grief or anger over feeling marginalized or misunderstood by his family or community, the word civilian may connote frustration, sarcasm, disdain, and despair. This invites defensive counter-transference and perhaps vain attempts at compensation, rather than empathic recognition of the authenticity of such feelings. The relational social worker must be able to bridge the divide between us (combat survivors) and them (civilians) with the therapeutic relationship. The relationship can be a template of here-and-now lived experience of reintegration into civilian life which requires modification of the subordination, stoicism, and restricted expression of affect regarding self and others instilled in combat experience (Grossman and Christensen, 2008; Hoge 2010).

Intake and Assessment

In the initial intake and assessment, the clinician should be aware of her eye contact, body language, and tone when acquiring history and presenting problems (Brandell 2011). Authenticity and emotional presence, free of pressure to accomplish a clinical mission, allow mutuality and co-construction of engagement that must precede artic-ulation of a core treatment problem. If agencies require clinicians to use symptom checklists and scales during intake, the clinician should minimize note-taking that limits eye contact and weave the pursuit of specific information into a conversational tone. Thorough preparation by the clinician makes the exploration easier to conduct conversationally. A rigid Q and A conveys that the clinician, like society or the military, sees the veteran as just another number or as sick if they answer yes to symp-toms on a checklist (Hoge 2010; Watson 2009). Practitioners with trauma, including combat trauma, value the creation of space for issues to emerge (Goldstein et al. 2009). In this space, the relational social worker can assess safety and trust before pursuing details. Allowing details of trauma to emerge too early can result in emotional flooding and retraumatization, often ending treatment (Van der Kolk et al. 1996).

Problem Formulation and Treatment Planning

Many veterans report problems remembering appointments due to short-term memory and concentration loss, difficulty leaving home during episodes of hypervigilance, unexpected job interviews, childcare, and the like. Clinical social workers need flexibility and open recognition of the increased demands of the veteran's transition. Immediate return to comfort and confidence may not be possible. As noted above, relational theory does not ascribe contextual reality factors automatically to resistance or transference. Of course these may be present, and accommodations with all clients are meaningful; in this population, the potential for attrition is exaggerated by ambivalence about chain of authority and the complexities of reentry into civilian life. Collaboration on managing factors that interfere with treatment consistency involves not only scheduling but phone check-ins if symptoms are too intense. Addressing these context factors openly builds attachment free from authoritarian pressure

(Erbes et al. 2009). The relational social worker measures holding a frame of consistency against transference linked to anger at the government or to negative feelings toward nonmilitary persons. Maintaining balance for the relational clinician includes discussing issues related to the veteran's ambivalence as well as real-life issues with a clinical supervisor or administrator (Erbes et al. 2009).

Clinical interventions will also depend on whether a veteran is still on active duty or may be called backup for another deployment due to a reserve obligation. Psychoeducation on the importance of a soldier's defenses, such as psychic numbing and the avoidance of processing grief and traumatic experiences in the combat zone, should be discussed (Tyson 2007). Explicitly acknowledging the value of maintaining these normal adaptations can convey to the veteran that the clinical social worker is not going to impose the processing of difficult content or minimize the value of what otherwise might be primitive coping defenses, if he will be redeployed. Given the potential of additional trauma exposure, the clinician should elicit what the veteran feels would be most helpful to him, so he does not break down defenses that he feels are necessary to survive in a combat situation again. In this case, it might be necessary to take a here-and-now, supportive approach that focuses on normalizing why he is having difficulty readjusting as well as the relative value of temporary adjustment, in order to improve his social and emotional functioning with family and community.

The Course of Treatment

Many specific issues require attention with combat veterans seeking clinical services. Regarding space, the veteran may not want to have his back to the door, will need a clear exit, and may be sensitive to outside noises. Time management also is vital. A core military value is promptness, and if a veteran is kept waiting in a crowded waiting room, he may assume the clinician does not observe this value and leave treatment. The same is of control over the end of any session: keeping to agreed times shares control. Withdrawal may indicate fear of being asked about his combat experience, such as questions regarding whether they killed someone in action or witnessed the same. The relational clinician, while not the blank screen, must be prepared in her own countertransference so as not to overreact, judge, or offer sympathy for behaviors necessary for survival in a war zone (Castro 2004; Hoge 2010).

Self-Disclosure. The issue of self-disclosure, always controversial, combined with the authenticity of the interpersonal in relational practice, has special salience with combat veterans. Contemporary neuroscience reaffirms that self-disclosure of a clinician's affective experience helps the client increase his capacity for self-regulation, which assists in the reconfiguration of internal representations that may have been altered through traumatic experience (Quillman 2011; Porges 2011). For the clinician, this self-disclosure must be purposeful and contained. Client and clinician both constrict or expand the other's emotional experience in the bidirectional process (Stolorow and Atwood 2002). In relational social work treatment, the clinician making the implicit explicit should be to help the veteran move from the traumatic content per se to the discomfort of talking about it (DeYoung 2003), which resonates in all his interpersonal relationships.

Even positive relational moments can create intense defensive reactions and anxiety in the combat trauma survivor. The desire to dissociate and emotionally withdraw to ward off all feelings may be true for the clinician as well (Van der Kolk et al. 1996). As a relationship model for future possibilities of reconnection, the clinician must bring these things into awareness with empathy for the pull to disavow history. The veteran needs to see the clinician take risks and share her emotional experience in a non-defensive way to convey that the clinical relational space is a solid and the clinician is brave enough to contain his trauma narrative. Fosha (2000) states that in order for the clients to be willing to share their affects, the clinician must not only show the same but model that "affects are valuable, tolerable, enriching, and that they need not be draining, overwhelming, or shameful" (p. 214). Clinician "neutrality" (Mitchell 1988) can be an unbearable reminder of the veteran's experience with the civilian world in which he has perceived his affect was uncontainable by others and can trigger episodes of shame, rage, and dissociation, as there is no affective ground to which to anchor to (Stolorow 2007).

Rice and Greenberg (1984) suggest that *empathic prizing,* which is the unconditional positive regard the clinician has for her client, be made treatment specific, affirming the veteran's intrinsic worth and humanity. At the same time, affirmation may reveal ego deficits (DeYoung 2003; Wachtel 2007). Affirming positive qualities may trigger survivor guilt, rational guilt for behaviors in a war zone, or aspects of personality structure prior to combat experience. The relational clinician's emphasis on the here and now, including the bravery it takes to share difficult experience, can allow the veteran to become more aware of his adaptation to difficult circumstances rather than focus on affects like shame, guilt, and self-criticism (Stolorow 2007). As a corollary, the veteran's being apologetic, or hyper-focused on getting it right in the interaction with the clinician, may reveal a tendency for self-blame for any ruptures. A relational clinician will attend to her own part in any ruptures or misattunements (Mitchell and Aron 1999), indicating the mutuality of all interpersonal connection. Farber (2006) notes that new clinicians must not mistake authenticity in the relational approach for relentless self-disclosure or self-referencing. Silent listening is critical, with the gauge being intolerable withholding for the trauma survivor or clinician anxiety.

Transference Issues. A relational clinical perspective emphasizes what Hoffman (1994) refers to as *dialectical constructivism,* which posits that in a therapeutic relationship there is a reciprocal influence on both the parties subjectivity (Aron 1999). True neutrality, and uncontaminated transference, is not possible (Wachtel 2010). From this perspective, the classical concept of countertransference (the clinician's reaction to the client's transference) is not sufficient to capture the subjective interactions that occur in the bidirectional process. Mitchell and Aron (1999) argue that the term countertransference minimizes the impact of the clinician's behavior on the transference. Orange (1995) argues that the mutual reciprocal interaction of two subjectivities is better described as *co-transference.* Safran (2002) emphasizes that in-depth exploration of the client's experience that unfolds in the therapeutic space should not focus on interpretations about generalized relational patterns. All these concepts underscore the relational principle that the clinician is not an objective observer in the interaction. Rather, interpersonal reconnection through affective sharing with others, who are not combat veterans, can be accomplished through the co-transference in the relationship (Bragin 2010; Shay 2002). By the clinician modeling observation of her internal processes and actions, in the relationship as they are happening, the veteran and clinician cocreate a template for relationships outside the treatment room. As with all work with trauma survivors, the clinician may experience secondary trauma or reactivated traumas of her own past, such as being the helpless observer, perpetrator, and enactor (Neumann and Gamble 1995). Supervision to avoid unconscious reenactments is part of trauma practice (Herman 1992).

Compassion Fatigue and Shared Trauma. Clinicians working with combat veterans are at risk for secondary traumatic stress reactions, variously referred to as *compassion fatigue* (CF) (Figley 2002), *secondary traumatic stress disorder* (STSD) (Stamm 1999), and *vicarious traumatization* (McCann and Pearlman 1990; Pearlman and Saakvitne 1995; Sabin-Farrell and Turpin 2003). Affected clinicians can experience a syndrome of symptoms, which may parallel their client's diagnosis of PTSD (Adams et al. 2006). While it is an unavoidable occupational hazard for mental health professionals who are empathically immersed in their client's trauma narrative, these reactions cause alterations in a clinician's self-identity, cognitive schemas, interpersonal relationships, physical health, job morale, worldview, and spirituality (Figley 2002; Hesse 2002; Tyson 2007).

Relational social work, which emphasizes the intersubjective field between clinician and client (Stolorow and Atwood 2002), may specifically invite vicarious traumatization (Rasmussen 2005). The co-construction of the trauma narrative confronts the relational social worker with her vulnerability and may challenge her attitudes about aggression and killing (Tyson 2007). Munroe (1991) research found that clinicians who have themselves been exposed to combat-related PTSD had significantly more intrusion and avoidance symptoms. A relational social worker unaware of her emerging symptoms, or alterations in her cognitive schemas, is at risk for rupturing her empathic connection that bridges the client between the worlds of war morality and civilian morality (Tyson 2007).

Clinicians providing treatment to returning combatants of the wars in Iraq and Afghanistan are at increased risk for compassion fatigue. This group of veterans is younger, subjected to severe trauma exposure from multiple deployments, may be less able to return to their prewar occupation due to the present economic situation as well as individual psychological or emotional injury (Barnett and Sherman 2011; McDevitt-Murphy et al. 2010). Negative effects can be minimized by organizational changes, increased supervision and training, as well as clinician's awareness of potential overidentification (Zimering et al. 2003). At the same time, Tedeschi and Calhoun (2004) discuss at length the concept of *posttraumatic growth* that emphasizes the positive effects on the psychological growth of the clinician and client. Finding meaning and purpose in the work with combat veterans can increase *compassion satisfaction* (Linley and Joseph 2007).

The construct of *shared trauma* speaks to primary reactivation in the relational clinician of experience of similar trauma (Tosone 2006). Tosone (2006) states that shared trauma transforms a clinician's self-concept and impacts the therapeutic intimacy in the clinical dyad. She noted that in the aftermath of the September 11, 2001, terrorist attacks on the World Trade Center, employing emotional distancing "felt intolerable and inauthentic" (p. 93). This may be a similar hazard to the many social work clinicians themselves recently serving in military combat for whom retriggering of trauma is a risk. Shared traumas alter professional boundaries regarding a clinician's depth of caring and concern for a client, both productive and defensive. Tosone et al. (2003) noted that shared trauma may cause a clinician to feel desensitized, lack empathy, have less tolerance, and experience more anger at clients who express fear and anxiety that they are themselves warding off. Both the client and therapist may be in the process of mourning actual and ambiguous losses (Tosone and Bialkin 2004).

Relational Social Work: A Case Illustration

Tom is a young, white, 23-year-old male, who was brought into the community mental health center by a fellow marine 4 months after he returned from serving 4 years in the Active Duty Marine Corps. Tom had two intense combat tours in Iraq. He reported that he joined the military in his senior year of High School after 9/11 because he felt "it was the right thing to do". When Tom had completed his 4 years of service, he signed up for the Ready Reserve Unit of the Marine Corps because he felt he had to "finish the mission for my buddies, and this is the only skill set I have." At the initial intake, Tom was guarded, exhibited psychomotor agitation, pressured speech, restricted affect, and constantly watched the door. He reported he was "pissed off about being here," and only came to get his buddy "off his back." His friend, who was also a client at the agency, was asked by Tom to stay for the first intake. He initially gave Tom's history and reported why he was worried about Tom, while Tom remained stone faced at attention at the edge of his seat. It had been a common occurrence in my experience for one combat veteran to bring another veteran in for help. As in Tom's case, highly resistant and suspicious, he needed a friend with similar experience to reassure him there was no stigma attached, a concern I normalized for him.

Tom did not report symptoms when he was demobilizing: he had 3 years left in his reserve obligation, and he didn't want to be seen as "crazy" or as someone who would "get someone else killed." He was living at home with his parents and younger siblings, which was difficult, as he felt "civilians don't get it." Tom reported He could not sleep or stop checking the doors and locks, making sure " the perimeter was secure." He did not exhibit any psychotic processes and did not report any early childhood trauma or losses. Tom saw another clinician the first month he was back, when he could not sleep. Tom complained the clinician was stone faced and wrote notes with little eye contact, going down to checklists and wanting details of his traumatic stressors, suggesting a psychiatrist consultation. Tom stated,

"I don't think I hated myself or anyone else more than in that moment." He had stormed out, afraid he might hurt the clinician. I expressed empathy and contextual normalization, saying that it made sense why he, or anyone else who had been in combat, would have felt enraged. This seemed to relax him and his psychomotor agitation began to decrease. Tom felt he could not connect with friends he had before the Marine Corps who were "living the fairy tale that if you work hard, and do good things, nothing bad happens to you." He could not relax in public places, imaging things that might happen, so he spent most of his time in his parent's basement. He only felt comfortable talking to his battle buddies with whom he felt he was not "a freak." He said it is easier to be in combat than be with his family, as "they just want to pretend the last few years didn't happen." Tom engaged more freely as I validated how his own "just world" beliefs and sense of safety and meaning had been shattered. He acknowledged drinking heavily and getting into fights, which prompted his friend to bring him for treatment.

Tom's symptoms, including alterations in his schemas surrounding trust, safety, and meaning, met the criteria for PTSD. His hypervigilance, hyperarousal, emotional withdrawal, and isolation were ego-syntonic for him – uncomfortable but necessary. Most troubling and angering was his inability to connect with anyone outside of the military. He stated his problem was making some kind of sense out of everything that happened. Tom had survivor guilt over members of his squad who were killed and felt rage in his perception that he was now "like an outcast, that everyone is afraid of."

Keeping with the social work principle of meeting a client where he is, I stated that only someone who had been to battle would know what it was like for him, where anyone would have had to change and do what was necessary to survive. I offered that if it was all right with him, we could work together on skills to help him tolerate the uncomfortable feelings, assuring him that he was not going to lose anything that he needed if he was redeployed: this remained in my mind due to his reserve obligation. I asked his permission to add some goals that I thought might be helpful, rather than telling him what he needed. I expressed a core concern that his present symptoms, if left unchecked, could become chronic.

I was very careful not to elicit too much traumatic combat content during the early stages stages of engagement and assessment. I asked background questions to get to know him, keeping the tone conversational and avoiding clinical terms or diagnoses. I expressed curiosity about his life before the Marine Corps, what meaning and purpose it had for him to join after 9/11, and then what his experience of being home now was like. I wanted him to navigate his narrative, knowing that I would not tread anywhere that felt dangerous. I noted that there were differences because I was not in the military and asked how was it to talk with me, someone who had not been to combat. I encouraged him to let me know anytime he felt I was not "*getting it*." I acknowledged that I appreciated his service and commitment. I emphasized that I could not possibly know more about Tom, or what was right for him, than he already knew himself because he had the skills, strength, and resilience to make it through two deployments. We talked about the tremendous resources it took for all service men and women to get through basic training and combat.

I asked Tom to look at our collaboration as a safe place where he could unpack his bags, since, in his own words, he really "hadn't unpacked" yet and that we would make sure we would pack it all backup before he left each session. This was to reassure him that if he took the risk in letting his guard down in here, that did not mean he had to drop those defenses down anywhere else before he was ready. I kept good eye contact, asked permission to jot down a few dates and names. Tom would "Yes, Ma'am" a lot, even after I let him know he did not need to be so formal. I referred to Tom as "Sergeant" until he let me know he wanted me to call him by his first name.

I made attempts to understand what went on in the region where Tom was deployed, to show him that I really wanted to "get it." He appeared relieved that I gained working knowledge of what was going on during the time he was there, without having to explain it all to me. I used my tone of voice, facial expressions, and body language to help Tom begin to experience and regulate more of his affect, which was constricted except when he was angry. When things outside the room startled him, I confirmed that the noise bothered me too. One night, we were the last in the building and Tom insisted he walk me to my car, which I agreed to, instead of exploring it as a transference reaction. I knew he genuinely felt responsible for others' safety, and he might experience more distress over my refusal of something he could give back.

Early on, I employed education about physiological effects of stress on the body and the necessary adaptations required by the military and combat. This opened up his ambivalent feelings toward his superiors in the military and his frustration of not being able to integrate back to his prewar identity, without disavowing his combat experience. Tom agonized that his skills as a sniper would not transfer to anything but law enforcement. He often felt discouraged due to limited openings for the police academy. Other criminal justice positions he felt he might like required a college education. When feeling hopeless about his prospects, Tom would bring in an application to work as an independent security contractor, or mercenary, in Iraq or Afghanistan. Although I felt this was a terrible idea, I worked hard to control my judgment and offered support and validation regarding how it must feel like he was on an alien planet here and life in the paramilitary might seem easier. When Tom would become angry at something I missed or forgot, I acknowledged my error, and he appreciated my accountability. At times, when his symptoms exacerbated, he would cancel an appointment at the last minute or not show. I explored this casually with him and he agreed that if he could not tolerate leaving home, he would check in via phone. I wanted to express investment in our work rather than rules. Absences decreased over time, and we noted his strength at coming in on days that he wanted to bolt.

I used language that might bridge differences by suggesting we team up, together, perhaps come up with a new mission objective based on current values and strengths. Tom's mission objective was finding a meaningful pursuit that could incorporate his combat experience, so that the "before war me, and after war me, could hang in the same body." I self disclosed to Tom that if I had gone through the same things, I would probably feel the same way and reminded him that as difficult as things were now, he was the same person who could function under far worse circumstances.

Tom said one day, after a long silence, that he was ready to talk about "s**t" that went down, because he felt I "had his back." He was afraid not only to burden me but that I would be "weirded out, scared, or think he was crazy." I let him know the walls in my office had pretty much heard it all, and there was nothing he could say that I couldn't bear to hear or change the way I felt about him. I was honest in responding that some things might be scary or freak me out but that I was not afraid of him or his anger. If he had the courage to bear going through it for us all even when he was afraid, then, at the very least, I could help him hold some of this stuff, so he didn't have to carry it alone.

Tom welled up for the first time, and we sat in silence for a long while. Tom stated he felt he was "keeping secrets", that made him feel "afraid, and full of shame and guilt". He painfully disclosed he was hearing gunfire or his name being shouted by dead friends, when exposed to even the most innocuous stimuli, like a brand of water his buddy was drinking when he was hit. He also said he could not stop looking at video and photos of graphic material from events when he almost died or others were killed and injured. He felt he was seriously "f**d up," but worse, "couldn't feel anything at all." To him that meant he couldn't feel "like a human being again." I let him know how much it meant that he would trust me enough to share this difficult material, that I did not think he was crazy or wrong, and he was grieving for himself and others, and trying to make sense of it all. I had Tom bring in the video and photos, some extremely graphic, but many were pictures of his squad, smiling, in all their gear. These photos elicited great pride in Tom and he had a wider range of affect when he shared them, which I drew his attention to.

As we sat and looked at the pictures and videos, I employed mindfulness techniques, psychic numbing and cognitive distancing for myself, so I could be present for Tom without exhibiting distress. I helped him frame that it is normal for anyone to feel numb or that it didn't feel real, because it is too much for anyone to get their head around. I asked him to notice where he felt it in his body to help him reduce dissociation.

Over several sessions of normalizing his reactions, and how it was for me to witness his experiences, he began to exhibit more grief, and he reported less self-loathing. Tom's symptoms of hyperarousal did increase as his numbing decreased, but we worked together to figure out which skills for distress tolerance worked best for him. Gradually, Tom stopped reviewing the images daily. He understood why he was hearing his buddies' voices, though he still struggled with survivor guilt. Tom had frequent nightmares of combat operations gone bad and once dreamt that I was there with him while he was trying to get to his wounded buddies. I let him know how important it was to me that he had taken me in enough to be part of the rescue efforts. Because I not only heard his narrative but also saw pictures and video, I began to have nightmares of combat, felt vigilant at times, and began to experience alterations in my worldview. I had to pay close attention to my positive transference and genuine feelings of care for him that might interfere with my challenging him or acknowledging things that we both might be avoiding. Both the positive and negative aspects of the trauma work with Tom transformed both the relationship and my own narrative over time.

After 1 year, while the work still oscillated between trauma and supportive work, Tom was reactivated to deploy to Iraq. He had just begun community college, decreased his drinking, spent less time isolating, and found himself better equipped "to deal with civilians" who in his mind were "not all bad" anymore. I was careful not to burden Tom with worry about his safety, as he complained his family did. I genuinely thanked him for his service to our country and explored the positive and negative feelings hearing me say that brought up. I controlled my own reactions of wanting to get him out of the deployment due to his PTSD but knew how he felt about "wimping out." I reminded him of his strengths and inner resilience. I realistically stated that more exposure such as his first tour would have an impact on his neurophysiological system, and we brainstormed ways for him to cope, by reviewing what worked and didn't work for him before. I struggled in supervision with what type of contact might be beneficial while he was in the combat theater and decided to let him know that he could reach out if he felt like it. He jokingly remarked, "you are coming with me cause I always hear s**t in my head that you might say when I am stressed out." I knew at that remark that he had internalized me as someone not only whom he could look to for support but who understood him.

Several months after he deployed, I began receiving urgent voice mails from Tom from a cell phone in Iraq. I became vigilant in answering my phone to unknown numbers and found myself searching the Internet to see if he had been injured in action. My own narrative had been changed by the bidirectional relationship and the care and concern that evolved from our collaborative alliance. When Tom finally reached me, his speech was pressured and agitated. Tom said he called because he was struggling with rage at his command and feeling isolated in his reserve unit, after the one guy he connected with was killed. He stated he hoped my voice might help. I used our relationship, and regulation of my affect, to attempt to anchor him by stating he had been in bad situations before, and capable at his job, while validating his anger at his superiors. Although I was anxious, I was careful to let him know that we would work together on it all when he returned. Knowing his dark sense of humor, I told him to not do anything stupid, as I wouldn't visit him in the brig. Tom seemed to calm after a few minutes of my reframing, and validating how hard it must be to not be able to mourn his buddy while under fire.

The conversation abruptly cut off, due to what turned out to be a rocket and mortar attack. It was impossible to find out that he was safe for several days until I received an email from him. Other than processing it with my supervisor, I felt alone and helpless in my experience of anxiety and intrusive recollecting of the sounds of incoming mortars, yelling, and ensuing chaos before the phone cut off. My symptoms were more than a countertransference reaction and required more than supervision. I sought personal help to process the traumatic experience I had shared with Tom, a relational clinical recommendation particularly in work with trauma (Herman 1992).

When Tom returned, his symptoms were greatly exacerbated and he quickly resumed treatment. We co-constructed the narrative around our shared experience of his deployment. I limited self-disclosure to my concern for him, not the symptoms I experienced. He gave me a piece of twisted shrapnel, as a "souvenir of our shared combat." He reported that being connected to me had helped him navigate back and forth twice between combat and home in a way that he didn't have to cut off one part to exist in either place. He continues to remain engaged in treatment and able to grieve and work through his traumatic experiences. He also has become more amenable to my challenging cognitive distortions, such as his belief that he could have done more to save fellow marines that were killed. He adopted a survivor mission of reaching out to marines, or soldiers, he would meet at college and offer support, advice, or bringing them to the agency or to the VA for help.

Conclusion

The case of Tom illustrates how a clinical work utilizing a relational approach can help bridge the differences between a civilian clinician and combat survivor. Emphasis on a two-person perspective, in which differences are acknowledged and normalized with this population, can assist the returning soldier reintegrate back to his civilian environment through the co-construction of a future narrative that allows for the premilitary, military, and post-military aspects of identity to coexist. The process of the social work clinician, empathically responding to the combatant's real experience with real experiences of her own, is part of the mutual process that is direct and expressed in the treatment process, rather than artificially being relegated to transference and countertransference as a detached analysis. The therapeutic alliance becomes a template of safe interaction and connection to others, so that the veteran can create and share new meanings and adequately process grief and the traumatic experiences.

Study Questions

1. Describe how mutuality and co-construction of the core problem, as relational practice skills, are reflected in the case in this chapter. Describe how this does or does not reflect your own practice approach, now or previously.
2. Describe how the adaptations to a combat zone might be viewed in the classification organization of the DSM-IV. How would *context* be used to normalize defensive measures that have now become a problem.
3. Name two techniques the social work clinician used to promote a safe working space for the client. What role did self-disclosure play in engaging the resistant client?
4. Discuss how secondary trauma, or shared trauma, might impact you as the clinician? How would you address this issue with relational techniques?
5. Discuss the pros and cons of ongoing contact with past clients. Explain how the situation of redeployment of a combat veteran does or does not alter your view on ongoing contact.
6. Describe the role of internalization in the client's experience of the clinician being "with him" in redeployment and also in civilian life. What kind of impact does internalization have on how a relational clinician might anticipate and manage this type of experience?

References

Adams, R. E., Boscarino, J. A., & Figley, C. R. (2006). Compassion fatigue and psychological distress among social workers: A validation study. *The American Journal of Orthopsychiatry, 76*(1), 103–108.

Adler, A. (1992). *What life could mean to you* (C. Brett, Trans.). Oxford: One World. (Original work published 1931).

Adler, A. B., Huffman, A. H., Bliese, P. D., & Castro, C. A. (2005). The impact of deployment length and experience on the well-being of male and female soldiers. *Journal of Occupational Health Psychology, 10*(2), 121–137. doi:10.1037/10768998.10.2.121.

Aron, L. (1996). *A meeting of minds: Mutuality in psychoanalysis.* Hillsdale: Analytic Press.

Association American Psychiatric. (1994). *Diagnostic and statistical manual of mental disorders.* Washington, DC: American Psychiatric Association.

Barnett, J. E., & Sherman, M. D. (Eds.) (2011, February). Treating traumatized oef/oif veterans: How does trauma treatment affect the clinician? *Professional Psychology: Research and Practice, 42*(1), 79–86.

Berzoff, J., Flanagan, L., & Hertz, P. (2008). *Inside out and outside in: Psychodynamic clinical theory and practice in contemporary multicultural contexts.* New York: Jason Aronson.

Bonanno, G. A. (2004). Loss, trauma, and human resilience: Have we underestimated the human capacity to thrive after extremely aversive events? *American Psychologist, 59*(1), 1–25. doi:10.1037/0003-066x.59.1.20. 07/12/2011.

Bowlby, J. (1983). *Attachment* (2nd ed.). New York: Basic Books Classics.

Bragin, M. (2010). Can anyone here know who I am? Co-constructing meaningful narrative with combat veterans. In P. Rosen (Ed.), *Clinical Social Work Journal, 38*(3), 316–326.

Brandell, J. (2011). *Theory and practice in clinical social work* (2nd ed.). Los Angeles: Sage.

Bromberg, P. M. (1998). *Standing in the spaces: Essays on clinical process trauma and dissociation.* New York: Psychology Press.

Castro, C. A. (2004). *Walter reed army institute of research: Battlemind training I and II transitioning from combat to home,* Washington, DC.

Cozolino, L. (2002). *The neuroscience of human relationships: Attachment and the developing social brain.* New York: W.W. Norton & Company.

DeYoung, P. (2003). *Relational psychotherapy: A primer.* New York: Routledge.

Erbes, C. R., Curry, K. T., & Leskela, J. (2009). Treatment presentation and adherence of Iraq/Afghanistan era veterans in outpatient care for posttraumatic stress disorder. *Psychological Services, 6*(3), 175–183.

Farber, B. A. (2006). *Self-disclosure in psychotherapy.* New York: The Guilford Press.

Figley, C. R. (1978). *Stress disorders among Vietnam veterans: Theory, research and treatment.* London: Routledge.

Figley, C. R. (2002). *Treating compassion fatigue.* London: Routledge.

Fontana, A., & Rosenheck, R. (2005). The role of loss of meaning in the pursuit of treatment for posttraumatic stress disorder. *Journal of Traumatic Stress, 18*(2), 133–136.

Fosha, D. (2000). *The transforming power of affect.* New York: Basic Books.

Fosha, D., Siegel, D. J., & Solomon, M. (2009). *The healing power of emotion: Affective neuroscience, development and clinical practice.* New York: Norton.

Frankl, V. E. (1946). *Man's search for meaning.* New York: Simon & Schuster.

Freud, S. (1918). *Totem and taboo.* New York: Moffat, Yard & Co.

Goldstein, E. G., Miehls, D., & Ringel, S. (2009). *Advanced clinical social work practice: Relational principles and techniques.* New York: Columbia University Press.

Grossman, D., & Christensen, L. W. (2008). *On combat: The psychology and physiology of deadly conflict in war and in peace.* Illinois: Warrior Science Publications.

Herman, J. L. (1992). *Trauma and recovery: The aftermath of violence- from domestic abuse to political terror.* New York: Basic Books.

Hesse, A. R. (2002). Secondary trauma: How working with trauma survivors affects therapists. *Clinical Social Work Journal, 30*(3), 293–309.

Hoffman, I. Z. (1994). Dialectical thinking and therapeutic action in the psychoanalytic process. *Psychoanalytic Quarterly, 63*, 187–218.

Hoge, C. W. (2010). *Once a warrior–always a warrior: Navigating the transition from combat to home*. New York: GPP Life.

Hoge, C. W., Castro, C. A., Messer, S. C., McGurk, D., Cotting, D. I., & Koffman, R. L. (2004). Combat duty in Iraq and Afghanistan, mental health problems, and barriers to care. *The New England Journal of Medicine, 351*(1), 13–22.

Hoge, C. W., Auchterlonie, J. L., & Milliken, C. S. (2006). Mental health problems, use of mental health services, and attrition from military service after returning from deployment to Iraq or Afghanistan. *Journal of the American Medical Association, 295*(9), 1023–1032.

Janoff-Bulman, R. (1992). *Shattered assumptions: Towards a new psychology of trauma*. New York: The Free Press.

Jordan, J. V. (2010). In J. Carlson & M. Englar-Carlson (Eds.), *Relational–cultural therapy*. Washington, DC: American Psychological Association.

Laser, J., & Stephens, P. (2011). Working with military families through deployment and beyond. *Clinical Social Work Journal, 39*(1), 28–38.

Lifton, R. J. (1973). *Home from the war*. New York: Simon & Shuster.

Linley, P. A., & Joseph, S. (2007). Therapy work and therapists' positive and negative well-being. *Journal of Social and Clinical Psychology, 26*(3), 385–403.

McCann, I. L., & Pearlman, L. A. (1990). Vicarious traumatization: A framework for understanding the psychological effects of working with victims. *Journal of Traumatic Stress, 3*, 131–149.

McDevitt-Murphy, M. E., Williams, J. L., Bracken, K. L., Fields, J. A., Monahan, C. J., & Murphy, J. G. (2010). PTSD symptoms, hazardous drinking, and health functioning among U.S. OEF and OIF veterans presenting to primary care. *Journal of Traumatic Stress, 23*(1), 108–111.

Miller, J. B. (1989). *Connections, disconnections and violations* (Work in progress, Vol. 33). Wellesley: Stone Center Working Paper Series.

Miller, J. B., & Stiver, I. (1997). *The healing connection: How women form relationships in therapy and in life*. Boston: Beacon.

Mitchell, S. A. (1988). *Relational concepts in psychoanalysis: An integration*. Cambridge: Harvard University Press.

Mitchell, S. A. (2000). *Relationality: From attachment to intersubjectivity* (Vol. 20). New Jersey: The Analytic Press.

Mitchell, S. A., & Aron, L. (1999). *Relational psychoanalysis: The emergence of a tradition*. New Jersey: The Analytic Press.

Munroe, J. (1991). *Therapist traumatization from exposure to clients with combat related posttraumatic stress disorder: Implications for administration and supervision*. Ed.D. dissertation, Northeastern University, Boston. Dissertation Abstracts International, 52-03B, 1731.

Neumann, D. A., & Gamble, S. J. (1995). Issues in the professional development of psychotherapists: Countertransference, and vicarious traumatization in the new trauma therapist. *Psychotherapy, 32*(2), 341–347.

Orange, D. (1995). *Emotional understanding: Studies in psychoanalysis*. New York: Guilford Press.

Pearlman, L. A., & Saakvitne, K. (1995). *Trauma and the therapist: Countertransference and vicarious traumatization in psychotherapy with incest survivors*. New York: Norton.

Porges, S. W. (2011). *The polyvagal theory: Neurophysiological foundations of emotions, attachment, communication, and self-regulation*. New York: W.W. Norton & Company.

Quillman, T. (2011, January 18). Neuroscience and therapist self-disclosure: deepening right brain to right brain communication between therapist and patient. *Clinical Social Work Journal*. Retrieved from http://www.springerlink.com/content/103103u12873hlr5/fulltext.html. Accessed 12 July 2011.

Rasmussen, B. (2005). An intersubjective perspective on vicarious trauma and its impact on the clinical process. *Journal of Social Work Practice, 19*(1), 19–30.

Rice, L., & Greenberg, L. (1984). *Patterns of change: An intensive analysis of psychotherapeutic process*. New York: Guilford Press.

Saari, C. (2002). *The environment: Its role in psychosocial functioning and psychotherapy*. New York: Columbia University Press.

Sabin-Farrell, R., & Turpin, G. (2003). Vicarious traumatization: Implications for the mental health of workers? *Clinical Psychology Review, 23*(3), 449–480.

Safran, J. D. (2002). Brief relational psychoanalytic treatment. *Psychoanalytic Dialogues, 12*, 171–195.

Schamess, G. (2011, May 12). Mutual transformation in psychotherapy. *Clinical Social Work Journal*. Retrieved from http://www.springerlink.com/content/30730377846h8311/fulltext. html. Accessed 28 June 2011.

Schore, A. N. (2001). Minds in the making: Attachment, the self-organizing brain, and developmentally-oriented psychoanalytic psychotherapy. *British Journal of Psychotherapy, 17*(3), 299–328.

Shatan, C. F. (1978). Stress disorders among Vietnam veterans: The emotional context of combat continues. In C. R. Figley (Ed.), *Stress disorders among Vietnam veterans* (pp. 43–55). New York: Brunner/Mazel.

Shay, J. (1994). *Achilles in Vietnam*. New York: Scribner.

Shay, J. (2002). *Odysseus in America: Combat trauma and the trials of homecoming*. New York: Scribner.

Sherman, N. (2010). *The untold war: Inside the hearts, minds, and souls of our soldiers*. New York: W.W. Norton & Co.

Southwick, S. M., Gilmartin, R., McDonough, P., & Morrisey, P. (2006). Logotherapy as an adjunctive treatment for chronic combat-related PTSD: A meaning-based intervention. *American Journal of Psychotherapy, 60*(2), 161–174.

Stamm, B. H. (Ed.). (1999). *Secondary traumatic stress: Self-care issues for clinicians, researchers, and educators* (2nd ed.). Lutherville: Sidran Press.

Stern, D. N. (2000). *The interpersonal world of the infant*. New York: Basic Books.

Stolorow, R. D. (2007). *Trauma and human existence: Autobiographical, psychoanalytic, and philosophical reflections* (Vol. 23). New York: Routledge/Taylor & Francis Group.

Stolorow, R. D., & Atwood, G. E. (2002). *Contexts of being: The intersubjective foundations of psychological life*. London: Routledge.

Tedeschi, R. G., & Calhoun, L. G. (2004). Posttraumatic growth: Conceptual foundations and empirical evidence. *Psychological Inquiry, 15*(1), 2–17.

Teicholz, J. G. (2009). My relational self psychology. *Self and Systems, 1159*, 122–138.

Tosone, C. (2004). Relational social work: Honoring the tradition. *Smith College Studies in Social Work, 74*(3), 475–487.

Tosone, C. (2006). Therapeutic intimacy: A post-9/11 perspective. *Smith College Studies in Social Work, 76*(4), 89–98.

Tosone, C., & Bialkin, L. (2004). Mass violence and secondary trauma: Issues for the clinician. In S. L. Ashenberg-Straussner & N. K. Phillips (Eds.), *Understanding mass violence: A social work perspective* (pp. 157–168). Boston: Pearson.

Tosone, C., et al. (2003). Shared trauma: Group reflections on the September 11th disaster. *Psychoanalytic Social Work, 10*(1), 57–77.

Tyson, J. M. (2007). Compassion fatigue in the treatment of combat-related trauma during war-time. *Clinical Social Work Journal, 35*(1), 183–192.

Van der Kolk, B. A., McFarlane, A. C., & Weisaeth, L. (Eds.). (1996). *Traumatic stress: The effects of overwhelming experience on mind, body, and society*. New York: Guilford Press.

Wachtel, P. (2007). *Relational theory and the practice of psychotherapy*. New York: The Guilford Press.

Wachtel, P. L. (2010). One-person and two-person conceptions of attachment and their implications for psychoanalytic thought. *The International Journal of Psychoanalysis, 91*(3), 561–581.

Watson, P. J. (2009). *Understanding military culture when treating PTSD*. Retrieved from http://www.ptsd.va.gov/professional/ptsd101/course-modules/military_culture.asp

Watts, R. E. (2003). Adlerian therapy as a relational constructivist approach. *The Family Journal: Counseling and Therapy for Couples and Families, 11*(2), 139–147.

Wilson, J. P., Friedman, M. J., & Lindy, J. D. (2001). A holistic, organismic approach to healing trauma and PTSD. In J. P. Wilson, M. J. Friedman, & J. D. Lindy (Eds.), *Treating psychological trauma and PTSD* (pp. 28–56). New York: The Guilford Press.

Wrenn, L. J. (2003). Trauma: Conscious and unconscious meaning. *Clinical Social Work Journal, 31*(2), 123–137.

Zimering, R., Munroe, J., & Gulliver, (2003). *Secondary traumatization in mental health providers*. Psychiatric Times. 20(4). http://www.psychiatrictimes.com/p030443.html

Social Work Practice with Reentry from Incarceration

Thomas K. Kenemore

Introduction

This chapter describes and illustrates an application of relational social work practice with individuals in transition from prison or jail to their communities and to free society. These individuals constitute a vast, underserved, and oppressed population, making them a legitimate target population for social work practice (Specht and Courteny 1994). The reentry population is distinct, yet largely invisible; the invisibility maintained by social, political, and cultural forces that, by design, relegate individuals in this category to a permanent under-caste (Alexander 2010), and by neglect.

Reentry for individuals is an internal, interpersonal, cultural, and social transition from a highly controlled, predictable, and dangerous world in which compliance is paramount to a highly unpredictable, confusing, also dangerous world in which expectations are subtle and conflicting. Although most reentry individuals initially are on some form of parole supervision, that arrangement at best emphasizes compliance and does not effectively address the multiple needs of these individuals. The crisis of change involved for this population calls for proactive social work service that is humanizing, responsive, and demonstrative that successful reentry is an achievable goal, however complex. Relational clinicians are most likely to encounter reentry individuals in settings that focus on concrete services, though they may show up for services in a wide range of venues without their incarceration background being necessarily known. Regardless of setting, engaging them will require use of clinical social work skills, including a capacity for relational engagement. Practitioners have a window of opportunity to engage these disaffected and skeptical people in the reconfiguration of a meaningful way of living outside incarceration. This is a tall but necessary order. Relational theory offers a potential means of circumventing the clearly failing current pattern of either authoritarian or avoidant

T.K. Kenemore, Ph.D., LCSW, BCD (✉)
Master of Social Work Program, Chicago State University, Chicago, IL, USA
e-mail: thomas@kenemore.org

J.B. Rosenberger (ed.), *Relational Social Work Practice with Diverse Populations,*
Essential Clinical Social Work Series, DOI 10.1007/978-1-4614-6681-9_15,
© Springer Science+Business Media New York 2014

practices that reentry individuals ordinarily face (Maur and Chesney-Lind 2002). Without clinical practice knowledge, the social worker is apt to be acculturated to this dehumanizing approach.

Developing practice frameworks and approaches that are useful in guiding clinical social work with this population requires an understanding of the unique character- istics and experiences of individuals going through this transition. Individual pro- cesses of reentry are inseparable from the ecological, cultural, and political contexts within which they occur. How these contextual arrangements are internalized and processed by each reentering individual is highly idiosyncratic and unique and shapes the individual's experience and sense of self. Reentry follows involuntary and coercive segregation from the very society that social workers represent. Certainly, any practice model that implicitly or explicitly replicates the demands for client compliance to an imposed framework is problematic for people recently released from highly coercive conditions. Therefore, effective clinical social work with individuals transitioning from prison or jail to freedom requires development and use of practice skills and approaches that can be perceived as credible by the individuals and families receiving the help and that are demonstrably effective in facilitating change. This requirement – that the practices must yield practical results to meet often desperate concrete needs in order to establish credibility – is the rela- tional social worker's opportunity to create an interpersonal link that maintains the individual's willingness to engage and use help.

Thus, the relational clinician engaging in case management activities, resource finding, and other "concrete" service delivery is also necessarily engaged at the same time in a clinical relational process as the reentry individual struggles to nego- tiate successfully with an ecological situation that is experienced as incoherent, confusing, and hostile. If the clinician is able to conceptualize this active process as engagement in, and construction of, a specialized relationship, the reentry client can experience the clinician's active, stable, persistent, positive, and empathic attention as corrective and as a model for other relationships encountered in the reentry pro- cess. The client will, and should, remain skeptical and mistrustful of people and resources that are a part of managing reentry but can also begin to perceive and experience credible, trustworthy, and helpful relationships as well and to differenti- ate between potentially useful and potentially dangerous relationships. This process can ultimately facilitate development, maintenance, and enhancement of the client's cohesive self within non-cohesive social challenges.

The clinician can also learn, in the process, a great deal about relational practice in work with this challenging population. First and foremost, an artificial distinction between "concrete" services and "therapeutic" services can be effectively erased. The clinician can begin to perceive the relational processes as essential to the change process that is occurring with the client during reentry, and she can perceive and begin to manage the therapeutic activity that is occurring along with concrete service and case management delivery and correct a traditional and limited conceptualization of therapy as occurring only in a defined therapeutic space, e.g., the therapist's office (Altman 2010). Also, the relational clinician can actively engage in an introspective process that positions him/her to develop and maintain empathy with reentry clients, overriding traditional stereotypes about people with criminal backgrounds and incarceration experience. Within this clinician change process, the relational clinician can significantly enhance her cultural competence and capacity to work effectively with broader and more diverse populations. Finally, the challenging and challenged reentry population provides a vast resource for the clinician's development of relational practice skill. In this way, work with the reentry population demonstrates the relational model's constructivist value in being adaptable in order to establish and maintain connection.

The Reentry Population

The United States has the highest documented incarceration rate in the world. In 2009, the United States reported that 743 residents per 100,000 were incarcerated, followed by Rwanda at 595 per 100,000 and the Russian Federation at 559 (West et al. 2010). In 2009, over two million individuals were incarcerated in the USA (Glaze 2010). The total recorded correctional population in 2009 was over seven million, including those incarcerated, and just over 4.5 million under community supervision (approximately 3.8 million on probation and just over 700,000 on parole) (Glaze 2010). Allen Beck, Chief of the Bureau of Justice Statistics, Corrections Statistics Program, reported in 2006 that, overall, approximately 12 million jail admissions are processed each year (Beck 2006). Many of these are individuals who are arrested and awaiting trial, but not convicted of a crime. Incarceration rates of individuals convicted of a crime in the USA quadrupled between 1989 and 2003 and have leveled or declined slightly more recently (West et al. 2010). Analysis indicates "perhaps the single greatest historical force behind the growth of the prison population has been the national 'war on drugs'" (Human Rights Watch 2003).

The reentry population roughly mirrors the prison and jail population, as most of those incarcerated are eventually released. At least 95 % of state prisoners are released back to their communities at some point (Hughes and Wilson 2002). This suggests that a significant portion of social service populations include reentry individuals, whether identified as such or not. It also suggests that families and communities, particularly those that are urban and poor, are coping with issues related to reentry. Over five million adults were on probation or parole in 2009, accounting for approximately 80 % of the reentry population (Glaze 2010). In total, well over seven million individual adults were under some form of correctional supervision, including incarceration, supervision, and parole (1 in every 31 adults in the population, 1 in 18 men, 1 in 89 women, 1 in 11 African Americans, 1 in 27 Latinos, and 1 in 45 whites) (Bureau of Justice Statistics 2010). In addition, there were almost 93,000 youth held in juvenile facilities (Bureau of Justice Statistics 2010). African Americans accounted for over 39 % of the total prison and jail population and Hispanics (of all races) comprised nearly 21 % of the total (Bureau of Justice Statistics 2010). Together these two categories accounted for almost 60 % of the incarcerated population. Rates of incarceration varied by state, with Maine having the lowest ratio (150 per 100,000) and Oklahoma having the highest (657 per 100,000). Reliable national statistics on religion and incarceration are not available, but reports suggest that around 60 % of inmates are Christian (31 % Catholic and 28 % Protestant) and approximately 6 % are Muslim (Bureau of Justice Statistics 2011). These statistics, while indicating characteristics of incarcerated populations, are assumed to also be reflective of the released population, given the 95 % rate of release of those incarcerated. Breakdowns of the reentry population are much more scattered and partial, reflecting in part the relative absence of control over, and of national interest in, this category.

Mental illness is between two and four times higher among prisoners (thus among the reentry population) than in the general population (Hammett et al. 2001), suggesting the value of access to clinical services for this population. Three quarters of those returning from prison have a history of substance use disorders (Hammett et al. 2001), again suggesting the need for access to clinical services. Homelessness rates are significantly higher among this population, both before and after incarceration (Culhane et al. 2002; Metraux and Culhame 2004), with all the attendant clinical needs that accompany this devastating experience. Similarly, about two in five prison and jail inmates have not graduated high school, and many have low employment rates and earnings before incarceration (Harlow 2003; Holzer et al. 2003), leaving them especially vulnerable to failure and recidivism in the absence of proactive social work service. Education and employment opportunities are obviously severely limited after incarceration, as the individuals have a criminal history. These factors also add to recidivism rates, which are particularly high during the first 2–3 years after release (Bureau of Justice Statistics 2010). A large portion of reincarceration results from parole violations: Studies consistently indicate that around 68 % of prisoners released are rearrested within 3 years of release, and of these, around 35 % are returned to prison for parole violations (Bureau of Justice Statistics 2010; Lawrence 2008). The majority of inmates leave prison with no savings, no immediate entitlement to unemployment benefits, and few job prospects (Petersilia 2000). Taken as a whole, these factors indicate the critical role for social work practice, and particularly relational practice, of engaging individuals in a respectful, adequately complex, and cohesion-building experience, against great odds. Clinical assessment and treatment planning need to evolve to capture client individualization and strength and to resist the pull toward social and psychological pathological categorization of reentry clients.

The Reentry Process and Requirements of the Social Work Practitioner

According to Kupers (1999), over 90 % of ex-inmates will leave prisons with little or no discharge planning. This includes those with serious mental illnesses as well as drug histories and significant physical illness. Though planning prior to release is sometimes recognized as important, its implementation is ordinarily left to the whims of local prison administrations and is typically ignored. Common sense would suggest that relational clinicians should be involved with those incarcerated throughout their tenure in prison, be instrumental in helping inmates plan for a successful reentry, and be automatically available to help with the actual transition process. One can find promising examples of programs in prisons. There is a growing literature on counseling and other programs that help incarcerated individuals, including psychodynamic approaches (Kita 2012; Smith 2009; Hinshelwood 1993; Kupers 2005; Morris 2001; Saunders 2001). However, a range of macro- and mezzo-level ideological, policy, funding, administration, and other factors present deeply embedded barriers to this access. While not detailed here, they include punitive national policies, media stereotyping of individuals and groups who are involved in the criminal justice system, lack of funding resources for programming, policy variations in state and local governments, and cultural variations within local prisons (Beck 2006; Maur and Chesney-Lind 2002; Petersilia 2000).

The lack of discharge planning leaves access to any support or resources in the hands of community-based social services. Typically, those programs are organized around housing, employment, substance abuse treatment, or other specialized services, and the involvement of relational clinicians for engagement in a relational process is not valued. Without clinical engagement, the released individual is on his/her own to break an invisibility shield and actively pursue practices of engagement in order to receive needed help. This invisibility shield includes public disinterest and ignorance, the individual's efforts to hide his criminal background, and a hidden well of shame, fear, and anger. Left to fend for themselves, staying drug-free, keeping out of serious trouble, and successfully adjusting to the outside world all present significant challenges to this large population (Kupers 1999; Maur and Chesney-Lind 2002; Petersilia 2000).

Many ex-inmates have typically spent hours or days in solitary confinement or in segregated housing. Once outside, and without help in navigating unfamiliar territory through a reliable relationship of support, ex-inmates are ill prepared to deal with the social complexities facing them and will suffer from serious psychological, relational, and practical problems. Their legal history assigns them forever to a caste of individuals who carry a permanent criminal record that bars them from adequate housing, gainful employment, or opportunities for most forms of advancement (Alexander 2010; Jacobson 2005) Particularly if Black and male, they are subject to reproduction and maintenance of their oppression in daily discourse (Mullaly 2010), often including racist stereotyping (Alexander 2010; Rome 2004). When the default community position is either neglect or active distrust, a proactive social work agenda is required to establish some base of affiliation wherein individual recognition and ongoing support is developed to offset malevolent messages. Programs that do not include alliance with a primary relationship of respect and understanding may perpetuate the lonely, survival-based qualities of prison life.

The Subjective Experience: A Call for Relational Practice as Activism

There is limited research-based knowledge about the subjective experience of ex-prisoners entering our communities. This deficit in knowledge has been evident and largely unheeded for many years, despite long-standing concern about recidivism (Irwin 1970). There is typically no officially established relational arrangement immediately upon release, except with a probation officer. The failure to establish a clinical presence as part of discharge contributes to this dysfunctional service gap.

Services of relational clinicians built into the transition would offer a chance for a clinician to demonstrate an assertively constructivist intent. Clinical social work practice offers assessment, helping the reentering person to identify the clinician as an ambassador of free society, including relational follow-through with a treatment plan to demonstrate an interest in working with him/her to express goals, means to reach those goals, attention to external and internal issues the individual is struggling with, and exploration of options. The relational model does not ask or demand that the guarded person become a deep confidant as the basis of clinical social work. It rather inquires what he needs, how he can be assisted in pursing goals, and what he experiences in the clinical process. The practitioner in this process is also engaging actively in providing concrete services as needed, including educational and resource-finding activity. In this way, engagement allows the co-construction of a relational space that is attuned to the client's concerns and needs. Nancy McWilliams discusses this relational process as being attuned to people who "…need to talk to someone who will let that process happen without trying to cheer them up, distract them, join in their denial, or minimize their pain" (McWilliams 1999, p. 59). The clients she cites as needing such an attentive process include people in stigmatized minority groups who are legally incarcerated, or who have damaged children or failing parents or other consuming dependents, or who have lost jobs and are confronting an indifferent economic environment, or who are in financial distress that cannot be quickly fixed (McWilliams 1999, p. 59). The reentry client is such a person.

Maruna (2001), O'Brien (2001), and Kenemore and Roldan (2006) have conducted three of the few qualitative studies with ex-prisoners who have made successful adjustments to the outside world. Getting out of prison is described by the subjects of these studies as a traumatic, overwhelming experience. Coping with a varied and confusing range of internal experiences and feelings is an immediate assignment. Internal experiences emphasize lack of preparation for leaving the structured, predictable prison environment. The ex-prisoners' perceptions of the broader community, and of institutions within the community, are more abstract and tend toward mistrust.

A complex story emerges from ex-prisoners about keeping their lives on course or "staying straight." Common themes that emerge include the wish to engage with, and to contribute to, their families, their communities, and other ex-prisoners (Kenemore and Roldan 2006). They want to be of help to others who have been through similar experiences. These thematic aims become missions and are expressed in an ecological context that is experienced as dangerous and dominated by mistrust of people or institutions representing authority and requiring hypervigilant watchfulness. The challenge for the clinician, in this context, is to present herself, and her services as potentially useful in helping the individual client pursue his/her mission. This will require overcoming the service user's assumption that the clinician is a barrier to be overcome, avoided, or worked around. In the study by Kenemore and Roldan (2006), the ex-prisoners feel it is important to manage the relationships in their lives. They particularly value supportive attitudes, talking straight, and loyalty in the relationships they maintain. They convey an exceptional consciousness about daily life that reflects an unusual alertness to their own inner experience, ongoing interactions with other important people in their lives, and the positive and negative forces affecting their ability to stay on course. They are acutely alert to temptation and to the struggle against it (Kenemore and Roldan 2006).

Successful reentry appears to include important transformative narratives. Maruna (2001) argues that "to desist from crime, ex-offenders need to develop a coherent, pro-social identity for themselves. As such, they need to understand their criminal pasts (why they did what they did), and they also need to understand why they are now not like that anymore" (Maruna 2001, p. 7).

He describes this process of transformation as one of therapeutic rebiographing: "The ex-offender is able to justify one's past while also rationalizing the decision to go straight" (Maruna 2001, pp. 164–165). Maruna found that ex-offenders who desist from crime do not attempt to deny or hide their pasts. Instead, they tend to turn their tragic pasts into something positive. This rebiographing typically includes recognition that they were going down a destructive path, leading to a change in attitude and behavior. O'Brien (2001) similarly found that female ex-offenders who reenter society successfully discover meaning for their lives that they attribute to the prison experience itself. They often develop corrective intense caregiving relationships with their children upon release that are important to their progress in transition to freedom.

The study by Kenemore and Roldan (2006) describes how significant experiences of change have dramatically and positively affected the direction of their lives. In some instances, the change occurs when the person is first incarcerated, is shocked by the experience, realizes they have been operating in a way that has ensured their getting arrested and convicted, and vows to turn their life around. In other instances, it may be the experiences of being taken under the wing of an older inmate and being told how to change attitudes. In still other instances, change can involve a religious conversion to Islam or a Christian faith and becoming focused on biblical or Qu'ran theology. In another instance, it may be an incarcerated mother recognizing the impact of her absence and the shame experienced by her children after a prison visitation. It always is an event or moment in which the inmate or ex-offender recognizes being on a "bad" track and needing to change. These experiences are recounted as turning points by the subjects of these studies (Kenemore and Roldan 2006; Maruna 2001). Within a relational social work process, these experiences can potentially be captured, articulated, and utilized to help the client organize around a positive identity and to facilitate empowerment. Without involvement in a relational process, whether in clinical practice or within a social matrix, the experience can be dismissed, minimized, or lost. This argues for reentry individuals having access to clinical social work service with providers who are trained and skilled in utilizing a relational process.

The ex-prisoners maintain hope about the future, despite the past and current difficulties. They work at maintaining strong proactive, positive, and hopeful attitudes. Having a mission is central to feeling hopeful. The ex-offenders want to leave their mark on the world somehow. They express a strong desire to help others like themselves, particularly younger people who could use their wisdom to avoid the troubles they have experienced. They want to protect others from copying their errors. Spirituality, religion, belief in God as a protector, and the power of prayer are typically important aspects of their current experience and their hopefulness about the future (Kenemore and Roldan 2006).

Relational Social Work Practice with the Reentry Population

The unique experiences of the reentry population, summarized above, inform the proposed practice framework. Initial assumptions for engagement in clinical work with individuals in this population must be that people *do* want to have successful reentry experiences and that they *do* want help. Relational social work practice with individuals in a reentry transition, however, poses specific challenges to the clinician. Engagement with clients who mistrust authority and resist professional intervention is a central issue for practice with the reentry population. The relational clinician invariably represents the authority structure that has been in place during incarceration and threatens to be a major source of oppression. The clinician cannot expect otherwise. This requires her to be scrupulous in exploring self-knowledge of her perception of, and responses to, this population and to be proactive in introducing the issue of trust. Such engagement helps the clinician to position herself to establish authenticity of communication with the initially mistrustful client (McWilliams 1999).

Active Listening: Engaging the Potential Service User

In general, ex-prisoners express negative attitudes toward mental health services (Kenemore and Roldan 2006; O'Brien 2001; Petersilia 2000; Maur and Chesney-Lind 2002). While such attitudes are not unique to this population, the ex-prisoner carries an added layer of mistrust, skepticism, and fear about counseling and therapy, because the social worker, counselor, or therapist is, by definition, a representative of the dominant culture (Houston 2002; Mullaly 2010). The individual has ordinarily been directed by, compliant with, and resentful of a host of authority figures who are perceived as harmful and dangerous, since their arrest and conviction, and often before. On first contact, there is no reason for the individual to view the relational clinician as potentially helpful or interested in their experience.

Like other marginalized groups, many ex-offenders also believe that counselors who have not had similar experiences could not begin to understand them. They are most responsive to people who "talk straight," who can "hold their own," or are otherwise unafraid to challenge them (Kenemore and Roldan 2006). For those who have accessed mental health services, the experiences have been reported as generally disappointing and often have only served to foster the negative attitudes they already have. Most express that they cannot understand how talking about their fears and vulnerabilities can be helpful. This is augmented by the fact that they typically have spent a lifetime preoccupied with fending off anxieties. Many admit to having some awareness that something is wrong, and a wish to correct their lives (Kenemore and Roldan 2006). Even those more motivated to be candidates for clinical social work services tend to reenter the community trying to deal with their problems alone and unsupported (Petersilia 2000; Maur and Chesney-Lind 2002).

In a seeming contradiction, reentering individuals do feel that talking with someone about their feelings could be helpful if they could trust that their confidentiality would be respected. Despite skepticism about therapy or counseling, the ex-prisoners recognize in a profound way their need for help. Two quotes from ex-offenders in the study by Kenemore and Roldan (2006) illustrate this point:

> No matter what programs or services are out there when you get out of prison, the main thing is to have someone to talk to and rely on as you sort out all the changes...

> Most people wanna be well. Most people realize that something is wrong for them to be there [prison]. Most people realize that what they did is wrong. But most of them don't come out and get affiliated with any sort of therapy or any sort of organization that is gonna refer them to therapy. So they just come out and do the best they can.

The Intersubjective Perspective

The primary tool of practice is the clinician's management of the relationship with the service user over time (Perleman 1983; Tosone 2004; Goldstein et al. 2009). Two essential perspectives inform the development and maintenance of a therapeutic relationship with individuals experiencing transition from prison to freedom. The first is a relational and intersubjective perspective, which insists that the therapist is "...always a participant in the client's inner *and* interpersonal world" (Berzoff et al. 2011, p. 224). The relational, intersubjective stance in relation to the service user is an absolute requirement throughout. This stance assumes that both parties have and can share legitimate subjective experiences of themselves and each other within the relationship, thus cocreating a shared "space" in which change in experience, perception, feeling, attitude, and behavior can occur (Aron 1996; Mitchell 1997; Mitchell and Aron 1999; Curtis and Hirsch 2003).

A particularly useful reference for this stance is Altman's conceptualization of an adaptation of psychoanalytic principles to the ecological, social context (Altman 2010). It incorporates ecological, cultural, and social factors in a "two-person social-psychoanalytical perspective [that] is necessary to accommodate such intrinsically social factors as race and social class within a psychoanalytic frame of reference" (p. 390). He further insists that "one can think psychoanalytically and systemically at the same time, that unconscious transference/countertransference dynamics can be applied to multiperson and organizational systems as well as to individual minds and dyadic interactions" (p. 173).

The Anti-oppressive Perspective

The second essential perspective is an anti-oppressive stance. The reentry population primarily includes clients who experience extreme obstacles to a successful transition within the community. To whatever degree this situation was true before incarceration, it is invariably a dominant feature upon reentry. The anti-oppressive stance assumes that "unless we acknowledge the unassailable link between culture, social structure and social inequality, social work practice at best will prove to be ineffectual and at worst may serve to reproduce unwittingly the divisions [oppression] which it is attempting to remove" (Houston 2002, p. 156). At a personal level, this stance suggests "interventions that bridge the separation of existential freedom and socio-political liberty" (Mullaly 2010, p. 223). Built on an established pedagogy which critiques oppression and advocates liberation (Freire 1970, 1992) and empowerment traditions deeply embedded in social work practice ideology (Simon 1994), this stance is essential for work with individuals in transition from prison or jail to freedom.

Together, these perspectives position the relational clinician to engage meaningfully and effectively with individuals struggling against powerful internalized, interpersonal, cultural, and structural forces and thereby to help them become more empowered to achieve a relatively comfortable adaptation to freedom individually and within their families and communities. This work can be conceptualized as a process in which the client (service user) and relational clinician (facilitator) engage in a discourse aimed at helping the individual sort out all the changes that are occurring and being experienced, and to recognize the barrier to engagement that such terms as 'client and therapist' or 'clinician' create. The terms service user and facilitator are used in this context. The terms also are reminders of what is essential in the empowerment stance that the facilitator must take to establish credibility and ultimately to get inside the experience of the service user.

Stanley Houston (2002) utilizing four key constructs from French philosopher and sociologist Pierre Bourdieu's theory (Bordieu 1979, 1988, 1989; Bordeiu and Wacquant 1992) provides a four-step framework for a general anti-oppressive and culturally sensitive stance within which intersubjective processes between service user and facilitator can play out and move toward liberation. These components are isolated out here for discussion, but in practice they overlap and flow within the relational space that the clinician and client construct together. This framework is further elaborated in the case below, to illustrate the application of the relational/

intersubjective and anti-oppressive perspectives cited above, as central to direct relational social work practice with the reentry population.

The first step (Houston, pp. 156–159) involves expanding cultural competence with knowledge of the reentry population, the issues reentry individuals face, and the subordinated cultures within which these individuals operate. It also involves the relational clinician critically reviewing and consciously evaluating her own dominant cultural context. This expanded awareness must include knowledge of how oppression and privilege are internalized for both parties in the anticipated service user-facilitator relationship. The clinician is required to aspire to cultural competence by understanding: the habitus or internalized and embodied social structures, representing the dominant and subordinate cultures related to the client and to the clinician; the arrangements of capital, including resources available and held by both dominant and subordinate cultures; and the field, including the physical, economic, social, and cultural venue in which oppression related to the service users' and service providers' relationship are played out.

The second step, enhancing professional reflexivity (Houston, pp. 159–160), involves introspective application of this knowledge to self. The relational clinician must identify her social location as an agent of the dominant culture, how that location is internalized, and how it informs perception of the potential reentry individual service user. This exercise, prior to, or early in contact with the service user, reduces the opportunity for the clinician to reproduce and reenact an oppressive discourse with the service user. It also positions the facilitator to engage empathically with the service user. This process may overlap such concepts as countertransference and introspection in more traditional clinical practice literature, though these are inadequate terms for this reflective process, because they do not represent the actuality of the self as part of the social context. In relational theory, the clinician is required to have full acknowledgement of the realities of her own presence as a representative of the social order, as well as someone who has internalized much of that order.

The third step, developing cultural sensitivity, is about empathic engagement (Berzoff et al. 2011; Brandell 2011; Coady and Lehman 2008; Kohut 2000; Rogers 1961) with the reentry individual and together identifying opportunities for the reentry service user to transcend his cultural limitations and/or to transform limiting social arrangements. This step typically involves challenging and deconstructing problematic components of the individual's narrative and facilitating awareness of internalized oppression. This agenda goes beyond a traditional stance of empathy, as it assumes that facilitating overcoming oppression is an essential aim of the clinician. The mechanisms for such change initially are in the challenging and correction of assumptions held by both parties. This leads to creation of a potential space (Bollas 2008, 2009, 2011; Casement 1991; Winnicott 1965, 1969) in which both can together create an alternative narrative. The relational clinician must actively demonstrate an understanding, however limited, of the reentry individual's sociocultural experience and must also actively and effectively attend to concrete needs of the person. Therefore, it requires engaging in a process with the service user that enables getting inside their experience. The relational social worker uses empathy, inquiry, reflective listening, and a great deal of self-examination to track the ebb and flow of authentic connection, a step that requires exceptional thought and empathy on the part of the clinician. By engagement in an authentic relating to what exists at the outset, an opening occurs for something as yet unformulated to occur (Schafer 1980a, b, 1982; Stern 1985, 1998).

The fourth step, raising awareness and facilitating empowerment, involves a process of conscientization (Friere 1970), with the facilitator and service user critically examining oppressive social arrangements and internalization of these structures, systematically challenging internalized oppression and fatalism, and constructing narratives, relational patterns, and actions that will lead to increased empowerment.

A Representative Case Example: David

This representative case will illustrate each step in the clinical social work relational and anti-oppressive treatment of "David." This case illustrates the many therapeutic, research, and social experiences that are representative of work with individuals in transition from prison or jail to freedom. The case description isolates out the relational, intersubjective components of the process; it does not describe the complex activities that occur related to networking, case management, referral, legal assistance, financial assistance, employment and housing, and service programming in the social reentry process. Those activities, as indicated, are critical and intrinsic to working with the multiple concrete needs of this largely abandoned population and are concurrent with social work principles but are not the focus of this relational social work practice discussion. Therefore, the case description focuses on the essential clinical social work therapeutic relationship process that is core to any meaningful help.

Initial Engagement with David

David is a 38-year-old African American man, released from a prison complex on Chicago's south side three weeks prior to my contact with him. He was given $50 on his release and remembers the guard saying, "We'll see you later" as he walked out. He also remembers coming to a stoplight a couple of blocks from the prison and not having any idea what to do next. He ended up in a shelter after a couple of days of wandering around. The shelter staff sent him to an organization that helps individuals getting out of prison. The counselor he met with at the shelter suggested that because of the torture he reported, he might use some counseling. He was referred to me.

David had served 12 years for a conviction on an attempted murder charge and claimed that he had been tortured by police into confessing to this crime, which he had not committed. He had been silent during the court proceedings and throughout his incarceration about the torture, being ashamed of having let the police intimidate him. However, he remembers the torture like it was yesterday. During his time in prison, he had been moved twice and had generally faded into the prison population in each site. He had befriended an older man, a "lifer," in the last prison, who had talked to him a lot about getting his life together when he was released.

David had been a junior member of the Blackstone Rangers gang prior to his imprisonment. He was living with a wife and a two-year-old son prior to his arrest. He had had some erratic contact with his wife and child during his imprisonment, and his wife had made contact with him about a month prior to his release. She wondered if he wanted to see his son, now 14 years old. He had looked forward to being met by them when he was released, but made no specific plans. His wife had given no indication of her availability and did not meet him upon his release. He had still not had contact with any family members since his release at the time he and I first met. He had worked some in construction before his incarceration and was interested in finding an adult education program where he could learn some skills and maybe get a bachelor's degree. These plans were amorphous, and David was completely without information or guidance as to how to pursue any such goals.

Step One: Intersecting Structures. Before I met David, I had to think about David's social world as I imagined it. Being White, suburban, middle class, and professional, I had little relational knowledge of people from the Chicago neighborhood where David grew up, who were convicted of murder and imprisoned for many years, or who were poor or Black. I had no experience of torture or other police brutality. I did, however, have plenty of ideas from the media. Black men were supposed to be dangerous, poor, and harbor hatred of White people.

I also had to think about my role as a relational clinician in a relatively large social service organization, funded by a mixture of government and private resources, and with a mission of helping poor families stabilize. In sum, I had to recognize that my access to David's experiential world was severely limited and compromised by my being embedded in this, my own, social context.

Step Two: Relational Clinician as Agent of the Dominant Culture. I anticipated that David would approach me with skepticism, fear, and anger as a therapist who would likely relate to him as a stereotypical Black, view him in pathological terms and who would want to influence his mind in some way. Recognizing that interpersonal relating means that both parties bring their histories to the encounter, I anticipated that I would tend to relate to him in some ways that would validate these expectations, despite my claim of openness, antiracism, and concern. I would likely be defensive and overly careful and would probably feel awkward and "professional" in my stance as a White man. I recognized the need to contain and/or get these issues on the table with David early in our contact. The nuances of relational social work required me to consider how to do this in a way that was not concealing my own defensiveness or inspiring a minimization of defensiveness in a man who had every reason to be suspicious and on guard.

Step Three: Cultural Sensitivity. David presented as a short, stocky, dark-skinned man who seemed very jumpy and anxious. After an initial introduction at the agency, David explained he was here because he told the case manager at the shelter that he was tortured, and the woman seemed worried about some psychological damage. He was supposed to talk to a therapist to find out if that was true. I recognized that the issue of being damaged by the torture represented broader issues of damage done to him. It also represented an internalization of the referring agent's perception of him as damaged, i.e., pathological, subordinate, and incapacitated.

I knew I had to change the course of the discussion very quickly to avoid being locked into an expert, dominant role. I told him that rather than explore the question of damage, as it was the question of the referring agent and not his own experiential question, I wanted to begin to understand him as a person and as a man. I let him know immediately that I knew he had spent a long time in prison, that he was recently released, that he was facing a White professional stranger, and that I knew nothing about his experience. I also let him know that I believed he probably knew little about me and might wonder about my credibility or potential usefulness. I told him I wanted him to check me out and try to discover if I might be of some use to him and that I would be as forthcoming and truthful as possible with him. This stance is illustrative of McWilliams' (1999) suggestion to invite questions and direct feedback in all initial encounters with clients. It also reflects relational theory guidance to social work clinicians to be proactive in clarifying the mutuality of the relationship (Tosone 2004).

I told David I was aware that I could not possibly know his experience but that I would work very hard at listening to whatever he could or would share and try to learn about his experience. I indicated I wanted to explore his experience of being confronted with an older White clinician and that I would be forthcoming with him about my experience of being confronted with a younger African American man just out of prison. This required my being active and explanatory rather than listening passively. In relational social work with oppressed populations, initiation of this discourse is necessary to override learned suppression.

This offer was followed by a few weeks of back and forth negotiation that came to be understood as being about who was in charge of the direction of the conversation. I repeatedly insisted that he was, but of course he continued to test this stance. Also tested was whether I could be trusted if he shared his stories with me. I insisted that he should remain skeptical, as he had no historical reason to expect trustworthiness. Here again, clarifying the accuracy of doubts and distrust keeps the dialogue less defensive. The relational clinician is always alert to defensiveness in self and other, as expected and useful in interpersonal recognition.

During this engagement process with David, I was alert to how his story was unfolding in fits and starts, giving me pieces of material that I would need to assemble for assessment. My sense was that we were developing a potentially workable alliance in which I could be potentially useful to him. Over several weeks, David shared stories of growing up, of being harassed by police, of being a junior gang member, of getting arrested and tortured, of confessing to an attempted murder, and of his time in prison. He also began to talk about being released, being overwhelmed, and of feeling fearful about being free and back in his community. He had made some attempts to get in touch with his wife but was repeatedly frustrated and disappointed. He was able to apply for, and get accepted into, a new residential program for men getting out of prison. I offered help with his application for the residential program, but my help was not needed. I listened, followed his stories, and focused on learning about his life.

David then began to talk about secretly and privately feeling very ashamed. His shame, once he identified it, was palpable in the room and began to feel overwhelming to me. My initial impulse was to offer reassurance and to minimize the feeling. He reacted quickly to this response with a return to stories about his frustrations with employment agencies, service personnel, and people who disappoint him. As I identified my inappropriate response, explained it as a defensive response to feeling overwhelmed by what he was sharing, apologized for not listening more carefully, and redirected my attention back to his experience, David returned to his theme of shame. In relational social work practice, this process illustrates evoked resistance, which caused me to revert to my own experience, which I then corrected by identifying the error, sharing my internal experience as explanation, and returning to an attentive focus on his experience. This interchange also illustrates the therapeutic power of mutuality, humility, and vulnerability to error as part of the clinician's process and thereby a humanizing of the mutually constructed helping relationship.

Over time we were able to construct explicitly together a space in which David could share these difficult and embedded feelings and in which I could tolerate them without defensive withdrawal. Only then could we begin to work together to discover what was driving and maintaining them. Allowing myself to know my own experience as the listener, I could begin to understand my own intense feelings of guilt. I felt absolutely responsible for his oppression. I did not share details of these feelings but identified for David my initial reactions as defensive and attending to my own internal experience. I was prepared to discuss my feelings, but only if such sharing were essential for our return to our shared attention on his distress. It was important to let the client know of my recognition of a relational error and of my struggle and intent to return to a truly listening focus.

Throughout this initial period, my input in these discussions was primarily intense listening, asking questions to clarify if I was understanding him correctly, and sometimes sharing my overwhelmed and guilty feelings in response to his stories. I had to balance any confessional sharing with selective use of my own responses in the relationship. The guideline was to maintain a stance of mutuality. Our thematic discussions repeatedly focused on his experience of shame, attached to many historical and current issues and events, including his disappointing his child and himself, his creating difficulties for his mother, his lack of skill, his hidden anger at helpers (including me) and employers, and his current unsettled social state. Thus, we both expressed and assessed similar arenas of experiences of shame and guilt, being overwhelmed, and our efforts to avoid being controlled by these experiences.

Over time, the iconic experience of being tortured by White police officers, leading to his confession, became central in our sessions. David described the torture in detail, remembering specific events and sequences and elaborately describing his feelings of terror, rage, and pain. He did not express particularly strong current feelings about these events. He had remained silent about these events after his

confession and throughout his 12-year incarceration. He had told nobody about
what had happened to him.

Step Four: Transformation and Empowerment. The co-constructed story that
emerged over time between David and me was about his internalized oppression, in
particular as a poor Black man, as a man with a criminal record, and as a failed son,
gang member, provider, husband, and father. An important part of the constructed
story was about my internalization of White privilege, middle-class status, professionalism, and guilt. This co-construction provided a venue for achieving important
alterations in David's and my narratives.

As a young recruit to a street gang, David had internalized the party line that
White cops were not to be trusted and were out to get young Black kids. Gang
recruits were oriented to be strong and never give in to White authority figures,
especially the police. David had believed this ideology, and his belief had consistently been reinforced by police harassment of gang members. The torture experience he had after his arrest was systematic, brutal, and unrelenting for 2 days,
leading to his giving up and being willing to do anything to stop the pain, fear, and
isolation. Thus, all the party line elements were confirmed for David. Immediately
afterward he was overcome with feeling ashamed, because he had failed to be
strong, such that he could never talk about the experience throughout his incarceration and until his release. He had faded into the prison culture and operated as an
ordinary prisoner. He had adapted compliantly to prison regimens and culture, and
maintained marginal social relationships with other imprisoned gang members. He
had remained troubled by his experiences with the police but had never shared his
story about these experiences with anyone until sometime after his release.

My initial reactions to David's sharing of this story included the experience of
outrage at the police and at his treatment. I questioned whether he might be exag-
gerating to get my sympathy. I wondered if he actually did attempt murder. I had a
chronic feeling of guilt that White people were harming young Black men. I also
became somewhat fascinated by the details of the torture experience that he shared.
I had to recognize that all of these reactions were familiar ones within my internalization of White privilege. They were reactions informed by my more traditional
clinical social work practice experience with White clients, by the media's stereotyping of poor Black men, and by my attraction to stories that seemed exotic from
my privileged perspective. My professional experience was to struggle with the
impulse to distance emotionally from the material and from my emotional reactions
and to formulate trauma-driven explanations for David's status. I also wanted at
times to comfort him and to minimize the intense focus on shame and perhaps to
change the subject to something more practical or productive. My relational clinical
training allowed me to recognize that all such shifts away from the relational connection would have given me a place to hide from my own experiences of guilt and
powerlessness, but at the price of distancing from David as a fellow human being.
Even the construct of parallel process – both of us being powerless, guilty, and
ashamed – had to be modified in the relational perspective to be identified as real
and immediate experiences, not "illustrations" of a psychodynamic phenomenon.

A turning point occurred as I was "helping" David make sense of his experiences. He held his hand up and said, "Remember, this is about me. I don't want your sympathy and do-gooder help. I want to stop feeling so ashamed." David's instructions clearly demonstrated his participation in the relationship at this point as a coauthor of the developing narrative. It required that I dismiss my White privilege guilt and sympathy and pay attention, i.e., take a more present and empathic stance toward him and away from my own internal struggles. We were able, together, to explore openly and as current internalization his experiences, historical and current, and to begin to connect these experiences with his overall internalized oppression. This shift signaled the progression in the relational social work process to core problem identification and to contracting about the work to be done.

David's disappointing his mother by joining a gang and getting into repeated conflicts with police and school authorities while growing up, his abandonment of his wife and child resulting from his incarceration, his spending so much of his life in prison, and his struggling so much since his release were all connected to a primary feeling of being ashamed of himself. Carrying the burden now of a man with a criminal background, besides presenting significant concrete barriers to his life adjustment to freedom, was also a current and constant source of disappointment in his sense of self. Eventually this also got connected to his own father's abandoning the family when David was 6 years old and stories about how Black men are irresponsible and immature. His agenda had always been to be strong and responsible, not like his mythical father, and he had failed. This sense of failure had supplied meaning to his experience of torture and about everything else in his life.

As this material emerged, my input was to begin to challenge his personal failure explanations. By this point I had achieved some credibility with David as a consistent listener and as a person who reliably worked with him to open up and share his experience and begin to understand it. He was able to consider the possible value of some of the alternative explanations that I began to offer, including ecological conditions, such as the poverty he lived in, the racism that was a daily experience with White authority figures including police, and including the negative stereotyping of Black men by African American adults in his community. Ultimately the torture experience became a "laboratory" we shared to explore his belief in his responsibility in getting tortured as constructed out of his guilt rather than as a social reality. His recognition of these forces, both internalized and in his environment, as contributing to his life experiences did not directly challenge or dismiss his feeling of shame, but instead began to provide alternative references. During this process, I gradually became recognized as a White man with some authority, who was not abandoning or negatively judging him. In response, I was able to feel more competent in my ability to stay focused on his experience and in the ability to engage with him in challenging problematic components of his narrative.

David began to be able to talk about experiences he had in prison with an older African American man who "took me under his wing" soon after his incarceration and who "talked straight" to him about his life. The man had some sort of political agenda, he thought, and was not religious, but told him he needed to change and that this experience was "a wakeup call."

David had been protected by his relationship with this man from activating his gang relationships in prison. Though he did connect with the gang members, he was able to stay on the periphery, because everyone respected the man who took him in. This man served a role that was missing in his childhood due to his absent father, a person with some authority and credibility helping him navigate a dangerous social world. In our discussions he also revisited his wife's contact with him before his release and decided there was a supportive element to her contact, though she didn't follow through. He also began to connect with other men who claimed they had been tortured since his release and began to explore legal action with a law firm in the city that was taking on police torture cases. He reconnected with his wife and began discussions with her about meeting with his son.

Progressive Clinical Social Work Practice

Some progressive, anti-oppressive social work practice approaches, currently gaining attention, view intrapsychic, intrapersonal change as positively counteracting personal and intrapsychic damage associated with oppression; a key component is interpersonal active involvement in the struggle for liberation (Mullaly 2010; Hicks et al. 2005; Pease and Fook 1999; Grey and Webb 2009). Though authors of postmodern social work approaches criticize use of the "expert" position by the practitioner in traditional approaches, and some dismiss therapeutic work as oppressive, many also incorporate individual clinical social work as a legitimate practice mode, as long as it does not aim to help the individual adapt to oppressive conditions. The relational clinician's focus on not only the client but the professional and the larger social order as implicated in oppression and its reversal is a prime example of client and clinician in situation. The situation is not the microlevel professional dyad; rather, the dyad is a microcosm of the mezzo- and macro-level forces impacting client and clinician alike.

Robert Mullaly's (2010) practice framework, for example, describes social work practice at the personal level as making links between personal problems and structural causes and between therapeutic insights and conscious deeds that enable people to change themselves and social conditions. This perspective is quite compatible with social work's historical "person-in-situation" perspective and with the profession's essential ecological stance. It is also compatible with relational social work practice theory, as it requires that the therapist facilitates the uncovering of subjective reality and attends primarily to the experience of the service user.

Within Mullaly's (2010) anti-oppressive framework, clinical social work practice can be utilized to enable consciousness-raising and for uncovering subjective reality and opening it to reflection, as a step toward liberation from internalized oppressive assumptions. According those anti-oppressive, critical, and progressive practice models and approaches which do integrate clinical social work treatment as a potential component, practitioners who use a clinical model must not help service users adapt to an oppressive status quo; rather, they must facilitate liberation. In order to do this, the clinician must understand the oppression as an active force and be able to name its agents. It also involves uncovering the subjective reality of the oppression reproduction and opening it to critical reflection (Mullaly 2010). In other words, anti-oppression requires both external and internal exploration. Given the association of internal exploration with blaming the victim, the social work clinician has to have conviction and clarity about the need for both and to recognize their mutual contributions to a relational social work course of treatment. Essential relational skills utilized in this process, and described above, include:

- Cultural sensitivity and competence
- Introspection and recognition of one's self as representing the dominant culture
- Management of transference and projective perceptions of a population that is largely people of color, poor, disenfranchised, and negatively stereotyped
- Establishing credibility in engagement
- Achieving a relational discourse that enables co-construction of meaning
- Facilitation of awareness of oppression and transformation of negative narratives
- Utilization of internalized, interpersonal, and ecological strengths to support change
- Maintaining a therapeutic stance with the client throughout the transformation process

An ecological assessment context embraces these skills and creates and ensures a holistic understanding of the client's experience and situation. This complex understanding and orientation is utilized to facilitate client engagement. These characteristics require active relational intervention strategies and an empowerment stance, to address inevitable client resistance of interpersonal distrust and to learn from the clients their concerns, needs, and goals.

Treatment planning emphasizes transition from submission and survival to achievement and empowerment.

Conclusion

Clinical social work practitioners who are capable of expanding their cultural competence to include successful engagement with individuals who are going through the reentry from incarceration process are essential to a successful reentry process for many of this large and neglected segment of social work practice. As described, an anti-oppressive stance and the application of relational theory principals are essential components of that capacity in the individual relational clinician. The established need for "someone to talk to and rely on as you sort out all the changes" (Kenemore and Roldan 2006) is an opportunity for the therapeutic agent to engage in an arrangement that facilitates the critical internal changes. These changes are directed to enable the clinician to begin to attend to his internalized oppression, to reconstruct attitudes and behaviors that are consistent with his hopeful aims, to become organized around liberation and freedom, to develop strategies and relationships that facilitate overcoming social and psychological barriers, and to participate successfully in their communities. Individuals who are in this population, if successfully engaged, have much to teach us as relational clinicians about how to work with them.

Study Questions

1. What assumptions do you bring to practice about prisoners, people with criminal backgrounds, poor people, Black people, prisons and jails, the justice system? Use these assumptions to discuss their origins, reinforcements, and maintenance in current social context.
2. What expectations do you bring to practice about yourself and your role as a clinician with clients in situations like reentry? How might the relational social worker use self-awareness of these expectations in their clinical role?
3. How might you go about identifying the "accuracy" of certain assumptions, as opposed to accepting assumptions that are based on stereotypes?
4. Do a brief role-play of how you pursue engagement with a client whose experience instills suspicion and other forms of resistance. Discuss some relational techniques (not knowing, authenticity, and the like) and how they have worked, or not, in practice.
5. What are essential assessment and empowerment principles in social work practice, and how can they be applied differentially in work with reentry clients?
6. Discuss how you can implement the four steps described in this chapter in actual practice situations. Use a situation that you have encountered in your own practice to illustrate this process.

References

Alexander, M. (2010). *The new Jim crow: Mass incarceration in the age of colorblindness*. New York: The New Press.
Altman, N. (2010). *The analyst in the inner city* (2nd ed.). New York: Routledge.
Aron, L. (1996). *A meeting of minds*. Hillsdale: The Analytic Press.
Beck, A. (2006). *The importance of successful reentry to jail population growth*. Presented at the Urban Institute's Jail Reentry Roundtable, June 27, 2006. Retrieved from www.urban.org/projects/reentry-roundtable/upload/bedk.PPT.
Berzoff, J., Flanagan, L., & Hertz, P. (2011). *Inside out and outside in: Psychodynamic clinical theory and psychopathology in contemporary multicultural context* (3rd ed.). Lanham: Rowman & Littlefield.
Bollas, C. (2008). *The evocative object world*. New York: Routledge.
Bollas, C. (2009). *The infinite question*. New York: Routledge.
Bollas, C. (2011). *The Christopher Bollas reader*. New York: Routledge.
Bordieu, P. (1979). *Distinction: A social critique of the judgement of taste*. London: Routledge.
Bordieu, P. (1988). *Homo academicus*. Cambridge: Polity Press.

Bordieu, P. (1989). Social space and symbolic power. *Sociological Theory, 17,* 14–15.

Bordieu, P., & Wacquant, L. (1992). *An invitation to reflexive sociology.* Chicago: University of Chicago Press.

Brandell, J. (Ed.). (2011). *Theory and practice in clinical social work* (2nd ed.). Los Angeles: Sage.

Bureau of Justice Statistics. (2010). *Total correctional population, correctional populations in the United States,* 2009. Retrieved from http://bjs.ojp.usdoj.gov/index.pbdetail&iid=2316.

Bureau of Justice Statistics. (2011). *Reentry trends in the U.S.: Recidivism.* Retrieved from http://bjs.ojp.usdoj.gov/content/reentry/recidivism.cfm.

Casement, P. (1991). *Learning from the patient.* New York: The Guilford Press.

Coady, N., & Lehmann, P. (Eds.). (2008). *Theoretical perspectives for direct social work practice: A generalist-eclectic approach* (2nd ed.). New York: Springer.

Culhane, D., Metraux, S., & Hadley, T. (2002). The impact of supportive housing for homeless people with severe mental illness on the utilization of public health, corrections, and emergency shelter systems: The New York initiative. *Housing Policy Debate, 13*(1), 107–163.

Curtis, R., & Hirsch, I. (2003). Relational approaches to psychoanalytic psychotherapy. In A. Gurman & S. Messer (Eds.), *Essential psychotherapies.* New York: Guilford.

Freire, P. (1970). *Pedagogy of the oppressed.* New York: Continuum.

Freire, P. (1992). *Pedagogy of hope: Reliving pedagogy of the oppressed.* New York: Continuum.

Glaze, L. (2010). Correctional populations in the United States, 2009. *Bureau of Justice Statistics Bulletin,*NCJ231681.Retrievedfromhttp://frobjs.ojp.usdoj.gov/index.cfm?ty=pbdetail&iid=2316.

Goldstein, E., Miehls, D., & Ringel, S. (2009). *Advanced clinical social work practice: Relational principles and techniques.* New York: Columbia University Press.

Gray, M., & Webb, S. (Eds.). (2009). *Social work theories and methods.* Los Angeles: Sage.

Hammett, T., Roberts, C., & Kennedy, S. (2001). Health related issues in prisoner reentry. *Crime and Delinquency, 47*(3), 390–409.

Harlow, C. (2003). *Bureau of justice statistics special report: Education and correctional populations,* NCJ 195670. Washington, DC: US. Retrieved from http://bjs.oip.usdoj.gov/bjs/.

Hicks, S., Fook, J., & Pozzuto, R. (Eds.). (2005). *Social work: A critical turn.* Toronto: Thompson Educational Publishing.

Hinshelwood, R. (1993). Locked in the role: A psychotherapist within the social defense system of a prison. *Journal of Forensic Psychiatry, 4*(3), 427–440.

Holzer, H., Raphael, S., & Stoll, M. (2003). *Urban institute roundtable: Employment dimensions of reentry: Understanding the nexus between prisoner reentry and work.* Washington, DC: The Urban Institute.

Houston, S. (2002). Reflecting on habitus, field and capital: Towards a culturally sensitive social work. *Journal of Social Work, 2*(2), 149–167.

Hughes, T., & Wilson, D. (2002). *Reentry trends in the United States.* Washington, DC: U.S. Department of Justice/Bureau of Justice Assistance.

Human Rights Watch. (2003). *Incarcerated America.* Retrieved from www.hrw.org/legacy/backgrounder/use/incarceration/.

Irwin, J. (1970). *The felon.* Berkeley: University of California Press.

Jacobson, M. (2005). *Downsizing prisons: How to reduce crime and end mass incarceration.* New York: New York University Press.

Kenemore, T., & Roldan, I. (2006). Staying straight: Lessons from ex-offenders. *Clinical Social Work Journal, 34*(1), 5–21.

Kita, E. (2012). Making it thinkable: A psychodynamic approach to the psychosocial problems of prisons and prisoners. In J. Berzoff (Ed.), *Falling through the cracks: Psychodynamic practice with vulnerable and oppressed populations.* New York: Columbia University Press.

Kohut, H. (2000). *Analysis of the self: Systematic approach to treatment of narcissistic personality disorders.* International Universities Press, New York.

Kupers, T. (1999). *Prison madness: The mental health crisis behind bars and what we must do about it.* San Francisco: Jossey-Bass.

Kupers, T. (2005). Posttraumatic stress disorders in prisoners. In S. Stojkovic (Ed.), *Managing special populations in jails and prisons* (pp. 10–21). Kingston: Civic Research Institute.

Lawrence, A. (2008). *Probation and parole violations: State responses.* National conference of State Legislatures, Denver CO.

Maruna, S. (2001). *Making good: How ex-convicts reform and rebuild their lives.* Washington, DC: American Psychological Association.

Maur, M., & Chesney-Lind, M. (Eds.). (2002). *Invisible punishment: The collateral consequences of mass imprisonment.* New York: The New Press.

McWilliams, N. (1999). *Psychoanalytic case formulation.* New York: The Guilford Press.

Metraux, S., & Culhane, D. (2004). Homeless shelter use and reincarceration following prison release: Assessing the risk. *Criminology and Public Safety, 3*(2), 201–222.

Mitchell, S. (1997). *Influence and autonomy in psychoanalysis.* Hillsdale: The Analytic Press.

Mitchell, S., & Aron, L. (1999). *Relational psychoanalysis: The emergence of a tradition.* Hillsdale: The Analytic Press.

Morris, M. (2001). Grendon Underwood: A psychotherapeutic prison. In J. Saunders (Ed.), *Life within hidden worlds: Psychotherapy in prisons* (pp. 89–112). London: Karnac.

Mullaly, B. (2010). *Challenging oppression and confronting privilege* (2nd ed.). New York: Oxford University Press.

O'Brien, P. (2001). *Making it in the free world.* New York: State University of New York Press.

Pease, B., & Fook, J. (Eds.). (1999). *Transforming social work practice: Postmodern critical perspectives.* London: Routledge.

Perleman, H. (1983). *Relationship: The heart of helping.* Chicago: The University of Chicago Press.

Petersilia, J. (2000). When prisoners return to the community: Political, economic, and social consequences. University of California, Irvine School of Social Ecology, prepared for *Sentencing and Corrections: Issues for the 21st century* (9): 1–8.

Rogers, C. (1961). *On becoming a person: A therapist's view of psychotherapy.* London: Constable.

Rome, D. (2004). *Black demons: The media's depiction of the African American male criminal stereotype.* Westport: Praeger.

Saunders, J. (Ed.). (2001). *Life within hidden worlds: Psychotherapy in prisons.* London: Karnac.

Schafer, R. (1980a). Action and narration in psychoanalysis. *New Literary History, 12,* 61–85.

Schafer, R. (1980b). Narration in the psychoanalytic dialogue. *Critical Inquiry, 7,* 29–53.

Schafer, R. (1982). The relevance of the 'here and now' transference interpretation to the reconstruction of early development. *The International Journal of Psychoanalysis, 63,* 77–82.

Simon, B. (1994). *The empowerment tradition in American social work: A history.* New York: Columbia University Press.

Smith, L. (1999). Individual and institutional defences against primitive anxieties: Counseling in prison. *Psychodynamic Counseling, 5*(4), 429–442.

Specht, H., & Courteny, M. (1994). *Unfaithful angels: How social work has abandoned its mission.* New York: The Free Press.

Stern, D. (1985). *The interpersonal world of the infant.* New York: Basic Books.

Tosone, C. (2004). Relational social work: Honoring the tradition. *Smith College Studies in Social Work, 74*(3), 475–487.

West, H., Sabol, W., Greenman, S. (2010, December). Prisoners in 2009. *Bureau of justice statistics bulletin.* Retrieved from http://bjs.ojp.usdoju.gov/content/pub/pdf/p09.pdf.

Winnicott, D. (1965). *Maturational processes and the facilitating environment: Studies in the theory of the emotional development.* London: Hogarth Press.

Winnicott, D. W. (1969). The use of an object. *The International Journal of Psychoanalysis, 50,* 711–716.

Relational Theoretical Foundations and Clinical Practice Methods with People Experiencing Homelessness

Daniel C. Farrell

Introduction

This chapter describes theoretical foundations and practice methods for relational social work practice with people experiencing homelessness. Its relevance to the study of practice with diversity lies in the internally transformative impact of homelessness, past or present, in clients' lives, that infuses their perceptions, functioning, and interactions with social services of all kinds, deeply altering the framework the clinician must apply to begin a relational therapeutic process. The chapter starts by contextualizing homelessness, summarizing its place in American history leading up to the current landscape of this devastating occurrence. The chapter then explores the deleterious effects of homelessness from multiple perspectives, including a social and legal framework, culminating in the subjective meaning of homelessness and housing from a relational perspective. It strives to describe the complexity of an individual's or family's varied experiences of being homeless. Diverse issues include age, ethnicity, gender, family composition and background of the homeless population, and the impact of length and depth of time of homelessness as these factors shape internalization of the multiple experiences within a life of homelessness.

The chapter then discusses the clinical social work practitioner's role in co-constructing an understanding of the client's experiences in order to build the therapeutic alliance, which in the most challenging cases is the primary catalyst for change. Although many variables and factors shape how a person internalizes the multiple experiences of homelessness, some common themes germane to clinical practice emerge. For example, critical to the clinical practitioner's preparedness to work with this population is knowing that people who are chronically homeless may hold deep distrust of systems and programs that are supposed to assist them to

D.C. Farrell, LCSW (✉)
NYU Silver School of Social Work, New York, USA
e-mail: danielcfarrell@gmail.com

J.B. Rosenberger (ed.), *Relational Social Work Practice with Diverse Populations*,
Essential Clinical Social Work Series, DOI 10.1007/978-1-4614-6681-9_16,
© Springer Science+Business Media New York 2014

obtain housing. From a relational practice point of view, clarity about clients' context supports the establishment of engagement and mutuality of understanding, so that transference and countertransference become a useful tool in the co-construction of meanings and methods of work with this vulnerable, disenfranchised, and largely invisible population. This section outlines the tools, both concrete and clinical, for practice with this underserved population.

Lastly, this chapter will discuss macro-level contributions to homelessness: the practitioner must be aware of policy decisions that have directly led to the explosion of homelessness in America over the past 30 years and their continuing impact on clients' realities in the present. A basic understanding of multiple etiologies of homelessness assures that the clinical practitioner has a well-rounded understanding of external forces, as well as internal forces, to help explain and address the existence of this abhorrent social condition.

The Person Experiencing Homelessness: Understanding Context and Scope

The definition of homelessness used in this chapter is the most updated version of the original McKinney-Vento Act of 1987 (42 U.S.C.§ 11301), which is applied by Housing and Urban Development (Department of Housing and Urban Development [HUD] 2012).

- *Literally homeless* – an individual or family who lacks a fixed, regular, and adequate nighttime residence, meaning the individual or family has a primary nighttime residence that is a public or private place not meant for human habitation or is living in a publicly or privately operated shelter designed to provide temporary living arrangements. This category also includes individuals who are exiting an institution where he or she resided for 90 days or less who resided in an emergency shelter or place not meant for human habitation immediately prior to entry into the institution.
- *Imminent risk of homelessness* – an individual or family who will imminently lose (within 14 days) their primary nighttime residence provided that no subsequent residence has been identified and the individual or family lacks the resources or support networks needed to obtain other permanent housing.
- *Homeless under other federal statutes* – unaccompanied youth (under 25) or families with children and youth who do not otherwise qualify as homeless under this definition and are defined as homeless under another federal statute, have not had permanent housing during the past 60 days, have experience persistent instability, and can be expected to continue in such status for an extended period of time.
- *Fleeing/attempting to flee DV* – any individual or family who is fleeing, or attempting to flee, domestic violence, dating violence, sexual assault, or stalking.

The devastating occurrence of homelessness affects millions of Americans annually. An estimated 636,017 experienced homelessness on a given night in 2011 (National Alliance of Homelessness [NAEH] 2012). In 2009 close to 1.6 million Americans utilized a homeless shelter (HUD 2010). The total number of homeless people probably is much higher, as these counts do not reflect those who are housing-unstable and living doubled up with others. The number of people in this country who experienced at least one episode of homelessness in 1 year may be as high as 3.5 million (National Coalition for the Homeless 2009).

American homelessness is not a recent, localized, or demographically selective occurrence. It has been well documented since the antebellum period (Kuhlman 1994; Kusmer 2002). Homelessness crosses urban, suburban, and rural communities. It affects single adults, youth, and families. As certain subsets of people who experience homelessness have declined, including people who are chronically homeless, overall numbers of people who experience homelessness in rural and suburban communities have increased (HUD 2010). Nationally, families experiencing homelessness increased by 13 % since 2007 (United States Interagency Council on Homelessness [USICH] 2010). Homeless youth without their families, defined as young people ranging in age between 12 and 24 who have spent at least one night on the streets, in a public space, or a shelter without their family, may be the largest growing cohort among the total homeless population. It is estimated that as many as two million youth leave home without parental permission and experience at least one night of homelessness (Witkin et al. 2005). Although the number of homeless youth is hard to measure owing to methodological issues, one study estimates that one in twenty youth is homeless at least one point during the calendar year (Ringwalt et al. 1998).

Homelessness has shifted and changed over the years as the demographic composition of homelessness has greatly expanded. The earlier homeless person was economically destitute and usually drifted in and out of homelessness and flophouses (Varcarolis 1990). Today, however, homelessness is varied and complex. For many, homelessness is transient, a single episode of short duration that ends as quickly as it began (Coalition for the Homeless 2008). For others, it is episodic, experienced many different times over an extended period. For this subgroup, housing instability is a common thread. The last subgroup is comprised of people who are chronically homeless as they typically experience a single episode of homelessness over a long period of time or multiple episodes of long duration that may be interrupted by a short period of housing (Kertesz and Weiner 2009).

Enduring Destructive Effects of Homelessness

The devastation of homelessness for an individual or family is experienced on multiple levels, and restoration of housing in many cases will not reverse the effects. This is a critical point in orienting the clinical social worker. The relational practitioner must recognize this intrapsychic impact, relating to the individual's deeply personal experience rather than being focused on concrete services alone. People at risk for homelessness live on the margins of society, in a state of economic instability that tears away the cohesion of self or family. People who have fallen into homelessness suffer harm in social, legal, interpersonal, and intrapersonal arenas. For example, people in homelessness experience stigma and negative labeling at much higher rates than the non-homeless population, whatever their other characteristics (Phelan et al. 1997).

As homelessness exploded into the public consciousness in the early 1980s, prevailing ideas about causes were split between the general public and academia. Academics focused on a person-centered perspective (Buck et al. 2004), with research not presenting homelessness as a social problem (Best 2010). Yet, the public perception focused on structural, not individual, causes. Lee et al. (1991) reported that most Americans placed homeless people into a "deserving poor category" (p. 657). Recently public perception, being unstable, has shifted to viewing homeless people as lazy, irresponsible, unmotivated, and dependent (Williams 2003). This perspective reflects Goffman's (1963) definition of stigma as discrediting, disqualifying one from full social acceptance, and culminating in the belief that the stigmatized person is "not quite human" (p. 5). The individual deficit model, though not based on empirical knowledge (Shier 2010) and disregarding macro influences of policymaking, expands social and psychological implications to the marginally housed who are at great risk for homelessness and therefore exposed to the stressors and social rejection of the prevailing myopia. The relational clinician's advantage, and imperative, is the assertive reconnection of the individual client's distress and coping strengths and needs to her social vulnerability.

Being homeless strips basic liberties and equalities, as people experiencing homelessness lack basic acknowledgment by society (Wright 2007–2008). It means being subjugated by the law in virtually all capacities, especially with many local anti-solicitation ordinances that have recently been enacted (Iwamoto 2007–2008). People who are homeless lose the right to property, personhood, and protection against illegal search and seizure, as these legal protections are contingent on having a private, personal space (Stec 2006). The lack of legal protections applies whether the individual is living on the street or in a shelter. This loss of fundamental freedoms and options is hard for non-homeless people to fully comprehend. The relational practitioner is doubly equipped for meaningful clinical as well as practical responses. Being oriented toward not knowing as a way of creating a mutual narrative, the relational social work clinician can engage the client authentically in addressing her intrapsychic state in concert with validation and interventions regarding macro-level needs. This integration of contextual social conditions with individual suffering allows the social worker to demonstrate the fundamental precepts of meaning clinical practice.

Practice Beyond Housing

Upon descent into homelessness, people face multiple risk factors that increase the likelihood of increased symptom formation. This population has higher rates of substance abuse and mental health issues, with attendant social costs including frequent use of emergency shelter, medical and mental health services, and public corrections (Padgett et al. 2009; Stein et al. 2008; Culhane 2002). For a person who is chronically homeless in a shelter setting, all medical and social service utilization rates are higher than for people who are transiently or episodically homeless (Culhane et al. 2002). Not unlike all clients, people who are homeless accept treatment options more frequently when benefits accrued to them, both social and economic, outweigh the consequences of not accepting treatment (Abel and Cummings 1993). Substance abuse may, in some cases, be the *result* of homelessness and not related to the cause (Johnson et al. 1997). In sum, the clinical social worker's charge is to create a treatment plan that encompasses not only the most evident reason for seeking intake but also the surrounding conditions that make any treatment plan viable. Problem definition and treatment contracting with a person struggling with homelessness, even when this is not the presenting problem, emerges from a thorough relational assessment and engagement of the client as a whole person.

Young children who experience homelessness face challenges beyond the normal scope for non-homeless families. Negative effects include delays in cognitive and emotional development that can be devastating if protective micro and macro interventions are not implemented (Hart-Shegos 1999). For homeless youth, themes that are prevalent include greater levels of sexual and physical abuse both at home and on the street (Rew et al. 2002; Zeber et al. 2008). While the ever-present threat of violence persists for all people experiencing homelessness, the threat for women is greater (Wenzel et al. 2001). Veterans may face distinct challenges: single homeless veterans experience medical illness at great rates than non-homeless veterans (O'Toole et al. 2010). Female veterans are overrepresented among homeless women (Gamache et al. 2003), and younger veterans are homeless at greater numbers as compared to their older counterparts (Tessler et al. 2003). Lastly, homeless veterans who experienced combat are at greater risk for comorbid symptoms (Benda et al. 2001).

Homelessness is not a unifying concept for those who experience it, although commonalities of experience exist across age, gender, family size, and geographic landscape. A person's life in homelessness takes varied shapes and forms and is dependent on many variables, some of which may be controllable, but many of which are not. The meaning of one's housing is closely tied to economic and emotional vitality. The recent mortgage crisis, with millions of people propelled into homelessness by the false promise of the American dream of home ownership beyond their actual means, demonstrates the power of housing in the social mind. The circumstances that lead to homelessness, such as age of onset and support systems or lack thereof, as well as duration of homelessness, disruptions of employment, education, and the like, and how one is able to survive or possibilities to exit out of homelessness, may vary the degree of devastation, but regardless of these variables, the resulting threat to economic, familial, and emotional vigor is quite real. The clinical social work perspective is therefore inextricable from the concrete services necessary to restore housing security.

The deleterious effects of homelessness will, to varying degrees, negatively affect the homeless person's ability to navigate both the world and the treatment setting. Clinicians encounter people who are homeless in multiple settings because of associated problems, but it is a mistake to presume those problems are *causative* of their homelessness. As people living in homelessness are living on the edge, service provision needs to have demonstrable value relative to the way services are provided. In other words, the services must take into account the varied and complex day-to-day struggle inherent in the lives of people experiencing homelessness. While this is true for clinical social work with all vulnerable populations, services must be clinically oriented to appreciate the depth of individual struggles with attendant aspects that are salient and transcendent of homelessness, such as substance abuse or mental health issues. Simultaneously, the relational practitioner must be flexible in treatment planning to help the person navigate homeless service systems and ensure that basic needs are met: clinical efficacy requires a safe place to sleep and certainty about from where and when one's next meal is coming.

Relational Social Work Practice Perspectives on the Impact of Homelessness

The sense of self of the clinical social work client is a shifting amalgam of states, the understanding of which requires the social work practitioner to make a global assessment of all factors impinging on her immediate range of needs and capacities, including the needs and capacities in the clinical relationship. Inborn human potential is actualized in a supportive, thriving, and interactive environment, and innate qualities and capabilities are enhanced or thwarted by experience (Fosshage 2003). Neurological research highlights that development is "experience-dependent" (Siegal 2001, p. 72). People seek out others for meaningful relationships and experiences to serve developmentally appropriate functions through their interactive experience (Tolpin 1986). Relational theory takes this one step further, adding a wider array of interpersonal factors, to state that experience is context dependent (Bromberg 1996; Orange et al. 1997). Thus, relational theory asserts that inner life cannot be characterized by simple organization or concretized representations of others (Jordan 1995). Developmental health therefore is neither exclusive of one's larger environment nor determined by a linear and cumulative set of interpersonal experiences.

Living in homelessness requires a radical change of one's outlook and navigation in the world. It shifts focus internally and interactively to moment-to-moment survival, which eclipses openness to higher-level implications of relationship. For instance, empathic attunement, a mainstay of clinical relationship building, means attunement to the client's constricted focus on basic needs. The experience of homelessness for long periods produces adaptive and coping strategies for survival within hostile environments. Experience is organized by creating a version of normalcy in the seemingly chaotic world of homelessness. The highly charged adaptive state required of homelessness becomes a constant experience of being. As such, for many who experience chronic homelessness, there may be a pull to the lifestyle of homelessness despite a deeply held wish to end one's life of homelessness. While not precisely equivalent, this is similar to the chronic substance abuse lifestyle, wherein the fluctuations of desperation and euphoric relief become self-experiences to which sobriety, with all its promise of safety and accomplishment, seems abstractly desirable but distant and alien from immediate experience.

For the clinical social worker, the overwhelming significance of a person being homeless may detract from the challenging task of establishing a humanizing and individualizing focus of relational work. Homelessness may seem like a unifying concept, and therefore working with people who are homeless could seem straight-forward with regard to interventions. As mentioned, there exist commonalities to the experiences of homelessness. However, based on the multiple variations within the homeless population, and risk factors preceding or accompanying it, the clinician needs to be aware of countertransference generalizations that only add to the stigmatizing reduction of the person to this single variable. More appropriately, the clinician can be mindful of the postmodern notion that people subjectively move through experiences in a manner that is completely unique to them, so there can be no overarching way of uniformly working with "homeless people."

Challenges to the Clinician. Working with people in homelessness requires the clinician to monitor in herself the preconceived notions and attitudes about homelessness that pervade public consciousness. Social workers are not immune to the prevailing individual-deficit, reductive assumptions and need to be open to their own a priori conceptions. This countertransference assessment requires reframing the positivist stance of assuming we can objectively know and understand social phenomena, to a more humble attitude of acceptance that we cannot fully know others as we know ourselves (Slavin 2002). This post-positivist relational belief system opens the door to empathic attunement to the other's individual experience, irrespective of its unfamiliarity to the clinician. The relational model, itself postmodern and not positivist, opens the door for the clinician to witness her own biases and expectations, even her priorities, while she engages the individual client experiencing homelessness as she would any client.

While openness may seem obvious, the anxiety of empathic attunement to a person whose conditions of living are distressing can destabilize the clinician's relational stance. Subjugated knowledge about the experience of the homeless thus refers not only to their voices being unheard but to the clinician's potentially suppressed assumptions about the homeless. Practical assistance is not to be disregarded and indeed may be an urgent focus for both client and practitioner, but such assistance must be pursued without diminishing the clinical centrality of an attuned pursuit of mutual understanding, problem definitions, and contracting for co-constructed goals. The case management dimension of relational practice with people experiencing homelessness must vary as the clinical social worker establishes the interaction of environmental and psychodynamic emphasis according to her client's changing self and situational needs (Kanter 2010).

The rich tradition of social work highlights that it is not only willing and able to work with people in very difficult and nontraditional settings but ethically committed to doing so. As Jane Addams, Nobel Peace Prize winner in 1931, stated, "The good we secure for ourselves is precarious and uncertain until it is secured for all of us and incorporated into our common life" (Addams 1910). Homelessness is, of course, no exception. The clinical social worker is oriented to both "the good," meaning concrete as well as intrapsychic needs, and "all of us," meaning each person's journey as an equally valued individual. Presenting situations outlined are unique to the individual(s) and should be appreciated as such in the clinical or casework situation. Only when clinical attention is not diverted to a host of fragmented interventions (Berzoff et al. 2011) is the client assisted in maintaining a cohesive self-experience alongside concrete services. The relational model of social work interventions models the ability to work successfully to ameliorate conditions both externally and internally for clients across a continuum of challenging situations.

Assessment of Cause and Effect. The postmodern relational framework is an excellent fit for both understanding and working practically with people who are homeless. The relational framework emphasizes working in the present, the here-and-now (Teicholz 1999). People experiencing homelessness are in acute distress and must live almost exclusively in the present, managing basic necessities on a day-to-day basis. Whether living on the streets or in a shelter, the homeless require proactive assistance to reorganize their normative experiences. While it may seem basic to note in a clinical context, people who are homeless have an issue with affordable housing regardless of other disabling conditions. The emphasis in recent years to focus resources on permanent housing with continuing relational support has proven effective, as documented by Gladwell (2006) in a *New Yorker* article titled "Million Dollar Murray: Why Problems like Homelessness May Be Easier to Solve than Manage." A clinical issue of mental illness, substance abuse, or physical health may exist, and chronic homelessness certainly induces such conditions, but these also can be misidentified as the cause rather than the effect, or some combination of both.

The clinician who views the assessment process from this fundamental perspective will facilitate engagement with her client, as it conveys a basic respect: the social pathology is acknowledged through an understanding that if this person lived in a society that had a guaranteed right to housing, or lived in a village where social networks ensured its members were taken care of by mutual responsibility, homelessness would not in most cases be an issue. This perspective and formulation sends the message that our sociopolitical system is a root cause of homelessness irrespective of other individual problems. Particularly in devastating life circumstances impacting the client, the clinical social worker applies the relational skills of mutuality in building an understanding of the issues at hand by demonstrating attunement to the macro context even while keeping track of micro contributing factors that are part of a larger framework. Once this empathic and clarifying foundation is firmly rooted in the clinician's way of thinking and confirmed related stance, the door is open for a wide array of relationally based interventions.

Nonspecific Clinical Interventions Based on the Relational Perspective. The value of the therapeutic alliance is the most important variable in the therapeutic process: there is ample evidence that an established therapeutic alliance in any treatment setting is of primary benefit for the client (Elvins and Green 2008; Zeber et al. 2008; Graybar and Leonard 2005; Smerud and Rosenfarb 2005; Martin et al. 2000;

Bordin 1979). More specifically, there is evidence that the one-to-one of fit between worker and client is an important component to positive outcomes. Consumer-driven studies confirm that the therapeutic alliance is highly valued and of primary importance to clients (Angell and Mahoney 2007; Bruck et al. 2006). Thirty-seven percent of veterans that experienced homelessness in New York City stated that intensive case management was a critical component to help sustain housing (Henderson et al. 2008). In a study of assertive community treatment (ACT) services in rural and semirural communities, consumers rate the program highly. ACT demonstrates the proactive stance of relational treatment, particularly germane to practice with clients in overwhelming circumstances, by placing the social work practitioner in the role of initiating the contact, reaching out to engage the client, and conducting assessment of all client needs as the clinician's concern (Substance Abuse and Mental Health Services Administration [SAMSHA] 2012). The primary complaints of clients were of staff turnover and having multiple workers (Redko et al. 2004), which confirms that factors that disrupt the therapeutic alliance are deleterious to the treatment. Furthermore, consumers stated that the most important factors of the relationship with their social worker are getting services, being social in terms of personal interaction, and that their worker to be there when needed (Buck and Alexander 2006). The literature is replete with studies that highlight that these characteristics of the therapeutic alliance have efficacy with respect to outcomes. These attributes of empathic continuity and acknowledgement of social pathologies are essential to successful outcomes and are primary components of the relational perspective.

The documentation of the ACT efficacy in rural communities does not minimize the efficacy of the principles of responsive, attuned, and continuous relational social work with all populations and settings. Locating the client in their homeless situation is more feasible in rural settings than in urban ones, and clients' ability to actually reach treatment facilities on their own is reduced geographically. However, the key clinical efficacy variables are the initial contact being a determined one, with the clinical social worker demonstrating credibility by active engagement, quick assessment and initiation of useful interventions, and persistent pursuit of dialogue to establish mutual problem definition and treatment progress (SAMHSA 2012). This proactive and pro-social posture is a centerpiece of relational practice: the clinician is fully aware of and prepared for the work establishing a climate of respect, contextual awareness and concern, and the need for an established contract for practice.

Specific Clinical Interventions with People Experiencing Homelessness Based on the Relational Theory Perspective. Whether the client is living on the street or in a shelter setting, the first contact should be made with utmost respect, deference, and nonintrusive curiosity about the person's varied and complex experiences of homelessness. People living on the street experience day-to-day concerns such as finding food, a place to urinate and defecate, and locating a "safe" place to sleep in a manner that is quite unfamiliar to non-homeless people. At the same time, those who are chronically homeless may have attained a level of adaptation and skills of survival that are not easily left behind (Farrell 2010). This adaptation should be understood as a strength and potential source of self-esteem by the clinical social worker.

They have more than survived: they have mastered a cultural migration that may be a source of relational interest and connection. For example, people experiencing long-term street homeless may have established a foothold in a community not overtly hostile to their existence and have figured out strategies for issues the clinician may never have imagined require a strategy. If necessary, and with permission, a clinician might seek contact with neighborhood people who know the person and can provide vital information that can help move a case forward.

A number of common themes have emerged from the literature with regard to providing effective clinical practice to people living on the street. Rowe et al. (2002) and Levy (2000) state that social workers need to understand that the beginning phase or the initial engagement will most likely occur over a continuum. Within the beginning phase there are two distinct stages: the pre-engagement and engagement stages. The longer the person has been living on the streets, the longer it may take to establish a baseline level of trust. The pre-engagement stage works toward establishing basic communication. In this stage, the social worker observes and attempts to make contact without any expectations from the person. Making verbal contact and conveying a level of respectful empathy characterize this stage. Empathy, in its full relational meaning, does not include projections or assumptions about the person's state or concerns, nor does it include impingement on personal space, concretely or psychologically. And while it may be tempting to sympathize with the plight of a person living on the street, the expression of sympathy is not appropriate as it signifies an inability to suspend one's own subjective experience which is antithetical to relational work (Fosshage 2003).

The engagement stage builds on the establishment of basic communication and attempts to foster a therapeutic alliance (Levy 1998). In the engagement stage, the role of the social worker is more clearly defined utilizing a variety of techniques, which allow for the expansion of the therapeutic alliance. This includes relationally based clinical skills such as a focus on the present, empathic and reflective listening, consistency of contact, maintaining a nonjudgmental attitude, and managing countertransference responses. Concrete services include an offer of practical benefits to include applying for low-income housing options, employment services, income-based assistance, the provision of hygiene kits, and medical and psychiatric services with an understanding that the person may or may not accept these services. As such, trust building and mutual understanding occur gradually and cannot be forced.

An additional theme in the literature includes maximum programmatic flexibility to meet the basic needs of the person who is street homeless and allowance for failure and regression in the treatment process (Pollio 1990). This perspective attempts to understand the lack of a total forward trajectory to housing as failures in the treatment. From a relational perspective, the notion of success and failure is reframed to be understood as the beginning realignment of internal organizing principles. There is no "regression" as previously understood. Especially for people who are chronically homeless, leaving a life of homelessness behind is neither a quick nor easy path. The day-to-day existence in a life of homelessness has, to an extent, been mastered (if not loathed), so leaving this familiarity of living may not come easily (Farrell 2012; Rowe 2005).

Similarly to street homelessness, the varied experiences of living in a homeless shelter are challenging for non-homeless people to comprehend. Length of stay is decided by the locality that funds the shelter and may be as short as 30 days. People living in homeless shelters are subjugated to a complex system that may not always work in their best interests and, some have argued, are vehicles of social control (Harnet and Postmus 2010). Living in a homeless shelter for long periods of time may produce its own institutional dysfunction. People who live in a shelter are subordinated in the homeless shelter hierarchy, as activities of basic daily living as controlled by the shelter. Shelters usually have specific times for meals and turning out lights and control use of television, computers, and any other recreation materials. In one qualitative study, people living in homeless shelters were asked about their experiences and many were highly critical of the services available to them (Hoffman and Coffey 2008). The notion of respect, dignity, and holding onto one's humanity was common but, according to respondents, not seen as important by shelter providers.

From a relational perspective, the homeless shelter may provide a variety of functions for a person. These functions can be healthy as related to social ties and networks one establishes or unhealthy as the threat of violence and intimidation by other residents or the possibility of institutionalization is a real especially for the most vulnerable. It is important for the social worker to become attuned to the multitude of functions the shelter provides for the person and the range of the continuum these functions provide – from healthy to unhealthy. For the most challenging to reach shelter resident, it is possible that a connection with a nonclinical, possibly off-shift staff member has been forged. It is important for management staff of the shelter and leadership of the organization to set the tone of inclusiveness so all staff understand and work toward the same goal – ending homelessness for all its residents. In this manner, the social worker should work with all nonclinical staff to determine who knows the resident well enough to act as a positive figure as begin to coax the hard-to-reach resident to work with clinical staff. It was imperative to be diligent in this way when supervising the social worker in the following case.

Case Example

Ms. Martin is a 36-year-old single female of mixed race origin. She has been living on the streets of a large urban city for 3 years surviving on the streets by panhandling and prostitution. She lost her housing stability after cycling in and out of substance abuse rehabilitation centers, thus losing her housing voucher. She became literally homeless as she relapsed after leaving her residential treatment program.[1] Ms. Martin had no income and lost her social supports, leaving her without any housing recourse. She came to the drop-in center when she needed basic services such as food, clean clothes, and to utilize a clean bathroom and a shower. Initially, she stated there was nothing else she needed that other than occasional basic necessities.

---

[1] This case was supervised by the author; the use of "we" indicates joint decisions of supervisor and social worker.

As Ms. Martin often slept within a few blocks of the drop-in center, her clinical social worker provided outreach services to her. We decided that she would visit her encampment one to two times per week just to check in on her. The check-ins were marked by consistency and a nonjudgmental attitude. We were mindful that she was not interested in coming inside and only worked to plan for safety, since her life on the streets was quite precarious (there were occasions when she was physically assaulted). In addition to her issues of addiction, social isolation, lack of income, and an inability to afford market rate housing, an attachment to the familiar experience of homelessness seemed to have taken hold.

Ms. Martin's social worker had to recognize the powerful draw that the streets represented Ms. Martin. At this moment in time of her life, she had a deep clinical need to experience relationships through a reconstructed interpersonal matrix. It is an interesting and helpful idea for the relational clinician to recognize that clients arrive with already co-constructed models of self and relationship: these are the products of the context of their lives, whether cultural, interpersonal, developmental, or other interactive fields. In the case of Ms. Martin, she was entering through a co-constructed experience as the context of one of abuse. Even though she was at times able to clearly articulate her desire for something more, something better for herself, the pull of the embedded construction required patient and mindful construction of an alternative construction, in which she was a cocreator rather than victim.

Ms. Martin's social worker had challenges holding her with unconditional positive regard as Ms. Martin reminded her of a close friend who was abused, and who also felt a draw, often unconscious, to abusive relationships in her own life. The meanings and representations of relationship abuse were present in her professional life and also stirred deep responses in her own personal life. The monitoring of her countertransference was imperative, even as she was able to use direct empathic understanding of the power of abusive internalizations from her own experiences. It posed unique challenges as she recognized her desire to save Ms. Martin. This manifested itself with strong protective feelings upon leaving the encampment, especially before a holiday weekend or a planned vacation. She felt that she would fail to protect her and feared that something terrible would happen to Ms. Martin in her absence.

My assessment was that it was not prudent to open a discussion of her internalized representational disjunction – person of worth; person of no worth – but to continue to present as a deeply caring person who wanted what is best for Ms. Martin. Ms. Martin's life on the streets and vulnerable position at this point in time of her life represented meanings beyond victimization, that her self-representation was cohesive around this degraded lifestyle, and that she could not easily extricate herself from this surrounding context without more time and dialogue in which she could get to know on her present terms. Her desire to save her had to be reconfigured in a relational practice model, in which she would develop with her co-constructed space where choices of her self-sense could be explored, not imposed.

In supervision, we discussed the relational-perspectivist view, namely, my reality and yours are equally valid and they mutually influence each other. Thus, her feelings of rescue were co-constructed to including part of my unconscious wish fantasy and perhaps part of Ms. Martin's wish to be rescued. Either way, working in the here-and-now required us to see Ms. Martin from a fully empathic point of view and for her to see herself from a vantage point that respected her coping and self-definition up to now. This prospect left her sometimes feeling uncomfortable, but knowing that despite the underlying rescue feelings, they were born out of authentic caring and concern for her and for this terribly vulnerable population we had chosen to work with.

In the 10 months her clinical social worker worked with Ms. Martin, a very good therapeutic relationship formed. Ms. Martin had become more closely related to her clinical social worker than with anyone else in the past 3–4 years. Ms. Martin began making slow yet steady strides toward healthy relational experiences. She agreed to accept a low dose of an antidepressant medication that was administered weekly by the drop-in center's nurse. She allowed staff to buy the clothing for her and slowly began to integrate some functions of the drop-in center by occasionally attending groups and eating meals with other residents. Her clinical social worker began working with Ms. Martin to obtain Public Assistance benefits, Medicaid, and vital identification documents, such as a birth certificate and Social Security card. Throughout the time that her clinical social worker provided ongoing clinical casework with Ms. Martin, slight yet significant changes in her behavior were noticeable. She began to talk more frequently about leaving her life of homelessness. Supportive housing applications were submitted with the hope that she would attend the interviews and be quickly accepted by the housing provider. However, for the first few housing interviews set up, Ms. Martin sabotaged them by not being at the location at the agreed upon time. The critical juncture revolved around the management of negative countertransference, as she was able to frame Ms. Martin's sabotage around the challenging aspects of being homeless as opposed to simply resistance to ending it.

Ms. Martin continues to struggle and has not yet ended her life of homelessness, but the instances of housing sabotage have greatly diminished. While Ms. Martin remains homeless, the case has progressed both clinically and concretely and it is expected that her life of homelessness will end in the near future.

As the therapeutic alliance emerges, the person in homelessness may not be able to sustain a consistent course toward housing. This can be expected: given the isolation many experience in homelessness, the person who is chronically homeless may be unfamiliar with someone taking an active and sustained interest in their situation. Additionally, the person may be testing the social worker to determine whether she is dependable over time. At these crucial moments, the relational skills of staying in the moment, maintaining consistency of contact, and a nonjudgmental attitude and respectful interpretation of the person's actions are most important. As a result, the therapeutic alliance is strengthened and allows the therapeutic process to continue to evolve and expand with the ultimate goal of ending homelessness.

Transference and Countertransference in the Relational Process with the Homeless

The clinical social worker seeking to engage the person experiencing homelessness needs a perspective similar to that of engaging a client from any unfamiliar culture. The practitioner's exploratory framework is not limited to the diagnostic: relational treatment requires the clinician to engage the client's direct narrative of experience with the goal of reflecting comprehension, attunement to meanings of the experience, and permission to seek a contract for work from an individual who already is under great duress. Specific benefits of this comprehensive assessment model include education about the relationship of symptom severity to length of homelessness (Chinman et al. 2000; Klinkenberg et al. 1998). In other words, the clinician who is embracing the whole of the client's experiential situation will seek to discern regression and malfunction directly linked to homelessness stressors rather than assessing symptomatology as presumptively independent of the client's journey. At the same time, the clinician will need to assess resource access when there is a co-occurring mental health or substance abuse problem.

While it is clear that many clinical treatment settings do not typically include people who are homeless, it is also true that many homeless services seek to exclude people with other kinds of problems. The value of the therapeutic alliance in this situation is especially vital. Enabling a client to gain eligibility to homeless services and to be able to maintain or improve functioning to continue that eligibility requires the social work clinician to create a treatment plan that encompasses the concrete and the psychodynamic needs. Clinicians working in relational treatment regarding intrapsychic and interpersonal issues are well advised to consider case managers and other service providers as part of an essential team.

Working with people who are homeless requires a more nuanced and textured approach toward building engagement and sustaining the treatment process. For people living in shelters, the clinical social worker, regardless of her own intentions and skill, is representative of a system that may not be concerned with the quality of a homeless person's life, but only ending their time in shelter as quickly as possible, sometimes without viable housing options. Suspicion, manipulation, denial, and the like are to be viewed through the relational lens as learned coping strategies rather than as classic resistance. The social services entitlement of shelter may not serve those most in need, as some people living on the street refuse to accept shelter owing to prior bad experiences with various institutions (Morse et al. 1996). For others, especially among the severe and persistent mentally ill, shelter is only one part of the larger institutional circuit to avoid (Hopper et al. 1997). It is analogous to jail or prison as institutional control is an important concern for the shelter provider, essentially relegating the shelter resident into a role of social disadvantage (Draine et al. 2002).

Part of the relational social worker's perspective is interest in, not aversion to, clients' attitudes toward herself and her work as an expression of their real-life experience. It is a collective countertransference temptation for the clinician to distance himself from social work as poorly serving many of the most vulnerable clients. Splitting clinical from social work is the opposite of the relational practitioner's aim. Rather, acceptance of the difficulty of establishing a trusting, mutually defined engagement and a fruitful treatment plan and process is at the heart of relational clinical social work: difficulty with these practice goals in a defined mental health population is no different than difficulty with a homeless population in terms of being a natural stage of the process.

Rehousing Process

The rehousing process may be as complex and varied for some as it may be simple and straightforward for others. For those who are suffering from severe and persistent mental illness or substance abuse issues, supportive housing may be the primary option. The standard model of supportive housing is based on the treatment first, continuum-of-care, or linear model. This model is typically congregate-style housing and is defined as permanent, affordable housing for low-income, disabled, and formerly homeless people (Supportive Housing of New York 2006). Evidence supports that mental health consumers derive great benefit from living in supportive housing, which has been effective with reducing homelessness, increasing housing stability, reducing hospitalizations, and an overall improved quality of life (Shern et al. 1997). As well, there is precedent that the continuum-of-care supportive housing model works well to successfully house and retain those who were chronically homeless (Culhane et al. 2002). However, for people experiencing homelessness with a major mental illness, the precursor of housing often means being "compliant" with prescribed treatment in order to be eligible for supportive housing.

The housing first model has become more prominent and has received much attention and funding in recent years. The philosophy of the housing first model is based on the idea that housing is an individual right for all homeless people regardless of their presenting situation (Tsemberis 2004). The housing first model is most often in the form of scattered-site apartments with assertive community treatment teams providing treatment services. Research regarding the housing first model and its efficacy for those who have mental illness and are chronically homeless is quite impressive as it consistently shows that retention rates are very high (Forchuk et al. 2008; Tsemberis et al. 2003).

For people living in homelessness, active rejection of housing opportunities may occur after calculating all factors and variables. While social workers and nonclinical staff may not understand why someone who is homeless would not accept almost any housing option made available, studies show that people experiencing homelessness prefer more freedom and autonomy related to housing options and may reject housing options that limit choice and are perceived as coercive (Tsembaris and Asmussen 1999; Tsemberis et al. 2004). One study found that many respondents made a conscious choice to reject housing if they had to accept a diagnosis of a mental illness, indicating that they would rather continue their life of homelessness than accept a diagnosis they believed was inaccurate (Luhrmann 2008). Respondents stated that being labeled with a mental illness could have severe repercussions, as this label was equated with weakness and vulnerability. Being labeled weak or vulnerable is antithetical to survival within homelessness. Another factor may be that life on the streets or in shelters is so precarious that the focus of one's intentions must be on day-to-day survival activities (Snow and Anderson 1993). Especially for homeless youth living on the street, the development and maintenance of social ties through the use of social capital, leaving homelessness may mean severing peer ties that have significant meaning (Stablein 2011). Living in homelessness, especially for a long period of time, can negatively affect housing outcomes as initial planning to leave homelessness may have been replaced by negative attitudes about one's ability or society's willingness to assist in homeless exiting (Wright 1998). Housing rejection is probably relatively rare, and the literature on this topic is limited.

While these housing models work well for the subpopulation for which they are intended, the majority of people who experience homelessness are not severely mentally ill. The shelter or homeless outreach provider must make placement into permanent housing a priority, whether or not funding sources require it. Homeless service providers should establish reasonable housing placement targets for staff and consistent housing placement meetings for staff and residents to ensure high fidelity to the targets. Agency and program leadership need to establish a culture of success which includes treating shelter residents with fairness and respect while emphasizing housing placements. This is achieved by hosting housing placement parties, instituting housing fairs for landlords in the community, housing tours for residents, etc. It is also important that nonclinical staff understands the larger mission of the organization and culture of the shelter. This is practically achieved by asking residents when they are moving into housing and if there is anything they can do to support this goal. This may seem like undue pressure by support staff, but if implemented firmly and empathically, it should be experienced by most residents as a support mechanism that is designed to assist in their exiting homelessness for permanent housing.

Conclusion

In more recent times, researchers and policymakers have moved away from the belief that micro factors are the primary causes for homelessness and have come to some agreement that causes of homelessness are multifaceted and are too often the result of a convergence of unfortunate events, on both the macro and micro levels (Early 2005; Lee et al. 2010). It is clear that the utter lack of a cogent housing policy and systematic dismantling of housing-based subsidies continues to reverberate across the country in rising homelessness for adults, families, and youth.

Many among the ranks of the homeless or marginally housed (living doubled up with others) could not afford housing based on 100 % of their income, so the resulting homelessness is based on earning power in today's economy and social subsidization (O'Flaherty and Wu 2006). For people living with an extreme low income, choices related to housing may be between utilizing a high proportion of their income on poor-quality housing and increasing expenditures on other fixed costs while sacrificing housing altogether (Quigley et al. 2001). As severely impoverished people face a scarcity of resources, opportunity costs, defined as "those costs associated with foregoing the next most attractive course of action" (Friedman and Hechter 1988, p. 202), may be the only viable option.

Homelessness exists on a continuum. The vast majority of people who experience homelessness do so at specific times and places in their lives. As such, homelessness should not be considered to be the single overarching theme unless germane to a case at a particular time. People experiencing homelessness have lived lives outside of homelessness in their past and will do so in the future. It is with this broad understanding of larger social forces coupled with clinically based relational skills that builds the therapeutic alliance that is an important component for the ultimate successful outcome of obtaining and retaining permanent housing. With this shift of emphasis, the focus on a right to and demand of affordable and sustainable housing becomes the most obvious intervention, making long shelter stays as antiquated and unnecessary as it is fiscally unsustainable and morally indefensible.

Study Questions

1. What makes relational social work well suited for working with people experiencing homelessness?
2. Describe the specific ways in which discrimination, marginalization, and stigmatization are addressed by the relational clinician.
3. Describe assumptions clinical social workers may have when beginning to work with people who are homeless. Identify the source of these assumptions.
4. Describe one or more challenges of the following subset of people experiencing homelessness:

   (a) Homeless youth
   (b) Homeless families
   (c) Unsheltered adults (street homeless)
   (d) People who are chronically homeless

5. Describe nonspecific interpersonal features and specific interventions a relational clinician utilizes to build a trusting relationship with her client. Give an example from your own practice of an intervention that has been successful in this area of treatment.
6. What further interventions could be utilized to further the case of Ms. Martin's successful transition from the streets to permanent housing? Discuss also the importance of resources, referrals, and support in any transition for a client.

References

Abel, M. H., & Cummings, P. (1993). A demonstration program for homeless male alcohol and other drug abusers. *Journal of Mental Health Administration, 20*(2), 113–125.

Addams, J. (1910). *Twenty years at hull-house with autobiographical notes*. New York: The MacMillan Company.

Angell, B., & Mahoney, C. (2007). Reconceptualizing the case management relationship in intensive treatment: A study of staff perceptions and experiences. *Administration and Policy in Mental Health and Mental Health Services Research, 34*, 172–188.

Benda, B. B., Rodell, D. E., & Rodell, L. (2001). Relative contribution of familial factors to comorbidity among homeless veterans. *Journal of Family Social Work, 6*(2), 3–24.

Berzoff, J., Flanagan, L. M., & Hertz, P. (Eds.). (2011). *Inside out and outside in: Psychodynamic clinical theory and psychopathology in contemporary and multi-cultural settings*. Lanham: Rowman & Littlefield.

Best, R. (2010). Situation or social problem: The influence of events on media coverage of homelessness. *Social Problems, 57*(1), 74–91. doi:10.1525/sp.2010.57.1.74.

Bordin, E. S. (1979). The generalizability of the psychoanalytic concept of the working alliance. *Psychotherapy: Theory, Research and Practice, 16*(3), 252–260.

Bromberg, P. A. (1996). Standing in the spaces: The multiplicity of self and the psychoanalytic relationship. *Contemporary Psychoanalysis, 32*(4), 509–535.

Bruck, E., Winston, A., Aderholt, S., & Muran, J. C. (2006). Predictive validity and therapist attachment and introject styles. *American Journal of Psychotherapy, 60*(4), 393–407.

Buck, P. W., & Alexander, L. B. (2006). Neglected voices: Consumers with serious mental illness speak about intensive case management. *Administration and Policy in Mental Health and Mental Health Services Research, 33*(4), 470–481. doi:10.1007/s10488-005- 0021-3.

Buck, P. O., Toro, P. A., & Ramos, M. A. (2004). Media and professional interest in homelessness over 30 years (1974–2003). *Analyses of Social Issues and Public Policy, 4*(1), 151–171.

Chinman, M. J., Rosenheck, R., & Lam, J. A. (2000). The case management relationship and outcomes of homeless persons with serious mental illness. *Psychiatric Services, 51*, 1142–1147.

Coalition for the Homeless. (2008). *Off target: A progress report on Mayor Bloomberg's five-year homeless plan*. Retrieved from http://www.coalitionforthehomeless.org/pages/policy-briefs-archive

Culhane, D. P. (2002). *New strategies and collaborations target homelessness*. Washington, DC: The Fannie Mae Foundation. Retrieved from http://content.knowledgeplex.org/kp2/img/cache/documents/14775.pdf.

Culhane, D. P., Metraux, S., & Hadley, T. R. (2002). Public service reductions associated with placement of homeless persons with severe mental illness in supportive housing. *Housing Policy Debates, 13*(1), 107–163.

Draine, J., Salzer, M. S., Culhane, D. P., & Hadley, T. R. (2002). Role of social disadvantage in crime, joblessness, and homelessness among persons with serious mental illness. *Psychiatric Services, 53*(5), 565–573.

Early, D. W. (2005). An empirical investigation of the determinants of street homelessness. *Journal of Housing Economics, 14*, 27–47. doi:10.1016/j.jhe.2005.03.001.

Elvins, R., & Green, J. (2008). The conceptualization and measure of therapeutic alliance: An empirical review. *Clinical Policy Review, 28*(7), 1167–1187. doi:10.1016/j.cpr.2008.04.002.

Farrell, D. C. (2010). The paradox of chronic homelessness: The conscious desire to leave homelessness and the unconscious familiarity of the street life. *Journal of Human Behavior in the Social Environment, 20*(2), 239–254. doi:10.1080/1091135090326975.

Farrell, D. C. (2012). Understanding the psychodynamics of chronic homelessness from a self psychological perspective. *Clinical Social Work Journal, 40*(3), 337–347. doi:10.1007/s10615-012-0382.

Forchuk, C., MacClure, S. K., Van Beers, M., Smith, C., Csiernik, R., Hoch, J., & Jensen, E. (2008). Developing and testing an intervention to prevent homelessness among individuals discharged from psychiatric wards to shelter and 'No fixed address'. *Journal of Psychiatry Mental Health Nursing, 15*, 569–575. doi:10.1111/j.1365-2850.2008.01266.x.

Fosshage, J. L. (2003). Contextualizing self psychology and relational psychoanalysis. Bi-directional influence and proposed syntheses. *Contemporary Psychoanalysis, 39*(3), 411–448.

Friedman, D., & Hechter, M. (1988). The contribution of rational choice theory to macrosociological research. *Sociological Theory, 6*(2), 201–218.

Gamache, G., Rosenheck, R., & Tessler, R. (2003). Overrepresentation of women veterans among homeless women. *American Journal of Public Health, 93*(7), 1132–1136.

Gladwell, M. (2006). Million Dollar Murray: Why problems like homelessness may be easier to solve than manage. *The New Yorker, 13*, 96–107.

Goffman, E. (1963). *Stigma: Notes on the management of spoiled identity.* New York: Simon and Schuster.

Graybar, S. R., & Leonard, L. M. (2005). In defense of listening. *American Journal of Psychotherapy, 59*(1), 1–18.

Harnet, H. P., & Postmus, J. L. (2010). The function of shelters for women: Assistance or social control? *Journal of Human Behavior in the Social Environment, 20*(2), 289–302. doi:10.1080/10911350903269948.

Hart-Shegos, E. (1999). *Homelessness and its effects on children.* Minneapolis: Family Housing Fund. Retrieved from http://www.fhfund.org.

Henderson, C., Bainbridge, J., Keaton, K., Kenton, M., Guz, M., & Kanis, B. (2008). The use of data to assist in the design of a new service system for homeless veterans in New York City. *The Psychiatric Quarterly, 79*(3), 3–17. doi:10.1007/s11126-007-9060-0.

Hoffman, L., & Coffey, B. (2008). Dignity and indignation: How people experiencing homelessness view services and providers. *The Social Science Journal, 45*(2), 207–222. doi:10.1016/j.soscij.2008.03.001.

Hopper, K., Jost, J., Hay, T., Welber, S., & Haugland, G. (1997). Homelessness, severe mental illness and the institutional circuit. *Psychiatric Services, 48*(5), 659–664.

Iwamoto, T. (2007-2008). Adding insult to injury: Criminalization of homelessness in Los Angeles. *Whittier Law Review, 29*, 515–539.

Johnson, T. P., Freels, S. A., Parsons, J. A., & Vangeest, J. B. (1997). Substance abuse and homelessness: Social selection or social adaptation? *Addiction, 92*(4), 437–445.

Jordan, J. V. (1995). A relational approach to psychotherapy. *Women and Therapy, 16*(4), 51–61.

Kanter, J. (2010). Clinical case management. In J. Brandell (Ed.), *Theory and practice of clinical social work* (pp. 561–585). New York: Columbia University Press.

Kertesz, S. G., & Weiner, S. J. (2009). Housing the chronically homeless: High hopes, complex realities. *Journal of the American Medical Association, 301*(17), 1822–1824. doi:10.1001/jama.2009.596.

Klinkenberg, W. D., Calsyn, R. J., & Morse, G. A. (1998). The helping alliance in case management for homeless persons with severe mental illness. *Community Mental Health Journal, 34*(6), 569–578.

Kuhlman, T. L. (1994). *Psychology on the streets. Mental health practice with homeless persons.* New York: Wiley.

Kusmer, K. L. (2002). *Down and out, on the road. The homeless in American history.* New York: Oxford University Press.

Lee, B. A., Link, B. G., & Toro, P. A. (1991). Images of the homeless: Public views and media messages. *Housing Policy Debate, 2*(3), 649–682.

Lee, B. A., Tyler, K. A., & Wright, J. D. (2010). The new homelessness revisited. *Annual Review of Sociology, 36*, 501–521. doi:10.1146/annurev-soc-070308-115940.

Levy, J. S. (1998). Homeless outreach: A developmental model. *Psychiatric Rehabilitation Journal, 22*, 123–132.

Levy, J. S. (2000). Homeless outreach: On the road to pretreatment alternatives. *Families in Society: The Journal of Contemporary Human Services, 81*, 360–368.

Luhrmann, T. M. (2008). "The street will drive you crazy": Why homeless psychotic women in the institutional circuit in the United States say no to offers of help. *The American Journal of Psychiatry, 165*(1), 15–20. doi:10.1176/appi.ajp.2007.07071166.

Martin, D. J., Garske, J. P., & Davis, K. D. (2000). Relation of the therapeutic alliance with outcome and other variables: A meta-analytic review. *Journal of Counseling and Clinical Psychology, 68*(3), 438–450.

McKinney-Vento Homeless Assistance Act of 1987, 42 U.S.C.§ 11302et seq. General definition of homeless individual.

Morse, G. A., Calsyn, R. J., Miller, J., Rosenberg, P., West, L., & Gilliland, J. (1996). Outreach to homeless mentally ill people: Conceptual and clinical considerations. *Community Mental Health Journal, 32*(3), 261–274.

National Alliance to End Homelessness. (2012). *The state of homelessness: A research report on homelessness in America.* Washington, DC: Homelessness Research Institute. Retrieved from http://www.endhomelessness.org/section/_search/?q=The+state+of+homelessness%3AA+research+%09report+on+homelessness+in+America

National Coalition for the Homeless (2009). *How many people experience homelessness?* Retrieved from http://www.nationalhomeless.org/factsheets/How_Many.pdf

O'Flaherty, B., & Wu, T. (2006). Fewer subsidized exits and a recession: How New York City's family homeless shelter population became immense. *Journal of Housing Economics, 15*, 99–125. doi:10.1016/j.jhe.2006.08.003.

Orange, D. M., Atwood, G. E., & Stolorow, R. D. (1997). *Working intersubjectively: Contextualism in psychoanalytic practice* (Psychoanalytic inquiry book series, Vol. 17). Mahwah: Analytic Press.

O'Toole, T. P., Buckel, L., Bourgault, C., Bluman, J., Redihan, S. G., Jiang, L., & Friedmann, P. (2010). Applying the chronic care model to homeless veterans: Effect of a population approach to primary care on utilization and clinical outcomes. *American Journal of Public Health, 100*(12), 2493–2499. doi:10.2105/AJPH.2009.179416.

Padgett, D. K., Stanhope, V., Henwood, B. F., & Stefancic, A. (2009). Substance use outcomes among homeless clients with serious mental illness: Comparing housing first with treatment first programs. *Advance online publication.* doi:10.1007/s10597-009-9283-7.

Phelan, J., Link, B. G., Moore, R. E., & Stueve, A. (1997). The stigma of homelessness: The impact of the label "homeless" on attitudes toward poor persons. *Social Psychology Quarterly, 60*(4), 323–337.

Pollio, D. (1990). The street person: An integrated service provision model. *Psychosocial Rehabilitation Journal, 14*, 57–69.

Quigley, J. M., Raphael, S., & Smolensky, E. (2001). Homelessness in California. *Working papers, Berkeley program on housing and urban policy, institute of business and economic research, UC Berkeley.* Retrieved from http://escholarship.org/uc/item/2pg3f4ns

Redko, C., Durbin, J., Wasylenki, D., & Krupa, T. (2004). Participant perspectives on satisfaction with assertive community treatment. *Psychiatric Rehabilitation Journal, 27*(3), 283–286.

Rew, L., Fouladi, R. T., & Yockey, R. D. (2002). Sexual practices of youth. *Journal of Nursing Scholarship, 34*(2), 139–145.

Ringwalt, C. L., Greene, J. M., Robertson, M., & McPheeters, M. (1998). The prevalence of homelessness among adolescents in the United States. *American Journal of Public Health, 88*(9), 1325–1329.

Rowe, C. (2005). *Treating the basic self: Understanding addictive, suicidal, compulsive, and attention-deficit/hyperactivity (ADHD) behavior.* New York: Psychoanalytic Publisher.

Rowe, M., Fisk, D., Frey, J., & Davidson, L. (2002). Engaging persons with substance abuse disorders: Lessons from homeless outreach. *Administration and Policy in Mental Health, 29*, 263–273.

Shern, D. L., Felton, C. J., Hough, R. L., Lehman, A. F., Goldfinger, S., Valencia, E., et al. (1997). Housing outcomes for homeless adults with mental illness: Results from the second-round McKinney program. *Psychiatric Services, 48*(2), 239–241.

Shier, M. L. (2010). Perspectives of employed people experiencing homelessness of self and being homeless: Challenging socially constructed perceptions and stereotypes. *Journal of Sociology and Social Welfare, 38*(4), 13–37.

Siegal, D. J. (2001). Toward an interpersonal neurobiology of the developing mind: Attachment relationships, "mindsight", and neural integration. *Infant Mental Health Journal, 22*(1–2), 67–94.

Slavin, M. O. (2002). Post-Cartesian thinking and the dialectic of doubt and belief in the treatment relationship. A discussion of Atwood, Orange, and Stolorow. *Psychoanalytic Psychology, 19*(2), 281–306.

Smerud, P. E., & Rosenfarb, I. S. (2005). The therapeutic alliance and family psychoeducation in the treatment of schizophrenia: An exploratory prospective change study process. *Journal of Counseling and Clinical Psychology, 76*(3), 505–510. doi:10.1037/0022-006X.76.3.505.

Snow, D. A., & Anderson, L. (1993). *Down on their luck.* Berkeley: University of California Press.

Stablein, T. (2011). Helping friends and the homeless milieu: Social capital and the utility of street peers. *Journal of Contemporary Ethnography, 40*(3), 290–317. doi:10.1177/0891241610390365.

Stec, J. (2006). Why the homeless are denied personhood under the law: Toward contextualizing the reasonableness standard in search and seizure jurisprudence. *Rutgers Journal of Law and Urban Policy, 3*(2), 321–353.

Stein, J. A., Dixon, L. D., & Nyamathi, A. M. (2008). Effects of psychosocial and situational variables on substance abuse among homeless adults. *Psychology of Addictive Behaviors, 22*(3), 410–416. doi:10.1037/0893-164X.22.3.410.

Substance Abuse and Mental Health Services Administration (2012). Retrieved from http://store.samhsa.gov/facet/Treatment-Prevention-Recovery/term/Assertive- Community Treatment

Supportive Housing of New York (2006). *What is supportive housing?* Retrieved from http://www.shnny.org/documents/Whatiss.h.NYC_000.pdf

Teicholz, J. G. (1999). *Kohut, Loewald, and the postmoderns: A comparative study of self and relationship* (Psychoanalytic Inquiry Book Series, Vol. 18). Mahwah: Analytic Press.

Tessler, R., Rosenheck, R., & Gamache, G. (2003). Homeless Veterans of the all-volunteer force: A social selection perspective. *Armed Forces and Society, 29*(4), 509–524.

Tolpin, M. (1986). The self and its selfobject: A different baby. In A. Goldberg (Ed.), *Progress in self psychology* (pp. 115–142). New York: Guilford.

Tsembaris, S., & Asmussen, S. (1999). From streets to homes: The pathways to housing consumer preference supported housing model. In K. J. Conrad, M. D. Matters, P. Hanrahan, & D. J. Luchins (Eds.), *Homeless prevention in treatment of substance abuse and mental illness* (pp. 113–131). Binghamton: The Haywood Press.

Tsemberis, S. J. (2004). Housing First. In *Encyclopedia of homelessness* (pp. 277–280). London: Sage.

Tsemberis, S. J., Moran, L., Shinn, M., Asmussen, S. M., & Shern, D. L. (2003). Consumer preference programs for individuals who are homeless and have psychiatric disabilities: A drop-in center and a supported housing program. *American Journal of Community Psychology, 32*(3–4), 305–317.

Tsemberis, S., Gulcur, L., & Nakae, M. (2004). Housing first, consumer choice, and harm reduction for homeless individuals with a dual diagnosis. *American Journal of Public Health, 94*(4), 651–656.

U.S. Department of Housing and Urban Development. (2010). *The 2009 annual homeless assessment report to Congress.* Retrieved from http://www.hudhre.info/documents/5thHomelessAssessmentReport.pdf

U.S. Department of Housing and Urban Development. (2012). Retrieved from http://www.endhomelessness.org/content/article/detail/3006

U.S. Interagency Council on Homelessness. (2010). *Opening doors: Federal strategic plan to prevent and end homelessness.* Retrieved from http://www.usich.gov/PDF/OpeningDoors_2010_FSPPreventEndHomeless.pdf

Varcarolis, B. (1990). *Psychiatric mental health nursing.* Philadelphia: W. B. Saunders.

Wenzel, S. L., Leake, B. D., & Gelberg, L. (2001). Risk factors for major violence among homeless women. *Journal of Interpersonal Violence, 16*(8), 739–752.

Williams, J. C. (2003). *A roof over my head: Homeless women and the shelter industry*. Boulder: University Press of Colorado.

Witkin, A. L., Milburn, N. G., Rotheram-Borus, M. J., Batterham, P., May, S., & Brooks, R. (2005). *Youth and Society, 37*(1), 62–84. doi:10.1177/0044118X04272811.

Wright, B. R. E. (1998). Behavioral intentions and opportunities among homeless individuals: A reinterpretation of the theory of reasoned action. *Social Psychology Quarterly, 61*(4), 271–286.

Wright, R. G. (2007-2008). Homelessness and the missing constitutional dimension of fraternity. *University of Louisville Review, 46*, 437–471.

Zeber, J. E., Copeland, L. A., Good, C. B., Fine, M. J., Bauer, M. S., & Kilbourne, A. M. (2008). Therapeutic alliance perceptions and medication adherence in patients with bipolar disorder. *Journal of Affective Disorders, 107*(1), 53–62. doi:10.1016/j.jad.2007.07.026.

Index

38448586R00174

Made in the USA
Lexington, KY
08 January 2015